Unabridged
Christianity

Unabridged Christianity

Biblical Answers to Common Questions About the Roman Catholic Faith

Fr. Mario P. Romero

"...Always be ready to give an explanation to anyone who asks you for a reason for your hope, but do it with gentleness and reverence..." (1 Peter 3:15-16)

Queenship
PUBLISHING COMPANY
P.O. Box 220 • Goleta, CA 93116
(800) 647-9882 • (805) 692-0043 • Fax: (805) 967-5843

Nihil Obstat:
The Very Reverend Kenneth R. Morvant, J. C. L., J. V.

Imprimatur:
The Most Reverend Edward J. O'Donnell, D.D.,
Bishop of the Roman Catholic Diocese of Lafayette, Louisiana

Library of Congress #: 97-076238

Published by:
    Queenship Publishing
    P.O. Box 220
    Goleta, CA 93116
    (800) 647-9882 • (805) 692-0043 • Fax: (805) 967-5843

Printed in the United States of America

ISBN: 1-57918-056-6

This book is dedicated to my parents,
Rosemary Bigler Romero
and the late Paul Romero, Jr.

Thank you, Mom and Dad,
for giving me physical life
and for introducing me to Jesus Christ —
the source of everlasting life.
Thank you for the rich spiritual inheritance
that you have left to our family.
I love you both with all of my heart.

About the Cover

The icon of the crucifixion of Jesus appearing on this book's front cover dates back to the 13th century and pictures our Lord flanked by the Blessed Virgin Mary and St. John as mentioned in John 19. Pictured in the four corners of the icon are "the four living creatures" who offer eternal praise to God referred to in Revelation 4. Some of the early Church Fathers saw these four "living creatures" as representing the four evangelists: Matthew, Mark, Luke and John.

Contents

Introduction

In the Gospel of Matthew Jesus tells His followers that, because they have been enlightened by God with the gift of faith, they are called to be "the light of the world" (Matt 5:14). Jesus then goes on to say to His disciples that they must "set [their faith] on a lampstand, where it [can give] light to all..." (Matt 5:15). This first book of mine is an attempt to put the beautiful "light" of my Roman Catholic faith "on a lampstand" in hopes that all people may draw nearer to the ultimate "light of the world" (John 8:12) — Jesus Christ our Lord and Savior. It is my wish that this book convey a warm invitation to all readers to prayerfully consider the wonderful truths espoused by the Roman Catholic Church — truths revealed to us by Jesus Christ and kept alive by the Apostles and their successors.

In my eight years of ministry as a parish priest, a number of my parishioners have forwarded to me various pamphlets and video tapes on the topic of "Roman Catholicism" that they have received from their well-intentioned evangelical Christian friends. The producers of the pamphlets and videos that I have seen thus far attempt to expose what they (mistakenly) believe to be the "false teachings" of the Roman Catholic faith. The unfortunate thing about many of these materials is that the Catholic faith is often presented in an incomplete manner — which can be *very* misleading to the uninformed reader/viewer. After assisting my Catholic parishioners time and time again in responding to their evangelical Christian friends and answering many of the same questions repeatedly, I had the idea of putting together a book that would respond to some of the common misunderstandings of the Roman Catholic faith and give a more accurate and complete explanation of what Roman Catholics *actually* believe and why we believe it.[1]

Some evangelical Christians will sometimes make the statement that certain Catholic beliefs and practices "are not found anywhere in the Bible." When a knowledgeable Catholic produces the requested Biblical backing, the objecting evangelical Christian will, oftentimes, still be unconvinced and take his objection to the next level: "I don't agree with the Catholic Church's interpretation of these particular Scriptural verses" (usually meaning: "The Catholic Church's interpretation of these Biblical verses doesn't square with my pastor's/denomination's interpretation so, obviously, you Catholics must be mistaken.")

Note that when a courtroom judge is hearing a case and lawyer "Smith" claims that a certain verse contained in the civil law book should be interpreted to mean one thing and lawyer "Jones" states that the same verse should, instead, mean something totally different, the judge looks back at the oldest rulings of previous judges and courts to see which lawyer's interpretation (if any) has *historical precedence*. The interpretation of the civil law that goes back the farthest is the one that the modern-day judge will adhere to. The same holds true with interpretations of passages from Sacred Scripture. Many Protestant Christians have converted to the Catholic faith after they researched the writings of the early Christians and discovered how "Catholic" their belief and practice was.

Using some of the commonly-heard misconceptions about the Catholic faith as points of departure, I will examine various key passages from Scripture, look at historical documentation found in secular sources and, at the end of each chapter, I will present quotes from the writings of the first generations of Christians to show that modern-day Catholic beliefs and practices have *solid* precedence in the beliefs and practices of the early Church.[2]

On the first day of classes in my freshman year at Catholic High School in New Iberia, Louisiana, our homeroom teacher took us on a tour of the school library. As I gazed at the thousands of books positioned on the shelves, I noticed a huge volume that must have measured over twelve inches thick. I made the comment to the librarian at the desk, "Wow! What kind of book is *that*?" "That is an unabridged dictionary," she responded. "Unabridged? What does that mean?" I said. "Go and look it up in the unabridged dictionary," the librarian told me. I opened up the massive book to the word "unabridged" and discovered that it meant: "the most complete of its kind." "The reason why it is such a large book," said the librarian, "is that it is the most comprehensive dictionary available. It presents truth in the most thorough manner possible — without abbreviating or omitting any of the important details like the other, more compact, dictionaries do."

When I was trying to choose a title for this book about the Biblical basis of some of the key doctrines of the Roman Catholic faith, the name "Unabridged Christianity" came to mind. Much like an unabridged dictionary found in a library, Roman Catholic Christianity offers its followers the *fullness* of Christian Truth — without abbreviating or omitting any of the important theological "details" like many of the other, more doctrinally "compact," Christian denominations do.

St. Paul writes to the Christians living in Corinth that there is "one Lord, *one faith*, [and] one baptism" (Eph 4:5). What St. Paul is saying is that, since our *one Lord* (Jesus Christ) instituted only *one Church,* that *one Church* holds only *one faith* (i.e., has one distinct set of beliefs).[3]

If one browses through one's hometown phone book, he will likely discover *scores* of different Christian denominations, most with their pastors holding doctoral degrees in Scripture, all claiming to be "led by the Holy Spirit" in their "plain, straightforward interpretation of the Bible." The teachings of these various Bible-believing Christian denominations vary *widely* on many crucial issues of doctrine, for example:

- What did Jesus mean when He declared at the Last Supper "this is my body...this is my blood..." (cf. Matt 26:26-28)? (i.e., What is the nature of Jesus' presence in Holy Communion?)
- How often (if ever) should a Christian receive Holy Communion?
- What does the Bible reveal God's Name to be?
- Do the Scriptures reveal God to be a Trinity of Persons?
- Who/what is the Holy Spirit? What does it mean to be "baptized in the Holy Spirit"? Is this necessary for a Christian and, if it is, how does this come about?

- What is the disposition of a faithful Christian's soul after the death of his body?
- What (if anything) are the saints in heaven able to do? What type of relationship (if any) should a Christian living on earth have with the saints in heaven?
- Are you and I conceived with original sin?
- How is one "saved" and, after he is saved, can he be unsaved if he backslides unrepentantly in a serious way? If a "saved" Christian backslides unrepentantly in a grave manner, does that mean that he only *thought* that he was saved when, in fact, he was never really saved at all?
- What does it mean to become "justified" and "righteous" in God's sight? Was the Protestant Reformer Martin Luther correct when he used Scripture to teach that Christians were like "dunghills covered with snow" *(meaning that "saved" Christians remained, internally, sinners displeasing to God but, externally, were "coated" with the righteousness of Jesus Christ — which would "hide" their true interior state from God the Father on Judgement Day and, thus, make them eligible for admittance into heaven immediately upon their death)*? How should 2 Cor 5:17 be interpreted?
- Was the Protestant Reformer John Calvin right when he used the Bible to teach that God has already pre-destined/pre-determined which people will go to heaven and which will not?
- What was Jesus referring to when He spoke in John 3:3-5 about the necessity of being "born again"?
- What did St. James mean when he wrote, "See how a person is justified by works and not by faith alone" (James 2:24)? What was the author of the Book of Revelation saying when he wrote "...All the dead were judged according to their deeds" (Rev 20:12-13)?
- What was St. Paul speaking about when he wrote "...stand firm and hold fast to the traditions that you were taught, either by an oral statement or by a letter of ours" (2 Thess 2:15) and "...hold fast to the traditions, just as I handed them on to you" (1 Cor 11:2)? What role should "tradition" *(as spoken about by St. Paul in the previously-mentioned Scripture passages)* play in Christianity?

- Should the divorce and re-marriage "exception clauses" found in Matt 5:31-32 and Matt 19:9 be seen as a modification of the absolute prohibition of divorce and re-marriage found in Mark 10:11-12, Luke 16:18, and 1 Cor 7:10-11? What situation was St. Matthew referring to when he used the word "unlawful" (Greek: *porneia*) in Matt 5:31-32 and Matt 19:9?
- Must one possess the gift of tongues to be considered a true Christian?
- In the light of our revolutionary Lord deliberately choosing all male Apostles (cf. Luke 6:13-16) and personaly commissioning them to consecrate the Holy Eucharist "in memory of [Him]" (cf. Luke 6:19-20), was it our Lord's intention for women to assume ordained ministry?
- How will the end of the world unfold? (i.e., How should Revelation Chapter 20 be interpreted?)
- What does the Bible teach about "the tribulation" and "the millennial reign"? Have they begun yet? Are we in them now? Are they yet to come?
- Will there be a "rapture" of the faithful into heaven before the Second Coming of Christ so that the faithful are protected from "the tribulation"?
- Who/what is the anti-Christ? Is he/she/it alive now?
- How are your worship services structured? What elements do they contain?
- How is your church leadership structured?
- When disagreements arise among members of your church over one of the many difficult-to-understand passages contained in Scripture, how are they resolved? Which person or group has the final say if a unanimous consensus cannot be reached?
- Is water baptism necessary and, if it is, what is required to be validly baptized? If water baptism is necessary, should it be done "in the name of the Father, and of Son and of the holy Spirit" as mentioned in Matt 28:19 or should it be done "in the name of Jesus Christ" as mentioned in passages such as Acts 2:38?
- Are infants eligible to be baptized?
- How many Christian "Sacraments" are there and (if there are any) what are they and what do they accomplish?
- Is there any correlation between financial prosperity and faithfulness to God? Does God desire His faithful followers to be

materially well-off? Explain Luke 6:24 & Matt 19:24.

- Is abortion a morally acceptable option for a Christian? If it is morally acceptable, under what condition(s)? At what point does a fertilized human ovum become a human being? If you believe that human life begins at the moment of conception, should the innocent human baby in the womb be eligible to receive the death penalty if his mother was the unfortunate victim of rape or incest?
- Through the use of artificial birth control, may a Christian married couple dictate to God when He can create new life and when He cannot? Which Scripture(s) teach this? What made God so mad in Gen 38:6-10?
- What about the moral permissibility of euthanasia (i.e., premeditated "mercy killing" of the sick)?
- What about the morality of *in vitro* fertilization (i.e., a lab technician force-fertilizes a human ovum in a laboratory dish and, thus, manufactures a human being on demand)?
- Is homosexual sexual acting-out morally acceptable for a Christian if he claims that that is the orientation that God created Him with? Why or why not? If homosexual acting-out is morally acceptable, should homosexual marriages be allowed?
- May an ill Christian seek treatment from a medical doctor? May an ill Christian receive a blood transfusion if it is deemed medically beneficial to him?
- Numerous times the Bible speaks out strongly against the sin of abusing alcoholic beverages and becoming drunk (e.g., 1 Cor 6:9-10). May a responsible non-alcoholic Christian adult have an occasional beer or glass of wine? How should God's command in Deut 14:26 be interpreted?
- Do the Scriptures permit a Christian couple to dance in a modest fashion? Was David sinning in 2 Sam 6:14-16?
- Please show me the traceable historical link that your church has to Jesus Christ and the Apostles who lived in the first century A.D.? Which of the early Church Fathers belonged to your church and believed as you do? Please show me writings from members of your church dating from 100, 500 and 1000 A.D.
- Which of the aforementioned doctrinal issues affect one's salvation and which are simply unimportant peripheral matters that Christians are free to disagree on?

Certain Christian groups in existence today (who quote the Scriptures extensively) stand out because of their unique interpretations of various Bible passages: One well-known congregation uses the Bible to teach that Jesus Christ was not God (cf. John 14:28, etc.) and that only 144,000 "elect" members of their congregation will experience the fullness of salvation in heaven (cf. Rev 7:4). Another large Christian group uses the Bible to teach that God is not a Trinity of Persons — but one Diving Being who switches into various modes/roles as necessary (cf. Deut 6:4, etc.). Yet another familiar group uses the Bible to support the novel scenario that, at one point in history, the risen Jesus lived among "other sheep" (cf. John 10:16) — whom they believe to be the native Indians in North America.

In studying the wide diversity of interpretations of Scripture being proposed today, one can clearly observe that the Bible, by itself, is not self-interpreting. The basic question boils down to: *"To whom have you given the authority to interpret the Bible for you? (i.e., Whose interpretations of Scripture [and resulting doctrinal mix] have you chosen to adopt?)"*

Since every Christian should desire to follow Jesus Christ as intimately as possible, he should long to hold fast to the *one faith* that was taught by Jesus and the Apostles and to belong to the *one Church* that was historically instituted by our Lord Himself. The question that every thinking Christian must eventually ask is: "Which one of the *thousands* of different 'Holy-Spirit-guided,' 'Bible-based' Christian Churches in existence today (which run the theological and doctrinal gamut) is the one established by Jesus Christ Himself"? Since contradictory teachings cannot simultaneously be true, which Christian Church has *the fullness* of the objective Truth proclaimed by Jesus and the Apostles? This brief book is an attempt to share some of the Scriptural and historical "evidence" that the contemporary Roman Catholic Church and the Apostolic Church founded by Jesus Christ circa 30 A.D. are one and the same.

In the Vatican II Document, *Unitatis Redintegratio*, we read the following about the deep love and respect that the Catholic Church has for Christians of all denominations:

"From her very beginnings there arose in this one and only Church of God certain rifts (cf. 1 Cor 11:18-19; Gal 1:6-9; 1 Jn 2:18-19), which the apostle strongly censures as damnable (cf. 1 Cor 1:11 ff.; 11:22). But in subsequent centuries more widespread disagreements appeared and quite large Communities became separated from full communion with the Catholic Church — developments for which, at times, men of both sides were to blame. However, one cannot impute the sin of separation to those who at present are born into these Communities and are instilled therein with Christ's faith. The Catholic Church accepts them with respect and affection as brothers. For men who believe in Christ and have been properly baptized are brought into a certain, though imperfect, communion with the Catholic Church...They therefore have a right to be honored by the title of Christian, and are properly regarded as brothers in the Lord by the sons of the Catholic Church."[4]

It would literally take *libraries* of books to speak in depth about each and every tenet of the Roman Catholic faith. Rather than doing an exhaustive study of the Catholic faith, what I have attempted to do in this short book is to give Catholics a few starting points for Biblically-based discussions of various key doctrines of their faith. At the beginning of each chapter of this book I present the official teaching of the Catholic Church as it appears in the authoritative *Catechism of the Catholic Church* (published in 1994 by the Vatican).

Speaking about the Catholic faith, former Presbyterian minister *(now Roman Catholic apologist)* Dr. Scott Hahn once said: "The Catholic faith is like a lion; it doesn't need us to defend it so much as it needs us to unlock its cage and let it out. Once out it can take care of itself." [5] My hope is that this brief book can instruct Catholics and other interested Christians on how to begin to "let the lion out."

As I sat down and began to put this book together, I wanted to acknowledge the sources of the ideas and information that I was to present. Obviously, when one is speaking about ancient Christian beliefs that date back 2,000 years, there are not too many new ideas that haven't already been expressed by someone else. Although many of the ideas and methods of presentation in this book are my own, a number of analogies and examples are "borrowed" from professors that I have had in the seminary, lectures that I have attended, audio and video tapes that I have listened to, books that I have read, etc. Whenever possible, I will cite the source of my idea, information, or analogy. My intention is certainly not to plagiarize anyone's work but to compile information about our Catholic faith into what I think is a meaningful and user-friendly format. I certainly consider myself to be more of a "compiler" than an original author.

My heartfelt thanks go out to the many friends who have looked over various parts of this book and have offered some excellent recommendations for its improvement: Fathers Lloyd Benoit, Michael Champagne, C.J.C., Ronnie Groth, Kirk Mansel, S.J., Randy Moreau, Kenneth Morvant, Robie Robichaux, Terry Tekippe, and Tom Voorhies. I wish to thank Mr. Bob Schaefer of Queenship Publishing Company for his tremendous patience and understanding. I would also like to thank Mrs. Darlene Broussard for her editorial assistance and encouragement.

I certainly would welcome any suggestions as to how I could improve this book to give a more clear and accurate presentation of our Roman Catholic faith. If you wish, please correspond with me c/o Queenship Publishing Company.

November 30, 1998
Feast of Saint Andrew the Apostle

Fr. Mario P. Romero

NOTE: Also available for sale from Queenship Publishing Company is a pamphlet that I have created entitled *Catholic Pocket Evangelist*. This small booklet is a handy Scriptural quick-reference guide that can be stored in the back of one's Bible and referred to easily whenever one wants to share the Biblical basis of his Catholic faith with others.

P. S. — The reader will notice that this book contains a good number of endnotes at the end of each chapter. Please refer to them when you see the endnote numbers in the book's text because they contain many worthwhile "goodies."

Endnotes

1   Throughout this book I use the terms "evangelical Christian" and "fundamentalist Christian." Because Protestant Christianity has splintered into so many different sects (who differ from one another on various points of Biblical interpretation, doctrine and religious practice), it is difficult to state precisely what groups/individuals could be considered "evangelicals" and which could be considered "fundamentalists." The term "evangelical" is derived from the Greek word *evangelion* (which means "good news.") In verses such as Matt 5:14-15, Jesus calls *every* Christian to be an "evangelical Christian" — one who is actively engaged in the sharing of the Good News of his salvation in Christ. Nowadays the term "evangelical Christian" is usually used to refer to Protestant Christians who adhere to the theological tenets promoted by the 16th century Protestant Reformers. Many (though not all) evangelical Christians are very respectful of the Roman Catholic faith and view Catholic Christians as fellow brothers and sisters in the Lord. In popular usage, the term "fundamentalist Christian" is often used to refer to a staunch subset of evangelical Protestants. A number of (though not all) "fundamentalist Christians" strongly oppose the Roman Catholic faith and believe the "Church of Rome" to be a non-Christian "religion" that leads people astray from the simple saving message of the Gospel of Jesus Christ.

2   An excellent series of books that has been very helpful to me in my research of the faith of the early Christians has been the 3-volume set *The Faith of the Early Fathers*, edited and translated by William A. Jurgens and published by The Liturgical Press in Collegeville, MN. I would highly recommend this series which contains a very helpful doctrinal index in the back of each volume.

3   In the Gospel of Matthew, Jesus says: "And so I say to you, you are Peter, and upon this rock I will build my *church*..." (Matt 16:18-19). Note that the word "church" is singular. Jesus didn't intend to found numerous *churches* that believed a variety of things about crucial doctrinal issues. Jesus wanted His followers to "be one, [as He and His Father] are one" (John 17:22).

4   Walter M. Abbott, S.J. (General editor), *The Documents of Vatican II*, (Piscataway, NJ: Association Press, New Century Publishers, Inc., 1966), Chapter 1, paragraph 3, p. 345.

5   Frank Sheed, Mazie Ward, *Frank Sheed & Mazie Ward's Catholic Evidence Training Outlines*, (Ann Arbor, Michigan: Catholic Evidence Guild, 1992), quote appears on un-numbered page in book's Foreword.

Guide to Abbreviations of Biblical Books

	Old Testament			
1) Genesis	(Gen)	24) Proverbs	(Prov)
2) Exodus	(Exod)	25) Ecclesiastes	(Eccl)
3) Leviticus	(Lev)	26) Song of Songs	(Songs)
4) Numbers	(Num)	27) **Wisdom**	(Wisdom)
5) Deuteronomy	(Deut)	28) **Sirach**	(Sirach)
6) Joshua	(Josh)	29) Isaiah	(Isaiah)
7) Judges	(Judges)	30) Jeremiah	(Jer)
8) Ruth	(Ruth)	31) Lamentations	(Lam)
9) 1 Samuel	(1 Sam)	32) **Baruch**	(Baruch)
10) 2 Samuel	(2 Sam)	33) Ezekiel	(Ezek)
11) 1 Kings	(1 Kings)	34) Daniel	(Dan)
12) 2 Kings	(2 Kings)	35) Hosea	(Hosea)
13) 1 Chronicles	(1 Chron)	36) Joel	(Joel)
14) 2 Chronicles	(2 Chron)	37) Amos	(Amos)
15) Ezra	(Ezra)	38) Obadiah	(Obad)
16) Nehemiah	(Neh)	39) Jonah	(Jonah)
17) **Tobit**[1]	(Tobit)	40) Micah	(Micah)
18) **Judith**	(Judith)	41) Nahum	(Nahum)
19) Esther	(Esther)	42) Habakkuk	(Hab)
20) **1 Maccabees**	(1 Macc)	43) Zephaniah	(Zeph)
21) **2 Maccabees**	(2 Macc)	44) Haggai	(Hag)
22) Job	(Job)	45) Zechariah	(Zech)
23) Psalms	(Psalms)	46) Malachi	(Mal)

New Testament	1) Matthew	(Matt)	15) 1 Timothy	(1 Tim)
	2) Mark	(Mark)	16) 2 Timothy	(2 Tim)
	3) Luke	(Luke)	17) Titus	(Titus)
	4) John	(John)	18) Philemon	(Philemon)
	5) Acts	(Acts)	19) Hebrews	(Heb)
	6) Romans	(Rom)	20) James	(James)
	7) 1 Corinthians	(1 Cor)	21) 1 Peter	(1 Pet)
	8) 2 Corinthians	(2 Cor)	22) 2 Peter	(2 Pet)
	9) Galatians	(Gal)	23) 1 John	(1 John)
	10) Ephesians	(Eph)	24) 2 John	(2 John)
	11) Philippians	(Phil)	25) 3 John	(3 John)
	12) Colossians	(Col)	26) Jude	(Jude)
	13) 1 Thessalonians	(1 Thess)	27) Revelation	(Rev)
	14) 2 Thessalonians	(2 Thess)		

[1] Note that Catholic and Protestant Bibles contain the exact same twenty-seven New Testament books. The difference between Catholic and Protestant Bibles lies in the seven Old Testament books that are highlighted in the above Old Testament list. These seven books, absent from Protestant Old Testaments, are usually referred to by Catholics as "the Deuterocanonical Books" and by Protestants as "the Apocrypha." Also included in the Catholic "Deuterocanonical Books" are fuller versions of the Old Testament books of Daniel and Esther. *(Cf. Chapter 2 of this book for a discussion of why these seven firmly-established Old Testament books, repeatedly declared by numerous early Christian Councils [393, 397, 417 A. D., etc...] to be the inspired Word of God, were later deleted from the "Protestant" Old Testament canon decided upon by Martin Luther and successive Reformers more than eleven centuries later.)*

Guide to Abbreviations Appearing in Footnotes Taken From the *Catechism of the Catholic Church*:

AAS: *Acta Apostolicae Sedis*

DS: Denzinger-Schonmetzer, *Enchiridion Symbolorum, definitionum et declarationum de rebus fidei et morum*

DV: *Dei Verbum*

CDF: Congregation for the Doctrine of the Faith

CIC: Codex Iuris Canonici

LG: *Lumen gentium*

MC: *Marialis cultus*

MF: *Mysterium fidei*

PL: J. P. Migne, ed., Patrologia Latina (Paris: 1841-1855)

PG: J. P. Migne, ed., Patrologia Graeca (Paris: 1857-1866)

PO: *Presbyterorum ordinis*

SC: *Sacrosanctum concilium*

STh: Summa Theologiae

Chapter 1

"What Do You Mean *Father* Mario Romero?"

A True Story

Recently, I purchased a radio from a local department store and, upon returning to the Church rectory, I discovered that it didn't work properly. I returned, once again, to the store where I had bought it and asked the sales clerk if I could exchange it for another one. She said that that would be fine but first she had to fill out a defective goods return form. "What is your name?" she asked me as she began to fill out the paperwork. "Father Mario Romero," I replied. She paused a little while and responded, "What do you mean *Father* Mario Romero? Aren't you Catholics aware that in the Bible Jesus says, 'Call no one on earth your father; you have but one Father in heaven' (Matt 23:9)? I'll record your name as *Reverend* Mario Romero. O.K.?"

A Catholic Response

A widely-accepted approach that Catholic and Protestant Bible scholars often use to determine the meaning of a particular passage from Scripture is to do a "word study." A "word study" is a search of the Scriptures to see if key words in the particular passage being considered appear elsewhere in the Bible and, if they do, discovers what meaning(s) these words have when they are used in these other places. If Jesus' words in Matt 23:9 are supposed to mean that He has forbidden Christians to use the title "father" (Greek: *pater*) to refer to another human being, there shouldn't be any other places in the New Testament where that title is used to refer to a person—right?

If one opens a Bible concordance and looks under the word "father," one will discover 124 instances in the New Testament alone where human beings are called "father" (Greek: *pater*)![1] A small sampler include the following:

- Jesus Christ Himself calls human beings "father" (Greek: *pater*) numerous times:

  - "What *father* [Greek: *pater*] among you would hand his son a snake when he asks for a fish" (Luke 11:11)?
  - "...a *father* [Greek: *pater*] will be divided against his son and a son against his *father* [Greek: *pater*]..." (Luke 12:53).
  - "If anyone comes to me without hating his *father* [Greek: *pater*] and mother...he cannot be my disciple" (Luke 14:26).
  - "'honor your *father* [Greek: *pater*] and your mother...'" (Matt 19:19).

- In his Letter to the Romans, St. Paul calls Abraham (a human being) "father": "...[F]ollow the path of faith that our *father* [Greek: *pater*] Abraham walked..." (Rom 4:12).

- In the Acts of the Apostles, St. Stephen calls human beings "father": "...My brothers and *fathers* [Greek: *pater*], listen. The God of glory appeared to our *father* Abraham while he was in Mesopotamia..." (Acts 7:2).

In his First Letter to the Corinthians, St. Paul, an early celibate Christian minister who did not have any natural-born children of his own (cf. 1 Cor 7:8),[2] uses the title "father" to refer to himself: "...[F]or I became your *father* in Christ Jesus through the gospel. Therefore, I urge you, be imitators of me. For this reason I am sending you Timothy, who is *my beloved and faithful son in the Lord...*" (1 Cor 4:15-17).

From the incredible number of times that human beings are called "father" (Greek: *pater*) in the New Testament, it appears that there is absolutely nothing wrong with the title in-and-of-itself. Why, then, did the unmarried St. Paul call himself "father" (cf. 1 Cor 4:15-16) and why do Catholics often call their priests "father"?

- Traditionally, a father provides food for his family. In calling a priest "father" the Catholic community is recognizing that he is feeding them with God's Word in the Holy Scriptures (cf. Acts 6:4) and with Jesus' Body and Blood in the Holy Eucharist (cf. Luke 22:19-20).

- Traditionally, a father brings new life into the world. In calling a priest "father" the Catholic community is recognizing that, at the baptismal font, he, in the name of God *(whom Jesus reveals in Matt 28:19 to be Father, Son, and Holy Spirit),*[3] is, supernaturally, bringing new Christians into the world (cf. John 3:1-5, 22).

- Traditionally, a father counsels and encourages members of his family to lead good and upright lives. Scripture speaks about St. Paul performing this important aspect of fatherhood for the Christian community: "As you know, we treated each one of you *as a father treats his children*, exhorting and encouraging you and insisting that you conduct yourselves as worthy of the God who calls you into his kingdom and glory" (1 Thess 2:11-12). One can clearly see how Catholic priests "father" in the spiritual realm in much the same way that natural fathers "father" in the secular realm.[4]

Note that in the Scriptures, Jesus makes the clear statement that He is *the* Good Shepherd (cf. John 10:14) while at the same time he also commissions *certain human beings* to shepherd His people in His physical absence (cf. John 21:15-17; Eph 4:11). In the Scriptures, Jesus is identified as *the* great High Priest (cf. Heb 3:1) while at the same time we read that *all* Christians are invited to share in Christ's priesthood (cf. 1 Pet 2:5 9; Rev 1:6). In the

Scriptures Jesus is identified as *the* King of kings (cf. 1 Tim 6:15) while at the same time the Bible says that Jesus will share His Kingship with *all* faithful Christians (who in Rev 3:21 are pictured wearing crowns and sitting on thrones and "reigning" right next to Jesus, the Lord of lords and the King of kings).[5] In exactly the same way, a Catholic "father" (a priest) shares in a small and totally subordinate way in the Fatherhood of God as he exercises his ministry, in Jesus' name, to God's people.[6]

Actually, in speaking about the often-hypocritical Scribes and Pharisees in Matt 23:1-10, Jesus prohibits the use of *three* titles in reference to them: "rabbi" *(meaning: "teacher")*; "father" *(in the spiritual sense)*; and "master" *(meaning: "leader")*. Jesus tells the sometimes spiritually-misguided Scribes and Pharisees that, since they were presently failing to carry out their appointed roles of *teaching* Divine truths to God's people, spiritually *fathering* them, and *leading* them in the pursuit of holiness, they are currently undeserving of their titles of "father," "master," or "rabbi."

From looking at the *whole* of the New Testament, it appears that what Jesus is saying in Matthew 23:9 is simply a restatement of the First Commandment: "You shall not have other gods besides me" (cf. Exodus 20:3; Deut 5:7). Or, in other words, remember that there is only one *heavenly* Father (who is the source of all earthly fatherhood).[7]

When Catholics call their priests "father" they are certainly not saying that they are equal to God the Father in heaven *(believe me, I am far from it!)*. It simply says that, like St. Paul in his God-given role as spiritual "father" of various early Christian communities (cf. 1 Cor 4:15-16), the priest is also exercising a spiritual "fatherly" role as he feeds his congregation with the Holy Eucharist and with the Word of God, as he brings new Christians into the world through the waters of Baptism, and as he encourages and exhorts members of his spiritual "family" to lead holy and upstanding lives.[8]

The minute that any Catholic priest starts to become hard-hearted and begins to behave like a little "god" himself, Jesus would give to him the same message that He gave to the Scribes and Pharisees in Matt 23:9: "Since you are not now acting as the true spiritual 'father' that you were called by God to be, you are presently undeserving of the title that the members of your faith community use to address you."[9]

Let us pray for all Catholic priests and ministers of all Christian denominations. May we never be "pharisaical" but always live like the committed spiritual "fathers," "leaders," and "teachers" that God calls us to be.[10]

Did the Early Christians Use the Title "Father" (Greek: *pater*) to Refer to Both Natural Human Fathers *AND* "Spiritual Fathers" of the Christian Community?

- As was discussed previously, the New Testament authors called human beings "father" (Greek: *pater*) an amazing 124 times in their Biblical writings!: Cf. Matt 3:9; Luke 1:32; John 4:12, etc. Refer to any Bible concordance for a complete listing of the remainder of these Scriptural citations.[11]

Endnotes

[1] Cf. *The Eerdmans Analytical Concordance to the Revised Standard Version of the Bible* (compiled by Richard E. Whitaker), (Grand Rapids, Michigan: William B. Eerdmans Publishing Co., 1988), pp. 360-362.

[2] Cf. Chapter 19 of this book for a discussion of the Biblically-rooted vocation of celibacy.

[3] To read more about the Biblical reality of the Blessed Trinity cf. John 14:25-26; Matt 28:19; Luke 3:21-22; 2 Cor 13:13; Jude 1:20-21; Gen 18:1-2; Gen 1:26. (Cf. also Chapter 22 of this book.)

[4] Although they are usually not called "father" by members of their congregation, most Protestant ministers spiritually "father" their congregation in many of these same ways.

[5] Cf. Patrick Madrid, "Any Friend of God Is A Friend of Mine," *This Rock* Magazine, (September, 1992 issue), p. 11.

[6] St. Paul's role of spiritual "father" is clearly displayed as he writes to Timothy: "[T]o Timothy, *my true child in faith*: grace, mercy, and peace from God the Father and Christ Jesus our

Lord" (1 Tim 1:2).

7   St. Paul writes about God the Father being the source of all earthly fatherhood: "...I kneel before the Father, from whom every family in heaven and on earth is named..." (Eph 3:14-15).

8   Note how, in the Old Testament, priesthood involved spiritual "fatherhood": "...Be a father and priest to me..." (Judges 17:10); "Come with us and be our father and priest..." (Judges 18:19).

9   Note that Jesus' prohibition regarding the use the title "father" to refer to the often self-serving Jewish Scribes and Pharisees (cf. Matt 23:9) could not have possibly referred to New Testament priests since, at that point in Jesus' ministry, the New Testament priesthood had not yet been established by Him. Only later do we read the Scriptural account of Jesus commissioning ("ordaining") the twelve Apostles and commanding them to offer the Eucharistic Bread and Wine (which He declared to be His Body and Blood) "in memory of [Him]" (cf. Matt 26:26-28; Luke 22:19-20). Cf. chapter 6 of this book to read about the sacrificial nature of the Eucharistic Meal established by Christ— which would necessitate the ministry of a priest.

10   As a Catholic priest, I personally have no problem with a non-Catholic Christian refusing to refer to me as "father." Since I am not currently feeding him with Jesus' Body and Blood in the Holy Eucharist (cf. John 6:48-68) and God's Word in the Holy Scriptures (Acts 6:4), since I am not currently baptizing him and the other members of his family so that they can become "born again" as children of God (cf. John 3:1-5, 22) *(cf. chapter 22 of this book)*, and since I am not currently counseling and encouraging him to lead a holy and upright life (cf. 1 Thess 2:11-12), I am not presently spiritually "fathering" him. Hopefully, one day, through the grace of the Holy Spirit, he will become a Catholic and then I will have the opportunity to minister to him in those ways. The non-Catholic Christian should not deny, though, that I, in Jesus' Name, rightfully spiritually "father" the members of the Catholic Christian community.

11   Cf. *The Eerdmans Analytical Concordance to the Revised Standard Version of the Bible* (compiled by Richard E. Whitaker), (Grand Rapids, Michigan: William B. Eerdmans Publishing Co., 1988), pp. 360-362.

Chapter 2

Catholic Bibles and Protestant Bibles: What's the Difference and Why the Difference?

What Does the Catholic Church Teach?

"This complete list is called the canon of Scripture. It includes forty-six books for the Old Testament...and twenty-seven for the New.⁹¹" (*Catechism of the Catholic Church*, #120.)

"...[T]he Church from the very beginning accepted as her own that very ancient Greek [Septuagint] translation of the Old Testament which is named after seventy men⁵¹..." (Vatican II document, *Dei Verbum*, #22.)[1]

Common Objection #1

"The Old Testament used by Protestants and Jews contains thirty-nine books while the Old Testament used by Catholics contains forty-six books. The Bible clearly states that if someone adds to Scripture: 'God will add to him the plagues described in this book' (cf. Rev 22:18). Why did you Catholics *add* seven books to your Old Testament?"

A Catholic Response

The Roman Catholic Church and the Eastern Catholic Churches in union with Rome have forty-six books in their Old Testament while the Jews and the Protestant Churches have thirty-nine books in their Old Testament. *(Note that Catholic and Protestant New Testaments are identical and each contain the exact same twenty-seven books.)*[2]

Some Protestant Christians will quote Rev 22:18 and ask us why we Catholics have *added* seven books to our Old Testament. The Catholic question to our Protestant brothers and sisters should, instead, be something like: "The verse immediately following Rev 22:18 says that one should not *take away* from the Scriptures: '... if anyone takes away from the words in this prophetic book, God will take away his share in the tree of life and in the holy city described in this book' (Rev 22:19). Why did Martin Luther and successive Protestant Reformers *delete* seven books from the firmly-established Christian Old Testament canon[3] in the 16th century when these seven books had been repeatedly declared to be the inspired Word of God by numerous 4th and 5th century Christian Church Councils?"[4]

Because most of the first Christians spoke Greek, the twenty-seven books of the New Testament were originally written in the language they could understand. When the dispersed Greek-speaking Jews translated the existing Hebrew Scriptures into Greek for their own use *(the Hebrew Scriptures were not yet formulated into a closed canon at that point)*, the Greek-speaking Christians readily embraced and adopted it for use in their own work of evangelization. The following are excerpts from the writings of historians and Scripture scholars that detail the circumstances that led the early Christian Church to decide on one Old Testament canon and the Jews to decide on another:

- Jerome Kodell, O.S.B., in his book, *The Catholic Bible Study Handbook* writes:

    "...[B]esides the thirty-nine [Old Testament] books revered as inspired by Protestant Christians (and Jews), Catholics include seven additional books: Baruch, Judith, 1 Maccabees, 2 Maccabees, Sirach (Ecclesiasticus), Tobit, and Wisdom... These books are known by Catholics as the 'Deuterocanonicals' and by Protestants as 'The Apocrypha'..."

...The current differences among Christians stem from the unsettled state of the Jewish scriptural canon in the early days of the [Christian] Church. A final decision on the contents of the Old Testament was not made in Judaism until the second or third century after Christ...

...[T]he group of books known as the 'Torah' was accepted as the word of God by 400 B.C., and the 'Prophets' by 200 B.C. But the canonicity of a later group of books known as the 'Writings' remained unsettled for many years. The writings were used in teaching and eventually in the liturgy by various Jewish communities, but there was no pressure to decide which of them should be ranked on a level with the Torah and Prophets. That rabbis finally did establish a definitive collection owed less to the internal needs of Judaism than to pressure from the outside: Christians had began quoting some of the disputed books as scripture and were implicitly canonizing writings which belonged to the Jews.

...Alexander the Great ended Persian rule at the Battle of Issus (Syria) in 333 B.C. He established Greek rule and cultural influence by setting up a series of military colonies and founding Greek-style cities, the most important of these being Alexandria (331 B.C.) in Egypt. The Greek language and way of life began to penetrate the eastern Mediterranean world.

...The Jews, in spite of the tenacity of their own religious and cultural traditions, were also affected by this Hellenistic movement, particularly those scattered beyond the confines of Palestine.

...A Greek translation of the Biblical books appeared in Alexandria around 200 B.C. This became known as the Septuagint (from the Latin for 'seventy'), because of the legend that the translation had been done by seventy-two translators, six from each of the twelve tribes. The Septuagint became the Bible of the Jews of the Diaspora (those 'dispersed' in foreign lands). It was later adopted by Christian missionaries when they took the Gospel into the Hellenistic world of the Roman Empire. The New Testament, written in Greek, records 300 of its 350 quotations from the Septuagint version of the Old Testament instead of in direct translation from the Hebrew.

The Septuagint translation was written during the period when the validity of the 'Writings' was still in question. Besides the Torah and Prophets, the Greek translators included other religious books used in synagogue worship...Recent textual evidence shows that the Septuagint was not translated all at once but over a period of time and by different individuals or groups. But by the first century A.D. [the Septuagint] had achieved widespread circulation and authority in the Greek-speaking Jewish world. By this time also, more recent Jewish books used in teaching and worship had become part of the Septuagint. Some of these are the books now disputed among Protestants, Catholics, and Jews... All of these [deuterocanonical] books circulated among the Greek-speaking Jews as Scripture for many years, including all during the lifetime of Jesus. Debate about their canonicity arose later...

While the Septuagint became the Jewish Bible of the Greek-speaking Mediterranean world, in Palestine the Hebrew Bible remained the standard. The Palestinian collection did not contain some of the books used at Alexandria, but there was no concern about a uniform edition. Jews used the writings which met the needs of their local communities. All of these books, Hebrew or Greek or Aramaic in origin, were considered part of the sacred writings...

...During the formative days of the Christian Church, the Jews did not possess a formal or explicit canon of Old Testament books. The Christian writers quoted the broad library of sacred writings used among contemporary Jews. The Jews continued their own discussions about the sacred books, and in the late second or early third century A.D. canonized the shorter collection that Jews and Protestants use today. Modern study by all parties to the current debate have raised questions about the correctness of this late Jewish decision to exclude some of the books which had been accepted as Scripture for more than 200 years.

The Christians did not establish their Old Testament canon as early as the Jews. Apparently, they did not consider the question of great importance to the Church, and continued to use the Hebrew writings as before. Christian attention was probably diverted by the far more crucial question of the contents of the New Testament canon.

...The question of the Old Testament canon rested during the next 1,000 years until it was raised again by the reformers in the sixteenth century. In his translation of 1534, Martin Luther grouped the deuterocanonical books together at the end of the Old Testament as books which 'are not held equal to the sacred scriptures and yet are useful and good for reading.' The Reformers, in deciding to get back to the situation at the time of the Church's origin, wanted to adopt as scripture the books that made up the Old Testament used by the early Christians. They presumed that the books revered by the Jews of their own time had always been the canonical Old Testament, and so the shorter list of books became the Old Testament of the Reformers. They did not know that the decision for a shorter Old Testament canon had been late in coming, and that during the first century both Jews and Christians held a wider selection of Old Testament books. In reaction to the Reformers, the Council of Trent in 1546 [formally] defined the longer Old Testament canon as inspired scripture."[5]

- Lawrence Boadt, in his book, *Reading the Old Testament* states:

"[T]he Catholic...[Old Testament] canon contains forty-six books, seven beyond the thirty-nine in Hebrew. These forty-six books were first listed as the canon by local Church councils in North Africa in the fourth century: at Hippo in 393, and at Carthage in 397 and 417 A.D. But they were not given solemn approval by the Church until the Council of Trent in April of 1546, although they had been accepted as binding in practice from the time of the fourth century decisions.

...[F]or Christians at the time of Christ and in the early Church, the common book of the Scriptures was not the Hebrew Bible at all but the Septuagint Greek Bible. It had much wider use in the Roman world because most Jews lived far from Palestine in Greek cities, and because most Christians were Greek-speaking Gentiles and not Jews at all. Thus the Greek Bible, although mostly a translation of the Hebrew books, had almost as exalted a status as the Hebrew itself did. Sometimes scholars even speak of an 'Alexandrian canon' of forty-six books that was parallel and equivalent to the 'Palestine canon' of only thirty-nine books.

...We can at least say that the question of exactly how many books made up the canon of inspired Scriptures was still open at the end of the Old Testament period, and that, after a time, Jewish tradition went one way and Christian tradition went another. It was not until the reformers in the 16th century demanded a return to the Hebrew canon that Christians fought over two distinct canons."[6]

- Raymond Brown, Joseph Fitzmyer and Roland Murphy (editors) in *The New Jerome Biblical Commentary* write:

"...Actually, a good number of the deuterocanonical books were originally composed in Hebrew (Sir, Jdt, 1 Macc) or Aramaic (Tob). The Qumran discoveries prove that some of these books were in circulation in Palestine and were accepted by Jewish groups there. The fact that the codices of the [Septuagint] do not isolate the deuterocanonical books as a group but mix them in with the Prophets (Bar) and the Writings (Sir, Wis) show that there was no awareness that these books had a unique origin, as there would have been if they were thought to be later and foreign additions to an already fixed collection translated from Hebrew.

…It was not the Jews of Alexandria but the Christian Church that, working with the [Septuagint], ultimately drew up an exclusive canon.

…The conclusion that there was no rigidly closed canon in Judaism in the 1st and early 2nd centuries. A.D. means that when the Church was in its formative period and was using the sacred books of the Jews, there was no closed canon for the church to adopt.

…[I]n debating purgatory with J. Maier of Eck (1519), it was Luther who broke with Church tradition and began a new era in discussions on the Old Testament canon… Confronted by 2 Macc 12:46 as 'scriptural proof' for the doctrine of purgatory, Luther rejected 2 Macc as Scripture.

The early reformers were not eager to reject the…[deuterocanonical books] altogether, since they had been in ecclesiastical use for more than a millennium."[7]

- John McKenzie, S.J., in his book, *Dictionary of the Bible* writes:

"The [Septuagint] enjoyed great authority among the Jews of the Diaspora into the 1st century A.D. It was the Gk Bible, and for this reason it was adopted by Christians when they began to evangelize the Hellenistic world. Christians adopted it with even greater enthusiasm than the Jews; it became the Bible of the Church in the first generation of Christians, and 300 of the 350 citations from the Old Testament in the New Testament are quoted according to the [Septuagint]...

There is little doubt that the acceptance of the [Septuagint] and its use by Christians led the Jews to reject it...

The earliest manuscripts of the [Septuagint] are the fragments from Qumran, probably from the latter half of the 1st century AD.

From the time of Paul onwards there can be little doubt that the [Septuagint], with the deuterocanonical books, was the OT of the apostolic church; it was probably adopted because Greek was the common language of the Mediterranean lands. This acceptance of the sacred books as found in the [Septuagint] perseveres in all the ecclesiastical writers of the first three centuries A.D. except Melito of Sardis (+ about 193), who cites the Hb canon; the fact of a difference is mentioned by Origen (+ 254), who affirms the right of Christians to employ the deuterocanonical books, even though they are not accepted by the Jews. The same canon is found in all the official canons: the Cheltenham Canon, about 350; the canons of Hippo (393), Carthage (397), and Innocent 1 (405), except the canon of Laodicea (360)."[8]

- *The New Oxford Annotated Bible (Revised Standard Version)* states:

"During the early Christian centuries most Greek and Latin Church Fathers such as Irenaeus, Tertullian, Clement of Alexandria, and Cyprian (none of whom knew any Hebrew) quoted passages from the [deuterocanonical books] as 'Scripture,' 'divine Scripture,' 'inspired' and the like.

...In the controversies that arose at the time of the Reformation, Protestant leaders soon recognized the need to distinguish between books that were authoritative for the establishment of doctrine and those that were not. Thus, disputes over the doctrines of Purgatory and of the efficacy of prayers and Masses for the dead inevitably involved discussion concerning the authority of 2 Maccabees, which contains what was held to be scriptural warrant for them [cf. 2 Macc 12: 38-46].

The first extensive discussion of the canon from the Protestant point of view was a treatise in Latin, *De Canonicis Scripturis Libellus*, published at Wittenberg in 1520 by Andreas Bodenstein, who is commonly known as Carlstadt, the name of his birthplace."[9]

• Karl Keating, in his book, *Catholicism and Fundamentalism* writes:

> "...The fact is that the Council of Trent did not add to the Bible what Protestants call the apocrypha books. Instead, the Reformers dropped from the Bible books that had been in common use for centuries. The Council of Trent, convened to reaffirm Catholic doctrines and to revitalize the Church, proclaimed that these books always had belonged to the Bible and had to remain in it. After all, it was the Catholic Church, in the fourth century, that officially decided which books composed the canon of the Bible and which did not. The Council of Trent came on the scene twelve centuries later and merely restated the ancient position."[10]

Common Objection #2

"The seven Catholic Old Testament 'deuterocanonical books' are not quoted in the New Testament. That proves that they are not inspired by God and, therefore, should not be included in the canon of the Christian Bible."

A Catholic Response

A number of Old Testament books accepted by Protestants and Catholics alike are not directly quoted in the New Testament: (e. g., Ezra, Nehemiah, Esther, Ecclesiastes, Song of Songs).[11]

In *The New Oxford Annotated Bible (Revised Standard Version)* one reads:

> "...[S]everal New Testament writers make occasional allusions to one or more [deuterocanonical] books. For example, what seem to be literary echoes from Wisdom are present in Paul's Letter to the Romans (compare Rom. 1.20-29 with Wis 13.5,8; 14.24, 27; and Rom. 9.20-23 with Wis. 12.12, 20; 15.7) and in his correspondence with the Corinthians (compare 2 Cor. 5.1, 4 with

15

Wis. 9.15). The short Letter of James, a typical bit of 'wisdom literature' in the New Testament, contains allusions not only to the Old Testament book of Proverbs but to gnomic sayings in Sirach as well (compare Jas.1.19 with Sir.5.11; and Jas.1.13 with Sir.15.11-12)."[12]

One can see here that clear literary echoes of the Catholic deuterocanonical books certainly do appear in New Testament writings. Thus, one can see the considerable influence that these seven Old Testament deuterocanonical books had on the authors of the New Testament.

Not only are the Roman Catholic Church and the Eastern Catholic Churches "Full Gospel" Churches, they are full/complete Old Testament Churches as well!

What Books Were Included in the Earliest *Christian* Declaration of the Canon of Scripture?:

• Latin Text from the Council of Hippo *(Canon 36: Oct. 8, 393 A.D.)*

[Old Testament]: *"(Placuit) ut praeter **Scripturas canonicas** nihil in Ecclesia egatur sub nomine divinarum Scripturarum. Sunt autem canonicae Scripturae: Genesis, Exodus, Leviticus, Numeri, Deuteronomium, Iesu Nave, Iudicum, Ruth, Regnorum libri quatuor, Paralipomenon libri duo, Iob, Psalterium Davidicum, **Salomonis libri quinque**, Duodecim libri prophetarum, Esaias, **Ieremias**, Daniel, Ezechiel, **Tobias**, **Iudith**, Hester, Hesdrae libri duo, **Machabaeorum libri duo.***

[New Testament]: *Novi autem Testamenti: Pauli Apostoli epistolae tredecim, eiusdem ad Hebraeos una, Petri duae, Ioannis tres, Iacobi una, Iudae una, Apocalypsis Ioannis. Ita ut de confirmando isto canone transmarina Ecclesia consulatur. Liceat etiam legi passiones Martyrum, cum anniversarii dies eorum celebrantur."*[13]

What Did the Early Christians Believe About the Forty-six Book Old Testament Presently Used by Roman Catholics and the Eastern Catholic Churches?:

- In the writings of many of the early Church Fathers the seven Catholic "Deuterocanonical Books" are quoted side-by-side "protocanonical" Scripture.[14]

- "Ptolemy, the King of Egypt, when he had constructed a library at Alexandria, and had filled it by collecting books from everywhere, afterwards learned that ancient histories written in Hebrew letters had been carefully preserved. Desiring to know these writings, he sent for seventy wise men from Jerusalem who knew both the Greek and Hebrew languages, and appointed them to translate the books... He supplied attendants to care for their every need, and also to prevent their communicating with each other, so that it might be possible to know the accuracy of the translation, by their agreement one with another. When he found that the seventy men had given not only the same meaning, but even in the same words, and had failed to agree with each other by not so much as a single word, but had written the same things about the same things, he was struck with amazement and believed that the translation had been written with divine authority." St. Justin Martyr in his *Exhortation to the Greeks* (circa 275 A.D.)[15]

- "The process [of translating the Septuagint from the Hebrew text] was no invention of words and contrivance of human wisdom. On the contrary, the translation was effected by the Holy Spirit, by whom the Divine Scriptures were spoken..." St. Cyril of Jerusalem in his *Catechetical Lectures* (circa 350 A.D.)[16]

- Cf. decrees from the Council of Hippo (393 A.D.)

- Cf. decrees from Councils of Carthage (397 and 417 A.D.)

Endnotes

[91] Cf. DS 179; 1334-1336; 1501-1504.

[51] I.e., the Septuagint. *(Author's note: The "Septuagint" is the Roman Catholic Church and the Eastern Catholic Churches 46-book Old Testament).*

[1] Walter M. Abbott, S.J. (General Editor), *The Documents of Vatican II*, (Piscataway, NJ: Association Press, New Century Publishers, Inc., 1966), Chapter VI, Paragraph 22, pp. 125-126.

[2] Refer to the *Guide to Abbreviations* page in the front of this book for a complete listing of the Old Testament and New Testament books.

[3] The "canon" of Scripture refers to those Biblical books officially recognized by the Christian community as being Divinely inspired.

[4] Note that the early Christian Church had not decided what books belonged to the Old and New Testament canons until 393 A.D. at the Catholic Council of Hippo in Africa *(cf. a portion of the text from the Council of Hippo at the end of this chapter).* This "Catholic canon" was reaffirmed again at the Councils of Carthage in 397 and 417 A.D. What the author of the Book of Revelation *(which was composed circa 96 A.D.)* is saying in Rev 22:18-19 is that he wishes for no one to add or to delete from this particular writing of his — the Book of Revelation. Catholics have not added or deleted a single word from the Book of Revelation.

[5] Jerome Kodell, O.S.B., *The Catholic Bible Study Handbook*, (Ann Arbor, Michigan: Servant Books, 1985), pp. 41-47.

[6] Lawrence Boadt, *Reading the Old Testament*, (New York, NY: Paulist Press, 1984), pp. 16-18.

[7] Raymond Brown, Joseph Fitzmyer, Roland Murphy (editors), *The New Jerome Biblical Commentary*, (Englewood Cliffs, NJ: Prentice Hall, 1990), pp. 1040-1042.

[8] John McKenzie, S.J., *Dictionary of the Bible*, (New York, NY: Collier Books Macmillan Publishing Co., 1965), pp. 786-788, 119.

[9] Herbert G. May and Bruce M. Metzger (editors), *The New Oxford Annotated Bible, Revised Standard Version* (Introduction

to the Apocrypha), (New York, NY: Oxford University Press, 1962, 1973), pp. xiv-xvii.

[10] Karl Keating, *Catholicism and Fundamentalism*, (San Francisco, CA: Ignatius Press, 1988), pp. 46-47.

[11] H. B. Swete, *An Introduction to the Old Testament in Greek* (Revised by Richard Rusden Ottley), (Peabody, MA: Hendrickson Publishers, 1914, 1989), p. 26.

[12] Herbert G. May and Bruce M. Metzger (editors), *The New Oxford Annotated Bible, Revised Standard Version* (Introduction to the Apocrypha), (New York, NY: Oxford University Press, 1962, 1973), pp. xiv-xviii.

[13] *Enchiridion Biblicum*, (Rome, Italy: Apud Librariam Vaticanam, 1927), Concilium Hipponense, Canon 36 (Oct. 8, 393), pp. 4-5. Notice the Latin names for the seven Catholic Old Testament Deuterocanonical books: *"Tobias"* (Book of Tobit), *"Iudith"* (Book of Judith), *"Machabaeorum libri duo"* (Books of 1st and 2nd Maccabees), *"Ieremias"* (Jeremiah) and *"Salomonis libri quinque" (the Five Books of Solomon)*.

According to Dr. Gregory Vall, Scripture professor at Notre Dame Seminary in New Orleans, LA, in a letter to this book's author dated March 27, 1995: "a sort of shorthand [is used here in this list that is] found also in many other canon lists." Dr. Vall identifies "the Five Books of Solomon" as Proverbs, Ecclesiastes, Song of Songs, Sirach [a Catholic Deuterocanonical book], and Wisdom [a Catholic Deuterocanonical book]. Dr. Vall says, "It might seem odd to include Sirach in this group, since it is explicitly ascribed to an author other than Solomon. But this is just one more indication that Solomonic 'authorship' refers to the genre of a book (in this case what we would call 'wisdom literature') and to its authority (but not necessarily to an historical claim to authorship)." "As for Baruch," says Dr. Vall, "it is presumably included here as part of the Book of Jeremiah as are Lamentations and the Epistle of Jeremiah (Baruch chapter 6 in Catholic English Bibles)." Cf. also H. B. Swete's book, *An Introduction to the Old Testament in Greek* (Revised by Richard Rusden Ottley), (Peabody, MA: Hendrickson Publishers, 1914, 1989), pp. 267-268, 270, 274.

14   E.g., the Didache (circa 70 A.D.), The Letter of Barnabas (circa 74 A.D.), Pope Clement I (circa 80 A.D.), St. Polycarp of Smyrna (circa 135 A.D.), St. Irenaeus (circa 189 A.D.), St. Hippolytus (circa 220 A.D.), St. Clement of Alexandria (circa 225 A.D.), St. Cyprian of Carthage (circa 250 A.D.), etc. For extensive quotations of the early Church Fathers citing passages from the Greek Septuagint Old Testament visit the *Catholic Answers* Internet web site at <http://www.catholic.com> or the *Nazareth Resource Library* web site at <http://www.cin.org/users/james/index.htm>

15   William A. Jurgens (editor and translator), *The Faith of the Early Fathers (Volume 1)*, (Collegeville, MN: The Liturgical Press, 1970), p. 65.

16   *Ibid.*, p. 352.

Chapter 3

The Historical "Roots" of the Roman Catholic Church

What Does the Catholic Church Teach?

"The Lord Jesus endowed His community with a structure that will remain until the Kingdom is fully achieved. Before all else there is the choice of the Twelve with Peter as their head [168] '...When the work which the Father gave the Son to do on earth was accomplished, the Holy Spirit was sent on the day of Pentecost in order that He might continually sanctify the Church.' [174]... Particular Churches are fully catholic through their communion with one of them, the Church of Rome 'which presides in charity.' [315] 'For with this church, by reason of its pre-eminence, the whole Church, that is the faithful everywhere, must necessarily be in accord.' [316] Indeed, 'from the incarnate Word's descent to us, all Christian churches everywhere have held and hold the great Church that is here [at Rome] to be their only basis and foundation since, according to the Savior's promise, the gates of hell have never prevailed against her..'..' The Church knows that she is joined in many ways to the baptized who are honored by the name of Christian, but do not profess the Catholic faith in its entirety or have not preserved unity or communion under the successor of Peter."[322] (*Catechism of the Catholic Church*, #765, 767, 834, 838.)

Common Objection #1

"Our church was founded by Jesus Christ circa 30 A.D. but we went 'underground' after the year 313 A.D. *(when the Emperor Constantine stopped the persecution of Christians and allowed Christianity to be practiced in public).* During this time period, the leaders of the Christian Church couldn't properly teach the massive amounts of new converts asking for admittance into the Church and, as a result, all kinds of 'Catholic distortions' began to creep into the 'pure faith' of the first Christians *(e. g., the Real Presence of Jesus Christ in the Holy Eucharist, intercessory prayer with the saints in heaven, prayer for the deceased, purgatory, etc.)* Our denomination, that had existed underground for centuries, simply resurfaced again after the Protestant Reformation in the 16th century."

A Catholic Response

It doesn't take much researching of the writings of the first generations of Christians to discover that the doctrines described by some of our Protestant brothers and sisters as "Catholic distortions of the pure Apostolic faith" existed *way before* the Emperor Constantine legalized the public practice of Christianity in 313 A.D. Please refer to the ends of each chapter of this book and look at the dates that the early Christians are describing their beliefs in the Real Presence of Jesus Christ in the Holy Eucharist, intercessory prayer with the saints in heaven, prayer for the deceased, purgatory, etc. *If* the Catholic Church has erred in holding these beliefs, that means it was in error *way before* Constantine's legalization of Christianity. *If* Catholics are wrong in holding these doctrines this would mean that the Church apostatized before the end of the 1st century *(while a number of the Twelve Apostles were still alive!)* — a highly unlikely theory considering Jesus' promises of perpetuity and doctrinal protection of His Church: "And so I say to you, you are Peter, and upon this rock I will build my church, and the gates of the netherworld *shall not* prevail against it" (Matt 16:18). Had the "gates of the netherworld" almost instantly prevailed against Jesus' Church after His death? Had Jesus left the Church orphan after a generation or two when He promised that He would never do that: "I will not leave you orphans..." (John 14:18)? Had the Holy Spirit, whom Jesus promised to lead the Church into all truth, "checked out"?: I have much more to tell you, but you cannot bear it now. But when he comes, the Spirit of truth, he will guide you to all truth..." (John 16:12-13).[1]

Consider this example: People have been eating soup since before the time of Christ. What if the "Yummy Soup Company" located in Peoria, Illinois would make the claim that they were originally founded in 500 B.C. but existed "underground" until 1958 A.D. when they produced their first can of soup at their United States factory? One would probably say to the "Yummy Soup Company," "Prove it! Show me some concrete evidence, in black and white, of your existence in these past twenty five centuries!" That is the challenge that a Protestant Christian, who makes the claim that his church was founded by Christ circa 30 A.D. but went "underground" and simply "re-surfaced" after the 16th century Protestant Reformation, must answer. It only takes a little reading of the writings of the early Christians to discover that the Church Fathers were solidly *Catholic* in their beliefs and practices.[2]

Common Objection #2

"What about the checkered past of the Catholic Church? Look at all of its sinfulness in the past 2,000 years!"

A Catholic Response

The Old and New Testaments are, unfortunately and fortunately, *chocked full* of accounts of God's appointed leaders occasionally making public displays of their own personal sinfulness and brokenness: e. g., the immorality of King David (cf. 2 Samuel 11:1-27), the sinfulness of King Solomon (cf. 1 Kings 11:1-43), the wavering faith of "doubting Thomas" (cf. John 20:24-29), the betrayal of the Apostle Judas (cf. Luke 22:47-53), etc.

Protestant televangelist Joyce Meyer once said something to the effect that God allows His ministers to make public displays of their own personal brokenness and sinfulness every now and then to show the faithful that their faith is in the wrong place *(meaning that, if a Christian's faith ultimately lies in Jesus, the occasional public displays of the human brokenness of Jesus' ministers should not deter him at all from the active practice of his faith. Rather than becoming discouraged and disillusioned, the Christian should pray ever more fervently for the continued conversion and spiritual renewal of his pastor.)*

The fact that the Catholic Church has been around 2,000 years has given its members more than ample opportunity to make public displays of their own human brokenness. Pope John Paul II, in his recent Apostolic Letter *Tertio Millennio Adveniente*, humbly apologizes for the sinful behavior of the individual members of the Catholic Church throughout the two millennia of its existence:

> "Hence, it is appropriate that, as the Second Millennium of Christianity draws to a close, the Church should become more fully conscious of the sinfulness of her children, recalling those times in history when they departed from the spirit of Christ and his Gospel and, instead of offering to the world the witness of a life inspired by the values of faith, indulged in ways of thinking and acting which were truly *forms of counter-witness and scandal...*
>
> Although she is holy because of her incorporation into Christ, the Church does not tire of doing penance: before God and man *she always acknowledges as her own her sinful sons and daughters.* As *Lumen Gentium* affirms: 'The Church, embracing sinners to her bosom, is at the same time holy and always in need of being purified, and incessantly pursues the path of penance and renewal.'"[3]

As foretold in Sacred Scripture, it is certainly true that in the Church that Jesus founded there exists both "weeds" *and* "wheat" (cf. Matt 13:25-30). Monsignor Bob Guste says about individual members of the Church: "What the world needs is not another Church but the constant renewal of the Church Jesus established. The trouble with the Protestant Reformation was not that the baby didn't need a bath but that the original baby was thrown out with the bath water.

The fact is that the baby regularly needs a bath — constant conversion and renewal until the Lord comes again... (Eph 5:25-27)."[4]

Common Objection #3

"We are not a *new* church! In the 16th century we simply reformed the *original* Church founded by Jesus Christ circa 30 A.D. that had fallen into doctrinal error."

A Catholic Response

By studying the writings of the early Christians one can clearly see how "Catholic" their belief and practice was. At the Protestant Reformation in the 16th century, major doctrinal changes were introduced into the apostolic faith by the Protestant Reformers that had no precedence at all in the belief of the early Church. To say that the Protestant Reformers simply "reformed" the one original Church founded by Christ would be like a homeowner, who demolishes many of the main supporting walls and major foundations of his home, who moves his home to a different location and changes the occupants and heads of household of his home, saying that he doesn't have a new home but simply has "remodeled" his original dwelling place. After the homeowner makes such drastic alterations to his original home, he hasn't just "remodeled it," he has a different home.[5]

Common Objection #4

"If one looks at the Gospel of Matthew in the original Greek of the New Testament, Jesus says to Peter: 'And so I say to you, you are *Petros* and upon this *petra* I will build my Church...' (Matt 16:18). In Greek, Peter's name (*Petros*) means 'a little pebble' while the Greek word for 'rock' (*petra*) means 'a large boulder.' It is obvious, therefore, that the man Peter was not the 'rock' that Jesus was speaking about. What Jesus was really saying was that His Church was to be built upon Peter's confession of faith in Him (cf. Matt 16:16) and that He Himself was the Rock foundation on which His Church was to be built."

A Catholic Response

Refer to Chapter 13 in this book for a response to this objection.

Common Objection #5

"The word 'Pope' is not found anywhere in the Bible, why do you Catholics use that title to refer to the Bishop of Rome?"

A Catholic Response

According to Merriam-Webster's Collegiate Dictionary, the word "Pope" comes from the Latin word *papa* (which comes from the Greek word *pappas* — which means "daddy" or "papa").[6] Please refer to Chapter 1 of this book to see why it would be totally appropriate for Catholics to call the successor of St. Peter "papa," "daddy," or "father."

Common Objection #6

"What about the instances in history when there were two or three Popes in office at one time (e. g., 1159-1180 A.D.)?"

A Catholic Response

The fact is that there were *never* two or three Popes of the Catholic Church who were in office at the same time. At a few points in history there were a few individuals who *claimed to be* Pope during the same time period but the fact is that there was only *one* valid Pope of the Church. The individuals who claimed to be Pope are referred to as "anti-popes" because they stood in opposition to the officially-recognized Pope.[7]

Common Objection #7

"What about the moments in history where there were gaps and no one was Pope (e. g., between 304 and 308 A.D.)?"

A Catholic Response

Due to fierce persecutions of the Christians and civil unrests, there are a few instances in history where a Pope was not named instantly to replace his successor. However, when the persecutions or the unrests ceased and the new Pope was finally named, he was acknowledged to be the valid successor of the previous Pope.

Common Objection #8

"There is no indication in the Bible that Jesus intended for Peter to have successors. After Peter died his succession stopped."

A Catholic Response

T. L. Frazier, in the book, *Surprised by Truth*, speaks about apostolic succession:

> "It has long been recognized...that Matt 16:18-19 is modeled on Isaiah 22:20-25 where Eliakim is given the 'key of the house of David' to be prime minister over Israel, 'a father to those who live in Jerusalem and to the house of Judah.' This office, which some have compared to the office of vizier held by Joseph in Egypt (Gen 41:40; cf. 2 Kgs. 15:5; 18:18; 1 Kgs. 18:3), was second in prerogatives and authority only to the monarch himself and was hereditary (i.e., there were successors). If Peter's apostolic office was the fulfillment of this Old Testament type, I thought, then there could be little question that Peter's office also had successors."[8]

In his book *Born Fundamentalist Born Again Catholic*, David Currie writes:

> "[In Isaiah 22:22] Isaiah was speaking to Eliakim, a new 'prime minister' in Israel. Eliakim took over the office from an unworthy prime minister. God was telling Eliakim that he would be chief ruler in Israel, under

the king alone. Isaiah uses two images in his discussion, a key and a peg. It is evident in Isaiah 22:22 that the key has two important aspects. It is a symbol of the power to rule — authority, and it symbolizes permanence — intergenerational succession. The key existed prior to being given to Eliakim, and it would exist after Eliakim passed on. The key, the power to rule, passes from mortal to mortal.

Later in Isaiah a peg is used to signify the instability of Eliakim's personal position. The peg, Isaiah foretells, will be pulled down: Eliakim would be cut down in the prime of his rule. The peg relates to Eliakim on a personal level. But the key denotes an *office*, both powerfull and permanent.

It is significant that Jesus uses only the symbolism of the key with Peter and never the peg."[9]

The Scriptures tell us that the Apostle Judas Iscariot hung himself after betraying Jesus (cf. Matt 27:5) and, after this tragic event, the early Church felt a need to replace him *immediately* so that the structure of Twelve Apostles that Jesus had set up to represent His New Testament Chosen People would remain intact.[10] We read in the Acts of the Apostles about St. Peter presiding over the selection process of the successor to the Apostle Judas Iscariot (cf. Acts 1:15-26). If the early Church felt a need to replace the *unfaithful* Apostle Judas Iscariot almost instantly after his death, it would have been all the more pressing for them to choose a successor for the only Apostle who was singled out by Christ to receive the "keys of the Kingdom of heaven" and be called "rock" (cf. Matt 16:18-19). History shows this to be exactly what happened.

If Jesus clearly wanted His Apostles and His first disciples to have a specific appointed leader in His absence, surely He would want His expanding Church in future generations to have a particular leader as well so that the "gates of the netherworld shall not prevail" against His Church in any age (cf. Matt 16:18). Remember St. Paul's words to the Ephesians: "to [God] be glory *in the church* and in Christ Jesus *to all generations, forever and ever. Amen*" (Eph 3:21). St. Paul also writes: "And what you heard from me through many witnesses *entrust to faithful people who will have the ability to teach others as well*" (2 Tim 2:2).

Common Objection #9

"The Church that Jesus speaks about protecting in Scripture (cf. Matt 16:18-19) is an invisible, 'spiritual' Church, made up of all true believers throughout the world. Jesus' Church is not one particular visible institution."

A Catholic Response

In the Gospel of Matthew, Jesus says that the Church that He established is called to be "...A city set on a mountain [that] *cannot be hidden*" (Matt 5:14). This certainly does not sound like some invisible "spiritual" collection of all true believers from every Christian denomination throughout the world.

In the Acts of the Apostles we read about a Jew named "Saul" who was on a mission to persecute any members of the Christian Church that he could find when, suddenly, he was knocked to the ground by the risen Jesus who said to him, "Saul, Saul, why are you persecuting *me*" (Acts 9:4)? We can see here that Jesus clearly identifies Himself with a distinct *visible* body of believers.

The word "church" (Greek: *ekklesia*) appears over one hundred times throughout the New Testament and not once does it refer to an invisible international grouping of all true believers.[11]

Al Kresta states:

> "The Evangelical vision of the Church as the invisible union of all who genuinely trust in Christ seemed...[to be] a subtle form of Docetism. Docetists believed that the Word did not truly take flesh but only appeared to, the invisibilists similarly denied the materiality of Christ's Body, the Church. By refusing to accept the visible Church Protestantism denied the extension of the Incarnation."[12]

David Currie writes:

> "I understand the origin of the belief [that Jesus'
> Church is not a specific visible one but an intangible
> union of all true believers]. The [Protestant] reformers
> had to explain how a person's body could be part of the
> body of Christ and yet not appear to be in physical com-
> munion with another person...For fifteen hundred years
> it was the understanding of all Christians that the Church
> was a visible entity on earth. The Church was the physi-
> cal manifestation of the mystical body of Christ. This is
> a favorite theme of Paul. A majority of Christians still
> do believe this. But the [Protestant] reformers had to
> find a justification for splitting from that visible Church.
> They invented the notion of an invisible church. It cer-
> tainly has no explicit scriptural basis."[13]

Founders and Founding Dates
of Various Christian Churches:

Church:	Founder:	Date:
Roman Catholic[14]	Jesus Christ. (In Matt 16:18-19 Jesus calls St. Peter "rock," entrusts to him the "keys of the kingdom of heaven" and appoints him to be His "prime minister."[15] Early Christian writings tell us that St. Peter was later martyred for his faith in Rome. St. Peter's Basilica, the headquarters of the modern-day Roman Catholic Church, is built on top of the tomb of St. Peter.)	circa 30 A.D.
Oriental Orthodox Churches[16]	These Churches have Apostolic origin but later went into schism from the primal See of Rome due to a Christological dispute.[17]	431

Church:	Founder:	Date:
Greek Orthodox Churches[18]	These Churches have apostolic origin but later went into schism from the primal See of Rome due to increasing economic, political, and cultural tensions and a theological dispute concerning the Holy Spirit.[19]	1054
Lutheran[20]	Martin Luther	1517
Church of England[21]	King Henry VIII	1534
Presbyterian[22]	John Knox	1560
Baptist[23]	John Smyth	1609
Methodist[24]	John & Charles Wesley	1738
Episcopal Church (U.S.)[25]	Samuel Seabury	1789
Church of Christ[26]	Evangelical Presbyterians in Kentucky & Pennsylvania in distress over Protestant factionalism & loss of fervor.	1804
Disciples of Christ[27]	Thomas & Alexander Campbell	1827
Mormons[28]	Joseph Smith	1827
7th Day Adventists[29]	William Miller	1840
Jehovah Witnesses[30]	Charles Russell	1870
Pentecostal[31]	A reaction to loss of evangelical fervor among Methodists & other denominations.	1901
Church of the Nazarene[32]	Merging of 3 existing Holiness groups in the U. S.	1908
Assemblies of God[33]	Merging of various Pentecostal churches at Hot Springs, Arkansas.	1914

An interesting phenomenon that appears to be springing up lately are groups of Christians that refer to themselves as "non-denominational." This is peculiar because Christian denominations are characterized by their stances on various theological/doctrinal issues. If one asks a "non-denominational Christian" what his beliefs are about a variety of theological/doctrinal issues *(such as those mentioned in the Introduction section of this book)*, what one will get is a doctrinal profile that is very close, if not identical, to one of the "official" Protestant Christian denominations already in existence. If the theological profile of the "non-denominational" pastor's church happens to be different from all of the other previously-established denominations or if it is a doctrinal hybrid of them, a brand new Christian denomination is, thus, born.

Since the 16th century Protestant Reformation, experts estimate that over twenty-five thousand denominations have come into being. A "non-denominational Christian" might very well be nothing more than a non-affiliated Pentecostal, Presbyterian, Baptist, etc. Catholic convert Steve Wood writes: "The unwritten creed in non-denominational churches is whatever the pastor happens to believe. Woe to the member who crosses the line and disagrees with the pastor."[34]

The Roman Catholic Church:
From Jesus Christ to Pope John Paul II[35]

Jesus Christ (b. circa 6 B.C.–d. circa 30 A.D.)[36]

(The Catholic Church was founded when the Holy Spirit descended upon the Apostles at Pentecost [cf. Acts 2] circa 30 A.D. Christ had already pre-picked St. Peter to be the Prime Minister [later called "Pope"] of His Church [cf. Matt 16:18-19].)[37]

1. Saint Peter   30-67
2. Saint Linus   67-76

(The first Gospel [Mark] was written circa 70 A.D.)

3. Saint Anacletus (Cletus)   76-88
4. Saint Clement   88-97
5. Saint Evaristus   97-105

(The last New Testament writing was completed circa 100 A.D. Note that the New Testament Bible was a product of the already-existing Roman Catholic Church.)

6. Saint Alexander I   105-115
7. Saint Sixtus I   115-125
8. Saint Telesphorus   125-136
9. Saint Hyginus   136-140
10. Saint Pius I   140-155
11. Saint Anicetus   155-166
12. Saint Soter   166-175
13. Saint Eleutherius   175-189

(St. Irenaeus [circa 180 A.D.] gives the list of the popes who succeeded St. Peter in an unbroken line. Refer to his writings at the end of this chapter.)[38]

14. Saint Victor I   189-199
15. Saint Zephyrinus   199-217
16. Saint Callistus I (Calixtus)   217-222
17. Saint Urban I   222-230
18. Saint Pontian   230-235
19. Saint Anterus   235-236
20. Saint Fabian   236-250
21. Saint Cornelius   251-253
22. Saint Lucius I   253-254
23. Saint Stephen   254-257
24. Saint Sixtus II   257-258
25. Saint Dionysius   259-268
26. Saint Felix I   269-274
27. Saint Eutychian   275-283
28. Saint Caius   283-296
29. Saint Marcellinus   296-304
30. Saint Marcellus I   308-309
31. Saint Eusebius   309-309
32. Saint Melchiades   311-314

*(The public practice of Christianity was made
legal by the Emperor Constantine in 313 A.D.
with the Edict of Milan.)*

33. Saint Sylvester	314-335
34. Saint Mark	336-336
35. Saint Julius 1	337-352
36. Liberius	352-366
37. Saint Damasus 1	366-384
38. Saint Siricius	384-399

*(At the Council of Hippo in 393 A.D., the Catholic Church
first lists the Biblical books belonging to the Christian
Old and New Testament canons.[39] The forty-six book O. T.
and the twenty-seven book N. T. were recognized as being
inspired by God. Refer to the end of this chapter to read a
segment from the Council of Hippo's declaration.)*

39. Saint Anastasius 1	399-401
40. Saint Innocent I	401-417
41. Saint Zosimus	417-418
42. Saint Boniface I	418-422
43. Saint Celestine I	422-432

*(In 431 A.D., Nestorius and other like-minded bishops
break with the primal See of Rome over a Christological
dispute and form separate Churches which came to be
known as the Oriental Orthodox Churches.)[40]*

44. Saint Sixtus III	432-440
45. Saint Leo I	440-461
46. Saint Hilary	461-468
47. Saint Simplicius	468-483
48. Saint Felix III (II)	483-492
49. Saint Gelasius	492-496
50. Anastasius II	496-498
51. Saint Symmachus	498-514
52. Saint Hormisdas	514-523
53. Saint John I	523-526

54. Saint Felix IV (III)	526-530
55. Boniface II	530-532
56. John II	533-535
57. Saint Agapitus	535-536
58. Saint Silverius	536-537
59. Vigilius	537-555
60. Pelagius I	556-561
61. John III	561-574
62. Benedict I	575-579
63. Pelagius II	579-590
64. Saint Gregory I	590-604
65. Sabinian	604-606
66. Boniface III	607-607
67. Saint Boniface IV	608-615
68. Saint Deusdedit	
(Adeodatus I)	615-618
69. Boniface V	619-625
70. Honorius I	625-638
71. Severinus	640-640
72. John IV	640-642
73. Theodore I	642-649
74. Saint Martin I	649-655
75. Saint Eugene I	654-657
76. Saint Vitalian	657-672
77. Adeodatus II	672-676
78. Donus	676-678
79. Saint Agatho	678-681
80. Saint Leo II	682-683
81. Saint Benedict II	684-685
82. John V	685-686
83. Conon	686-687
84. Saint Sergius I	687-701
85. John VI	701-705
86. John VII	705-707
87. Sisinnius	708-708
88. Constantine	708-715
89. Saint Gregory II	715-731

90. Saint Gregory III	731-741
91. Saint Zacharias	741-752
92. Stephen II (III)	752-757
93. Saint Paul I	757-767
94. Stephen III (IV)	768-772
95. Hadrian I	772-795
96. Saint Leo III	795-816
97. Stephen IV (V)	816-817
98. Saint Paschal I	817-824
99. Eugene II	824-827
100. Valentine	827-827
101. Gregory IV	827-844
102. Sergius II	844-847
103. Saint Leo IV	847-855
104. Benedict III	855-858
105. Saint Nicholas I	858-867
106. Hadrian II	867-872
107. John VIII	872-882
108. Marinus I	882-884
109. Saint Hadrian III	884-885
110. Stephen V (VI)	885-891
111. Formosus	891-896
112. Boniface VI	896-896
113. Stephen VI (VII)	896-897
114. Romanus	897-897
115. Theodore II	897-897
116. John IX	898-900
117. Benedict IV	900-903
118. Leo V	903-903
119. Sergius III	904-911
120. Anastasius III	911-913
121. Landus	913-914
122. John X	914-928
123. Leo VI	928-928
124. Stephen VII (VIII)	928-931
125. John XI	931-935
126. Leo VII	936-939

127.	Stephen VIII (IX)	939-942
128.	Marinus II	942-946
129.	Agapitus II	946-955
130.	John XII	955-964
131.	Leo VIII	963-965
132.	Benedict V	964-966
133.	John XIII	965-972
134.	Benedict VI	973-974
135.	Benedict VII	974-983
136.	John XIV	983-984
137.	John XV	985-996
138.	Gregory V	996-999
139.	Sylvester II	999-1003
140.	John XVII	1003-1003
141.	John XVIII	1004-1009
142.	Sergius IV	1009-1012
143.	Benedict VIII	1012-1024
144.	John XIX	1024-1032
145.	Benedict IX	1032-1044
146.	Sylvester III	1045-1045
147.	Benedict IX	1045-1045
148.	Gregory VI	1045-1046
149.	Clement II	1046-1047
150.	Benedict IX	1047-1048
151.	Damasus II	1048-1048
152.	Saint Leo IX	1049-1054

(The Eastern Orthodox Churches became independent Churches in 1054 A.D. Eastern Catholic Bishops broke away from the primal See of Rome because of increasing economic, cultural and political tensions and a theological dispute concerning a statement about the Holy Spirit elaborated upon by Rome in the Creed.)[41]

153.	Victor II	1055-1057
154.	Stephen IX (X)	1057-1058
155.	Nicholas II	1058-1061
156.	Alexander II	1061-1073

157. Saint Gregory VII	1073-1085
158. Blessed Victor III	1086-1087
159. Blessed Urban II	1088-1099
160. Paschal II	1099-1118
161. Gelasius II	1118-1119
162. Callistus (Calixtus) (II)	1119-1124
163. Honorius II	1124-1130
164. Innocent II	1130-1143
165. Celestine II	1143-1144
166. Lucius II	1144-1145
167. Blessed Eugene III	1145-1153
168. Anastasius IV	1153-1154
169. Hadrian IV	1154-1159
170. Alexander III	1159-1181
171. Lucius III	1181-1185
172. Urban III	1185-1187
173. Gregory VIII	1187-1187
174. Clement III	1187-1191
175. Celestine III	1191-1198
176. Innocent III	1198-1216
177. Honorius III	1216-1227
178. Gregory IX	1227-1241
179. Celestine IV	1241-1241
180. Innocent IV	1243-1254
181. Alexander IV	1254-1261
182. Urban IV	1261-1264
183. Clement IV	1265-1268
184. Blessed Gregory X	1271-1276
185. Blessed Innocent V	1276-1276
186. Hadrian V	1276-1276
187. John XXI	1276-1277
188. Nicholas III	1277-1280
189. Martin IV	1281-1285
190. Honorius IV	1285-1287
191. Nicholas IV	1288-1292
192. Saint Celestine V	1294-1294
193. Boniface VIII	1294-1303

194. Blessed Benedict XI	1303-1304
195. Clement V	1305-1314
196. John XXII	1316-1334
197. Benedict XII	1334-1342
198. Clement VI	1342-1352
199. Innocent VI	1352-1362
200. Blessed Urban V	1362-1370
201. Gregory XI	1370-1378
202. Urban VI	1378-1389
203. Boniface IX	1389-1404
204. Innocent VII	1404-1406
205. Gregory XII	1406-1415
206. Martin V	1417-1431
207. Eugene IV	1431-1447
208. Nicholas V	1447-1455
209. Callistus (Calixtus) (III)	1455-1458
210. Pius II	1458-1464
211. Paul II	1464-1471
212. Sixtus IV	1471-1484
213. Innocent VIII	1484-1492
214. Alexander VI	1492-1503

(Columbus discovered America in 1492.)

215. Pius III	1503-1503
216. Julius II	1503-1513
217. Leo X	1513-1521

*(The Protestant Reformation begins in 1517. Protestant
denominations begin to be formed after that. Martin
Luther adopts the thirty-nine book O. T. as authoritative
for Protestants and, thus, goes against over a
millennium of ancient Christian practice.)*

218. Hadrian VI	1522-1523
219. Clement VII	1523-1534
220. Paul III	1534-1549
221. Julius III	1550-1555
222. Marcellus II	1555-1555

223. Paul IV	1555-1559
224. Pius IV	1559-1565
225. Saint Pius V	1566-1572
226. Gregory XIII	1572-1585
227. Sixtus V	1585-1590
228. Urban VII	1590-1590
229. Gregory XIV	1590-1591
230. Innocent IX	1591-1591
231. Clement VIII	1592-1605
232. Leo XI	1605-1605
233. Paul V	1605-1621
234. Gregory XV	1621-1623
235. Urban VIII	1623-1644
236. Innocent X	1644-1655
237. Alexander VII	1655-1667
238. Clement IX	1667-1669
239. Clement X	1670-1676
240. Blessed Innocent XI	1676-1689
241. Alexander VIII	1689-1691
242. Innocent XII	1691-1700
243. Clement XI	1700-1721
244. Innocent XIII	1721-1724
245. Benedict XIII	1724-1730
246. Clement XII	1730-1740
247. Benedict XIV	1740-1758
248. Clement XIII	1758-1769
249. Clement XIV	1769-1774
250. Pius VI	1775-1799

(The U. S. Constitution was written in 1776.)

251. Pius VII	1800-1823
252. Leo XII	1823-1829
253. Pius VIII	1829-1830
254. Gregory XVI	1831-1846
255. Pius IX	1846-1878
256. Leo XIII	1878-1903
257. Saint Pius X	1903-1914

258. Benedict XV	1914-1922
259. Pius XI	1922-1939
260. Pius XII	1939-1958
261. John XXIII	1958-1963
262. Paul VI	1963-1978
263. John Paul I	1978-1978
264. John Paul II	1978-Present

The Roman Catholic Church, the Eastern Catholic Churches in union with Rome, and the (currently schismatic) Greek and Oriental Orthodox Churches are the *only* Christian Churches that can trace their historical roots, in black and white, right back to Jesus Christ Himself![42] (Author's note: The reason that I choose to be a Roman Catholic is because it was the original way to be a Christian and is not in schism with the primal See of St. Peter.)[43]

Circa 180 A.D. St. Irenaeus *(who was a disciple of St. Polycarp — who was a disciple of St. John the Apostle)*, in his *Against Heresies*, writes about the line of apostolic succession in the early Church:

"The blessed Apostles [*Peter* and Paul], having founded and built up the Church [of Rome], they handed over the office of the episcopate to *Linus*. Paul makes mention of this Linus in the Epistle to Timothy. To him succeeded *Anencletus*; and after him, in the third place from the Apostles, *Clement* was chosen for the episcopate... To this Clement, *Evaristus* succeeded; and *Alexander* succeeded Evaristus. Then, sixth after the Apostles, *Sixtus* was appointed; after him, *Telesphorus*, who also was gloriously martyred. Then *Hyginus*; after him, *Pius*; and after him, *Anicetus*. *Soter* succeeded Anicetus, and now, in the twelfth place after the Apostles, the lot of the episcopate has fallen to *Eleutherus*. In this order, and by the teaching of the Apostles handed down in the Church, the preaching of the truth has come down to us."[44]

Consider this visual picture of the formation of the Church and the Bible:

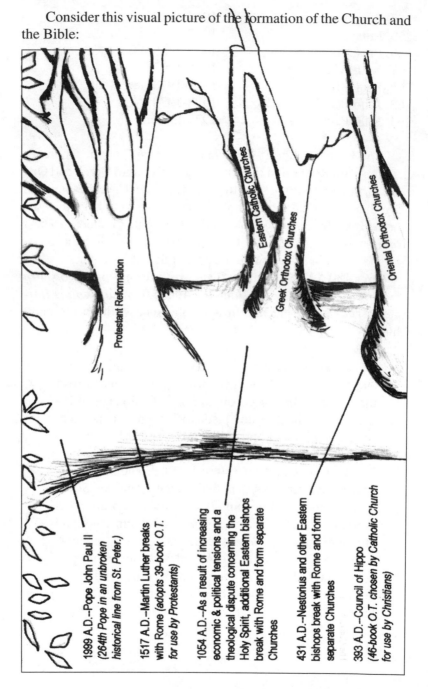

Protestant Reformation

Eastern Catholic Churches

Greek Orthodox Churches

Oriental Orthodox Churches

1999 A.D.--Pope John Paul II (264th Pope in an unbroken historical line from St. Peter.)

1517 A.D.--Martin Luther breaks with Rome (adopts 39-book O.T. for use by Protestants)

1054 A.D.--As a result of increasing economic & political tensions and a theological dispute concerning the Holy Spirit, additional Eastern bishops break with Rome and form separate Churches

431 A.D.--Nestorius and other Eastern bishops break with Rome and form separate Churches

393 A.D.--Council of Hippo (46-book O.T. chosen by Catholic Church for use by Christians)

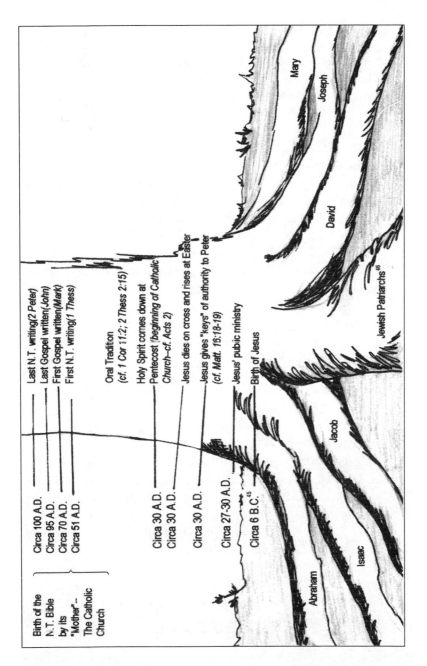

Birth of the
N. T. Bible
by its
"Mother"—
The Catholic
Church

Circa 100 A.D.   Last N.T. writing(2 Peter)
Circa 95 A.D.   Last Gospel written(John)
Circa 70 A.D.   First Gospel written(Mark)
Circa 51 A.D.   First N.T. writing(1 Thess)

                        Oral Tradition
                        (cf. 1 Cor 11:2; 2 Thess 2:15)

Circa 30 A.D.   Holy Spirit comes down at
Circa 30 A.D.   Pentecost (beginning of Catholic
                        Church–cf. Acts 2)

Circa 30 A.D.   Jesus dies on cross and rises at Easter

                        Jesus gives "keys" of authority to Peter
                        (cf. Matt. 16:18-19)

Circa 27-30 A.D.   Jesus' public ministry

Circa 6 B.C.[45]   Birth of Jesus

Mary
Joseph
David
Jewish Patriarchs[46]
Jacob
Isaac
Abraham

43

Endnotes

[168] Cf. *Mk* 3:14-15.

[174] LG 4; cf. *Jn* 17:4.

[315] St. Ignatius of Antioch, *Ad Rom.* 1, 1: *Apostolic Fathers*, II/2, 192; cf. LG 13.

[316] St. Irenaeus, *Adv. haeres.* 3, 3, 2: PG 7/1, 849; cf. Vatican Council I: DS 3057.

[322] LG 15.

[1]   Patrick Madrid (editor), *Surprised by Truth*, (San Diego, CA: Basilica Press, 1994), p. 130.

[2]   Cf. Chapter 23 of this book for the meaning of the word "Catholic" and its early application to the Church founded by Christ.

[3]   Pope John Paul II, Apostolic Letter *Tertio Millennio Adveniente*, (Boston, MA: St. Paul Books & Media, 1994), #33, p. 38. *(Author's note: I would like to offer to everyone my own apologies for the many times when my personal weaknesses and sinfulness have failed to show forth the love and compassion of Jesus Christ.)*

[4]   Monsignor Bob Guste, *The Gift of the Church*, (Santa Barbara, CA: Queenship Publishing, Co., 1993), p. 3.

[5]   In the 1500's, the Protestant Reformers "scraped off" what they *(mistakenly)* perceived to be theological "barnacles" that had attached themselves to the "hull" of the apostolic "ship" *(Church)*. By studying the writings of the early Church Fathers, we can clearly see that the Reformers actually removed entire foundational "planks" from the "hull" of the Church founded by Christ. Fifteen centuries after the founding of Jesus' Church (cf. Matt 16:18-19), the Reformers doctrinally re-designed the "ship" launched by Jesus Christ and appointed new "captains" to navigate it.

[6]   *Merriam-Webster's Collegiate Dictionary (Tenth Edition)*, (Springfield MA: Merriam-Webster, Inc., 1994), p. 906.

[7]   Cf. J. N. D. Kelly's book *The Oxford Dictionary of Popes* (published by Oxford University Press) to read accounts of the various "anti-popes" contending for the Papal Office.

[8]   *Surprised by Truth*, p. 203.

9   David B. Currie, *Born Fundamentalist Born Again Catholic*, (San Francisco, CA: Ignatius Press, 1996), p. 80.

10 The reason that Jesus chose twelve Apostles in the New Testament (cf. Luke 6:13-16) was to mirror the twelve Tribes of Israel (God's Chosen People) in the Old Testament (cf. Num 1:1-15). The twelve Apostles are God's "New Covenant Chosen People."

11 *Surprised by Truth.*, pp. 120-121.

12 *Ibid.*, p. 265.

13 *Born Fundamentalist Born Again Catholic*, p. 152.

14 Frank S. Mead (Revised by Samuel S. Hill), *Handbook of Denominations in the United States*, (Nashville, TN: Abingdon Press, 1988), p. 223.

Note that the Roman Catholic Church is the largest single Christian denomination in the world with approximately 1 billion members (cf. Robert Famighctti [editor], *The World Almanac and Book of Facts [1996 Edition]*, [Mahwah, NJ: World Almanac Books, 1995], p. 646).

15 Cf. Chapter 13 of this book for a discussion of the "prime ministry" given to St. Peter by Jesus.

16 Instead of believing that Jesus Christ was one Divine Person who possessed a human nature and a Divine nature, Nestorius held that Jesus' human nature constituted one distinct person and His Divine nature constituted another separate and distinct person. Due to this Christological dispute Nestorius, along with other bishops who ascribed to his theology, broke with the primal See of Rome after 431 A.D. and formed separate Churches which came to be known as the "Oriental Orthodox Churches."

17 A "See" refers to the jurisdiction of a particular bishop. Cf. Chapter 13 of this book for a discussion of the preeminence of the See of the Bishop of Rome (the "Pope").

18 *Handbook of Denominations in the United States*, p. 183.

19 To further articulate the scriptural truth that the Holy Spirit proceeds also from God the Son: "Indeed I shall continue to rejoice, for I know that this will result in deliverance for me through your prayers and support from the Spirit of Jesus Christ" (Phil 1:18-19), the Latin Church's Creed was expanded to read: "We believe in the Holy Spirit, the Lord, the Giver of Life, who proceeds from the Father *and the Son*..."

[20] Robert Famighetti (editor) *The World Almanac and Book of Facts (1996 Edition)*, (Mahwah, NJ: World Almanac Books, 1995), pp. 652-653.

[21] *Ibid.,* pp. 652-653.

[22] *Ibid.,* pp. 652-653.

[23] *Ibid.,* pp. 652-653.

[24] *Ibid.,* pp. 652-653.

[25] *Ibid.,* pp. 652-653.

[26] *Ibid.,* pp. 652-653.

[27] John A. O'Brien, *The Faith of Millions*, (Huntington, IN: Our Sunday Visitor, Inc., 1974) p. 68.

[28] *The World Almanac and Book of Facts (1996 Edition)*, pp. 652-653.

[29] *Handbook of Denominations in the United States*, p. 22.

[39] *The World Almanac and Book of Facts (1996 Edition)*, pp. 652-653.

[31] *Ibid.,* pp. 652-653.

[32] *Handbook of Denominations in the United States*, p. 92.

[33] *Ibid.,* p. 195.

[34] Patrick Madrid (editor), *Surprised by Truth*, (San Diego, CA: Basilica Press, 1994), p. 84. Author's note: The phrase "Non-denominational" usually means "our church has only one location and our 'pope' resides here on the premises" *(meaning: the person who teaches our congregation how difficult and apparently contradictory passages from the Bible should really be interpreted is standing behind our pulpit).* Cf. Chapter 12 of this book to read about the scriptural truth that the Bible is not self-interpreting.

[35] Cf. *Encyclopedia Americana* (Volume 21 - "Papacy" article), (Danbury, CT: Grolier, Inc., 1995) p. 369. Cf. also *Encyclopedia Britannica Micropedia* (Volume 9 - "Papacy" article), (Chicago, IL: Encyclopedia Britannica, Inc., 1993), p. 123. Cf. also *The World Book Encyclopedia* (Volume 15 - "Pope" article), (Chicago, IL: World Book, Inc., 1992 edition), p. 670. Cf. also Robert Famighetti (editor), *The World Almanac and Book of Facts (1996 Edition)*, (Mahwah, NJ: World Almanac Books, 1995), p. 650.

[36] *New American Bible With Revised New Testament*, (New York, NY: Catholic Book Publishing Co., 1986), Introduction to Bible chart p. 41. (Author's note: The reason why Jesus' birth is dated "circa 6 B.C." is due to an accidental miscalculation by the monk Dionysius Exiguus who formulated a new calendar in 533 A.D. that was intended to be based on the year of Christ's birth.) Cf. *The New Jerome Biblical Commentary* (Raymond E. Brown, S.S., Joseph A. Fitzmyer, S.J, Roland E. Murphy, O. Carm., (editors), (Englewood Cliffs, NJ: Prentice Hall, Inc., 1990, 1968), p. 1247.

[37] Cf. Chapter 13 of this book for a discussion of the "prime ministry" given to St. Peter by Jesus.

[38] St. Irenaeus was a disciple of St. Polycarp — who was a disciple of St. John the Apostle.

[39] This listing of Old and New Testament canonical books was later re-affirmed at the Councils of Carthage in 397 and 417 A.D.

[40] Cf. endnote #16 of this chapter to read about Nestorius and his Christology.

[41] Cf. Chapter 23 of this book.

[42] In the second century Tertullian writes, "Let them produce the origin of their church. Let them exhibit the succession of their Bishops, so that the first of them may appear to have been ordained by an Apostle, or by an apostolic man who was in communion with the Apostles." St. Augustine (d. 430 A.D.) writes to the Donatists, "Come to us, brethren, if you wish to be engrafted in the vine. We are afflicted in beholding you lying cut off from it. Count over the Bishops from the very See of St. Peter, and mark, in this list of Fathers, how one succeeded the other. This is the rock against which the proud gates of hell do not prevail." Cf. James Cardinal Gibbons, *The Faith of Our Fathers*, (Rockford, IL: TAN Books and Publishers, Inc., 1980), pg. 41-42.

[43] Cf. Chapter 13 of this book for a discussion of the primacy of the See of St. Peter. Roman Catholic convert *(and later Cardinal)* John Henry Newman, once said something to the effect that "knowledge of Church history spells the end of Protestantism."

44   William A. Jurgens (editor and translator), *The Faith of the Early Fathers (Volume 1)*, (Collegeville, MN: The Liturgical Press, 1970), p. 90. (Italics added by author.)

45   *New American Bible With Revised New Testament*, Introduction to Bible Chart, p. 41. Cf. also *King James Bible*, (Nashville, TN: Holman Bible Publishers, Inc., 1979), "Chart of the Life of Jesus Christ" located on an unnumbered page in the back of the Bible in the "Helps to Bible Study" section.

46   Cf. Matt 1:1-16.

Chapter 4

Is Faith in Jesus *"ALONE"* All That is Necessary For a Christian to Go to Heaven?

What Does the Catholic Church Teach?

"Justification has been *merited for us by the Passion of Christ* who offered himself on the cross as a living victim, holy and pleasing to God, and whose blood has become the instrument of atonement for the sins of all men... Our justification comes from the grace of God. Grace is *favor*, the *free and undeserved help* that God gives us to respond to his call to become children of God, adoptive sons, partakers of the divine nature and of eternal life[46]...With regard to God, there is no strict right to any merit on the part of man. Between God and us there is an immeasurable inequality, for we have received everything from him, our Creator...The merit of man before God in the Christian life arises from the fact that *God has freely chosen to associate man with the work of his grace.* The fatherly action of God is first on his own initiative, and then follows man's free acting through his collaboration, so that the merit of good works is to be attributed in the first place to the grace of God, then to the faithful. Man's merit, moreover, itself is due to God, for his good actions proceed in Christ, from the predispositions and assistance given by the Holy Spirit...

The merits of our good works are gifts of the divine goodness.[61] Grace has gone before us; now we are given what is due... Our merits are God's gifts."[62] (*Catechism of the Catholic Church*, #1992, 1996, 2007–2009.)

Common Objection #1

"In the Bible, St. Paul clearly says: 'For we consider that a person is justified by faith *apart from works of the law*' (Rom 3:28) and: 'For by grace you have been saved through faith, and this is not from you; it is the gift of God; *it is not from works*, so no one may boast' (Eph 2:8-9). To communicate the truth that Christians are justified by *faith alone*, Martin Luther popularized the Biblical doctrine of *"sola fide"* (which is Latin for *'faith alone'* and means that, by faith in Jesus *ALONE*, a Christian enters into a right relationship with God the Father and, thus, becomes immediately eligible for admittance into heaven).

You Roman Catholics, on the other hand, seem to believe that you can 'work your way to heaven' through your un-Biblical system of salvation that is based heavily upon the accomplishment of good deeds apart from the freely-given grace of God."

A Catholic Response

When a person "justifies" his typing on a computer word processor, he hits the appropriate key to make the words on the left and right margins line up straight *(as I have done in this book)*. Likewise, a "justified" person is one who is "straight" with God and, thus, eligible for admittance into heaven. *Merriam Webster's Collegiate Dictionary* defines "justification" as: "to...regard...as righteous and worthy of salvation."[1]

Romans 3:28 is a typical verse that fundamentalists will often use to speak about their understanding of the role of works in justification: "For we consider that a person is justified by faith apart from works [Greek: *ergon*] of the law" (Romans 3:28).

On the other hand, here is how St. James understands the role of works in justification: "See how a person is justified by works [Greek: *ergon*] and *not* by faith alone" (James 2:24).

At first glance, these two passages appear to be diametrically opposed. Romans 3:28 seems to be saying that a Christian is justified by faith *apart from works* while James 2:24 seems to be teaching that works play a role in justification and, therefore, a Christian is not justified by *faith alone*.

Although the same Greek word for "works" is used in both verses (*ergon*), the word is used to refer to two totally different things. When taken in context *(read all of Romans Chapter 3 and 4)* St. Paul, in Romans 3:28, is speaking about the works/observances of the Jewish religion *(i.e., circumcision, dietary regulations, purification rituals, etc.)*. St. Paul is telling Jewish Christians that they are not bound to continue to follow their former Jewish religious practices to be in right relationship with God.

On the other hand, when James uses the word "works" ("See how a person is justified by works and not by faith alone" — James 2:24), he is not speaking about Jewish religious observances but about the Christian corporal and spiritual works of mercy.[2] James teaches that, after the reception of the free gift of faith from God by grace, the Christian is called to serve Him in concrete ways and these tangible spiritual and corporal "works" give Him an indication of the intensity and vibrancy of the Christian's invisible, internal faith ("The dead were judged according to their deeds" — Rev 20:12-13).

How is one "justified" (made "straight" with God)? The phrase "faith alone" appears only once in the Bible and it is in the book of James: "See how a person is justified by works and *not by faith alone*" (James 2:24). In order to Biblically substantiate his doctrine of "*sola fide*" (meaning that a person is "made straight with God" and is, thus, eligible to enter into heaven, by a mere profession of faith in Jesus 'alone'), Martin Luther added the word "alone" to his German translation of Romans 3:28 — even when the word did not appear in the Greek scriptural manuscripts. Thus, by promoting his doctrine of "*sola fide*," Martin Luther broke his doctrine of "*sola scriptura*" (meaning that all that is necessary for Christian belief and practice is contained exclusively in the written Bible). In September of 1530, Martin Luther writes the following stinging letter to his friend Wenceslaus Link in a tract entitled *Sendbrieff von Dolmetzschen* concerning his addition to the words of St. Paul in Romans 3:28:

> "You tell me what a great fuss the Papists are making because the word 'alone' is not in the text of Paul. If your Papist makes such an unnecessary row about the word 'alone,' say right out to him: 'Dr. Martin Luther will have it so,' and say: 'Papists and asses are one and the same thing.' I will have it so, and I order it to be so, and my will is reason enough. I know very well that the word 'alone' is not in the Latin or the Greek text, and it was not necessary for the Papists to teach me that. It is true those letters are not in it, which letters the jackasses look at, as a cow stares at a new gate...It shall remain in my New Testament, and if all the Popish donkeys were to get mad and beside themselves, they will not get it out."[3]

If one studies the official Roman Catholic teaching on justification (cf. the beginning of this chapter), one can clearly see that the Catholic Church certainly does *not* believe that a Christian can "work his way to heaven" or "earn his own salvation" apart from the grace of God. Verses such as Romans 3:28 and Ephesians 2:8-9 are commonly cited as the Biblical basis for Luther's doctrine of *"sola fide."* Let us see if verses such as these warrant Luther's teaching on salvation.

Let us read Romans 3:28 within its Biblical context: "For we consider that a person is justified by faith apart from works of the law. Does God belong to Jews alone? Does he not belong to Gentiles, too? Yes, also to Gentiles, for God is one and will justify the circumcised on the basis of faith and the uncircumcised through faith" (Roman 3:28-30). It is clear that when St. Paul teaches in Romans 3:28-30 that "a person is justified by faith *apart from works of the law...,*" he is referring to the issue of whether or not New Testament Christians were bound to abide by Old Testament Jewish rituals contained in "the Torah" (commonly referred to as "the Law"). In Romans 3:28-30, St. Paul is instructing New Testament

Christians that it was *not* necessary for them to observe the traditional Jewish religious laws and rituals to be saved. St. Paul is absolutely right in teaching the New Testament Christians that they are justified (regarded as righteous in God's eyes and, therefore, eligible for salvation in heaven) by their faith in Jesus Christ without the obligation of having to live according to Jewish Old Testament religious laws.

Ephesians 2:8-9 is another verse that is frequently cited to back up Luther's doctrine of "*sola fide*." Nowhere in Ephesians (or anywhere else in the Bible) does it say that "*faith in Jesus ALONE* is all that is necessary for a Christian to go to heaven." Ephesians 2:8-9 does clearly teach that our Christian faith is a gracious gift from God and that this free gift cannot be earned by our good works. In the very next verse in Ephesians, St. Paul goes on to teach about salvation: "...we are...created in Christ Jesus *for the good works* [Greek: *ergon*] that God has prepared in advance, that we should live in them" (Eph 2:10). These Biblical truths are totally compatible with the teaching of the Catholic Church on justification presented at the beginning of this chapter.

The Bible and the Catholic Church clearly condemn the notion that a Christian can achieve heavenly salvation by his "works alone" apart from the grace of God. Roman Catholics believe that good works come *after* and *pre-suppose* the existence of a solid personal relationship with Jesus Christ. Martin Luther's simplistic "faith alone" ("*sola fide*") formula is an incomplete description of what the Bible teaches about what is necessary for a Christian's salvation. Let us look at what Scripture teaches about the necessity of performing good works, accomplished by God's grace and assisted by the Holy Spirit, in the God-given faith life of the Christian:

- "What good is it, my brothers, if someone says he has faith but does not have works [Greek: *ergon*]? *Can that faith save him*" (James 2:14)?[5]

- "So also *faith of itself, if it does not have works* [Greek: *ergon*], *is dead*" (James 2:17).[6]

- "...I will demonstrate my faith to you *from my works* [Greek: *ergon*]" (James 2:18).

- "You see that faith was active along with [Abraham's] works [Greek: *ergon*], and *faith was completed by the works* [Greek: *ergon*]" (James 2:22).[7]

- "*See how a person is justified by works* [Greek: *ergon*] *and not by faith alone*" (James 2:24).[8]

- "...*faith without works* [Greek: *ergon*] *is dead*" (James 2:26).

- "...whoever brings back a sinner from the error of his way will save his soul from death and will cover a multitude of sins" (James 5:20).[9]

- "...if I have all faith so as to move mountains *but do not have love, I am nothing*" (1 Cor 13:2).

- "Let us not grow tired of *doing good*, for in due time we shall reap our harvest, *if we do not give up*" (Gal 6:9).

- "Behold, I am coming soon. I bring with me the recompense I will give to each *according to his deeds*" (Rev 22:12).

- "...God, who will repay everyone *according to his works* [Greek: *ergon*],[10] eternal life to those who seek glory, honor, and immortality through *perseverance in good works*, but wrath and fury to those who selfishly disobey the truth and obey wickedness" (Rom 2:5-7).[11]

- "For in Christ Jesus, neither circumcision nor uncircumcision counts for anything, but only faith *working through love*" (Gal 5:6).[12]

- At the General Judgement at the end of time, what will distinguish "the sheep" (who will be admitted into heaven by Jesus) from "the goats" (who will be eternally damned by Jesus) will be their *loving works* (i.e., feeding the hungry, welcoming the stranger, clothing the naked, caring for the ill, visiting the imprisoned). These loving works will help to exhibit the sincerity and the depth of the Christian's God-given faith life (cf. Matt 25:31-46).

- "For we must all appear before the judgement seat of Christ, so that each one may receive recompense, *according to what he did in the body, whether good or evil*" (2 Cor 5:10).

- In the Book of Revelation we read that the spiritual merits of earthly good works accompany the saints when they are finally admitted into heaven: "'...Blessed are the dead who die in the Lord from now on.' 'Yes,' said the Spirit, 'let them find rest from their labors, for *their works* [Greek: *ergon*] *accompany them*'" (Rev 14:13), "She was allowed to wear a bright, clean linen garment, The linen represents *the righteous deeds of the holy ones*" (Rev 19:8).

- The New Testament tells us that Christians will not be judged by their "faith alone" but by their actual deeds and the personal conduct that they exhibited while living on earth. "...All the dead were judged *according to their deeds* [Greek: *ergon*]" (Rev 20:12-13).[13]

- "Therefore, my beloved brothers, be firm, steadfast, always *fully devoted to the work of the Lord*, knowing that *in the Lord your labor is not in vain*" (1 Cor 15:58).

- "For God is not unjust so as to overlook your *work* and the *love you have demonstrated for his name by having served and continuing to serve* the holy ones" (Heb 6:10).

- "Not everyone who says to me, 'Lord, Lord,' will enter the kingdom of heaven, but only the one who *does the will of my Father in heaven*" (Matt 7:21).[14]

- In the Gospel of Matthew a rich young man asks Jesus, "...What good must I do to gain eternal life?" Rather than saying that the rich young man needed to have faith alone He tells him: "If you wish to enter into life, keep the commandments...If you wish to be perfect, go, sell what you have and give to the poor, and you will have treasure in heaven..." (Matt 19:16-21).[15]

- "...*work out your salvation* with fear and trembling. For God is the one who works in you both to desire and to work" (Phil 2:12-13).[16]

- "...The person who *acts in righteousness* is righteous..." (1 John 3:7).

- "Now if you invoke as Father him who judges impartially *according to each one's works* [Greek: *ergon*], conduct yourselves with reverence during the time of your sojourning..." (1 Pet 1:17).

- "...we have confidence in God and receive from him whatever we ask, because we *keep his commandments and do what pleases him*" (1 John 3:21).

Roman Catholic convert Julie Swenson shares with her readers in the book, *Surprised by Truth*:

> "As a staunch spiritual daughter of Calvin, I believed that the unregenerate man is ever in a state of rebellion against God, incapable of doing anything right and good in God's sight. Christians are not themselves righteous, but are merely clothed in the robe of Christ's righteousness — a righteousness that is merely imputed to them; they are not intrinsically made righteous by God's sovereign grace. I believed Luther's bleak dictum that 'We are dunghills covered over with snow.' No matter how pure we might appear on the outside, we're not really pure — we remain wretched sinners...The Lord began to show me that this view was a twisted combination of truth and error. It is true that I desperately need the grace of Christ to buoy me up above the inclination to sin that threatens to draw us all downward into ruin, but I also realized that God's grace is not to be presumed upon.

God created me a responsible, rational person who must continually reach out for his grace and, aided by that grace, turn away from sin in order to be saved."[17]

Alan Schreck, in his book, *Catholic and Christian*, says: "The Council of Trent clearly stated that of the two (faith and works), faith was the primary means of accepting salvation ('the beginning of human salvation' from our perspective). 'Good works' or charity is also important for salvation, but as a 'fruit' of genuine faith."[18] In other words, the truth is that Christians are justified by an alive faith that is characterized by loving works of obedience to God.

What Did the Early Christians Believe About the Necessity of an Alive Faith Characterized by Loving Works of Obedience to God?

- "Why was our father Abraham blessed? Was it not because of his deeds of justice and truth, wrought in faith?" St. Clement of Rome in his *Letter to the Corinthians* (circa 80 AD)[19]

- "When we hear, 'Your faith has saved you,' we do not understand the Lord to say simply that they will be saved who have believed in whatever manner, even if works have not followed." St. Clement of Alexandria in his *Stromateis* (circa 202 AD)[20]

- "Whoever dies in his sins, even if he profess to believe in Christ, does not truly believe in Him; and even if that which exists without works be called faith, such faith is dead in itself, as we read in the Epistle bearing the name of James." Origen in his *Commentaries on John* (circa 230 A.D.)[21]

- "And you who are a matron rich and wealthy, anoint not your eyes with the antimony of the devil, but with the collyrium of Christ, so that you may at last come to see God, when you have merited before God both by your works and by your manner of living." St. Cyprian of Carthage in his *Works and Almsgiving* (circa 253 A.D.)[22]

- To paraphrase the words of St. Augustine (circa 400 A.D.) concerning the importance of an active, alive faith: "God made us without us but He won't save us without us."[23]

Endnotes

[46] Cf. *Jn* 1:12-18; 17:3; *Rom* 8:14-17; *2 Pet* 1:3-4.

[61] Cf. Council of Trent (1547): DS 1548.

[62] St. Augustine, *Sermo* 298, 4-5: PL 38, 1367.

[1] *Merriam Webster's Collegiate Dictionary (10th edition)*, (Springfield, MA: Merriam-Webster, Inc., 1994), p. 636.

[2] Based on Matt 25:35-46, the Christian "corporal works of mercy" are: feeding the hungry, giving drink to the thirsty, clothing the naked, sheltering the homeless, visiting the sick, visiting the imprisoned, burying the dead. Based on various Old and New Testament admonitions, the Christian "spiritual works of mercy" are: counseling the doubtful, instructing the ignorant, admonishing the sinner, comforting the sorrowful, forgiving of injuries, bearing wrongs patiently, praying for the living and the dead.

[3] Patrick Madrid, *Surprised by Truth*, (San Diego, CA: Basilica Press, 1994), p. 129. Cf. also Hartmann Grisar, S.J. (E. M. Lamond, translator) *Luther (Volume V)*, (London, England: Kegan Paul, Trench, Trubner & Co. Ltd., 1916), p. 517.

[4] "The Law," "the Torah," "the Pentateuch" and "the Five Books of Moses" are all names for the first five books of the Old Testament: Genesis, Exodus, Leviticus, Numbers, Deuteronomy. The Ten Commandments (God's premier Laws given to Moses) appear in Exodus 20 and Deuteronomy 5 with many other Jewish laws and rituals appearing in the other books of the Torah.

[5] James asks a rhetorical question here. After reading James 2:14-26, we see that the answer to James' rhetorical question would be, "No, an inactive faith, by itself, cannot save a Christian because good works are a gauge that Jesus will use to detect the presence and the vitality of a person's God-given faith life."

[6] James says, in effect, "faith alone...is dead" — the reason being is because good works serve as a "faith monitor" that God views to get a gauge of the intensity of a Christian's interior spiritual commitment.

7 James says that "faith was completed by [Abraham's] works" because God did His part by freely and graciously giving Abraham the gift of faith. As a response to God's free gift, with the aid of the Holy Spirit, Abraham completed God's plan by using his free will and co-operating and collaborating with Him and responding with the fruit of his gift of faith, good works. James 2:22 clearly teaches that faith without works is incomplete — and an incomplete faith will not justify a person (cf. James 2:14).

8 Note that James 2:17, 24 directly contradicts Luther's doctrine of justification by "faith alone." Is it any wonder why he had so much difficulty accepting the canonicity of this New Testament book and called the Book of James "an epistle of straw"?

9 We see here that the loving deed of bringing a sinner back to Christ (with the help of the Holy Spirit, of course!) will have an offsetting effect on a person's sins and help to save him from damnation in hell.

10 The reason why St. Paul says that "God will repay everyone according to his works" is because a person's works are seen as the "pulse" of his faith. If a Christian performs no good works in response to God's free gracious gift of faith, it is very possible that his faith has died (cf. James 2:17).

11 Note that this Scripture passage appears in the chapter of Romans that precedes Romans 3:28 (one of the verses that is commonly used to back up Luther's doctrine of "sola fide").

12 In his Letter to the Galatians, St. Paul says that a Christian's good works are his loving response to God's free and gracious gift of faith. Consider this analogy: When the time is right, a boy who is seriously dating a girl will make the monumental statement: "I love you!" After that crucial statement the boy will perform various tangible expressions of his love for the girl (e. g., hold her hand, write her love letters, send her flowers). In directing these expressions of love toward the girl, the boy is certainly not trying to "buy" her affection but simply attempting to externalize his interior commitment to their relationship. If a boy told a girl that he loved her and then showed her no tangible signs of his love, the girl would soon begin to wonder if the feelings of love really ever existed. The same

thing applies to faith and good works. St. Paul says in Romans: "For, if you confess with your mouth that Jesus is Lord and believe in your heart that God raised him from the dead, you will be saved" (Rom 10:9). That profession of faith is the Christian's "I love you!" The loving works that follow after that crucial moment show Jesus, our Lover, that we truly do mean what we said.

13 Note that Scripture doesn't say that "All the dead were judged according to their faith alone." The reason that the Bible teaches that the dead will be judged according to their deeds is because a Christian's deeds are a tangible barometer of the depth of his intangible faith. We can clearly see here that a Christian is not justified (declared righteous and worthy of salvation in heaven) by "faith alone." A verbal profession of faith plays a primary and a foundational role in a Christian's salvation but is not the only response necessary for the believer to be saved.

14 Jesus says here that a simple verbal expression of faith alone (cf. Rom 10:9), will not justify a person and make him righteous in God's eyes and, thus, worthy of entering heaven. In Matt 7:21, Jesus is teaching Christians the truth that "*actions* speak louder than mere words."

15 Following the commandments and giving alms to the poor are good spiritual deeds that would give Jesus an indication of the intensity of the rich young man's God-given faith life. Catholics believe that true faith will express itself in a person's manner of living. The writer Kahlil Gibran once wrote that "Work is love made visible." In a similar manner, performing loving works of obedience to God are "faith made visible." Good works are the "heartbeat" of an alive faith.

16 The *Catechism of the Catholic Church* echoes St. Paul's teaching found in Phil 2:12-13: "Man's merit, moreover, itself is due to God, for his good actions proceed in Christ, from the predispositions and assistance given by the Holy Spirit...The merits of our good works are gifts of the divine goodness. Grace has gone before us; now we are given what is due...Our merits are God's gifts." (*Catechism of the Catholic Church*, #2008).

17 *Surprised by Truth*, pp. 140-141. Cf. Chapter 10 of this book for a discussion of the Catholic view of justification as com-

pared to the Protestant view.

[18] Alan Schreck, *Catholic and Christian*, (Ann Arbor, Michigan: Servant Books, 1984), p. 27.

[19] William A. Jurgens (editor and translator), *The Faith of the Early Fathers (Volume 1)*, (Collegeville, MN: The Liturgical Press, 1970), p. 9.

[20] *Ibid.*, p. 184.

[21] *Ibid.*, p. 202.

[22] *Ibid.*, p. 225.

[23] William A. Jurgens (editor and translator), *The Faith of the Early Fathers (Volume 3)*, (Collegeville, MN: The Liturgical Press, 1979), p. 29.

Chapter 5

"My Lord and My God!"[1]: The Real Presence of Jesus Christ in the Holy Eucharist

What Does the Catholic Church Teach?

"The mode of Christ's presence under the Eucharistic species is unique...[199] In the most blessed sacrament of the Eucharist 'the body and blood, together with the soul and divinity, of our Lord Jesus Christ and, therefore, *the whole Christ is truly, really, and substantially* contained.'[200] 'This presence is called 'real' — by which is not intended to exclude the other types of presence as if they could not be 'real' too, but because it is presence in the fullest sense: that is to say, it is a *substantial* presence by which Christ, God and man, makes himself wholly and entirely present.'[201] ...The Council of Trent summarizes the Catholic faith by declaring: 'Because Christ our Redeemer said that it was truly his body that he was offering under the species of bread, it has always been the conviction of the Church of God, and this holy Council now declares again, that by the consecration of the bread and wine there takes place a change of the whole substance of the bread into the substance of the body of Christ our Lord and of the whole substance of the wine into the substance of his blood. This change the holy Catholic Church has fittingly and properly called transubstantiation."[204] (*Catechism of the Catholic Church*, #1374, 1376.)

Common Objection #1

"At the Last Supper Jesus told His Apostles: '...do this in *memory* of me' (Luke 22:19-20) and '...do this in *remembrance* of me' (1 Cor 11:24-25). The Eucharist is, therefore, simply a *memorializing* and a symbolic *remembering* of what Jesus did at the Last Supper 2,000 years ago. There is no way that His actual body and blood can be present to Christians here and now!"

A Catholic Response

The New Testament contains the following four narrative accounts of Jesus' words over the bread and wine at the Last Supper:[2]

1) "... this **is** my body ...this **is** my blood ..." (Matt 26:26-28).
2) "... this **is** my body ... This **is** my blood ..." (Mark 14:22-24).
3) "... This **is** my body ... do this in memory of me ... This **is** ... my blood ..." (Luke 22:19-20).
4) "... This **is** my body ... do this in remembrance of me ... This cup **is** ... my blood ... drink it, in remembrance of me ..." (1 Cor 11:24-25).

Please note that Jesus doesn't say anywhere in the four scriptural accounts of the Last Supper that the Eucharistic Bread and Wine were intended to serve as "symbols" or "representations" of His Body and Blood. It is interesting to observe how some Christian denominations claim to interpret the Bible's words in their plain, straightforward, literal sense in every other place but, when it comes to this crucial teaching of Jesus concerning the nature of His presence in the Holy Eucharist, they come up with their own explanations of why the word "**is**" spoken by Christ over the bread and wine at the Last Supper should not really, literally, mean "**is**."[3]

Protestant Christian denominations differ *widely* in their beliefs about the nature of Christ's presence in the Holy Eucharist. The Eucharistic belief of each Protestant denomination depends upon which Protestant Reformer's theology their church has chosen to adopt. Dr. Ludwig Ott, in his book *Fundamentals of Catho-*

lic Dogma, gives a brief overview of the broad variety of Eucharistic theologies developed by some of the major Protestant Reformers in the 16th century:

> "The Reformers...were not agreed on the question of the Real Presence...
>
> **Luther** admitted the Real Presence, but only during the celebration of Holy Communion. In contrast to the Catholic doctrine of Transubstantiation, he assumed a co-existence of the true Body and Blood of Christ with the substance of the bread and the wine (consubstantiation).
>
> **Zwingli** denied the Real Presence, and declared the bread and wine to be mere symbols of the Body and Blood of Christ. Holy Communion is, according to him, only a commemoration of our Redemption through the death of Christ, and a confession of Faith by the community.
>
> **Calvin** took a middle path. He rejected the substantial presence of the body and blood of Christ, but accepted a presence of power (dynamic presence). Through the use of bread and wine, a power proceeding from the transfigured Body of Christ in heaven, is conferred on the faithful.
>
> **Liberal Protestantism** of the present day denies that Christ intended to institute the Eucharist, and maintains that Jesus' Last Supper was a mere parting meal."[4]

How should modern-day Christians interpret Jesus' word "**is**"? In his First Letter to the Corinthians (written circa 56 A.D.),[5] St. Paul communicates to his readers the Eucharistic belief held during the first twenty-six years of the Church's existence. In First Corinthians, St. Paul gives his readers the earliest written account of how the infant Church understood the crucial word "**is**" spoken by Jesus over the Eucharistic Bread and Wine at the Last Supper: "The cup of blessing that we bless, is it not a participation in the blood of Christ? The bread that we break, is it not a participation in the body of Christ?" (1 Cor 10:16) Note well that St. Paul identifies the cup of wine, not as a "symbol" or a "representation," but as the "blood of Christ" and the bread, not as a "symbol" or a "representation," but as the "body of Christ." The original Greek word that is translated as "participation" in 1 Cor 10:16 is *koinonia* (which is often translated as "communion" in English).[6] What St. Paul is saying in 1 Cor 10:16 is that when the early Christians received Holy "Communion" they were participating, not in ordinary bread and wine, but in the Body and Blood of Jesus Christ Himself.

St. Paul goes on to instruct his early Christian readers about the Eucharistic Bread and Wine in First Corinthians: "...whoever eats the bread or drinks the cup of the Lord unworthily will have to answer for the body and blood of the Lord. A person should examine himself, and so eat the bread and drink the cup. For anyone who eats and drinks without discerning the body, eats and drinks judgment on himself. That is why many among you are ill and infirm, and a considerable number are dying" (1 Cor 11:27-30).[7] If the bread and the wine were merely symbols or representations, why does St. Paul stress so strongly the importance of the Christian being spiritually fit to receive them? If it were merely bread and wine, it wouldn't matter what the condition of a Christian's soul was. If, however, the bread and wine were truly the Body and Blood of Jesus Christ, shouldn't a Christian take a thorough spiritual inventory of himself before coming forward to receive them? That is exactly what St. Paul is instructing the early Christians to do so that they don't commit a sacrilege by ingesting Jesus Christ, the Holiest of the Holy, into a heart and soul full of serious sin (cf. *Catechism of the Catholic Church*, #1385.)

Karl Keating, in his book *Catholicism and Fundamentalism*, goes back to the original Greek language of the New Testament and gives his modern-day Christian readers a clue on how to correctly interpret Jesus' crucial 2,000-year-old statement over the Eucharistic Bread and Wine at the Last Supper: "This **is** my body."

> "The Greek [words used in all of the narrative accounts of Jesus' words at the Last Supper] all translate as 'This is my body.' The verb *estin* is the equivalent of the English 'is' and can mean 'is really' or 'is figuratively.' The usual meaning of *estin* is the former, just as, in En-

glish, the verb is usually taken in the real or literal sense. Fundamentalists, of course, insist Christ, in saying, 'This is my body,' spoke only a trope. This interpretation is precluded by Paul's discussion of the Eucharist in 1 Cor [11:23-34] and by the whole tenor of John 6, the chapter where the Eucharist is promised. The Greek word for 'body' in John 6 is '*sarx*,' which can only mean physical flesh, and the word for 'eat' translates as 'gnaws' or 'chews.' This is not the language of metaphor. The literal meaning cannot be avoided except through violence to the text — and through the rejection of the universal understanding of the early Christian centuries...

Aramaic [Jesus' native language] has about three dozen words that can mean 'represents,' so Christ would have had no difficulty at all in giving an unmistakable equivalent of 'this represents my body.'"[8]

Concerning the correct interpretation of the word "**is**" spoken by Jesus at the Last Supper, Fr. John A. O'Brien, in his book, *The Faith of Millions*, reminds his contemporary American readers: "...the phrase, 'to eat the flesh and drink the blood,' when used figuratively among the Jews, as among the Arabs of today, meant to inflict upon a person some serious injury, especially by calumny or false accusation. To interpret the phrase figuratively then would be to make our Lord promise life everlasting to the culprit for slandering and hating Him, which would reduce the whole passage to utter nonsense."[9]

In the four narrative accounts of Jesus' words over the bread and wine at the Last Supper, note that the words "do this in memory of me" that are found in Luke 22:19-20 and 1 Cor 11:24-25 *follow* Jesus' words "This **is** my body" and mean that, after the priest or bishop would make Jesus' Body and Blood truly present under the appearance of bread and wine (after it "**is**"), the Christian community was to remember Him. Jesus' words "do this in memory of me" that *follow* the word "**is**" certainly does not negate His Real Presence in the Holy Eucharist.

Some Christian denominations conclude that to "remember" someone is simply to look back and nostalgically recall an inaccessible historical character who is not able to be present to us here and now. Is this always the case? Does "remembering" someone require that person to be absent? Consider this example: A few years ago I attended my high school class reunion and I arrived a little bit early. When I arrived at the reunion I noticed that a few of my former classmates had already gotten there so we sat down and began to remember "the good old days." "Do you remember our former classmate Mark and how mischievous he was?" said one person. "Do you remember our former classmate Steven with his flaming red hair?" said another person. As we were in the midst of our "remembering," the front door swings open and, lo and behold, Mark and Steven come over and sit down with us at our table. As we continued to "remember" the various things that Mark and Steven and the rest of us did and said many years ago, we all sat back and enjoyed being in one another's company once again. Do you see how it is entirely possible to remember in the presence of someone whom you are remembering? At the Eucharist, Catholics are not simply recalling the life of an inaccessible historical figure but remembering in the Real Presence of the One being remembered: Jesus Christ.[10]

Because his Gospel was the last to be written, the Apostle John chose not to repeat the narrative account of Jesus' words over the Eucharistic Bread and the Wine found in the Gospels of Matthew, Mark and Luke. In John Chapter 6, however, the Apostle John *(who, in John 13:23, reclined right next to Christ at the Last Supper)* reveals Jesus' teaching on the Holy Eucharist. In the beginning of Chapter 6, John reports that: "The Jewish feast of Passover was near." (John 6:4) This verse puts John Chapter 6 in the context of the Jewish Feast of Passover *(which would be the future setting of the Last Supper).*[11]

After performing the miracle of the multiplication of the loaves and the fishes (cf. John 6:1-15) and after performing the miracle of walking on water (cf. John 6:16-21) Jesus, in the context of the Jewish feast of Passover, gives His teaching on the promised Holy Eucharist in John 6:51-68. Consider John 6:51-68 laid out in dialogue form:

Jesus proclaims His teaching on the Holy Eucharist to a crowd of listeners:	"...the bread that I will give is my flesh for the life of the world" (John 6:51).
Obviously understanding Jesus' words in their plain, literal sense, a number of the shocked listeners respond:	"...How can this man give us his flesh to eat" (John 6:52)?
Rather than seizing this first opportunity to clarify His tough words if the crowd (who was taking His speech literally) was understanding Him wrongly, Jesus goes on to make even stronger statements to the crowd about the Holy Eucharist:	"...unless you eat the flesh of the Son of Man and drink his blood, you do not have life within you" (John 6:53).[12] "...my flesh is true food and my blood is true drink" (John 6:55).
Obviously still taking our Lord's words literally, a number of Jesus' stunned listeners respond:[13]	"...This saying is hard; who can accept it" (John 6:60)?
Jesus, fully aware that His listeners were understanding His teaching in a literal sense, chooses not to seize His second opportunity to make clarifications of His harsh words if they were being interpreted incorrectly, doesn't back down an inch and responds to the unbelievers in the crowd:	"...Does this shock you" (John 6:61)?
Narrator:	"As a result of this, many [of] his disciples returned to their former way of life and no longer accompanied him" (John 6:66).
Risking His whole mission, Jesus turns to His most intimate disciples (the Twelve Apostles) and says to them:	"Do you also want to leave" (John 6:67)?
St. Peter speaking on behalf of the Twelve Apostles:	"Master, to whom shall we go? You have the words of eternal life" (John 6:68).[14]

Note that, when the unbelieving disciples began to walk away from Jesus, He makes no attempt at all to clear up any misunderstanding *(as He had done immediately with Nicodemus in John 3:1-5, 22 when he misunderstood about the necessity of being "born again" in the waters of Baptism, as He had done immediately with His disciples in Matt 16:5-12 when they misunderstood what He meant when He spoke about the "leaven" of the Pharisees and Sadducees, and as He had done immediately in John 10:6-16 where He had to reexplain to His perplexed disciples the metaphoric image of Him being the "gate of the sheepfold.")* Jesus didn't have to clear anything up in John 6 because He had plainly said what He meant. Jesus clearly teaches the doctrine of His Real Presence in the Holy Eucharist and then He tells His listeners, in effect, "If you can't accept the essential teaching that I have just proclaimed to you, please pull the door behind you on your way out" (cf. John 6:61). Jesus then turns to His closest followers (the Twelve Apostles) and says to them, in effect, "And if you also have a problem accepting my teaching on the Eucharist, you can catch your hats as well" (cf. John 6:67)! Following this, Peter, acting as spokesman for the rest of the Apostles, instantly responds to Jesus: "Master, to whom shall we go? You have the words of eternal life" (John 6:68).[15]

John 6:66 recounts the first time that people leave the Church because of a disagreement over doctrine.[16] Fr. Peter Stravinskas writes about John 6:

> "Holy Communion is so important to us Catholics because we have taken to heart the insights of John 6, an early and comprehensive treatment on the significance of the Eucharist, especially in terms of its ability to keep us one with Christ and to lead us to everlasting life... John the Evangelist is more emphatic than any other New Testament writer in asserting the necessity of the Eucharist for salvation (see 6:53), for he was dealing with Gnostics, a heretical sect that had allergic reactions to the visible or sensible signs of divinity, whether manifested in sacraments or an 'institutional' Church, and claimed to have access to the Lord in 'spiritual' ways, independent of the ecclesial Body of Christ.

They were attempting to have Communion without communion. John's response to such a suggestion is a resounding No, for it pleased Christ to make Himself available to His Church through the outward signs of bread and wine, transformed through the faithful sacramental action of His Church. The union was to be real and tangible — body entering body."[17]

A few years ago a friend of mine shared with me that, while he was on a business trip in southeast Texas, he stopped in at this one particular Catholic Church for Mass. In this Church the pastor had placed three life-sized statues so that their backs faced the tabernacle area where the Blessed Sacrament is kept. The fronts of these statues were positioned so that they faced the side exit doors of the Church. At the conclusion of Mass my friend, puzzled as to what these oddly-placed statues might be, went over to get a closer look at them. On the base of the statues of the departing disciples an inscription read: "Does this shock you? — John 6:61." *(A Biblical reference recounting Jesus' words to those unbelieving followers who chose not to accept the teaching of His Real Presence in the Holy Eucharist.)*[18]

In the Eucharistic chapter of John (John 6), Jesus says: "It is the spirit that gives life, while the flesh is of no avail" (John 6:63). Some Christian denominations will claim that what Jesus is saying here is that His Eucharistic Flesh is of no value. Is that really what Jesus was saying? Not at all. Jesus uses the word "flesh" in John 6:63 in the same way that St. Paul uses it throughout the New Testament — to speak about the fallen sinful nature of human beings apart from God: "Now the works of the *flesh* are obvious: immorality, impurity, licentiousness... In contrast, the fruit of the *Spirit* is love, joy, peace..." (Gal 5:19-23). When Jesus says in John 6:63 that "It is the Spirit that gives life, while the flesh is of no avail," He is comparing our fallen sinful human nature apart from God (our "flesh") to His supernatural Divine Nature — shared with human beings through His Eucharistic Flesh, the source of everlasting spiritual life (cf. John 6:54).[19]

In his First Letter to the Corinthians, St. Paul speaks about the fallen sinful nature of human beings apart from God when he says:

"...flesh and blood cannot inherit the kingdom of God, nor does corruption inherit incorruption" (1 Cor 15:50). St. Paul is saying here that living human beings and human beings who have already died, must have their fallen sinful human nature spiritually transformed by God before they can enter into everlasting life in heaven.[20] St. Paul is certainly not referring to Jesus' Divine Eucharistic Body and Blood when he says in 1 Cor 15:50 that "...flesh and blood cannot inherit the kingdom of God."

In Luke 24:13-35 the Bible tells us that, after His death and resurrection, Jesus appears in His Divine/human glorified body to two of His disciples who were traveling down the road to the city of Emmaus. When it begins to get dark at day's end, the two disciples invite the risen Jesus (whom they don't yet recognize) to share a meal with them. As Jesus was truly present to His disciples in His Divine/human glorified body, Scripture tells us: "...he took bread, said the blessing, broke it, and gave it to them" (Luke 24:30). Note that the same words: "took," "blessed," "broke," and "gave" are the exact same words in the exact same order that are used in every narrative account of Jesus' words over the Bread and Wine at the Last Supper — sometimes referred to as "the First Mass."[21] Then, after the meal in the presence of the risen and glorified Jesus, we read in the Gospel of Luke: "...the two [disciples] recounted...how [Jesus] was made known to them in *the breaking of the bread*" (Luke 24:35). According to the footnote in the *New American Bible With Revised New Testament* for Acts 2:42-47, the phrase "breaking of the bread" was a common term used by the early Christians to refer to the celebration of the Eucharistic liturgy.[22] Christ's risen and glorified Body and Blood couldn't be more fully present than that at a Mass!

Fr. John A. O'Brien, in his book *The Faith of Millions*, speaks about the Catholic belief in the Real Presence of Jesus Christ in the Holy Eucharist:

"Such was the faith not only of the Apostles and of the early Church, but remains to this day after the lapse of nineteen centuries the faith of all branches of Christianity save only Protestantism, which appeared upon the scene only in the sixteenth century. For the Greek

Church which seceded from the Catholic Church about a thousand years ago, the present Russian Church, the schismatic Copts, Armenians, Syrians, Chaldeans, and in fact all the Oriental sects, even though no longer in communion with the see of Rome, still hold fast to the teaching of Christ and the belief of His Apostles in the real presence of the body and blood, soul and divinity of our Lord in the Holy Eucharist...

For 1500 years all Christendom was united in the literal understanding of the Savior's words. In the sixteenth century it became the fashion to give new and arbitrary interpretations to passages in the Scriptures in accordance with one's private whim and fancy. The amount of religious anarchy and confusion which was brought about by this practice is evident from the fact that within seventy-five years [after the Protestant Reformation] over 200 different interpretations were given to the clear, simple words of Christ: 'This is My body.'"[23]

How Can Jesus' Body and Blood be Truly Present in the Holy Eucharist if They Cannot be Seen?: An Attempt to Speak About the Miracle of "Transubstantiation"

What makes you you? Is it your facial features? Is it your skin color? Is it the accent with which you speak? What if your face was badly burned in a fire and, after all of the bandages were removed, your face looked totally different? Would you still be you? Certainly. What if you went to the beach and got a dark sun tan? Would you still be you? Sure. What if you lived in another part of the world for a number of years and began to pick up different speech patterns? Would you still be you? Absolutely.

What makes bread bread? Is it its color? Is it its taste? Is it its shape? If a person put a few drops of food coloring into bread dough before baking it and it came out of the oven with a blue tint, would it still be bread? Certainly. If slices of banana were placed in bread dough before baking it and it came out of the oven tasting very differently, would it still be bread? Sure. If a person took a knife and cut up a loaf of bread into various patterns, would it still be bread? Absolutely.

After thinking through questions such as these, the Greek philosopher Aristotle (circa 300 B.C.) realized that the reality of a person or an object is not necessarily linked to any observable properties that the person or the object may outwardly exhibit. Aristotle tried to answer the questions "what makes you you?" and "what makes a thing a thing?" and developed some philosophical language to speak about the intangible, invisible, inner reality of a person or an object that makes it it.

The intangible, invisible, interior reality of a person or an object that makes it it, Aristotle called its "substance." Everything else that is associated with the person or the object that is external (e.g., a person's facial features, skin color, accent, or the bread's color, taste, shape), Aristotle called its "accidents."

Note how, in the Book of Exodus, Moses encounters God under the appearance of a burning bush (cf. Exod 3:2-6) and under the appearance of a column of cloud and fire (cf. Exod 13:21-22); the people who witnessed Jesus being baptized in the River Jordan encounter the Spirit of God under a dove-like appearance (cf. Matt 3:16); and Abraham encounters "the Lord" under the appearance of "three men" (cf. Gen 18:1-2). We can see from these scriptural examples how God has chosen, on numerous occasions, to make Himself truly present to His people under the appearance of various created things. Or, in other words, God does not have to *look* like God to *be* God. Of course, the most awesome example of this was when the world had the incredible privilege of encountering God under the humble appearance of "the carpenter's son" (cf. Matt 13:55; 1 John 5:20).

There is no example that one can cite from our experience of the world that exactly illustrates the miracle of transubstantiation.[24] Consider, however, these common everyday examples of how two things that look identical on the outside can actually contain very different interior properties: I have two photographs of myself as a young baby, taken about a month apart. In each photo I am wearing the same outfit, my hair is combed the same way, and I have an identical expression on my face. The reality that the photos reveal, however, is very different. In the earlier photo I had not yet been baptized. In the later photo I had been baptized and, thus, was "born again" as a child of God through "water and Spirit" (cf. John 3:1-5, 22). (Cf. Chapter 22 of this book.) Although my outer appearance looked exactly the same in the two photos, my inner status had changed dramatically in that my "old self" had "died with Christ" so that I could, in turn, be united with Jesus one day in His glorious resurrection (cf. Rom 6:4-6).

Obviously, St. Paul didn't *look* any different outwardly after being knocked to the ground by Jesus (cf. Acts 9:4) on his journey to Damascus but the reality of who he was *internally* changed dramatically after his powerful conversion experience. Along the same lines, don't identical twins *look* the same on the outside but have very different *interior* identities? Externally, doesn't a magnet *look* the same as a regular piece of metal but *interiorly* contain a totally different reality?

Fr. John A. O'Brien writes about the invisible presence of Jesus Christ under the appearance of the Eucharistic Bread and Wine:

> "In the Eucharist the substance of Christ's body has none of the sensible qualities or appearances of a human body. A striking analogy can be found in the manner in which the human soul, a spiritual substance, is present in the body. The soul, like all other spiritual beings, has no [tangible physical characteristics]; yet it animates the body which occupies space."[25]

The reason that I am speaking about this philosophical system that was developed circa 300 B. C. by Aristotle is because in the 1200's A.D., St. Thomas Aquinas borrowed this philosophical language and used it to describe what happens to the bread and the wine in the Holy Eucharist after the prayer of consecration. The question that St. Thomas sought to answer was: "How can our ancient Christian belief in the Real Presence of Jesus Christ in the Eucharist be explained if one cannot readily observe any external change?"

Consider this visual diagram of what happens to the bread and wine at the Eucharistic consecration:

	Before Consecration	After Consecration
"Accidents" of bread & wine (its outer, observable properties)	Its specific color, taste, shape.	Identical color, taste, shape.
"Substance" of bread & wine (its intangible, invisible, inner reality)	Common everyday food that sustains natural bodily life.	In every scriptural account of the Last Supper, Jesus takes common bread and wine and then, amazingly, teaches His Apostles: "this is my body...this is my blood..."[26] As a result of Christ's extraordinary proclamation, the inner reality (the "substance") of the common bread and wine is transformed ("transubstantiated") into the inner reality (the "substance") of Jesus' risen and glorified Body and Blood — which supernaturally sustains the Christian's soul spiritually into eternal life with God (cf. John 6:51, 54).

St. Thomas Aquinas used the phrase "transubstantiation" to further articulate the early Christian belief in the Real Presence of Christ in the Eucharist. By borrowing Aristotle's philosophical language of "substance" and "accidents," St. Thomas spoke about how the interior reality of the bread and wine can be transformed into the interior reality of the Body and Blood of Jesus Christ even though the outer properties (the "accidents") of the bread and wine still look the same to the naked eye.

When we Catholics receive Holy Communion, we are receiving the entire inner reality of Jesus Christ — Body, Blood, Soul, and Divinity *(His Body, Blood, and Soul are what make up His human nature and His Divinity makes up His Divine nature.)* Catholics are receiving that which makes Jesus Jesus while the outer external properties of bread and wine linger on. In the awesome Sacrament of the Holy Eucharist looks are, indeed, deceiving because "what you see is *not* what you get!"[27]

Former evangelical Christian (now Roman Catholic apologist), Mark P. Shea in his book, *This IS My Body: An Evangelical Discovers the Real Presence*, says the following about the Holy Eucharist: "I saw at once that regular biblical fellowship and regular Holy Communion were both a form of ritual; both 'means of grace.' The only difference is that in the former, God transubstantiates paper, ink and the human voice into His Word; whereas in the latter, according to Catholics, He changes the bread and wine into something even more impressive."[28]

Consider this simple truth: The ordinary food and drink that human beings consume daily is continually transformed by our bodily organs into our literal flesh and blood. If our feeble human organs can accomplish the amazing feat of invisibly transforming inanimate food and drink into living human flesh and blood, why couldn't Jesus, the Creator of humanity (cf. John 1:3), perform a similar *(but even more awesome)* invisible transformation of inanimate bread and wine into His risen and glorified Divine Flesh and Blood?[29]

A number of times over the past 2,000 years there have been reports of visible Eucharistic miracles where the bread and the wine were transformed into the observable Flesh and Blood of Jesus Christ.[30] It appears that, every now and then, Jesus sends us these extraordinary Eucharistic miracles to help deepen our belief in His Real Eucharistic Presence. The basis for the Roman Catholic belief in Jesus' Real Eucharistic Presence, however, is the faith of the Apostles, the liturgical practice of the early Church, and the witness of Holy Scripture. Extraordinary visible Eucharistic miracles, when God sends them to us, simply serve to reinforce the faith and practice of the Apostolic Church.[31]

Common Objection #2

"Old and New Testament Scripture clearly forbid anyone to partake of blood: '...if anyone...partakes of any blood, I will...cut him off from among his people' (Lev 17:10-12); '...avoid pollution from idols, unlawful marriage, the meat of strangled animals, and blood' (Acts 15:20). The Catholic belief that Jesus' Body and *Blood* are able to be consumed by believers in the Holy Eucharist is, therefore, a direct violation of this Biblical command."

A Catholic Response

The Old Testament passage cited above from Leviticus 17:10-12 refers to religious dietary regulations observed by the Jews. In the New Testament Jesus declared that *all* food was fit to eat and, thus, He did away with any requirement that Christians follow Old Testament Jewish dietary regulations: "Do you not realize that everything that goes into a person from outside cannot defile, since it enters not the heart but the stomach and passes out into the latrine? Thus he declared all foods clean" (Mark 7:17-19). The New Testament passage from Acts 15:20 cited above that suggests that Christians abstain from blood echoes St. Paul's teaching found in 1 Cor 8:7-9 and Rom 14:14-15 where he says that, in-and-of-itself, all food is clean and is able to be eaten by Christians. The only reason a Christian should refrain from eating any type of food, St. Paul says, is if it creates a hardship on a newly-converted Christian believer who is not yet mature in his faith.[32] Note that a number of the first Christians were of Jewish ancestry and, as a result, came from a background where dietary regulations played an extremely important role in the practice of their faith. St. Paul was asking non-Jewish (Gentile) Christians to be considerate in their dining habits whenever they are in the presence of newly-converted Jewish Christians. Although, technically, Christians are not bound to any type of dietary restrictions, for a Gentile Christian to consume a pork dinner right in front of a newly-converted Jewish Christian could shake that person up because he comes from a religious background where that kind of activity was strictly forbidden.

Not too many modern-day Christians would have a problem going to a restaurant and ordering a rare (bloody) steak or eating gravy (cooked blood) with their rice or potatoes. Wouldn't that be considered "partaking of blood" and, thus, go against Biblical teaching?[33] According to Jesus' New Testament teaching found in Mark 7:17-19, certainly not!

Note that the Bible says that Jesus was born in a manger (cf. Luke 2:7). It is interesting to note that, in French, the word *manger* means "to eat." A manger was a feed trough where animals came to eat. Later on in His life, the adult Jesus would tell His followers: "Whoever *eats* my flesh and drinks my blood has eternal life, and I will raise him on the last day" (John 6:54). A coincidence? The town where Jesus was born was called "Bethlehem" (cf. Luke 2:1-7). In Hebrew, the word "Bethlehem" means "house of bread."[34] A coincidence?

Common Objection #3

"If the doctrine of the Real Presence were true and you Catholics were really eating the body and blood of Jesus Christ you would be cannibals!"

A Catholic Response

Actually, there is a huge difference between a cannibal and a Catholic. A cannibal is a human who eats *human* flesh and blood, in its natural state, along with the accompanying muscle tissue, organs, veins, etc. On the other hand, a Catholic is a human who eats Jesus' *Divine* Flesh and Blood, in its risen and glorified supernatural state, as per His instructions found in the Gospel of John: "...Amen, amen, I say to you, unless you eat the flesh of the Son of Man and drink his blood, you do not have life within you. Whoever eats my flesh and drinks my blood has eternal life, and I will raise him on the last day. For my flesh is true food, and my blood is true drink" (John 6:53-55).[35] Please refer to the "Transubstantiation" section of this chapter for an explanation of the nature of Jesus' presence in the Holy Eucharist in the Catholic Church.

Concerning the topic of cannibalism, Catholic apologist Fr. Peter Stravinskas reminds his readers that: "both Tertullian and Minucius Felix...give considerable attention in their second-century writings to the charge of cannibalism being leveled against the Church. A belief in the Real Presence thus clearly existed in the Early Church, for no 'simple memorial supper' would have evoked such specific and violent charges from the general pagan population."[36]

Common Objection #4

"I would have to see Jesus' flesh and blood with my own two eyes to believe it!" one of my evangelical Christian friends told me.

A Catholic Response

I thought for a while and replied: "Have you ever seen God?" "No" my friend replied. "How can you believe in Him?" I asked. "Through faith, that's how I believe in Him" was my friend's reply. "Exactly! Through faith in Jesus' words found in Scripture is how we Catholics can believe in something that we cannot readily perceive with our feeble human eyes." Or, in the words of St. Paul: "...we walk by faith, not by sight" (2 Cor 5:7). Or, in the words of Jesus to "doubting Thomas": "...Have you come to believe because you have seen me? Blessed are those who have not seen and have believed" (John 20:29). Or, in the words of St. Peter: "Although you have not seen him you love him; even though you do not see him now yet believe in him, you rejoice with an indescribable and glorious joy, as you attain the goal of [your] faith, the salvation of your souls" (1 Pet 1:8-9).

As Catholics, our faith in Jesus is not restricted to what our limited human eyes and minds can fully comprehend. Although Peter did not fully intellectually comprehend Jesus' Eucharistic teaching recounted in John Chapter 6, he looked at Jesus with a heart full of trust and faith and, on behalf of the rest of the Apostles, exclaimed: "We have come to believe and are convinced that you are the Holy One of God" (John 6:69).

In his book *Catholic and Christian*, Alan Schreck speaks about the awesome mystery of Jesus' Real Presence under the appearance of the Eucharistic Bread and Wine:

"Should it surprise us that Jesus' body and blood are present in the eucharistic bread and wine? We believe that the fullness of God can take the form of a mere man — Jesus. Why should it be more difficult to believe (at Jesus' word) that God can be fully present in another part of his creation — bread and wine? If God submitted to be crucified for our salvation, is it any harder to believe that God would allow us to receive him into our bodies and spirits through a very basic human act, eating? The miracle of God's presence in the bread and wine of the Eucharist is comparable to the miracle of his presence among us in Jesus Christ. They are both beyond our comprehension, and reveal to us the depth of his love and his humility in placing himself at the disposal of his creatures, for the sake of our salvation."[37]

Common Objection #5

"But the Bible says that Jesus Christ '...has taken his seat at the right hand of the throne of the Majesty in heaven' (Heb 8:1-2) and is not in a 'tabernacle...made by hands' (Heb 9:11), therefore, He cannot be present in the hundreds of thousands of tabernacles in Catholic Churches throughout the world."

A Catholic Response

In the Book of Exodus, God (who was in heaven) says to His Chosen People on earth: "They shall make a sanctuary for me, that I may dwell in their midst" (Exodus 25:8). Could God dwell in an earthly sanctuary and also dwell in heaven at the same time? Sure He could and He did.[38] In the Gospel of Luke, the twelve-year-old Jesus is found by Mary and Joseph in the Jewish Temple and He tells them: "Did you not know that I must be in my Father's *house*"

(Luke 2:49)? Here again, we see that God the Father resides in heaven and He also has a "house" (a dwelling place) on earth so that He could be present to His people in an intimate way. One of the qualities of God (who is Father, Son, and Holy Spirit) that human beings don't possess is omnipresence *(the ability to be present in all places at once).*

The objection that Jesus couldn't be in heaven and also in a tabernacle in a Catholic Church assumes that Jesus' Divine/human glorified body is identical to our purely human body and can only be in one place at a time. Because Jesus' Divine/human glorified Body is not limited by the restrictions of our merely human bodies,[39] Jesus' glorified Body can be present at many different places on earth at the same time while He is also seated at the right hand of the Father in heaven.[40] Jesus dwells in your heart and mine and we both live in different places on earth don't we? If Jesus can dwell in different people's hearts *(fleshy tabernacles)* (cf. John 14:23) throughout the world, it would seem logical that He could also dwell in metal tabernacles in Catholic Churches throughout the world.

In Scripture, Jesus tells every one of His followers: "For where two or three are gathered in my name, there am I in the midst of them" (Matt 18:20). The only way that Jesus could be seated at the right hand of the Father in heaven and accomplish the amazing feat of being simultaneously present to every group of praying Christians living anywhere in the world is if He were omnipresent. Jesus also tells all Christians, "...And behold, I am with you always, until the end of the age" (Matt 28:20). Again, Jesus is promising to be present at every moment to every Christian living in every place on earth. Because Jesus is omnipresent, He can still accomplish this incredible act while He is seated, simultaneously, at the right hand of the Father in heaven.

Jesus says in every narrative account of the Last Supper that what may look like bread "**is**" really His Flesh and what may look like wine "**is**" really His Blood. Therefore, it follows that wherever the excess Consecrated Bread and Wine are kept after the Eucharist is concluded (a Catholic tabernacle), there "**is**" Jesus' Body and Blood. The Bible never once says that, after the celebration of the Eucharist is concluded, the Consecrated Bread and Wine cease to be Jesus' Body and Blood.

Common Objection #6

"In the Bible, Jesus says that He **is** "the gate" (John 10:9) and He **is** "the vine" (John 15:5). Certainly no Christian believes that He is literally a part of a fence or a type of garden plant. When Jesus said in John 6 that His flesh **is** bread and His blood **is** drink He was simply using a figure of speech to metaphorically compare Himself to those objects."

A Catholic Response

As most people do, Jesus certainly used figures of speech in His conversation. The above passages from John 10:9 and John 15:5 are certainly examples of His doing that. In the Gospel of John, Jesus asks His followers to "eat His flesh and drink His blood" (cf. John 6:51-68). Jesus worked long and hard to attract the few faithful followers that He had. Would it be likely that He would have let them walk away (cf. John 6:66) from the long-awaited Messiah because they happened to poorly comprehend one of His metaphoric figures of speech? It would seem very illogical. Being the extraordinary teacher that He was, Jesus would have had the moral obligation to immediately clear up His follower's misunderstandings if they failed to accurately grasp a crucial teaching that He was trying to communicate to them.

Consider this example that Catholic apologist Patrick Madrid sometimes uses to illustrate the importance of the correct interpretation of a text: Take the sentence: *"I never said that you stole the money."* At face value, this simple sentence seems to be pretty straightforward and easy to understand, right? But is it? The way one interprets the words of this sentence can, actually, change its meaning dramatically:

- *"I* never said that you stole the money" could imply that *you* never made such a statement — but *another person* may have said it.
- "I never *said* that you stole the money" could imply that you didn't make this statement *orally* — but you may have *written it* in a letter or *implied it* through some type of innuendo.

- "I never said that *you* stole the money" could imply that you didn't say that *this particular person* stole the money — but *another person* may have stolen it.
- "I never said that you *stole* the money" could imply that you never accused the person of actually stealing the money — but the money may have been lost through *accident or negligence*.
- "I never said that you stole the *money*" could imply that you didn't say that *money* was stolen by the person — but *another type of asset* could have been stolen by the person in question.

Do you see how it is quite possible to interpret an apparently simple sentence in a wide variety of ways? Who would be in the best position to correctly interpret the statement "this is my body ... this is my blood" spoken by Jesus at the Last Supper? The early Christians who lived in Biblical times and who knew the Apostles personally and witnessed firsthand what the infant Church's beliefs and practices were. Please refer to the end of this chapter to see that the Eucharistic belief of the first Christians in the Apostolic Church is the Eucharistic belief of the Roman Catholic Church.

Common Objection #7

"If you Catholics were truly eating and drinking the body and blood of Jesus Christ at Mass, when you would go to the restroom you would be placing Jesus' body and blood into the sewerage system. What a sacrilege that would be!"

A Catholic Response

From comments such as this, it is clear that the Catholic doctrine of transubstantiation is often very misunderstood among some Christians of other denominations. Catholic teaching clearly states that the "substance" (the interior reality) of Jesus' Body and Blood remains in the Eucharistic elements only as long as the "accidents" (the outer observable properties) of the Consecrated Bread and Wine remain. The *Catechism of the Catholic Church* (#1377) states: "The Eucharistic presence of Christ begins at the moment of the consecration and endures as long as the Eucharistic species subsist..."[205]

If one were to analyze bodily waste in a laboratory, one would discover various acids and chemicals expelled by the human body after the digestion process has already been fully completed. Any waste products that come from consuming the Eucharist would come from the "accidents" of the Consecrated Bread and Wine (the wheat, water, grapes and alcohol making up the outer appearances of the Consecrated Bread or Wine.) Obviously, the invisible, intangible, inner substance (the interior core reality) of Jesus in the Holy Eucharist, Body, Blood, Soul, and Divinity is not able to be broken down by a human stomach and expelled as waste by the human body.

Common Objection #8

"You Catholics believe that you are partaking of Jesus' glorified and risen body and blood when you receive Holy Communion. If Jesus was able to give His Apostles His glorified and risen body and blood to eat at the Last Supper on Holy Thursday (before His crucifixion on Good Friday), there would have been no reason for Him to go through the agony of offering His flesh and blood on the cross the next day."

A Catholic Response

Jesus was certainly really, truly, and entirely present to His Apostles at the Last Supper Body, Blood, Soul, and Divinity. As a matter of fact, at the Last Supper, His Body, Blood, Soul, and Divinity (His complete person) was able to interact with all who gathered for the meal. In Jesus' words in all of the narrative accounts of the Last Supper, He takes the bread and the cup and tells His followers: "This **is** my body, this **is** my blood." He does *not* say that the bread and wine that He was to give them was to "represent" or "symbolize" His Body and Blood. Jesus' Body and Blood were in glorified and risen form only after His Resurrection at Easter. What the Apostles ate and drank at the Last Supper on Holy Thursday was Jesus' Body and Blood in the state that it was in at that moment, Body, Blood, Soul, and Divinity.[42] How did Jesus give His Body and Blood to His Apostles to eat on Holy Thursday before His Body and Blood were in glorified and risen form? Scripture doesn't give us the mechanics of *how* Jesus did it, it only tells us *that* Jesus did it. The New Testament recounts scores of Jesus' supernatural miracles without giving readers the details of *how* Jesus accomplished them, the reader is only informed *that* Jesus accomplished them. Remember the words of the angel Gabriel to the puzzled Virgin Mary: "For *nothing* will be impossible for God" (Luke 1:37).[43] In his commentary on the Last Supper St. Augustine (d. 430 A.D.) declared that, in a mystical way, Christ held Himself in His hands at the Last Supper.

Jesus still had to die on the cross for our sins the next day in order to redeem the human race: "In [Jesus] we have redemption by his blood, the forgiveness of transgressions, in accord with the riches of his grace..." (Eph 1:7, cf. also Heb 9:22). Jesus' crucifixion on Good Friday, thus, reconciled us to God and re-opened the gates of heaven that were closed by the sin of Adam and Eve (cf. Eph 2:13; Gen 3:1-24).[44]

Common Objection #9

"I used to be Catholic but, when my first marriage ended in divorce and I remarried again, the man-made laws of the Catholic Church told me that I could no longer receive Holy Communion. The Catholic Church rejected me at a painful time in my life so, therefore, I found another more compassionate church who allowed me to receive holy communion with them."

A Catholic Response

Cf. Chapter 25 of this book to answer this objection.

Common Objection #10

"We have holy communion in our church also!"

A Catholic Response

Some Christian denominations (e. g., some Episcopalians[45] and Lutherans) believe in the Eucharistic doctrine of *"consubstantiation."*

The doctrine of consubstantiation holds that, after consecration, the "substance" (the inner core reality) of Jesus is present alongside the "substance" (the inner core reality) of common bread and wine (i.e., they exist side-by-side). This Eucharistic belief differs significantly from the Roman Catholic, Eastern Catholic and Oriental and Greek Orthodox doctrine of "transubstantiation" in that Roman Catholic, Eastern Catholic and the Oriental and Greek Orthodox Churches believe that, after the words of consecration, the "substance" (the inner core reality) of the common bread and wine cease to exist and only the "substance" of Jesus Christ (His inner core reality) remains (along with the outer observable properties of bread and wine). How can Roman Catholics, Eastern Catholic and Greek and Oriental Orthodox Christians believe such a thing? In all of the narrative accounts of Jesus' words at the Last Supper, Jesus takes the bread and the wine and then declares: "This **is** my body ... this **is** my blood." Note that Jesus doesn't say, "This is my body and also bread besides" or "This is my blood and also wine besides" *(which is what the Eucharistic doctrine of "consubstantiation" holds.)*

Various fundamentalist Christian denominations will occasionally partake of common bread and wine *(some drink grape juice to avoid the alcohol)* in an attempt to nostalgically re-enact Jesus' 2,000 year-old actions at the Last Supper.[46] However, fundamentalist Christian denominations certainly *do not* believe that the complete and entire Body, Blood, Soul, and Divinity of Jesus Christ is actually present in the Holy Eucharist.

St. Ignatius of Antioch (circa 110 A.D.) writes in his *Letter to the Smyrnaeans* about valid celebrations of the Holy Eucharist: "The sole Eucharist you should consider valid is one that is celebrated by the bishop himself or by some person authorized by him. Where the bishop is to be seen, there let all his people be, just as wherever Jesus Christ is present, there is the Catholic Church."[47]

Common Objection #11

"Why doesn't the Catholic Church have an 'open Communion' where any Christian of good will can receive the Holy Eucharist? Isn't the Catholic Church being elitist by not allowing other Christians to receive Holy Communion in their Church?

A Catholic Response

Notice how the word "Communion" looks very much like a combination of two regularly-used English words: "common" and "union." When one receives Communion in the Catholic Church he is saying that he shares a "common union" of belief with us. Since no other Christian denomination (besides the Oriental and Greek Orthodox and Eastern Catholic Churches in union with Rome) share our foundational belief as to what the Holy Eucharist actually is, they are not yet in common union (communion) with us. When a Catholic approaches the Eucharistic minister to receive Holy Communion at Mass the minister will say: "The Body of Christ" *(which is, essentially, a shortened form of the question: "Do you believe that this is truly the Body of the risen Jesus Christ in its entirety — Body, Blood, Soul, and Divinity?")* If the person does believe this about the Eucharist, he makes a profession of faith by responding: "Amen!" Note that Protestant Christians, when asked this question about their belief in the Holy Eucharist, could not respond "Amen" because no other Christian denomination (besides the Oriental and Greek Orthodox and Eastern Catholic Churches) believes what the Roman Catholic Church believes about the Holy Eucharist (cf. the "Transubstantiation" section of this chapter.) Cf. Matt 5:23-24.

Speaking about the issue of the reception of Holy Communion in the Church circa 150 A.D., St. Justin Martyr in his *First Apology* states: "We call this food Eucharist; and no one is permitted to partake of it, except one who believes our teaching to be true..."[48]

Common Objection #12

"Why do I need to receive Jesus in Holy Communion when He is already constantly dwelling within me?

A Catholic Response

Numerous times in the New Testament we are presented with the image of Jesus as a "bridegroom" who is seeking total union with His "bride" — the Church (cf. Rev 19:7-9). Why do married couples share the marital act with each other even though they already constantly dwell in one other's presence? Spouses dwell in each other's presence constantly but share the marital act at certain extraordinary moments to renew and reaffirm their covenant of love in the most intimate exchange possible. The reception of Holy Communion is to a Christian's relationship with Jesus what the marital act is to a married couple — a total giving and receiving and a reaffirmation of our covenant relationship in the most intimate expression possible.

What Does Heavenly Worship Look Like?[49]

In the Book of Revelation we read about a vision of heavenly worship experienced by St. John. These are some of the things that he saw taking place in heaven on "the Lord's day" (cf. Rev 1:10):[50]

- Jesus is dressed in the liturgical garb of the high priest (cf. Rev 1:13; Exod 28:4).
- Worshippers are promised the New Testament "hidden manna" (i.e., heavenly Bread) to eat (cf. Rev 2:17; John 6:48-51; Rev 3:20).[51]
- Worshippers in the sanctuary are dressed in white robes (cf. Rev 4:4).
- The *Sanctus* ("Holy, Holy, Holy") prayer is prayed by the worshippers (cf. Rev 4:8; Isaiah 6:1-3).
- The perpetual sacrificial nature of the worship is evident because Jesus, in His risen, glorified body in heaven *(where Scripture says we will be made whole again)* still looks like "a Lamb that seemed to have been slain" (cf. Rev 5:6; Rev 21:4; 1 Cor 5:7-8; 1 Cor 11:26).[52]
- The "Great Amen" is proclaimed by the worshippers (cf. Rev 5:14).
- Worshippers kneel (cf. Rev 5:14).
- An altar is used (cf. Rev 8:3).
- The theology of the Communion of Saints is clearly displayed as the inhabitants of heaven constantly offer prayers of worship to God and petition Him to respond to their earthly concerns (cf. Rev 6:9-10; Rev 8:3-4).
- Incense is regularly used (cf. Rev 5:8; Rev 8:3-4)
- The body and soul of the Blessed Virgin Mary *(the "Ark of the New Covenant" where God the Son dwelt for nine months)* is seen assumed into heaven[53] (cf. Rev 11:19–12:5; Psalm 2:9, Rev 19:15).

- We are told that "the woman" *(the Blessed Virgin Mary)* was/is totally protected from the devil's influence[54] (cf. Rev 12:14; Exod 25:10-11).
- Faithful virgins who follow Christ wherever He goes are given special honor (cf. Rev 14:4). (Note how Rev 14:4 is beautifully fulfilled in the lifestyle of modern-day Roman Catholic clergy who have embraced the consecrated celibate life in an attempt to free themselves to do the work of the Lord with an undivided heart.)
- White linen cloth is used to represent the righteous deeds of the saints (cf. Rev 19:8).
- The liturgy of the Word (the proclamation of the Scripture readings) comprises the first part of the worship (cf. Rev Chapters 5-8; Luke 24:27), and is followed by the liturgy of the Eucharist (the Sacred Meal) (cf. Rev 19:9; Acts 2:42, 46; Luke 24:30).

We can see here how the Roman Catholic Church has patterned its liturgy to mirror the heavenly worship recounted in Scripture.[55] Faithful Catholics strive to worship God here on earth in the same way that they will worship Him, with the angels and the saints, for an eternity in heaven.[56]

Jesus prayed that His followers "may be one, as [He and the Father] are one" (John 17:22). Let us continue to pray that one day all Christians will be in common union (communion) of belief in the Real Presence of Jesus in the Holy Eucharist and, thus, be able to share together in the one Bread and the one Cup of our Lord Jesus Christ (cf. 1 Cor 10:17, Matt 5:23-24). May all Christians, one day, be able to approach the Holy Eucharist and utter the words of the Apostle Thomas as he gazed in awe upon the Body of the risen and glorified Jesus: "My Lord and my God" (John 20:28)![57]

If you are not already a Roman Catholic, won't you consider becoming a member of our Church so that, besides having Jesus spiritually "in your heart," you can have the fullness of our Lord and Savior reside in your very body each and every time you receive the Holy Eucharist?

"Behold, I stand at the door and knock. If anyone hears my voice and opens the door, [then] I will enter his house and dine with him, and he with me (Rev 3:20)."

What Did the Early Christians Believe About the Nature of Jesus' Presence in Holy Communion?[58]

- "Therefore whoever eats the bread or drinks the cup of the Lord unworthily will have to answer for the body and blood of the Lord. A person should examine himself, and so eat the bread and drink the cup. For anyone who eats and drinks without discerning the body, eats and drinks judgement on himself. That is why many among you are ill and infirm, and a considerable number are dying." St. Paul in his *First Letter to the Corinthians* 11:27-30 (circa 56 A.D.)

- "The cup of blessing that we bless, is it not a participation in the blood of Christ? The bread that we break, is it not a participation in the body of Christ?" St. Paul in his *First Letter to the Corinthians* 10:16 (circa 56 A.D.)

- St. Ignatius of Antioch *(who was a disciple of St. John the Apostle)* stated that belief in the Real Presence of Jesus Christ in the Holy Eucharist was one of the litmus tests of orthodox belief. He writes about the Docetists — who were unbelievers in the Real Presence because they believed that Jesus only *appeared* to have a human body but never really became incarnate: "They abstain from the Eucharist and from prayer, because they do not confess that the Eucharist is the Flesh of our Savior Jesus Christ, Flesh which suffered for our sins and which the Father, in His goodness, raised up again. They who deny the gift of God are perishing in their disputes." St. Ignatius of Antioch in his *Letter to the Smyrnaeans* (circa 110 A.D.)[59]

- "I have no taste for corruptible food nor for the pleasures of this life. I desire the Bread of God, which is the Flesh of Jesus Christ, who was of the seed of David; and for drink I desire His Blood, which is love incorruptible." St. Ignatius of Antioch in his *Letter to the Romans* (circa 110 A.D.)[60]

- "For not as common bread nor common drink do we receive these; but since Jesus Christ our Savior was made incarnate by the Word of God and had both flesh and blood for our salvation, so too, as we have been taught, the food which has been made into the Eucharist by the Eucharistic prayer set down by Him, and by the change of which our blood and flesh is nourished, is both the Flesh and the Blood of that incarnated Jesus." St. Justin Martyr in his *First Apology* (circa 150 A.D.)[61]

- "He has declared the cup, a part of creation, to be his own blood, from which he causes our blood to flow; and the bread, a part of creation, he has established as his own body, from which he gives increase unto our bodies. When, therefore, the mixed cup [wine and water] and the baked bread receive the Word of God and become the Eucharist, the body of Christ, and from these the substance of our flesh is increased and supported, how can they say that the flesh is not capable of receiving the gift of God, which is eternal life — flesh which is nourished by the body and blood of the Lord and is in fact a member of him? St. Irenaeus in his *Against Heresies* (circa 189 A.D.)[62]

- "'Eat my flesh,' [Jesus] says, 'and drink my blood.' The Lord supplies us with these intimate nutrients, he delivers over his flesh and pours out his blood, and nothing is lacking for the growth of his children." St. Clement of Alexandria in his *The Instructor of Children* (circa 191 A.D.)[63]

- "'And she [Wisdom] has furnished her table' [Prov 9:1]...refers to his [Christ's] honored and undefiled body and blood, which day by day are administered and offered sacrificially at the spiritual divine table, as a memorial of that first and ever-memorable table of the spiritual divine supper [i.e., the Last Supper]." Hippolytus in his *Fragment from Commentary on Proverbs* (circa 217 A.D.)[64]

- "He [Paul] threatens, moreover, the stubborn and forward, and denounces them, saying, 'Whosoever eats the bread or drinks the cup of the Lord unworthily is guilty of the body and blood of the Lord' [1 Cor 11:27]. All these warnings being scorned and contemned — [lapsed Christians will often take Communion] before their sin is expiated, before confession has been made of their crime, before their conscience has been purged by sacrifice and by the hand of the priest, before the offense of an angry and threatening Lord has been appeased, [and so] violence is done to his body and blood; and they sin now against their Lord more with their hand and mouth than when they denied their Lord." St. Cyprian in his *The Lapsed* (circa 251 A.D.)[65]

- "After the disciples had eaten the new and holy Bread, and when they understood by faith that they had eaten of Christ's Body, Christ went on to explain and to give them the whole Sacrament." St. Ephraim in his *Homilies* (circa 350 A.D.)[66]

- "Do not, therefore, regard the Bread and Wine as simply that; for they are, according to the Master's declaration, the Body and Blood of Christ." St. Cyril of Jerusalem in his *Catechetical Lectures* (circa 350 A.D.)[67]

- "Having learned these things, and being fully convinced that the apparent Bread is not bread, even though it is sensible to the taste, but the Body of Christ; and that the apparent Wine is not wine, even though the taste would have it so..." St. Cyril of Jerusalem in his *Catechetical Lectures* (circa 350 A.D.)[68]

- "And when He Himself has affirmed and said, "This is my Blood," who can ever hesitate and say it is not His Blood?" St. Cyril of Jerusalem in his *Catechetical Lectures* (circa 350 A.D.)[69]

- "That Bread which you see on the altar, having been sanctified by the word of God, is the Body of Christ; that chalice, or rather, what is in that chalice, having been sanctified by the word of God, is the blood of Christ. Through that bread and wine the Lord Christ willed to commend His Body and Blood, which He poured out for us unto the forgiveness of sins. If you have received worthily, you are what you have received." St. Augustine in his *Sermon #272* (circa 400 A.D.)[70]

Endnotes

[1] The words of the Apostle Thomas as he gazed in awe at the risen and glorified body of Jesus Christ (cf. John 20:28).

[199] St. Thomas Aquinas, *STh* III, 73, 3c.

[200] Council of Trent (1551): DS 1651.

[201] Paul VI, *MF* 39.

[204] Council of Trent (1551): DS 1642; cf. *Mt* 26:26 ff.; *Mk* 14:22 ff.; *Lk* 22:19 ff.; *1 Cor* 11:24 ff.

[2] Note that, in all of the scriptural accounts of Jesus' words over the Eucharistic Bread and Wine, the Bible says that He "gave thanks" (cf. Matt 26:27; Mark 14:23; Luke 22:17; 1 Cor 11:24) The Greek word for "gave thanks" is *eucharistēsas* (which is where Catholics get the word "Eucharist" for our celebration of the Lord's Supper [i.e., the Mass]).

[3] A few other examples of the Roman Catholic Church interpreting Scripture in its straightforward, plain, literal sense include: "...you are Peter, and upon this rock I will build my church..." (Matt 16:18), "Whose sins you forgive are forgiven them..." (John 20:23), "...baptism...saves you now" (cf. 1 Pet 3:18-21). When faced with crucial passages such as these, many evangelical Christian denominations (who normally claim to adhere to the plain, literal sense of Scripture) are forced to come up with their own reasons of why these Bible passages should really mean something else than what they literally say. Cf. Patrick Madrid (editor), *Surprised by Truth*, (San Diego, CA: Basilica Press, 1994), p. 62.

[4] Dr. Ludwig Ott, *Fundamentals of Catholic Dogma (4ᵗʰ Edition)* (Rockford, IL: TAN Books and Publishers, Inc., 1960), pp. 372-373. (Bold print done by book's author for emphasis.)

[5] *New American Bible With Revised New Testament*, Introductory Article to First Corinthians, p. 243.

[6] Peter E. Fink, S.J. (editor), *New Dictionary of Sacramental Worship*, (Collegeville, MN: The Liturgical Press, 1990,) p. 395.

[7] Regarding St. Paul's words on the Eucharist found in 1 Cor 11:30, T. L. Frazier asks the question: "What other Christian 'symbol' ever carried the death sentence for its ill treatment?" Cf. *Surprised by Truth*, p. 195. Cf. also *Catechism of the Catholic*

Church, #1385.

8   Karl Keating, *Catholicism and Fundamentalism*, (San Francisco, CA: Ignatius Press, 1988), p. 247.

9   Rev. John A. O'Brien, *The Faith of Millions*, (Huntington, IN: Our Sunday Visitor, Inc., 1974), p. 215.

10   Note that, after His death and resurrection, Scripture tells us that Jesus often made Himself present to His followers in His risen, glorified body (cf. John 20:24-29; John 21:1-23; Luke 24:13-35).

11   Matt 26:17, Mark 14:12, and Luke 22:8 all state that the Last Supper was a traditional Passover meal held during the Jewish Feast of Passover.

12   Expounding upon the words of Jesus found in John 6:53-54, St. Ignatius of Antioch (d. 107 A.D.) writes that the Eucharistic Bread and Wine is the "medicine of immortality" and "the antidote to death." Is it possible for a mere "symbol" to impart eternal life to a Christian? Hardly. Only Jesus Christ Himself — truly present in the Holy Eucharist — could do that. Cf. James T. O'Connor, *The Hidden Manna*, (San Francisco, CA: Ignatius Press, 1988), p. 17.

13   The evangelical Christian interpretation of John 6 that holds that Jesus was simply speaking about accepting His Word when He asked His listeners to "eat His Flesh and Blood" could not be a correct one because, if the listeners were simply understanding Jesus to be metaphorically speaking about putting faith in Him, why their shocked responses? If the listeners chose not to put faith in Jesus' Word and they understood Him to be speaking about such, they would have simply said something like, "No, Jesus, we do not accept the truths that you are preaching to us and we choose not to follow you any more. Goodbye." That the listeners were taking Jesus literally is seen clearly in their responses: "How can this man give us [his] flesh to eat?" (John 6:52) and "This saying is hard; who can accept it" (John 6:60)? The fact that Jesus doesn't clear up His teachings after repeated shocked responses by the audience clearly indicates that He meant what He said to be taken literally — that one day His followers would be able to partake of His risen and glorified Flesh and Blood in the Holy Eucharist!

14   St. John tells us in John 6:68 that St. Peter was the first to pro-
      fess the ancient Christian belief that the Eucharistic Bread and
      Wine were not mere symbols but truly the Body and Blood of
      Jesus Christ Himself (cf. Chapter 13 of this book to read more
      about the prominent role of St. Peter in the early Church).

15   Catholic apologist Scott Hahn reminds us that the Last Supper
      was pre-figured by the Jewish Passover Meal, which was/is eaten
      by the Jews in commemoration of their Passover into freedom
      from their slavery in Egypt (cf. Exod Chapters 11-14). At the
      Passover Meal, God instructed His Chosen People to eat the
      actual flesh of the slain lamb (cf. Exod 12:3-7) and not some
      "symbol" or "representation" of the lamb's flesh (e. g., a lamb-
      shaped wafer). Cf. Scott Hahn, *Answering Common Objections
      Audio Tapes*, (West Covina, CA: St. Joseph Communications,
      Inc., (818) 331-3549).

16   Scott Hahn, *Eucharistic Day at Marytown Audio Tapes*, (West
      Covina, CA: St. Joseph Communications, Inc., (818) 331-3549).
      Cf. also Rev 13:17-18 and 2 John 7.

17   Rev. Peter M. J. Stravinskas, *The Catholic Church and the Bible*,
      (San Francisco, CA: Ignatius Press, 1987), p. 72.

18   The author of the Letter to the Hebrews speaks to early Jewish
      Christians and urges them strongly not to leave their Christian
      faith and revert back to Judaism: "For it is impossible in the
      case of those who have once been enlightened and *tasted the
      heavenly gift...* to bring them to repentance again" (cf. Heb 6:4-
      6). The footnote for Heb 6:4 in the *New American Bible With
      Revised New Testament* says that the reference to "tasting the
      heavenly gift" may, indeed, be a reference to the Holy Eucha-
      rist. The Biblical writer of Hebrews says that if a Christian truly
      realized what a treasure one had available in the Holy Eucha-
      rist, he would never *dream* of walking away from it.

19   *New American Bible With Revised New Testament*, Footnote
      for John 6:63, p. 155.

20   *Ibid.*, Footnote for 1 Cor 15:50, p. 263.

21   Cf. Matt 26:26-28; Mark 14:22-24; Luke 22:19-20; 1 Cor 11:24-
      25.

22   *New American Bible With Revised New Testament*, footnote to
      Acts 2:42-47, p. 183.

23 *The Faith of Millions*, p. 211, 214.
24 Note that, in His very first miracle at Cana (cf. John 2:1-11), Jesus not only transformed (transubstantiated) the substance (the interior reality) of water into the substance of wine, He even transformed the remaining "accidents" (the outer appearances) of water into wine as well!   One can clearly see from this amazing feat that our Divine Lord is quite capable of performing the miracle of transubstantiation!
25 *The Faith of Millions*, p. 220.
26 Cf. Matt 26:26-28; Mark 14:22-24; Luke 22:19-20; 1 Cor 11:24-25.
27 Speaking about the true bodily Presence of Jesus Christ in the Holy Eucharist, Pope Paul VI writes: "...since once the substance or nature of the bread and wine has been changed into the body and blood of Christ, nothing remains of the bread and wine except for the species — beneath which Christ is present whole and entire in His *physical* 'reality,' corporeally present, although not in the manner in which bodies are in a place." (*Mysterium Fidei*, #46) Cf. Claudia Carlen Ihm (Editor), *The Papal Encyclicals* (1958-1991 volume 5), Consortium/McGrath Publishing Company, 1981), p. 172.
28 Mark P. Shea, *This IS My Body: An Evangelical Discovers the Real Presence*, (Front Royal, VA: Christendom Press, 1993) p. 40.
29 Fr. Stefano Manelli, O.F.M. Conv., *Jesus Our Eucharistic Love*, (Brookings, SD: Immaculata Formation House, 1973), p. 72.
30 For further reading on reported Eucharistic miracles that were visible to the human eye, cf. Bob and Penny Lord's book, *This Is My Body, This Is My Blood: Miracles of the Eucharist (Volumes I and II)*, (Slidell, LA: Journeys of Faith, 1986, 1994).
31 Refer to the small sampler of writings from the early Church Fathers appearing at the end of this chapter.
32 *This IS My Body*, pp. 25-26.
33 Scott Hahn, *Eucharistic Day at Marytown Audio Tapes*.
34 Cf. John McKenzie, S.J., *Dictionary of the Bible*, (New York, NY: Collier Books Macmillan Publishing Co., 1965), p. 92.
35 When Catholics receive the Body and Blood of Jesus Christ at Mass, we do not receive them in the state that they were in on

Good Friday (i.e., in their "gory" form). When Catholics receive Holy Communion at Mass we receive Jesus' Body and Blood in their risen and glorified form as they were on Easter Sunday (which was "unbloody" and "non-gory").

[36] *Catholicism and Fundamentalism*, p. 251.

[37] Alan Schreck, *Catholic and Christian*, (Ann Arbor, Michigan: Servant Books, 1984), p. 132.

[38] Astounded that God would choose to dwell in the midst of His people in an earthly temple, King Solomon exclaims: "Can it indeed be that God dwells among men on earth? If the heavens and highest heavens cannot contain you, how much less this temple which I have built..." (1 Kings 8:27).

[39] Cf. John 20:26 where Jesus is able to pass through walls in His glorified Body.

[40] In the Old Testament, God dwelt in the Ark of the Covenant on earth (an ornate box described in Exod 25:10-22) and also in heaven at the same time.

[41] St. Cyril of Alexandria (d. 444 A.D.) writes to those in his day who were of the mistaken opinion that the Eucharistic Bread and Wine, if it were kept until the next day, would loose it's spiritual potency: "For Christ is not altered and His holy Body is not changed, but the power and force and life-giving grace of the blessing remain forever." Cf. Ronald Lawler, O.F.M. Cap., Donald W. Wuerl, Thomas Comerford Lawler, (editors), *The Teaching of Christ*, (Huntington, IN: Our Sunday Visitor, Inc., 1983), pp. 427-428.

[205] Cf. Council of Trent: DS 1641.

[42] The Apostles certainly did not chew on Jesus' arm or leg on Holy Thursday night because His Body and Blood were not yet in risen and glorified form. Please refer to the "Transubstantiation" section of this chapter to read about how the interior reality of a person or thing can be transformed without there being any observable outward change.

[43] In the Gospel of Mark, some Sadducees try to trap Jesus and pose to Him a difficult question that was impossible to answer using pure human reason alone. Jesus responds to the Sadducees: "...you do not know the power of God" (cf. Mark 12:18-24). When it comes to contemplating the profound spiri-

tual mysteries of our Christian faith, we must never say, "My human mind cannot figure out how God can accomplish this, therefore, it must be impossible for Him to do."

44 The reason why Catholics often display crucifixes in our homes and Churches is certainly *not* to make the statement that Christ hasn't risen from the dead but to visibly call to mind the words of St. Paul about the importance of Jesus' crucifixion to our salvation: "...we proclaim Christ crucified..." (1 Cor 1:23). The crucifix also vividly reminds Catholics that we are called by Jesus to "take up [our own] cross, and follow [Him]" (Matt 16:24).

45 Concerning the validity of Anglican orders, Rev. Peter Stravinskas writes: "The validity of the Sacrament of Orders depends on two things: correct intention and proper rite. After Henry VIII's break with Rome, various people (most notably Archbishop Cranmer) began to tamper with the liturgy. This became extremely problematic in regard to the ordination rite, in which words pertaining to the sacrificing priesthood were eliminated. The fact that they were dropped indicated a failure to believe that Holy Orders conferred the power to offer sacrifice. Therefore, the Anglican celebration of the sacrament was deficient because the words were lacking, but even more so, because the intention to ordain a sacrificing priest was lacking. The two defects combined to create a serious doubt in the mind of the Holy See that the Church of England had the priesthood as we know and understand it; that conclusion was formally reached in Pope Leo XIII's *Apostolicae Curae.*" Cf. Rev. Peter M. J. Stravinskas, *The Catholic Answer Book 2*, (Huntington, IN: Our Sunday Visitor, Inc., 1994), p. 58.

46 The sinless Jesus (cf. 1 Pet 2:22) apparently consumed alcoholic beverages in moderation during His lifetime (cf. Matt 11:19; John 2:1-12; Matt 26:26-28; Mark 14:22-24; Luke 22:19-20; 1 Cor 11:24-25). Cf. also Deut 14:26; 1 Tim 5:23; Hosea 2:10; Joel 2:24; Deut 7:13; Prov 3:10. The *abuse* of alcohol (drunkenness) is clearly condemned in Scripture (cf. Rom 13:13, Gal 5:21, etc.) Obviously, if one suffers from the disease of alcoholism, he is unable to consume alcoholic bev-

erages in moderation and should abstain from any and all beverages containing alcohol. Also, under-age children or individuals who plan to operate motor vehicles should not consume alcoholic beverages. Since alcohol can be so easily abused, its consumption should always be carefully monitored.

47 *Surprised by Truth*, p. 197.

48 William A. Jurgens (editor and translator), *The Faith of the Early Fathers (Volume 1)*, (Collegeville, MN: The Liturgical Press, 1970), p. 55.

49 Cf. *Catechism of the Catholic Church*, #1137-1139. Cf. also Scott Hahn, *The End: A Study of the Book of Revelation Audio Tapes*, (West Covina, CA: St. Joseph Communications, Inc. (818) 331-3549)).

50 The footnote in the *New American Bible With Revised New Testament* for Rev 1:10 identifies "the Lord's day" as Sunday — which was "the first day of the week" (cf. Acts 20:7; John 20:1; Gen 1:1–2:3).

51 "[The 'hidden manna' seems to be a] reference to Jewish apocalyptic tradition (see 2 Baruch 29:8) according to which the [Old Testament] manna will reappear as food of the messianic kingdom..." (Cf. Wilfrid J. Harrington, O.P., *Sacra Pagina Series: Revelation*, Collegeville, MN: The Liturgical Press, 1993), p. 62-63.

In John 6:49-57 Jesus teaches us that *He* is the new "manna" — hidden under the appearance of bread and wine in the Holy Eucharist: "While they were eating, Jesus took bread, said the blessing, broke it, and giving it to his disciples said, 'Take and eat; this is my body'" (Matt 26:26).

The reason why Holy Communion is available daily in most Catholic Churches is because, in the New Testament, the first Christians gathered *daily* to listen to the Word of God and to receive the Holy Eucharist (cf. Acts 2:42, 46). In the Old Testament, God fed His people *daily* with manna — the bread from heaven (cf. Exod 16:4-15; John 6:48-51). Also in the New Testament, Jesus instructs Christians to pray to our heavenly Father for the reception of "our daily bread"/spiritual nourishment (cf. Luke 11:3).

52 Cf. Chapter 6 of this book.

53 Cf. Chapter 17 of this book to read about the Catholic doctrine of the Assumption of Mary into heaven, body and soul, by the power of God and the identification of "the woman" described in Rev 12 as the Blessed Virgin Mary.

54 Cf. *Catechism of the Catholic Church*, #1137-1139. Cf. chapter 16 of this book to read about the Catholic doctrine of the Immaculate Conception of Mary in her mother's womb without the stain of original sin.

55 Just as the Roman Catholic liturgy is an imitation of the heavenly liturgy (cf. *Catechism of the Catholic Church* #1137–1139), King Solomon realized that the earthly temple that God had instructed him to build was a copy of the Heavenly Temple: "You have bid me build a temple on your holy mountain and an altar in the city that is your dwelling place, a copy of the holy tabernacle which you had established from of old" (Wisdom 9:8).

56 The reason why Catholics use the finest materials available in the construction of their Churches is to lift the worshipper's hearts and minds to God and to invite them to get a small glimpse of the grandeur and majesty of the Kingdom to come (cf. Rev 21:21). Note how God ordered the Jewish people to construct a magnificent temple that would be a fitting place for the worship of the Almighty (cf. 1 Kings Chapters 6-7).

57 The prayers of the Roman Catholic Mass form a beautiful "scriptural collage." For an excellent line-by-line breakdown of the scriptural basis of the prayers prayed at the Roman Catholic Mass cf. Fr. Peter Stravinskas, *The Mass: A Biblical Prayer*, (Huntington, IN: Our Sunday Visitor Inc., 1989).

58 Note well that none of the early Christian writers disputed the doctrine of the Real Presence of Jesus Christ in the Holy Eucharist, Body, Blood, Soul, and Divinity. If this was not the belief of the infant Church there would have been volumes written by the early Church Fathers protesting it. The first questioning of the doctrine of the Real Presence of Jesus Christ in the Holy Eucharist began in the 11th century with Berengar of Tours.

59 *The Faith of the Early Fathers (Volume 1)*, p. 25.

60 *Ibid.*, p. 22.

61 *Ibid.*, p. 55.

62 Karl Keating (editor), *This Rock* Magazine, "The Fathers Know Best," (San Diego, CA: Catholic Answers, Inc., Sept. 1996), pp. 38-39.

63 *Ibid.*

64 *Ibid.*

65 *Ibid.*

66 *The Faith of the Early Fathers (Volume 1)*, p. 311.

67 *Ibid.*, p. 361.

68 *Ibid.*, p. 361.

69 *Ibid.*, p. 360.

70 William A. Jurgens (editor and translator), *The Faith of the Early Fathers (Volume 3)*, (Collegeville, MN: The Liturgical Press, 1979), p. 30.

Chapter 6

"A Participation in the Blood of Christ"[1]: The Sacrifice of the Mass

What Does the Catholic Church Teach?

"The Eucharist is thus a sacrifice because it re-presents (makes present) the sacrifice of the cross, because it is its *memorial* and because it *applies* its fruit:

> [Christ], our Lord and God, was once and for all to offer himself to God the Father by his death on the altar of the cross, to accomplish there an everlasting redemption. But because his priesthood was not to end with his death, at the Last Supper 'on the night when He was betrayed,' [he wanted] to leave to His beloved spouse the Church a visible sacrifice (as the nature of man demands) by which the bloody sacrifice which he was to accomplish once for all on the cross would be re-presented, its memory perpetuated until the end of the world, and its salutary power be applied to the forgiveness of the sins we daily commit."[187]

(Catechism of the Catholic Church, #1366.)

Common Objection #1

"We read in Hebrews 7:27 that '[Jesus] has no need, as did the high priests, to offer sacrifice day after day, first for his own sins and then for those of the people; he did that *once for all* when he offered himself.' If the Letter to the Hebrews says that Jesus offered His sacrifice *once for all*, how can you Catholics possibly teach that the Mass is both a meal *and* a sacrifice? Wasn't Jesus' *once for all* sacrifice good enough for you? Why do you insist on offering additional sacrifices at your numerous Masses when Jesus cried from the cross, 'It is finished.' (John 19:30)?"

A Catholic Response

In the Book of Leviticus we read about the procedure for offering a bloody sacrifice: "He shall then *slaughter* the bull before the Lord, but Aaron's sons, the priests, shall *offer up its blood* by splashing it on the sides of the altar..." (Lev 1:5). Gerry Mattatics reminds us that, in the Bible, there are two distinct parts to a bloody sacrifice:

1. The slaying of the sacrificial victim. *(This happened to Jesus, once-for-all-times-and-ages [perpetually], on Calvary 2,000 years ago).*[2]

2. After the death of the sacrificial victim has taken place, the priest offers the victim's flesh and the blood to God. *(Note that St. Paul teaches in 1 Cor 10:16 that the Holy Eucharist is not a mere "symbol" but an opportunity to truly participate in the Body and Blood of Jesus Christ, offered to the Father in thanksgiving (Greek eucharistesas), for the salvation of all humanity).*

Matt 26:17, Mark 14:12, and Luke 22:8 tell us that the Last Supper took place within the framework of a Jewish Passover meal. The Jewish Passover meal was structured as follows:[3]

1. The host began the meal with a prayer of thanksgiving. *(accomplished by Jesus on Holy Thursday)*

2. The 1ˢᵗ cup of wine was blessed and consumed.
    (accomplished by Jesus on Holy Thursday)

3. The bread was blessed and consumed. *(This is when Jesus took the bread and declared it to be His Body in Matt 26:26; Mark 14:22; Luke 22:19; 1 Cor 11:24).*
    (accomplished by Jesus on Holy Thursday)

4. The 2ⁿᵈ cup of wine was blessed and consumed.
    (accomplished by Jesus on Holy Thursday)

5. The Passover Lamb was sacrificed and eaten as described in Exodus 12:21-22. Jesus Christ, the Lamb of God (John 1:29), was sacrificed within the context of Jewish Passover Sacrifice the next day on the cross (cf. Matt 27:50; Mark 15:37; Luke 23:46; John 19:30). St. Paul says "For our paschal lamb, Christ, has been sacrificed. Therefore, let us celebrate the feast..." (1 Cor 5:7-8).
    (accomplished by Jesus on Holy Thursday and Good Friday)

6. The 3ʳᵈ cup of wine was blessed and consumed. *(This is when Jesus took the cup of wine and declared it to be His Blood in Matt 26:27; Mark 14:23-24; Luke 22:20; 1 Cor 11:25).*
    (accomplished by Jesus on Holy Thursday)

7. Psalms were sung in praise of God (i.e., "the Great Hallel") (cf. Matt 26:30).
    (accomplished by Jesus on Holy Thursday)

8. The 4ᵗʰ cup of wine was blessed and consumed (cf. John 19:29-30).[4]
    (accomplished by Jesus on the cross on Good Friday)

Note how the Sacrifice of Christ on Calvary and the Sacrificial Jewish Passover meal (the Last Supper) are intimately intermingled and *form one sacrificial unit.*[5] In Luke 22:19 and in 1 Cor 11:24 Jesus says "Do this [one sacrificial unit] in memory of me." By re-presenting the one sacrifice of Jesus (cf. Heb 10:12-14), Catholics are simply following the command of Christ found in Luke 22:19 and 1 Cor 11:24: "Do this in memory of [Him]."

The reason that Catholics oftentimes display the crucified Jesus in their homes and Churches is certainly *not* to make the statement that He hasn't risen from the dead but to visually illustrate the words of St. Paul: "...we proclaim Christ crucified..." (1 Cor 1:23).[6] Jesus certainly does not die again and again at Catholic Masses, rather, Catholics follow Jesus' command to partake of the Eucharistic Bread and Wine in order to perpetually partake of the fruits of His *one* sacrifice accomplished 2,000 years ago on Calvary.[7] An image of the crucified Jesus also vividly reminds Catholics of the Lord's command to pick up our own "crosses" and follow Him (cf. Mark 8:34).

James T. O'Connor, in his book *The Hidden Manna*, writes about the Holy Eucharist:

> "When Christ becomes present at Mass he does so not in order to repeat the sacrifice of the Cross but to draw us into it, to make us participants in his one sacrifice... The Last Supper and Calvary and the Mass are all the same sacrifice, not because the historical acts of the past are repeated ... but because of the intrinsic unity that all these actions, past and present, possess in the one Priest and Victim... The killing and offering of the Victim has passed; the Victim who was killed and offered remains, now alive but Victim still."[8]

In Heb 10:25-31 we read that, if we don't attend the Eucharist, we do not participate in the re-presentation of the *one* sacrifice of Christ on Calvary and, without Christ's Sacrifice, the Bible tells us that "there remains a fearful prospect of judgement and a flaming fire that is going to consume the adversaries." Wow! If that doesn't get a person off the couch on Sunday morning, I don't know what could! The Bible says that missing Mass and the reception of Jesus' Body and Blood in the Holy Eucharist is hazardous to a Christian's spiritual health.[9]

Consider these simple Scriptural truths about the Mass:

- The intentional boycotting of Mass by a Catholic Christian constitutes a deliberate rejection of the Holy Eucharist (Heb 10:25-31).
- The Scriptures tell us that the Holy Eucharist is the Body and Blood of Jesus Christ Himself (cf. Matt 26:26-28).
- Therefore, the intentional boycotting of Mass equals a rejection of Jesus Christ. The Scriptures teach that the penalty for knowingly and deliberately rejecting Jesus is quite severe: "Whoever rejects me and does not accept my words has something to judge him: the word that I spoke, it will condemn him on the last day" (John 12:48). (cf. *Catechism of the Catholic Church*, #2180-2181).

In his First Letter to the Corinthians, St. Paul teaches about the Eucharistic Bread and Wine: "The cup of blessing that we bless, is it not a *participation* in the blood of Christ? The bread that we break, is it not a *participation* in the body of Christ" (1 Cor 10:16)? It follows logically that the *one* sacrifice of Jesus has to be present at the Eucharist if the Bible says that we are able to participate in it. The Greek word that is translated as "participation" in 1 Cor 10:16 is *koinonia* (which is often translated as "communion" in English). What St. Paul is saying is that, when we receive Holy *Communion* we are literally participating/communing in the Body and Blood of Jesus Christ.

In his First Letter to the Corinthians St. Paul speaks about the Eucharistic Bread and Wine: "For as often as you eat this bread and drink the cup, *you proclaim the death of the Lord* until he comes" (1 Cor 11:26). Surely St. Paul didn't believe that Jesus is killed again and again at every celebration of the Eucharist. What he was saying was that each Eucharist is a re-presenting (an eternal proclaiming and partaking) of Jesus' once-for-all-people-living-in-all-times-and-ages (i.e., perpetual) sacrifice on Calvary.[10]

In his First Letter to the Corinthians, St. Paul writes: "...For our paschal lamb, Christ, has been sacrificed. Therefore, let us celebrate the feast..." (1 Cor 5:7-8). Notice that St. Paul doesn't say, "For our paschal lamb, Christ, has been sacrificed. Therefore, there is nothing more that Christians are called to do..." The Catholic Mass is a re-presenting of the *one* sacrifice of Christ *(not a re-sacrificing!)* in which His saving merits are continually applied to the souls of individual Christians throughout the course of history. In the Catholic Mass we are following the command of Scripture and "celebrating the feast" of the paschal Lamb who has been sacrificed for our sins 2,000 years ago on Calvary.

The author of the Letter to the Hebrews tells us: "...because [Jesus] remains forever, [He] has a priesthood that does not pass away... since he lives forever to make intercession for them" (Heb 7:24-25). A priest is one who offers sacrifice and the author of the Letter to the Hebrews tells us that Jesus' priesthood "does not pass away."

New Testament Scripture tells us of the presence of an altar (a table of sacrifice) in heaven that is positioned before God's throne (cf. Rev 6:9, Rev 8:3; Rev 9:13; Rev 11:1; Rev 14:18; Rev 16:7). This heavenly altar of sacrifice was certainly not erected for the purpose of re-sacrificing Jesus again and again but to make the merits of His *one* sacrifice on Calvary perpetually accessible to Christians in all ages and places.

Catholic theologian F. J. Sheed writes about the Mass: "What still remains to be done is not an addition to what was done on Calvary, but its application to each man — that each of us should receive for himself what Our Lord won for our race."[11] James Cardinal Gibbons says about the Mass: "On the cross He purchased our ransom, and in the Eucharistic Sacrifice the price of that ransom is applied to our souls. Hence, all the efficacy of the Mass is derived from the sacrifice of Calvary."[12]

The writer of the Book of Revelation describes his heavenly vision of "a Lamb that seemed to have been slain" (Rev 5:6). Why would Christ "appear to have been slain" in heaven *(where we are told in Rev 21:4 that we will be made whole)* long after the crucifixion took place? Certainly Christ is not slain again and again at each Mass but His *one* sacrifice is re-presented again and again as a way to continually renew His Covenant with His people.[13]

In the words of Mark P. Shea: "The key idea is not repetition of His death (which the Church plainly states is impossible), but our present participation in the one eternal sacrifice of Christ on Calvary. We drink each day from the well He dug once for all; we eat the one loaf He has prepared."[14]

We read clearly in preface number 23 in the Sacramentary *(the official book of prayers used in the Roman Catholic Mass)*: "...Christ is the victim who *dies no more*, the Lamb, *once slain*, who lives forever..."[15] At the Eucharist Catholics are tapping into the "perpetual pipeline" from Calvary in which the merits of Jesus' death and resurrection are made available to the faithful at all times and in all places. At the Mass, Catholics open the spiritual "pantry" where the abundant merits of Jesus' death and resurrection are perpetually accessible for the spiritual rejuvenation and nourishment of His people.[16]

If we committed a sin today, would the Blood of Christ (shed 2,000 years ago on Calvary) be available to us at this moment to wash away that sin? Surely it would! Do you see how Jesus' Blood can be present to us here and now even though we are 2,000 years removed from the sacrifice of the cross on Calvary?

David Currie writes:

> "The work of Christ on the Cross is finished. The crucifixion need never be repeated. But its benefits are applied to me in today's time-frame through the real sacrifice of the Eucharist. The concept of making Christ's past sacrifice efficacious in the present is not foreign to Evangelicals. This is precisely what Evangelicals believe happens when a person put his faith in Christ. One day Christ's work on the Cross has not yet benefited the person, and the next it has been applied through faith. Catholics believe their sacrifice of the Eucharist makes the grace of the Cross available today."[17]

Common Objection #2

"In the New Testament we read that *all* Christians are 'priests' (cf. 1 Peter 2:5; Rev 1:5-6). As a result, the notion of a sacrificing priesthood, like that of the Old Testament, is unnecessary and obsolete."

A Catholic Response

In the Old Testament, God told the entire Jewish community that they were "a kingdom of priests" (cf. Exod 19:6), while at the same time God also chose to set aside certain members of the faith community to serve His people in a *specialized priesthood* — a priesthood not participated in by the rest of the members of the Jewish community (cf. Exod 19:21-22).[18]

In exactly the same way in the New Testament, *all* Christians are called "priests" (cf. 1 Pet 2:5; Rev 1:5-6). However, certain members of the Christian community were authorized/ordained to serve God's New Covenant community in unique ways not shared by all Christians. In the Acts of the Apostles we read: "They appointed *presbyters* for them in each church and, with prayer and fasting, commended them to the Lord in whom they had put their faith" (Acts 14:23). The English word "priest" comes from the Latin word *presbyter* (which comes from the Greek word *presbyteros*.)[19] These "presbyters" *(priests)* were ordained to carry out special functions that were not carried out by the priesthood of all the faithful (cf. 1 Tim 4:14; 1 Tim 5:17).[20]

Consider the following diagrams of the various types of Old and New Testament priesthoods and how they closely parallel each another:[21]

Old Testament:

The High Priest
(cf. Lev 21:10;
Matt 26:57)
type of sacrifice offered:
the chief priest was designated to
enter the Holy of Holies and perform
the religious rites on the annual Day of Atonement
(cf. Lev 16)

Ordained,
Full-Time
Ministerial Priests
(Pre-Levitical - cf. Exod 19:21-22,
Levitical - cf. Exod 29ff)
type of sacrifice offered:
animal (cf. Exod 29:10ff), drink
(cf. Num 15:10), grain (cf. Lev 2:14ff), etc.

The Common Priesthood
Shared by All Jews
(cf. Exod 19:6)
type of sacrifice offered:
spiritual sacrifices to God *(cf. Hosea 14:2)*;
also commissioned ordained full-time ministerial
priests to offer ritual sacrifice to God on their behalf in
the Temple (cf. 2 Macc 12:43).

New Testament:

Jesus Christ
(our "eternal
High Priest"
- *cf. Heb 7:1-3*)
type of sacrifice offered:
His Body & Blood on the cross
for the atonement of the sins
of humanity *(cf. Luke 23:46)*

**Ordained, Full-Time
Ministerial Priests**
(cf. Luke 22:7-20; Rom 15:15-16)
type of sacrifice offered:
all of the sacrifices offered by the
members of the common priesthood of all
Christians plus the Holy Sacrifice of the Mass
— which makes available to individual Christian
souls, throughout the course of history, the merits
of the once-for-all Sacrifice of Jesus Christ
on Calvary *(cf. 1 Cor 10:16; 1 Cor 11:23-30)*

**The Common Priesthood
Shared by All Christians**
(cf. 1 Pet 2:5; Rev 1:6)
type of sacrifice offered:
spiritual *(cf. 1 Pet 2:5)*, bodies *(cf. Rom 12:1)*,
donations *(cf. Phil 4:18)*, praise, good deeds,
generosity *(cf. Heb 13:15-16)*;
also commissioned ordained full-time ministerial
Christian priests to offer the Sacrifice
of the Mass to God for their needs and intentions.

Common Objection #3

"In Gen 9:6 we read that God forbids human sacrifices and, yet, this is what Catholics teach that the Mass is!"

A Catholic Response

Remember that Jesus Christ Himself was a Divine/human sacrifice: "...For our paschal lamb, Christ, has been sacrificed. Therefore, let us celebrate the feast..." (1 Cor 5:7-8). The Mass is not a re-sacrificing of Christ but a *participation* in His *one* sacrifice: "The cup of blessing that we bless, is it not a participation in the blood of Christ? The bread that we break, is it not a participation in the body of Christ" (1 Cor 10:16)?[22]

James T. O'Connor writes about the Catholic Mass:

"To say that the Mass adds nothing to the sacrifice of the Cross is an imperfect understanding of how Christ effects our redemption. Jesus offered his sacrifice to the Father as a man, and as mankind's priest and representative. That sacrifice was sufficient for the reconciliation of the entire world. Nonetheless, Christ willed and wills to associate us with that sacrifice. St. Paul expresses this truth very strongly when he writes: 'Now I rejoice in what was suffered for you, and I fill up in my flesh what is still lacking in regard to Christ's afflictions, for the sake of his Body, which is the Church' (Col 1:24). By Christ's will, we bring more than Christ and his offering to the Father. As sacrificial offerings we also bring ourselves, and our own lives with their joys and sufferings. Taken up into the sacrifice of Christ, these too become part of the sacrifice of praise and propitiation presented to the Father. Thus, each Mass is a sacrifice in which something new is being offered, the constant accumulation of what the members of Christ offer with and in Him."[23]

Consider this illustration: suppose I took a black marker and made one dot on a rubber band. That one dot would be present at one point on that rubber band. Suppose, now, that I stretched that rubber band. What would happen to that one dot? It would be the same one dot but it would now become present at various points on the rubber band. The same thing holds true with the sacrifice of the Mass. It was done once by Jesus 2,000 years ago but is made present to Christians throughout the ages as a way to continually renew our covenant with Jesus.[24]

Common Objection #4

"To repeat an action again and again implies that something was lacking the first time the action was done *(e. g., to keep painting one's house every week would imply that something was wrong with the original paint job)*. When you Catholics offer the Sacrifice of the Mass again and again, you are implying that something was lacking in Jesus' original one perfect sacrifice. What a blasphemy!"

A Catholic Response

Note that a husband and a wife share the marital act again and again, not because something was lacking the first time they shared it on their honeymoon, but because they wish to continually renew their covenant of love with one another. The exact same thing holds true with the Sacrifice of the Mass in which God continually renews His New Covenant with His people.[25]

In the Old Testament the word "covenant" is used many times as God entered into relationship, time and time again, with the Israelite people through various appointed leaders. In the New Testament (the "New Covenant"), Jesus uses the word "covenant" only once — when He teaches the Apostles at the Last Supper that the Eucharistic Wine was "...the cup [of the] new covenant in [His] blood..." which they were instructed to drink "...in remembrance of [Him]" (1 Cor 11:25). Thus, each time Christians drink the Eucharistic Wine *(which Jesus declared to be His Blood)* they renew their covenant with God, first initiated by the shedding of Jesus'

Blood on Calvary 2,000 years ago.

As was mentioned earlier in this chapter, Jesus' sacrifice on Calvary is perpetual (i.e., unending.) Dr. Scott Hahn reminds us that "you can't repeat something that never ends."

Common Objection #5

"Jesus says in Matt 9:13 that He 'desires mercy and not sacrifice.' Therefore, the sacrifice of the Mass is not pleasing to Him."

A Catholic Response

What Jesus is saying here to the sometimes-hypocritical Pharisees certainly does not refer to the sacrifice of the Mass but, instead, condemns public displays of holiness whereby wicked people, who had no true interior conversion, offered public sacrifice to God: "The sacrifice of the wicked is an abomination to the Lord, but the prayer of the upright is his delight" (Proverbs 15:8).[26]

In the Old Testament Book of the prophet Malachi, Malachi delivers to the Jews in Judah a message that he had received from the Lord: "...I have no pleasure in you, says the Lord of hosts, neither will I accept any sacrifice from your hands, for from the rising of the sun, even to its setting, my name is great among the nations; And everywhere they bring sacrifice to my name, and a pure offering..." (Mal 1:10-11).[27]

What Did the Early Christians Believe About the Mass Being the Re-Presentation of the One Sacrifice of Jesus on the Cross?

- "On the Lord's Day of the Lord gather together, break bread and give thanks after confessing your transgressions so that your sacrifice may be pure." *Didache* (circa 70 A.D.)[28]

- "There are sacrifices now, sacrifices in the Church. Only the kind has been changed; for now the sacrifice is offered not by slaves but by free men." St. Irenaeus in his *Against Heresies* (circa 180 A.D.)[29]

- Referring to the offering to God of the Eucharistic Bread and Wine at Mass, the ancient Roman Canon states: "May your holy angel take this sacrifice to your altar in heaven." *The Roman Canon* (circa 230 A.D.)[30]

- "The order certainly is that which comes from his sacrifice and which comes down from it: because Melchisedech was a priest of the Most High God; because he offered bread; and because he blessed Abraham. And who is more a priest of the Most High God than our Lord Jesus Christ, who, when He offered sacrifice to God the Father, offered the very same which Melchisedech had offered, namely bread and wine, which is in fact His Body and Blood." St. Cyprian of Carthage in his *Letter to a Certain Cecil* (circa 250 A.D.)[31]

- "If Christ Jesus, our Lord and God, is Himself the High Priest of God the Father; and if He offered Himself as a sacrifice to the Father; and if He commanded that this be done in commemoration of Himself — then certainly the priest, who imitates that which Christ did, truly functions in place of Christ." St. Cyprian of Carthage in his *Letter to a Certain Cecil* (circa 250 A.D.)[32]

Endnotes

[1] In his First Letter to the Corinthians, St. Paul says that when Christians receive the Eucharistic Bread and Wine they are participating/communing with the true Body and Blood of Jesus Christ Himself: "The cup of blessing that we bless, is it not a participation in the blood of Christ? The bread that we break, is it not a participation in the body of Christ" (1 Cor 10:16)?

[187] Council of Trent (1562): DS 1740; cf. *1 Cor* 11:23; *Heb* 7:24, 27.

[2] Gerry Mattatics, *Question and Answer Audio Tape of a Talk Given at St. Pius X Catholic Church in Lafayette, LA*, (Lafayette, LA: Champions of Truth, 1994).

3   Cf. Bruce M. Metzger and Michael D. Coogan, editors, *The Oxford Companion to the Bible*, (New York, NY: Oxford University Press, 1993), p. 573.

4   Cf. Scott Hahn, *Eucharistic Day at Marytown Audio Cassette*, (West Covina, CA: St. Joseph Communications, Inc.).

5   Scott Hahn, *Eucharistic Day at Marytown Audio Cassette*, (West Covina, CA: St. Joseph Communications, Inc.).

6   Cf. *Catechism of the Catholic Church*, #1085. (Cf. also 1 Cor 11:26).

7   Catholic apologist James Akin reminds us, "...we know from Scripture that Christ's work is applied to us over time and not in one big lump (Phil 2:12; 1 Pet 1:9)." The Catholic Resource Network, James Akin, http://www.ewtn.com/library/ANSWERS/PRIMINDU.TXT.

8   James T. O'Connor, *The Hidden Manna*, (San Francisco, CA: Ignatius Press, 1988), p. 302.

9   A Catholic who goes to Mass every Sunday and receives the precious gift of the Body and Blood of Jesus Christ is giving back to God a whopping 0.6% of the time that God has given to him that week *(1 hour is 0.6% of the 168 hours contained in a week)*. Do we owe that to Jesus in light of what He sacrificed for us?

10 A priest, by definition, is one who is appointed to offer sacrifice. Note that, in the Old Testament, the priest Melchizedek offers bread and wine (cf. Gen 14:18). In the New Testament, Jesus is identified as "a priest in the line of Melchizedek" (cf. Heb 5:6). Just like His predecessor, He also offers Bread and Wine — but He declares it to be His Body and Blood (cf. Matt 26:26-28; Mark 14:22-24; Luke 22:19-20; 1 Cor 11:24-25).

11 F. J. Sheed, *Theology for Beginners*, (Ann Arbor, Michigan: Servant Books, 1981), p. 160.

12 James Cardinal Gibbons, *The Faith of Our Fathers*, (Rockford, IL: TAN Books and Publishers, Inc., 1980), p. 255.

13 In the Letter to the Hebrews we read: "Jesus Christ is the same yesterday, today, and forever" (Heb 13:8). The merits of His sacrifice on Calvary are accessible to believers in the past, in the present, and in the future.

14 Mark P. Shea, *This IS My Body: An Evangelical Discovers the Real Presence*, (Front Royal, VA: Christendom Press,

1993), p. 24.

[15] *The Sacramentary*, (New York, NY: Catholic Book Publishing Co., 1985), p. 419.

[16] To use a banking analogy: A "perpetuity" is when an investor sets up a fund that will generate income to his chosen beneficiaries forever. On Calvary, Jesus "deposited" into His "perpetuity" the necessary "assets" (His Flesh and Blood) that would yield an abundance of spiritual benefits of all of His followers forever. The Mass is simply an opportunity for an individual Christian to partake in a portion of his share of the spiritual merits of Jesus' crucifixion and applying them to himself for the forgiveness of his sins and for the fortifying of his soul. At a Mass the Catholic Christian receives a spiritual "dividend check" from the eternal "deposit" made by Christ on the cross some 2,000 years ago.

[17] David B. Currie, *Born Fundamentalist Born Again Catholic*, (San Francisco, CA: Ignatius Press, 1996), p. 46.

[18] Note the presence of pre-Levitical/pre-Mosaic priests in the Old Testament (cf. Gen 14:18; Exod 3:1; Exod 19:21-22). One could, therefore, not say that a specialized ministerial priesthood was instituted by God only in the Mosaic economy and, now that the Old Testament Mosaic economy has been fulfilled by Christ, there is no longer any need for ordained, ministerial priests.

[19] *Merriam-Webster's Collegiate Dictionary (Tenth Edition)*, (Springfield, MA: Merriam-Webster, Inc. 1994), pp. 921, 925. Also, note the presence of Christian "elders/priests" (Greek: *presbyteros*) around God's throne in heaven (cf. Rev 4:4). Cf. also Butler, Scott, Dahlgren, Norman, Hess, David, *Jesus, Peter & the Keys,* (Santa Barbara, CA: Queenship Publishing Co., 1996), pp. 187-188.

[20] Note that, in the official Rites Book for the Sacrament of the Anointing of the Sick, the Catholic Church translates "elders/presbyters/*presbyteros*" in James 5:14 as "priests." To read more about the use of another Greek word for priest (*hierus*) in the New Testament cf. pp. 13-20 of Raymond E. Brown's book *Priest and Bishop: Biblical Reflections*, published by Paulist Press of New York, NY.

[21] The Catholic Resource Network, James Akin, http://

www.etwn.com/library/ANSWERS/PRIEST3.TXT. *(Author's note: I have used triangles here, not to imply that ordained priests are somehow holier or better than the laity, but to use a graphic figure that illustrates one point on the top, fewer in the middle, and a larger number at the base.)*

22 *This IS My Body*, p. 18.

23 *The Hidden Manna*, pp. 309-310.

24 Philip St. Romain, *Audio Tape of Unknown Title* (listened to by this book's author at a retreat).

25 The author of the Letter to the Hebrews writes: *"We have an altar* from which those who serve the tabernacle have no right to eat...Through [Christ] [then] let us continually offer God a sacrifice of praise, that is, the fruit of lips that confess his name" (Heb 13:10, 15). The Biblical author teaches the Hebrew Christians that they, indeed, have an altar (a place where sacrifice is offered) which those who serve the tabernacle (the unbelieving Jews) have no right to eat. We can see here a clear foundation for the theology of the Mass being a re-presentation of Jesus' one sacrifice on Calvary.

26 Cf. Psalm 51:18-21.

27 "The imperfect sacrifices offered without sincerity by the Jews in Judah are displeasing to the Lord. He will rather be pleased with the offerings of the Gentile nations throughout the world *(from the rising of the sun, even to its setting)*, which anticipate the *pure offering* to be sacrificed in messianic times, the universal Sacrifice of the Mass, as we are told by the Council of Trent." Cf. *New American Bible With Revised New Testament*, (New York, NY: Catholic Book Publishing Co., 1986), footnote for Mal 1:10, pg. 1100.

28 William A. Jurgens (editor and translator), *The Faith of the Early Fathers (Volume 1)*, (Collegeville, MN: The Liturgical Press, 1970), p. 4.

29 *Ibid.*, p. 95.

30 *The Hidden Manna*, p. 230, 175.

31 *The Faith of the Early Fathers (Volume 1)*, p. 232.

32 *Ibid.*, p. 232-233.

Chapter 7

"All These Devoted Themselves to Prayer, Together With ... Mary the Mother of Jesus..."[1]: Intercessory Prayer With the Blessed Virgin Mary and the Other Saints in Heaven

What Does the Catholic Church Teach?

"Being more closely united to Christ, those who dwell in heaven fix the whole Church more firmly in holiness... [T]hey do not cease to intercede with the Father for us, as they proffer the merits which they acquired on earth through the one mediator between God and men, Christ Jesus... So by their fraternal concern is our weakness greatly helped.[493] ...Exactly as Christian communion among our fellow pilgrims brings us closer to Christ, so our communion with the saints joins us to Christ, from whom as from its fountain and head issues all grace, and the life of the People of God itself."[497] (*Catechism of the Catholic Church*, #956, 957.)

Common Objection #1

"In the Bible, St. Paul says: "...there is one God. There is also *one mediator* between God and the human race, Christ Jesus..." (1 Tim 2:5). Why, then, do you Catholics pray to Mary and the saints and ask them to mediate to God on your behalf? Mary and the saints are not Divine and Scripture clearly tells us that they are not supposed to serve as mediators. That's Jesus' job exclusively!"

A Catholic Response

A "mediator" can be defined as a person who serves as a go-between or an intermediary between two parties. In 1 Tim 2:5, St. Paul, indeed, teaches that Jesus Christ is the one mediator (the one go-between or intercessor) between God and the human race. Catholics certainly have no problem at all accepting this scriptural truth.

Consider this visual picture of what St. Paul is describing in 1 Tim 2:5:

Humanity   Jesus   The Father

In the four verses immediately preceding 1 Tim 2:5, St. Paul instructs Christians to regularly engage in the practice of praying to Jesus on behalf of each another: "...I ask that supplications, prayers, petitions, and thanksgivings be offered for everyone... This is good and pleasing to God our savior..." (1 Tim 2:1-4). A visual picture of St. Paul's instructions to Christians found in 1 Tim 2:1-4 would look like this:

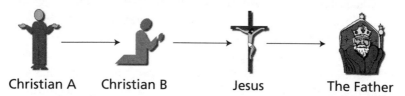

Christian A   Christian B   Jesus   The Father

In the previous diagram of 1 Tim 2:1-4, "Christian B," on be-half of "Christian A," would approach Jesus in prayer and would petition Him to grant the physical and spiritual needs of "Christian A." By praying in this fashion, "Christian B" would be serving as a go-between (a mediator/intercessor in prayer) to Jesus on behalf of "Christian A." St. Paul tells us that "This [type of prayer] is good and pleasing to God our savior..." (1 Tim 2:3).

Note that, in 1 Tim 2:1-5, St. Paul speaks about two different types of mediation. Let's give these two types of mediation names in order to differentiate them. Because Jesus' mediation is the fore-most and ultimate mediation between humanity and the Father let's call it *primary mediation*. Because our mediation/intercession in prayer on behalf of one another is subordinate to and totally de-pendent upon Jesus' primary mediation, let's call it *secondary mediation*.

In instructing Christians to pray to Jesus on behalf of one an-other, St. Paul is asking us to take on the role of *secondary media-tors* in prayer.[2] Obviously, our secondary mediation in prayer on behalf of one another is entirely dependent upon the primary me-diation of Christ.

Let's draw a visual picture of the two types of mediation that St. Paul speaks about in 1 Timothy 2:1-5:

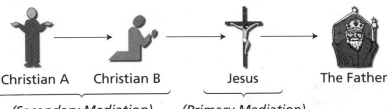

Christian A   Christian B   Jesus   The Father

(Secondary Mediation)   *(Primary Mediation)*
1 Tim 2:1-4   *1 Tim 2:5*

Catholic apologist Patrick Madrid writes:

> "Paul exhorts Christians to pray, supplicate, peti-tion, and intercede for all people... 'I urge you, broth-ers, by our Lord Jesus Christ and by the love of the Spirit, to join me in the struggle by your prayers to God on my behalf' (Rom 15:30-32).

'In [Jesus] we have put our hope that he will also rescue us again, as you help us with prayer' (2 Cor 1:10).

'We always give thanks to God, the Father of our Lord Jesus Christ, when we pray for you...we do not cease praying for you and asking that you may be filled with the knowledge of his will and all spiritual wisdom and understanding to live in a manner worthy of the Lord' (Col 1:4, 9-10).

If, while on earth, Paul could say, 'My heart's desire and prayer to God on their behalf is for salvation' (Rom 10:1) and 'I remember you constantly in my prayers, night and day...' (2 Tim 1:3), is there any reason to imagine that upon entering heaven Paul's charity and desire for other's salvation would be quenched and his prayers for others cease? Not at all. The Bible's many exhortations to mutual charity apply to all Christians, so they must apply to Christians in heaven...

A Protestant might object, 'These verses refer to Christians on earth only. They say nothing about those in heaven.'... Aren't the commandments of the Lord eternal, established in heaven as well as on earth?[3]

Rev. John A. O'Brien in his book, *The Faith of Millions*, writes about intercessory prayer with the Christian saints in heaven: "Whatever influence the saints possess comes from God and is traceable to their relationship with Him. Just as the moon borrows her light from the sun, so the saints borrow their light from the Sun of Justice, Jesus Christ..."[4]

Note that when a Christian minister has an "altar call" and he prays to the Lord on behalf of various members of his congregation who desire to turn their lives over to God, the minister himself is acting as a secondary mediator in prayer on their behalf. Is there anything wrong with that? Certainly not because the minister is serving as a *secondary* mediator in prayer to the Father while Christ remains the *primary* mediator.

When a Christian minister preaches a sermon, he is mediating the Word of God, written down in the pages of the Bible, to his congregation. The preacher is acting as a "go-between" between the paper, ink, leather and glue making up the Bible and the audible message that the preacher feels called to communicate to his church members. Is there anything wrong with that? Certainly not because the preacher is serving as a *secondary* mediator of God's Word while Jesus the Word become Flesh (cf. John 1:14) remains the *primary* mediator.

When a Christian minister conducts a healing service, he is serving as a go-between in that God is using him as an instrument to communicate His healing to particular members of His Church congregation. God could certainly heal these people directly but, sometimes, He chooses to mediate His healing through His human ministers. Is there anything wrong with that? Certainly not because the minister is serving as a *secondary* mediator of God the Father's healing while Jesus remains the *primary* mediator.

A misunderstanding that sometimes occurs in the minds of some Protestant Christians is that they think that we Catholics want to bump Jesus out of His role of primary mediator and then put Mary and/or the saints in His place. Nothing could be farther from the truth! When we Catholics ask Mary or the saints to intercede with us to Jesus we are asking them to act as *secondary mediators* in prayer on our behalf. There is no one, in heaven or on earth, who can take the spot of the primary mediation of Christ. Jesus is the "bridge" between heaven and earth and, as Christ tells us in the Gospel of John: "no one comes to the Father except through me" (John 14:6).

Consider this visual diagram of Mary's rightful place as a *secondary* mediator/intercessor in prayer to her Son, Jesus:

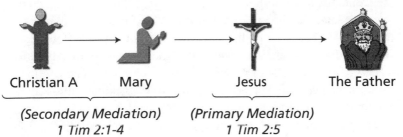

Christian A   Mary   Jesus   The Father

(Secondary Mediation)   *(Primary Mediation)*
1 Tim 2:1-4   *1 Tim 2:5*

Catholics do not pray *to* the saints. The word "to" can be misleading in that it can imply that something stops there (e. g., "I'm going *to* New Orleans" usually means that the person will stop when he arrives in New Orleans and will go no farther.) To say that Catholics pray *to* the saints could wrongfully imply that our prayer stops with the saints and goes no further. Nothing could be further from the truth! A more accurate way to speak about intercessory prayer might be to say that Catholics ask the saints to pray *with* us and *for* us as we pray *to* God who is Father, Son, and Holy Spirit. Catholics often pray *through* the saints *to* God. The rosary is not a prayer *to* Mary. It is a prayer *to* Jesus *through* Mary and *with* Mary (who we read in Rev 12:1-5 is looking upon the face of her Son Jesus in heaven.)[5]

Pope Paul VI, in his 1974 Apostolic Exhortation *For the Right Ordering and Development of Devotion to the Blessed Virgin Mary*, makes the following statement about the proper exercise of Catholic devotion to Mary: "In the first place it is supremely fitting that exercises of piety directed towards the Virgin Mary should clearly express the Trinitarian and Christological note that is intrinsic and essential to them ... in the expressions of devotion to the Virgin the Christological aspect should have particular prominence."[6] One can clearly see here that the Pope is reminding Catholics that devotion to Mary is a form of *secondary* mediation in prayer in which we are asking Mary to pray with us and for us to her Son, Jesus Christ, our primary mediator and Savior. Pope Paul VI rightly reminds us that all devotion to Mary must have a Trinitarian and a Christological focus because that was the focus of Mary's life: "...do whatever [my Son] tells you" (John 2:5).

The Blessed Mother and the saints are *not* Divine. We look to the saints for inspiration as we strive to live holy lives: "Remember your leaders who spoke the word of God to you. Consider the outcome of their way of life and imitate their faith" (Heb 13:7). Because the saints are in heaven with God, we ask them to pray for us and with us to God. In the Book of Revelation we read about the saints in heaven offering worship to God: "Another angel came and stood at the altar, holding a gold censer. He was given a great quantity of incense to offer, along with the prayers of all the holy ones, on the gold altar that was before the throne. The smoke of the incense along with the prayers of the holy ones went up before God from the hand of the angel" (Rev 8:3-5). Also, in the Book of

Revelation we read about the saintly worship taking place in heaven: "...Each of the elders held a harp and gold bowls filled with incense, which are the prayers of the holy ones" (Rev 5:8). Could it be conceivable that, while the saints in heaven are worshipping God constantly, that they could also offer prayers *(as they used to do so often while living on earth)* for their fellow Christians who are still struggling to be faithful to Jesus? It would seem logical.[7]

In the Book of the prophet Zechariah we read about the powerful intercession of heavenly beings with God on behalf of the living on earth: "Then the angel of the Lord spoke out and said, 'O Lord of hosts, how long will you be without mercy for Jerusalem and the cities of Judah that have felt your anger these seventy years?' To the angel who spoke with me, the Lord replied with comforting words. And the angel who spoke with me said to me, Proclaim: Thus says the Lord of hosts: I am deeply moved for the sake of Jerusalem and Zion, and I am exceedingly angry with the complacent nations; whereas I was but a little angry, they added to the harm. Therefore, says the Lord: I will turn to Jerusalem in mercy..." (Zech 1:12-16).

Can one pray directly to God? Sure! Catholics and Protestants alike offer prayer directly to God *and* also ask their fellow Christians to pray with them and for them. The big difference between Catholics and a number of Protestants is that Catholics don't restrict the term "Christian" to mean "only Christians living on earth."[8] Why did St. Paul (who was a spiritual giant in the early Church and a phenomenal pray-er) often ask others to pray for him when he could have very well prayed to God by himself?: "I urge you brothers, by our Lord Jesus Christ and by the love of the Spirit, to join me in the struggle by your prayers to God on my behalf" (Rom 15:30). By asking other Christians to pray for him (mediate for him) to Jesus, St. Paul was calling on his Christian "family" for spiritual support. St. Paul could have very well prayed to Jesus directly (and I'm sure he did at times) but he realized the value and the tremendous power of communal prayer.[9]

By asking the saints in heaven to pray with us, communities of faithful people are praying to God. In the words of Jesus: "For where two or three are gathered together in my name, there am I in the midst of them" (Matt 18:20). Why do a number of Catholics ask the saints in heaven to pray with us and for us to Jesus? For the same reason that a person would ask members of his family to pray to God for them in a time of need.[10] Does one *have* to tell the members of his family about a need that he has? No. Why do people often ask family members to pray for them? To gain support from the people who love them. The saints in heaven are still part of the spiritual family of Catholics even though their bodies have died and they are no longer physically present on earth.[11]

When we pray to Jesus directly there is one person praying. When we ask the saints to pray with us to Jesus, there are communities of people praying as the Bible requests (cf. 2 Cor 1:11). In the Acts of the Apostles, we read about the Christian community's prayer for St. Peter: "Peter thus was being kept in prison, but prayer by the church was fervently being made to God on his behalf" (Acts 12:5).

Roman Catholic convert Tim Staples speaks about intercessory prayer with the Christian saints in heaven:

> "...[I]n the Bible...Christians are commanded to help one another and love one another as members of a family, and to see their inter-dependence as members of a single body. Paul said, 'As a body is one though it has many parts, and all the parts of the body, though many, are one body, so also Christ. For in one spirit we were all baptized into one body...If one part suffers, all the parts suffer with it; if one part is honored, all the parts share its joy. Now you are Christ's body, and individually parts of it' (1 Cor 12:12-13, 26-27).
>
> ...Christians do not cease being members of Christ's body at death. I was taught as a Protestant that there is some sort of separation between Christians that occurs at death. 'We cannot pray to them or for them because they are with Jesus,' I was assured. Why does 'being with Jesus' mean they are separated from us? There is no Scripture that says this.
>
> A Christian is even more radically joined to God, and therefore more radically joined to the other members of the body of Christ, when he goes home to heaven.

He is freed from the constraints of sin; his faith has given way to perfect knowledge, and he is perfectly enabled to love and pray for other members of the Body of Christ.

Most importantly, since in heaven he has been perfected in righteousness by the blood of Christ, his prayers are very powerful, much more so than they ever could have been while he was here on earth. When this fact is seen in light of James 5:16 'The prayer of a righteous man has great power in its effects'the Catholic doctrine of asking the saints for their intercession is undeniably the biblical teaching.

2 Maccabees shows that long before Christ the Jews prayed for the deceased and knew that those who died in a state of friendship with the Lord could pray for them (cf. 2 Macc 12:42-46, 15:12-15). Even though I did not then accept the canonicity of 1 and 2 Maccabees, I had to acknowledge its historicity. Orthodox Jews still pray for the repose of the souls of their dead friends and relatives. Father [Pacwa] opened my eyes to see the souls in heaven are not dead; they are alive (cf. Luke 10:38) and they are intimately concerned with our spiritual welfare (Heb 12:1). Scripture confirms this again and again. On the mount of transfiguration in Luke 9:30-31, Moses and Elijah appear with Christ, and are involved with our salvation. Revelation 5:8 shows saints in heaven interceding with God for us and God responding to their prayers. Revelation 8:5 depicts the angels doing the same. Hebrews 12:22-24 tells us that when we 'come unto Mount Sion' in prayer, we do not just come to God, but also to 'the spirits of just men made perfect.' These are all members of our 'family in heaven' (Eph 3:15)...

I came to see that Mary's role as a heavenly 'prayer warrior' is completely biblical."[12]

Spiritual contact with our loved ones does not cease at death. In the Book of Revelation we read about the martyrs in heaven *(the saints)* who cry out to God and ask Him to act on their behalf: "How long will it be, holy and true master, before you sit in judgement and avenge our blood on the inhabitants of the earth" (Rev 6:9-10)? If the saints in heaven can plead with God and ask Him to take some negative action *(in this case to repay the individuals who were responsible for their deaths)*, would it also be possible for the saints in heaven to plead with God to take some positive action? It would seem reasonable that the holy saints in heaven would be more inclined to plead with God and ask Him for positive assistance for Christians still struggling to follow Jesus here on earth.

In the Second Book of Maccabees we read about the dream of Judas Maccabeus concerning the deceased Onias and the deceased prophet Jeremiah interceding in prayer for the Jewish people and for the Holy City: "...Onias, the former high priest, a good and virtuous man... was praying with outstretched arms for the whole Jewish community. Then in the same way another man appeared...Onias then said of him, 'This is God's prophet Jeremiah, who loves his brethren and fervently prays for his people and their holy city...'" (2 Macc 15:7-16). Here we see an example of the saints in heaven interceding for the living on earth.

In the Book of Tobit we read that an angel presents prayers to God and supports them with his own intercession: "I can now tell you that when you, Tobit, and Sarah prayed, it was I who presented and read the record of your prayer before the Glory of the Lord; and I did the same thing when you used to bury the dead" (Tobit 12:11-12). Here also we see an example of a heavenly being (an angel) interceding for the living on earth.[13]

In the parable of the rich man and Lazarus found in Luke we read about what kind of interaction a soul can have after the death of a person's body: "...send Lazarus to dip the tip of his finger in water and cool my tongue, for I am suffering torment in these flames..." (Luke 16:19-31). Lazarus and the rich man, after the death of their bodies were certainly not "sleeping." The "dead" rich man intercedes *(unsuccessfully in this case)* to Abraham in heaven on behalf of his five unfaithful brothers still living on earth.[14]

Protestant denominations differ *widely* in their beliefs about the disposition of a Christian's soul after his bodily death. Some Christian denominations understand St. Paul's imagery in First Thessalonians literally and they believe that, once a person dies, his soul is in a state of "sleep" and is not able to communicate at all with anyone or anything: "We do not want you to be unaware, brothers, about those who have fallen asleep, so that you may not grieve like the rest, who have no hope. For if we believe that Jesus died and rose, so too will God, through Jesus, bring with him those who have fallen asleep" (1 Thess 4:13-14). When St. Paul uses the term "falls asleep" he is simply saying that the person's physical body has died. We certainly cannot compare our earthly experience of sleeping to the activity that a spiritual soul can have after the death of the body. What about all the apparitions of the Blessed Mother throughout the centuries? She surely isn't sleeping![15] Jesus says in the Gospel of Luke: "...[H]e is not God of the dead, but of the living, for to him all are alive" (Luke 20:38). St. Paul tells the Romans about the dead: "For I am convinced that neither *death nor life* ... will be able to separate us from the love of God in Christ Jesus our Lord" (Rom 8:38-39). Since death does not destroy the bonds of Christian unity,[16] the ties between living and deceased Christians endure even after death.[17] In the Gospel of Luke Jesus says about the inhabitants of heaven: "...there will be rejoicing in heaven among the angels of God over one sinner who repents" (Luke 15:10). It appears that these heavenly inhabitants are very much aware of and in communion with the lives of fellow Christians struggling to be faithful to Jesus here on earth.[18]

Catholic apologist Patrick Madrid writes:

> "Many Protestants *delight* in being asked for intercessory prayer, and they actively encourage it in others, especially in those they consider 'prayer warriors," righteous Christians renowned for the efficacy of their prayers. ('The fervent prayer of a righteous person is very powerful') (James 5:16). Christians in heaven are *perfected* in righteousness. Should their prayers be discounted? To ignore their role as 'prayer warriors' makes no scriptural sense."[19]

Common Objection #2

"The Bible plainly says that the deceased are not able to do anything after the death of their bodies: 'For who among the dead remembers you?...' (Psalm 6:6); '...there will be no work, nor reason, nor knowledge, nor wisdom in the nether world where you are going' (Eccles 9:10). Therefore, to request the dead to intercede for us here on earth would be useless."

A Catholic Response

It is easy to observe how the Jewish understanding of the afterlife develops throughout the Old Testament. The writers of the passages from Psalm 6 and Ecclesiastes quoted above seem to be saying that the deceased are unable to do anything because their physical and spiritual existence has been forever blotted out by death.

In other Old Testament writings we read about the condition of the dead and the hope of resurrection: "Many of those who sleep in the dust of the earth shall awake..." (Dan 12:2-3); "But your dead shall live, their corpses shall rise; awake and sing, you who lie in the dust..." (Isaiah 26:19); "For do not abandon me to Sheol, nor let your faithful servant see the pit. You will show me the path to life, abounding joy in your presence, the delights at your right hand forever" (Psalm 16:10-11).

Of course, the New Testament has *numerous* passages that indicate the active status of the deceased: Cf. the parable of the rich man and Lazarus in Luke 16:19-31: (Cf. Rev 6:9-10 and read about the dead in heaven pleading with God in regards to earthly concerns.) Jesus says in the Gospel of Mark that God is "...not God of the *dead* but of the *living*..." (Mark 12:26-27). In the Gospel of Luke, Jesus is transfigured in between two very active "dead" saints — Moses and the prophet Elijah (cf. Luke 9:28-36). Refer to Heb 11-12:1 and notice how the "dead" saints in heaven are able to witness the faith journey of earth-dwelling Christians and "cheer us on" to victory.[20]

Common Objection #3

"The Bible clearly says that one who 'consults...spirits or seeks oracles from the dead' is 'an abomination to the Lord' (Deut 18:10-14) and, yet, isn't that what you Catholics do when you try to communicate with Mary who died almost 2,000 years ago?"

A Catholic Response

Mark Miravalle, in his book, *Introduction to Mary*, writes:

"[We must draw] the distinction between 'being God' and 'participating in the power of God.' Mary, especially since she is not bound by the limits of time and space in heaven, can participate in God's power to become visible to a person on earth, to communicate, and even to be present in her assumed body in a type of three dimensional apparition. Scripture attests to a vision or apparition by persons who have died and have risen in Christ; this is recorded in Matthew 27:52-53: '...and the graves were opened and many bodies arose out of them, bodies of holy men gone to their rest; who, after his rising again, left their graves and went to the holy city, where they were seen by many.' If the dead who rise in Christ can appear in bodily form to others, certainly the Mother of Jesus, whose body is gloriously assumed into heaven, can appear to her earthly children with Gospel messages encouraging greater faith, prayer, penance, conversion and peace."[21]

When I hear of the phrases "consulting spirits" or "seeking oracles from the dead" I think of some movies that I have seen on television where people are seated around a table with a crystal ball placed in the middle of them and the curtains blowing. These people, through the aid of a medium, are asking the spirit of someone who has died to return to them and to speak to them in order to reveal some message.

When Catholics ask Mary to pray for us and with us in heaven to Jesus (like the saints in Rev 8:3-4 and Rev 5:8 were doing) we are not asking Mary's spirit to return to earth so that she can reveal unknown secrets or messages to us. Actually, Catholics would much rather Mary stay in heaven where she is looking upon the face of God (cf. Rev 12:1-5) and offer our prayers to Him in person. If God wishes for Mary to return to earth to deliver some type of message to us *(as she has done in a number of apparitions)*, that is

His prerogative. Catholics don't pray for that, though, it is a free gift from God. Mary's basic message in every Church-approved apparition has been, "Repent from your sins and turn to Jesus before it's too late." Sounds like pretty solid Biblical advice to me (cf. Luke 12:35-40)![22]

Actually, the "dead" Christian saints are far more *alive* than what they were while living on earth. Jesus says in the Gospel of Mark: "As for the dead being raised, have you not read in the Book of Moses, in the passage about the bush, how God told him, 'I *am* the God of Abraham, [the] God of Isaac, and [the] God of Jacob? *He is not God of the dead but of the living...*" (Mark 12:26-27).

Common Objection #4

"Nowhere in the Bible do living Christians honor deceased saints in heaven."

A Catholic Response

The author of the Book of Revelation honors deceased saints in heaven: "These are they who were not defiled with women; they are virgins and these are the ones who follow the Lamb wherever he goes. They have been ransomed as the firstfruits of the human race for God and the Lamb" (Rev 14:4).[23]

In the King James Bible we read about St. Paul honoring living Christian saints: "Paul and Timotheus, the servants of Jesus Christ, to all the *saints* in Christ Jesus which are at Philippi, with the bishops and deacons... I thank my God upon every remembrance of you, always in every prayer of mine for you all making request with joy, for your fellowship in the gospel from the first day until now..." (Phil 1:1-7).[24] If Christians can honor a living saint on earth, would it not be all the more fitting for Christians to honor a saint who has reached his final destination and ultimate fulfillment in the Kingdom of heaven? Sure it would![25]

In the Book of Revelation the writer describes a vision of heaven: "Then God's temple in heaven was opened, and the ark of his covenant could be seen in the temple...a woman clothed with the sun, with the moon under her feet, and on her head a crown of twelve stars. She was with child... She gave birth to a son, a male child, destined to rule all the nations with an iron rod" (Rev 11:1912:5).[26] Speaking about "the woman" *(who the Church's Magisterium sees as a vision of the Virgin Mary, assumed body and soul, into heaven)*,[27] we read a few verses down in Chapter 12 of the Book of Revelation: "Then the dragon became angry with the woman and went off to wage war against *the rest of her off-spring, those who keep God's commandments and bear witness to Jesus*" (Rev 12:17). The Bible tells us that "those who keep God's commandments and bear witness to Jesus" are the offspring (the children) of Mary.[28] If the Book of Revelation tells us that Mary is the spiritual mother of all Christians aren't we supposed to follow the Fourth Commandment (cf. Exod 20:12; Deut 5:16) and "honor our father and mother?"

Note also that "honor" does *not* mean "worship." (For example, to call a judge "your honor" is simply acknowledging his important role in the community. To "honor" a teacher for his/her years of dedicated service is to express our appreciation for that person's valuable contributions. To "honor" our father and mother [cf. Exod 20:12] is to give them the respect and appreciation that they rightfully deserve. When a student makes the "honor roll" in school, his/her excellence in academics is publicly recognized and applauded and held up to others as a role model. Because of her spiritual excellence in being totally obedient to God's plan of salvation in Christ, Mary has made the spiritual "honor roll" and has become the supreme role model of faith for all Christians as we seek to tell Jesus every day: "May it be done to me according to your word" [Luke 1:38]. When we "honor" Mary, we are simply acknowledging the vital role that she played in the life of her Son, Jesus Christ.) Jesus says in the Gospel of John: "...The Father will *honor* whoever serves me" (John 12:26). I can't think of any follower who served Jesus more fully than His mother (who was faithful to Him from the moment of His first breath in the manger in Bethlehem to the moment of His last breath on the cross on Calvary).[29]

There is an important distinction between *worshipping* God and *honoring* the excellent accomplishments of His creatures. The traditional theological term *latria* refers to the worship that is due to God alone. This worship stems from the recognition that God is the Divine source and sustainer of all creation.

The traditional theological term *dulia* refers to the honoring of one of God's creatures for possessing some God-given gift (e. g., the Nobel Peace Prize, the Academy Awards, an Olympic medal). Since the earliest times, human beings have honored one another by acknowledging and recognizing some exceptional contribution that certain people have made to society. This grateful acknowledging and recognizing of people for their exemplary accomplishments in no way detracts from the worship due to God alone. Would an artist be offended if someone would come up to him at an art show and acknowledge the excellence of one of his created works of art? No, the artist would probably be flattered because someone was recognizing the beauty of one of his creations. The same thing would hold true with God. When someone acknowledges the beauty of one of His creatures (i.e., a saint in heaven) God must say to Himself: "I really did well when I created that person, didn't I!"

Every four years the Olympics are held and the top three finishers are honored (*"dulia"*) with medals. The third place finisher stands on the lowest platform and receives a bronze medal. The second place finisher stands on a higher platform and is awarded a silver medal. The first place finisher stands on the highest platform and receives a gold medal. If we were ranking the accomplishments of human beings throughout the history of the world, we would remember many individuals who have contributed greatly to the betterment of our world: (E.g., Dr. Jonas Salk discovered the polio vaccine and helped to save the lives of many people and was given many medical awards. Thousands of military soldiers have risked their very lives during wars to save their fellow soldiers and were awarded the Purple Heart medal. Steven Speilberg has produced some wonderful movies that have provided some fine entertainment and has received numerous Academy Awards.) These are all great accomplishments and these people are rightly honored (*"dulia"*) for their contributions to the betterment of humanity. Among these awesome accomplishments, where would we rank the person who brought forth the promised Messiah who would give the whole world the opportunity to be saved from eternal death? If we were setting up a three-tier Olympic platform to rank human beings for their contributions to the well-being of the world it might look something like this:

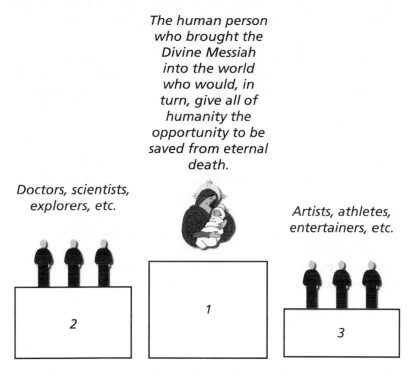

The human person who brought the Divine Messiah into the world who would, in turn, give all of humanity the opportunity to be saved from eternal death.

Doctors, scientists, explorers, etc.

Artists, athletes, entertainers, etc.

Because Mary was chosen by God to be, in the words of St. Francis, "the spouse of the Holy Spirit" (cf. Luke 1:34-35) and, thus, the vessel through which "the Word would become Flesh," her accomplishment *far surpasses* the importance of any other human accomplishment.[30] The theological term *hyper-dulia* is used to describe the highest type of honor (*dulia*) that she deserves. Note well that the honoring of Mary is not *latria* (the worship due to God alone). As a human being, Catholics simply recognize the magnitude of Mary's role in bringing about God's plan of salvation for the world.[31]

Consider this Biblical argument for honoring Mary: Did Jesus follow the Ten Commandments during His lifetime? Yes, had He not, He would not have been sinless (cf. 1 Pet 2:22). Does the 4th Commandment say that we should "Honor our father and mother?"

Yes, it does (cf. Exod 20:12; Deut 5:16). Does that mean that Jesus honored His mother, Mary, throughout His lifetime? Yes (cf. Luke 2:51)! Does the Bible say that all Christians are called to imitate Jesus? Yes (cf. 1 Cor 11:1). By honoring Mary, Christians are simply doing what Jesus Himself did![32]

To worship anyone but God would be idolatry. Catholics worship God alone. Mary and the saints are not divine, they are simply excellent spiritual role models who are united with God in heaven.[33]

Common Objection #5

"What do you mean in your quotation from the *Catechism of the Catholic Church* at the beginning of this chapter that, 'the [saints in heaven] do not cease to intercede with the Father for us, as they proffer the merits they acquired on earth...'?[34] A Christian will not get to heaven on his own merits or works. The Bible tells us that we will be saved only through faith: 'For by grace you have been saved through faith, and this is not from you; it is the gift of God; it is not from works, so no one may boast'" (Eph 2:8-9).

A Catholic Response

In the Book of Revelation we read about the merits that the deceased saints carry along with them into heaven: "...'Blessed are the dead who die in the Lord from now on.' 'Yes' said the Spirit, 'let them find rest from their labors, *for their works accompany them*'" (Rev 14:13). "'She was allowed to wear a bright, clean linen garment.' The linen represents the righteous deeds of the holy ones" (Rev 19:8). "...All the dead were judged according to their deeds" (Rev 20:13).

In the Book of James we read about the place of meritorious good deeds in the life of the Christian believer: "So also faith of itself, if it does not have works, is dead... I will demonstrate my faith to you from my works...faith was completed by the works... See how a person is justified by works and not by faith alone[35] ...faith without works is dead" (James 2:17, 18, 22, 24, 26).

What is the place of works in the life of a Christian? The Bible says that the Christian is justified by faith *and* by the works of

Christ, accomplished in him, through the inspiration of the Holy Spirit.[36] Did the saints, while they were living on earth, co-operate in an extraordinary way with the Holy Spirit to accomplish the works of Christ? Yes! As a result of their holy lives, the Book of Revelation tells us that they carry stored-up merit into heaven with them. It would make sense that the saints could beseech God to use some of their stored-up merit (fruits of their faithfulness) and apply it to spiritually assist the Christians still battling against the devil on earth. To use an analogy, the saints in heaven are kind of like our rich relatives who live in another "state" and have the capability of sending us aid when our resources are becoming depleted. The saints in heaven are our "cheering section" in the clouds, if you will, who do everything they can to boost us on until we can join them in their celestial home.[37] St. Paul writes to the Christian community at Corinth: "...God has exhibited us apostles as the last of all, like people sentenced to death, since *we have become a spectacle to the world, to angels and human beings alike*" (1 Cor 4:9). We can see here that heavenly inhabitants are, somehow, able to observe the living on earth.

Common Objection #6

"A number of times in the New Testament, Jesus deals with Mary in a rather sharp manner *(e. g., at the Cana wedding feast recounted in John 2:4, and in Luke 11:27-28 when Jesus speaks about who is truly blessed).* These incidents clearly show that Mary deserves no special honor from us."

A Catholic Response

Note what happened when Mary interceded with her Son on behalf of the newly-married couple at Cana (cf. John 2:1-12). Mary pled with Jesus on behalf of the couple (mediated/interceded to Him on their behalf), "They have no wine." Jesus responds to Mary, "Woman, how does your concern affect me?" Was Jesus being rude to His mother in responding this way? No, not at all. What He was saying to Mary was that He takes His cues from His Father and, as of yet, His Father had not instructed Him to reveal Himself to the people in this way. Can't you just picture Jesus, after having just been asked by Mary to help the couple in need, looking up to heaven and speaking to His Father, "Well, Father, you heard her? What do you think? Is now the right time to perform this miracle?" The Father then, in some way, communicates to Jesus: "Yes, Son, now's the time—heed your mother's request and go ahead and do it now." We can see here the loving influence that Mary has, not only with her Son but with God the Father as well, as He allows His Son to grant Mary's intercessory request.

In the Gospel of Luke we read: "While [Jesus] was speaking, a woman from the crowd called out and said to him, 'Blessed is the womb that carried you and the breasts at which you nursed.' He replied, 'Rather, blessed are those who hear the word of God and observe it' (Luke 11:27-28). Isn't Mary the model, *par excellence*, of the believer who hears the word of God and observes it? Mary not only *heard* the word of God she *carried* the Word of God and was with Him from His first breath to His last! Far from belittling Mary, Jesus is saying to His followers, "Yes, my mother is blessed (cf. Luke 1:48) and, if you are faithful to God, you have the opportunity to be blessed also."

Common Objection #7

"How can Mary and the saints possibly hear and understand the millions of simultaneous prayers being offered to them in different languages throughout the world?"

A Catholic Response

This objection assumes that there is some kind of big "switchboard" in heaven that can be overloaded with spiritual "calls" from people living on earth. Patrick Madrid writes:

"...[I]t's silly to think the abilities of the saints in heaven are as paltry as are ours. Our inability to understand *how* the saints hear so many prayers is hardly a reason to deny that they *can* hear them. In their glorified state the saints are capable of doing things we can barely imagine: 'Eye has not seen, and ear has not heard, [nor has it] entered the human heart, what God has prepared for those who love him' (1 Cor 2:9). Those in heaven rejoice over the repentance of even *one* sinner (Luke 15:7-10), but we have no details about how they can know about individual repentances.

We know that in heaven we'll be transformed into the image of Christ's glorious, resurrected body. 'We shall be like him,' Paul assures us (Phil 3:20-21). John says, 'We are God's children now; what we shall be has not yet been revealed. We do know that we shall be like him, for we shall see him as he is' (1 John 3:2). In his resurrected, glorified body, Jesus did all sorts of incredible things... heaven is an amazing place filled with people who, by God's infinite grace, are capable of doing amazing things."[38]

What Did the Early Christians Believe About Honoring the Saints in Heaven and Asking Them to Intercede in Prayer to God on Their Behalf?

- "Christ we worship as the Son of God; but the martyrs we love as disciples and imitators of the Lord; and rightly so, because of their unsurpassable devotion to their own King and Teacher. With them may we also become companions and fellow disciples." *The Martyrdom of St. Polycarp* (circa 155 A.D.)[39]

- "But not the high priest [Christ] alone prays for those who pray sincerely, but also the angels...as also the souls of the saints who have already fallen asleep." Origen in his *On Prayer* (circa 233 A.D.)[40]

- "Aschandius, my father, dearly beloved of my heart, with my sweet mother and my brethren, remember your Pectorius in the peace of the Fish [Christ]." Pectorious in his *Epitaph* (circa 250 A.D.)[41]

- "Let us remember one another in concord and unanimity. Let us on both sides always pray for one another. Let us relieve burdens and afflictions by mutual love, that if one of us, by the swiftness of divine condescension, shall go hence the first, our love may continue in the presence of the Lord, and our prayers for our brethren and sisters not cease in the presence of the Father's mercy." Cyprian in his *Letters* (circa 252 A.D.)[42]

- "Lawrence and Ignatius, though they fought betimes in worldly camps, were true and spiritual soldiers of God; and while they laid the devil on his back with their confession of Christ, they merited the palms and crowns of the Lord by their illustrious passion. We always offer sacrifices for them, as you will re-call, as often as we celebrate the passions of the martyrs by commemorating their anniversary day." St. Cyprian of Carthage in his *Letter of Cyprian to His Clergy and to All His People* (circa 250 A.D.)[43]

- "You say in your book that while we live we are able to pray for each other, but afterwards when we have died, the prayer of no person for another can be heard...But if the apostles and martyrs while still in the body can pray for others, at a time when they ought still to be solicitous about themselves, how much more will they do so after their crowns, victories, and triumphs." St. Jerome in his *Letter Against Vigilantius* (circa 406 A.D.)[44]

- "If the Apostles and martyrs while still in the flesh and still needing to care for themselves, can pray for others, how much more will they pray for others after they have won their crowns, their victories, their triumphs. Moses, one man, obtains God's pardon for six hundred thousand armed men, and Stephen prays for his persecutors. When they are with Christ will they be less powerful? St. Paul says two hundred and seventy-six souls were granted to his prayers, whilst they were in the ship with him. Shall he close his lips after death, and not mutter a syllable for those who throughout the world have believed in his gospel?" St. Jerome (d. 420 A.D.)[45]

- "Neither are the souls of the pious dead separated from the church, which even now is the kingdom of Christ. Otherwise there would be no remembrance of them at the altar of God in the communication of the Body of Christ." St. Augustine in his *The City of God* (circa 420 A.D.)[46]

Endnotes

[1] In Acts 1:14 we read that, after the Ascension of Jesus into heaven, the Apostles and the first Christian disciples made it a point to include the Virgin Mary as one of their "prayer partners" as they fervently prayed for the coming of the promised Holy Spirit. Between the Ascension of Jesus into heaven and the coming of the Holy Spirit at Pentecost there is a nine day span. The Latin word for "nine" is *novem* (which is where we get the word "novena"). Following the example of the first Christians, a Catholic "novena" is prayer for a period of nine days asking for a fresh outpouring of God's Holy Spirit.

[493] LG 49; cf. *1 Tim* 2:5.

[497] *Martyrium Polycarpi*, 17: *Apostolic Fathers* II/3, 396.

[2] Cf. Gen 20:17 and Job 42:8 and read about Abraham and Job prayerfully interceding with God on behalf of others.

[3] Patrick Madrid, *Any Friend of God Is A Friend of Mine*, (San Diego, CA: This Rock Magazine, September 1992 issue), pp. 8-9.

[4] Rev. John A. O'Brien, *The Faith of Millions*, (Huntington, IN: Our Sunday Visitor, Inc., 1963, 1974), p. 327.

[5] Cf. Chapter 17 of this book.

[6] Pope Paul VI, *For the Right Ordering and Development of Devotion to the Blessed Virgin Mary*, (Boston, MA: Daughters of St. Paul, 1974), p. 23.

[7] In Eph 6:18-20 St. Paul instructs all Christians to pray for one another. Since God's laws are binding not only on earth but in heaven as well, the heavenly saints are also charged with the task of carrying out this Biblical admonition. Cf. also Rom 15:30-32; 2 Cor 1:10; Col 1:4, 9-10; Rom 10:1; 2 Tim 1:3, etc.

[8] *Any Friend of God Is A Friend of Mine*, p. 10.

9   Rev. Jude O. Mbukanma, *Is It In The Bible?*, (Clifton, VA: M.
    E. T. Ltd., 1987), p. 50.

10 Note how, in many of their television broadcasts, evangelical
    Christian ministers will often give their viewers a phone num-
    ber on the screen to call so that they can pray along with a
    "prayer partner" from their church. Couldn't the viewers just
    pray directly to Jesus on their own? Yes, but many choose to
    take advantage of these special "prayer partners" to gain spiri-
    tual support and companionship. In the same way, Catholics
    could pray directly to Jesus by themselves but, many times,
    they choose to invite a heavenly "prayer partner" to pray along
    with them (cf. Acts 1:14).

11 Catholic apologist Patrick Madrid writes, "If asking Christians
    in heaven to pray for us conflicts with Christ's mediatorship,
    asking Christians on earth to pray for us conflicts for the same
    reason. If 1 Tim 2:5 eliminates intercession by the Christians in
    heaven, it eliminates intercession by Christians on earth." Cf.
    Any Friend of God Is A Friend of Mine, p. 10.

12 Patrick Madrid (editor), *Surprised by Truth*, (San Diego, CA:
    Basilica Press, 1994), pp. 229-231.

13 James Cardinal Gibbons writes, "If our friends, though sinners,
    can aid us by their prayers, why cannot our friends, the saints
    of God, be able to assist us also? If Abraham and Moses and
    Job exercised so much influence with the Almighty while they
    lived in the flesh, is their power with God diminished now that
    they reign with Him in heaven?" Cf. *The Faith of Our Fathers*,
    p. 129.

14 In the Book of Genesis, Jacob asks an angel in heaven to inter-
    cede for him to God on behalf of his grandchildren: "The An-
    gel who has delivered me from all harm, bless these boys that
    in them my name be recalled... And they may become teeming
    multitudes upon the earth" (Gen 48:16).

15 In the Gospel of Matthew we read about the very real possibil-
    ity of deceased saints making bodily apparitions before the Sec-
    ond Coming of Christ: "tombs were opened, and the bodies of
    many saints who had fallen asleep were raised. And coming
    forth from their tombs after his resurrection, they entered the
    holy city and *appeared to many*" (Matt 27:52-53).

[16] Note how St. Paul scolds Christians who think that they don't need each another: "Now the [Body of Christ] is not a single part, but many... The eye cannot say to the hand, 'I do not need you,' nor again the head to the feet, 'I do not need you...'" God has so constructed the body as to give greater honor to a part that is without it, so that there may be no division in the body, but that the parts may have the same concern for one another" (cf. 1 Cor 12:14-26). When considering Scripture passages such as this, it is easy to see how Christians on earth still need the spiritual fellowship of Christians in heaven. Along the same lines, Christians in heaven are called not to forget about the Christians who are still struggling to be faithful followers of Jesus on earth.

[17] In Chapter 11 of the Letter to the Hebrews, the Biblical author mentions the names of many of the deceased Old Testament saints and then he says: "Therefore, since we are surrounded by so great a *cloud of witnesses*, let us rid ourselves of every burden and sin that clings to us and persevere in running the race that lies before us" (Heb 12:1). One can see here that these saints are not dead but very alive and are, somehow, able to observe and to "cheer on" the Christians currently living on earth.

[18] St. Paul tells the Christians in Corinth that heavenly beings can, indeed, observe the faith journeys of Christians on earth: "...we have become a spectacle to the world, to angels and human beings alike" (1 Cor 4:9).

[19] *Any Friend of God Is A Friend of Mine*, p. 12.

[20] The "Internet" is an "**inter**connected **net**work" of computers in which people have the ability to share resources with one another online. The biblically-rooted doctrine of the "Communion of Saints" reveals to us the existence of a "spiritual internet" in which God's People, living and deceased, are able to share spiritual resources with those who are in need of them in a sort of "prayer web."

[21] Mark Miravalle, *Introduction to Mary*, (Santa Barbara, CA: Queenship Publishing Company, 1993), pp. 171-172.

[22] "Throughout the ages, there have been so-called 'private' revelations, some of which have been recognized by the authority

of the Church. They do not belong, however, to the deposit of faith. It is not their role to improve or complete Christ's definitive Revelation, but to help live more fully by it in a certain period of history..." Cf. *Catechism of the Catholic Church*, #66-67.

23   Cf. Chapter 19 of this book to read more about the biblically-based vocation of celibacy for the sake of freeing oneself to spread God's Kingdom.

24   *The King James Bible*, (Nashville, TN: Holman Bible Publishers, 1979), p. 130.

25   "...You have approached Mount Zion and the city of the living God, the heavenly Jerusalem, and countless angels in festal gathering, and the assembly of the firstborn enrolled in heaven, and God the judge of all, and the *spirits of the just made perfect*..." (Heb 12:22-24). We see here that the saints in heaven are *perfected in righteousness*. James tells us that "the fervent prayer of a righteous person is very powerful" (James 5:16). Should a Christian living on earth discount the power of the prayers of the saints in heaven who are *perfectly righteous* and who are eternally living in the presence of God?

26   Note how Mary is identified as the "Ark of the New Covenant" in the Book of Revelation. Note how, in 2 Sam 6:16, King David "leaps" before the Ark of the Covenant in the Old Testament. In Luke 1:41 John the Baptist "leaps" in his mother's womb when Mary—the "Ark of the New Covenant"—comes into his presence. Cf. Chapter 17 of this book for a more in-depth discussion of Mary as the "Ark of the New Covenant."

27   Cf. also the (mostly Protestant) *Harper's Bible Commentary*, James L. Mays (General Editor), (San Francisco, CA: Harper & Row Publishers, 1988), p. 1312.

28   Cf. John 19:26-27 where Jesus gives His mother Mary to John (a symbol of giving Mary to the Church).

29   Speaking about devotion to the Blessed Virgin Mary, Rev. John A. O'Brien writes, "Can anyone expect to please even an earthly son by showing a lack of reverence to His Mother? How much less, then, can such a course be pleasing to the Son of God..." Cf. *The Faith of Millions*, p. 370. Mark Miravalle writes about Mary: "...[T]he Blessed Mother gave the '*carne*' to the Incarnation. She gave flesh to the 'Word made Flesh... Just having

the physical presence of Jesus in the womb of Mary for nine months is like having the Eucharist constantly present within a person for nine complete months, constantly sanctifying its human tabernacle day and night by its spiritual and physical presence. All other saints, even St. Joseph, no matter how closely associated with the Incarnation, had at best an external relationship with God becoming man for our salvation... For these...reasons and several more, the Blessed Virgin Mary rightly receives a singular and unique place of special devotion in the Church which is higher than that of the saints and angels, but always humbly below the adoration due to God alone." Cf. *Introduction to Mary*, pp. 13-14.

[30] St. Paul writes to the Christian community in Philippi and encourages them to imitate other Christians who have set good spiritual examples: "Join with others in being imitators of me, brothers, and observe those who thus conduct themselves according to the model you have in us... [W]hatever is true, whatever is honorable, whatever is just, whatever is pure...if there is any excellence and if there is anything worthy of praise, think about these things..." (Phil 3:17; 4:8-9).

[31] *Introduction to Mary*, pp. 9-11.

[32] Scott Hahn, *A Biblical Understanding of Mary Audio Cassette*, (West Covina, CA: St. Joseph Communications, Inc. (818) 331-3549).

[33] Through her unfaithfulness to God, Eve shut all of her children out of paradise. Mary, on the other hand, through her supreme faithfulness to God, gave birth to Jesus our Savior who, in turn, opened wide the gates of paradise to His followers!

[34] Cf. *Catechism of the Catholic Church*, #956.

[35] This Scripture passage from James 2:24 directly contradicts the doctrine of *sola fide* promoted by Martin Luther.

[36] Cf. Chapter 4 of this book.

[37] In Hebrews 11 we read about numerous "dead" Old Testament saints: Abel (v. 4), Abraham (v. 8), Moses (v. 24), Gideon, Samson, David, Samuel, and the prophets (v. 32) and then we read: "Therefore, since we are *surrounded by so great a cloud of witnesses*, let us rid ourselves of every burden and sin that clings to us and persevere in running the race that lies before

us" (Heb 12:1). It appears here that the saints in heaven can, indeed, cheer us on as we seek to "fight the good fight of faith" here on earth.

38 Patrick Madrid, *This Rock* Magazine, (September, 1992 issue), p. 13.

39 William A. Jurgens (editor and translator), *The Faith of the Early Fathers (Volume 1)*, (Collegeville, MN: The Liturgical Press, 1970), p. 31.

40 Karl Keating (editor), *This Rock* Magazine, "The Father's Know Best," (San Diego, CA: Catholic Answers, Inc., May 1994, pp. 36-37.

41 *Ibid.*, pp. 36-37.

42 *Ibid.*, pp. 36-37.

43 *The Faith of the Early Fathers (Volume 1)*, p. 229.

44 *Catholic and Christian*, p. 157.

45 Rev. John A. O'Brien, *The Faith of Millions*, (Huntington, IN: Our Sunday Visitor, Inc. 1963, 1974), p. 326.

46 Alan Schreck, *Catholic and Christian*, (Ann Arbor, Michigan: Servant Books, 1984), p. 160.

Chapter 8

The "Hail Mary"[1]: A Scriptural Prayer Dissected

What Does the Catholic Church Teach?

"...The Church rightly honors 'the Blessed Virgin with special devotion. From the most ancient times the Blessed Virgin has been honored with the title 'Mother of God,' to whose protection the faithful fly in all their dangers and needs... This very special devotion ... differs essentially from the adoration which is given to the incarnate Word and equally to the Father and the Holy Spirit, and greatly fosters this adoration.'[514] The liturgical feasts dedicated to the Mother of God and Marian prayer, such as the rosary, an 'epitome of the whole Gospel,' express this devotion to the Virgin Mary."[515] (*Catechism of the Catholic Church*, #971.)

Common Objection #1

"The 'Hail Mary' prayer is not found anywhere in the Bible and is, therefore, an un-scriptural man-made Catholic invention."

A Catholic Response:

Let's examine the "Hail Mary" verse by verse and discover how it is, indeed, a solidly Biblical prayer:

- **"Hail Mary, full of grace, the Lord is with thee"**

This is the angel Gabriel's greeting to Mary found in Luke 1:28 — "Hail, full of grace, the Lord is with you."[2]

Please note that "hail" *does not* mean "worship." "Hail" is simply a greeting. "All hail the king," for example, simply means "let us welcome and greet the king." When a person "hails" a cab, he attempts to greet the taxi cab driver so that he can stop and give the person a ride.

- **"Blessed art thou among women and blessed is the Fruit of thy womb, Jesus"**

This is Elizabeth's statement about Mary found in Luke 1:42 — "Blessed are you among women, and blessed is the fruit of your womb." In this verse the name "Jesus" is added to more explicitly identify the Person who was "the Fruit of Mary's womb."

- **"Holy Mary"**

Because of her crucial role in bringing our long-awaited Savior into the world, this is what Mary realizes about herself in Luke 1:48 — "From now on will all ages call me *blessed*." "Blessed" and "holy" are synonyms.

- **"Mother of God"**

In the Gospel of Luke, Elizabeth says to Mary: "And how does this happen to me, that the Mother of my *Lord* [Greek: *Kyrios*] should come to me" (Luke 1:43)? Many times in the New Testament, the Greek word *Kyrios* is used as a title for God the Father (cf. Luke 1:6; Luke 1:9; Luke 1:11).[3] Because Mary was bearing a Divine Being in her womb, Elizabeth is, thus, rightfully saying to her in Luke 1:43: "And how does this happen to me, that the Mother of my...[God/*Kyrios*] should come to me?" Elizabeth and her baby (St. John the Baptist) rejoice when she hears that Mary was to give birth to the Second Person of the Blessed Trinity (who was/is God) and who has now taken on Flesh in the course of human history.

Mary is the mother of Jesus Christ in His entirety. The Scriptures tells us that Jesus is fully Divine (cf. 1 John 5:20) *and* that Jesus is fully human (cf. 1 Timothy 2:5). (An example that I sometimes use to show that Mary is the Mother of Jesus in His entirety is this: I put one drop of blue food coloring in a glass of clear water and that symbolizes that Jesus is fully Divine (cf. 1 John 5:20). To the blue water I add a drop of yellow food coloring to symbolize that Jesus is fully human (cf. 1 Tim 2:5). I stir the water up and a new combination is created in the course of history that wasn't there before: green water. Mary gave birth to the "new Divine combination created in the course of history that didn't exist before"— the Incarnation.)[4]

The Second Person of the Blessed Trinity has, indeed, always existed (cf. John 1:1-2). The unique Divine merger of the Second Person of the Blessed Trinity with human flesh and blood, however, was born in the course of history (cf. John 1:14). One could not say that Mary was the mother only of Jesus' human nature.[5] That would be like saying that our mothers could be the mother of *only* our bodies or *only* our souls. Our mothers are the mother of our *entire being*.[6] Mary is, at the same time, the mother of Jesus *and* the Mother of God. Of course this certainly does *not* imply that Mary pre-existed in heaven as God the Father's female parent!

To call Mary the Mother of God is simply making a statement about Jesus' Divinity. St. Paul tells us about Jesus: "For in Him dwells the whole fullness of the deity bodily..." (Col 2:9). To call Mary the Mother of God is simply to say that she gave birth, in the course of human history, to the child in which "the whole fullness of the deity [God] dwelt bodily."

Fr. Peter Stravinskas, in his book *The Catholic Answer Book,* gives some historical background on the origin of Mary's title: "Mother of God":

> "The fifth-century Council of Ephesus insisted on according Mary the title of "Theotokos" (God-bearer), rather than "Christotokos" (Christ-bearer) to emphasize Jesus' divinity.
>
> In other words, early heretics had argued that Jesus was not coeternal with the Father, and they attempted to demonstrate this by pointing to Jesus' origin in time

from a human mother. The Church responded by distinguishing the Son's existence as the Second Person of the Blessed Trinity from all eternity and His assumption of a human nature from Our Lady in the Incarnation. To stress the continuity between the Lord's divine preexistence and His existence in time, and His uninterrupted state of divinity (not lost in the Incarnation), the council saw the appropriateness of regarding Mary as the Mother of God, that is, the Mother of the Second Person of the Blessed Trinity in His earthly life."[7]

Mark Miravalle in his book, *Introduction to Mary*, goes on to say:

"Nestorius refused to call Mary "Mother of God" not primarily because of a mariological error, but because of a Christological error (an error concerning the true doctrine of Jesus.)

Nestorius erroneously divided the one person of Jesus Christ into two separate persons, and thus Mary would be Mother only of the 'human person of Jesus,' and not the Mother of God. The Ephesus definition of Mary as the *Theotokos* is actually a protection of the revealed truth about Jesus: that Jesus is one divine person with two natures, one divine nature and one human nature, and that the two natures are inseparably united in the one and only divine person of Jesus. We see then at Ephesus a case in point of the truth that authentic Marian doctrine will always protect and safeguard authentic doctrine about Jesus Christ."[8]

In Rev 11:19–12:5 the Biblical writer is describing a heavenly vision that he is having. First he sees the Ark of the Covenant in heaven *(the place where God dwelled with His Chosen People in the Old Testament — cf. Exod 25:1-40).*[9] Rather than describing an ornate box made of acacia wood, the Biblical writer describes a vision of "a woman clothed with the sun, with the moon under her feet, and on her head a crown of twelve stars... She gave birth to a son, a male child, destined to rule all the nations with an iron rod."[10]

Scripture presents Mary as the "Ark of the New Covenant" because God (the Second Person of the Blessed Trinity) would literally dwell in her for nine months before being born.

Mary's womb was the first tabernacle[11] (cf. Rev 11:19–12:1) because she housed God (the Word made Flesh). Since Mary carried and gave birth to the Divine Person of Jesus Christ in the course of history she, indeed, deserves the title "Mother of God."[12]

Consider this simple theological syllogism:[13]

1. Mary is the mother of Jesus *(cf. John 2:1)*.
2. Jesus is God *(cf. 1 John 5:20)*.[14]
3. Therefore, Mary is the Mother of God *(cf. Luke 1:43)*.

- **"Pray for us sinners now and at the hour of our death." Amen.**

St. Paul writes to Timothy: "I ask that supplications, prayers, petitions, and thanksgivings be offered for everyone..." (1 Tim 2:1-4). Does the Bible ask us to pray for one another? You bet. From her place in heaven, can Mary bring prayers and requests to Jesus on our behalf like she used to do on earth (cf. John 2:1-11)? You bet! (Cf. Rev 6:9-10 and read about the saints in heaven [cf. Rev 12] pleading with God and asking for Him to act on their behalf. Cf. also Rev 8:3-4 and read about the saints in heaven holding an eternal worship service before God.)

Common Objection #2

"Scripture tells us that God is eternal and has existed ever since the beginning of time: "...from eternity to eternity you are God" (Psalm 90:2). How could God possibly have a mother? She would have had to pre-exist Him!"

A Catholic Response

John 1:1 tells us that, from all eternity, "the Word" (the second Person of the Blessed Trinity) existed within the Godhead. In Matt

28:19 the Persons making up the Godhead are named (the Father, the Son, and the Holy Spirit.) Circa 6 B.C.,[15] "the Word" *(the second Person of the Blessed Trinity)* became flesh and dwelt among us (cf. John 1:14). To call Mary the "Mother of God" is simply saying that, at a particular point in history (circa 6 B.C.), she became the mother, not of God the Father or of God the Holy Spirit, but of the Word made Flesh in the course of history (whom the Bible identifies as "God"). Mary is the mother of a Divine being, who was named "Jesus," who is called "God" in the Scriptures, and who took on flesh at a certain point in human history. To call Mary the "Mother of God" is certainly *not* making the statement that she pre-existed the Blessed Trinity in heaven.

Was the "Hail Mary" invented by human beings? The piecing together of the Biblical texts was done by human beings but, doesn't every modern-day preacher, when giving a sermon or offering a prayer for a church member, piece together various texts from the Bible?

What Did the Early Christians Believe About Mary Truly Being the "Mother of God"?

- "For our God, Jesus Christ, was conceived by Mary in accord with God's plan..." St. Ignatius of Antioch in his *Letter to the Ephesians* (circa 110 A.D.)[16]

- "The Virgin Mary, being obedient to His word, received from an angel the glad tidings that she would bear God." St. Irenaeus in his *Against Heresies* (circa 180 A.D.)[17]

- "We acknowledge the resurrection of the dead, of which Jesus Christ our Lord became the firstling; who bore a body not in appearance but in truth, derived from Mary the Mother of God." *Encyclical Letter of Alexander to Another Bishop Alexander and to All Non-Egyptian Bishops* (circa 324 A.D.)[18]

- "The Archangel Gabriel bears witness, bringing good tiding to Mary. The Virgin Mother of God bears witness." St. Cyril of Jerusalem in his *Catechetical Lectures* (circa 350 A.D.)[19]

- "He that is born in time here below, of the Virgin Mary, the Mother of God." St. Athanasius in his *On the Incarnation of the Word of God and Against the Arians* (circa 365 A.D.)[20]

Endnotes

1   "Hail Mary" is the greeting given to Mary by the angel Gabriel right before he announces to her that she had been hand-picked by God to be the mother of the long-awaited Messiah (cf. Luke 1:28 in the *Douay Rhiems Bible*, (Rockford, IL: TAN Books and Publishers, Inc., 1971, 1989), p. 65.)

514 LG 66.

515 Cf. Paul VI, MC 42; SC 103.

2   *Douay Rheims Bible*, p. 65.

3   John L. McKenzie, S. J., in his book *Dictionary of the Bible*, (Collier Books Macmillan Publishing Co., 1965), p. 517, says, "The use of *Kyrios* in the Synoptic Gospels...is also a designation of God in quotations from the [Catholic "Septuagint" Old Testament] or as a substitute for the name of God."

4   Any analogy that we humans use to speak about God limps to some degree. My analogy of two different colors combining to form a new third color falls way short in speaking about the awesome mystery of Jesus' human nature and His Divine nature coming together in His one Divine Person. The Church teaches that these two natures of our Lord come together in His Divine Person "without confusion, change, division, or separation." Cf. *Catechism of the Catholic Church*, #467-468.

5   Catholic convert Tim Staples in the book, *Surprised by Truth*, Patrick Madrid (editor) (San Diego, CA: Basilica Press, 1994), p. 232, says, "I also objected to the title "Mother of God," arguing that since Mary only gave Jesus his humanity; she was only his mother "after the flesh." But Elizabeth addressed her as the "mother of my *Lord*," not "the mother of my Lord's body."

6   James Cardinal Gibbons writes: "Did the mother who bore us have any part in the production of our *soul*? Was not this nobler part of our being the work of God alone? And yet who would for a moment dream of saying 'the mother of my body,' and not

'*my* mother?' The comparison teaches us that the terms parent and child, mother and son, refer to the persons and not to the part or elements of which the persons are composed. Hence no one says: 'The mother of my *body*,' 'the mother of my *soul*;' but in all propriety 'my mother,' the mother of me who live and breathe, think and act, *one* in my personality, though uniting in it a soul directly created by God, and a material body directly derived from a maternal womb." James Cardinal Gibbons, *The Faith of Our Fathers*, (Rockford, IL: TAN Books and Publishers, Inc., 1980), p. 137.

7   Fr. Peter M. J. Stravinskas, *The Catholic Answer Book*, (Huntington, IN: Our Sunday Visitor Publishing Co., 1990), p. 42.

8   Mark Miravalle, *Introduction to Mary*, (Santa Barbara, CA: Queenship Publishing Co., 1993), p. 35.

9   Just as the Old Testament Ark of the Covenant contained manna, the staff of the priest Aaron, and the tablets of the Commandments (cf. Heb 9:3-4), Mary, the New Testament "Ark of the Covenant," contained "the Bread of Life" (cf. John 6:48), "the eternal High Priest" (cf. Heb 7:24), and "the Word of God" (cf. John 1:14).

10   Psalm 2:9 says of the promised Messiah: "With an *iron rod* you shall shepherd them..." The Gospels tell us that the woman who gave birth to the promised Messiah was named "Mary" (cf. Luke 2:1-7).

11   Circa 730 A.D., St. John Damascene writes about Mary: "And her body, which had been the Tabernacle of God, after chanting of the angels and of the Apostles was finished and last respects were paid, was placed in a coffin in Gethsemani." William A. Jurgens (editor and translator), *The Faith of the Early Fathers (Volume 3)*, (Collegeville, MN: The Liturgical Press, 1979), p. 350.

12   St. Augustine (d. 430 A.D.) writes that Mary "gave milk to our Bread."

13   A syllogism is a logical method of deductive reasoning usually following the structure: if truth "a" equals truth "b," and truth "b" equals truth "c," then truth "a" equals truth "c."

14   For further Biblical passages that speak of the divinity of Jesus cf. 1 John 5:20; John 1:1; John 20:28; John 10:30; John 14:9;

John 5:18, 23; John 8:24, 58/Exod 3:14; Col 2:9; Phil 2:11; 2 Pet 1:3; Matt 1:21-23.

[15] *New American Bible With Revised New Testament*, (New York, NY: Catholic Book Publishing Co., 1986), Introduction to Bible Chart, p. 41.

[16] *The Faith of the Early Fathers (Volume 1)*, p. 18.

[17] *Ibid.*, p. 101.

[18] *Ibid.*, p. 301.

[19] *Ibid.*, p. 354.

[20] *Ibid.*, p. 340.

Chapter 9

The Rosary: The New Testament on a String

What Does the Catholic Church Teach?

"...The rosary [is] an 'epitome of the whole Gospel'..."[515] Meditation engages thought, imagination, emotion, and desire. This mobilization of faculties is necessary in order to deepen our convictions of faith, prompt the conversion of our heart, and strengthen our will to follow Christ. Christian prayer tries above all to meditate on the mysteries of Christ, as in *lectio divina* or the rosary. This form of prayerful reflection is of great value, but Christian prayer should go further: to the knowledge of the love of the Lord Jesus, to union with him." (*Catechism of the Catholic Church*, #971, 2708.)

Common Objection #1:

"The rosary is a man-made invention and not found anywhere in the Bible."

A Catholic Response

Throughout the centuries, Catholic priests and religious have prayed from the Bible's 150 Psalms as part of their daily prayer.

In order to imitate the prayer of the clergy and religious, a number of the lay people (many of whom were not able to read) memorized the scriptural prayer the "Our Father" (cf. Matt 6:9-13; Luke 11:2-4) and prayed it 150 times in place of reading from the Bible's 150 Psalms.[1]

In a parallel development, a number of lay people, who had a special devotion to our Lord's mother, Mary, memorized the scriptural prayer the "Ave Maria": "Hail Mary, full of grace, the Lord is with thee" (cf. Luke 1:28) and prayed that 150 times, asking Mary to pray along with them to her Son, Jesus.[2] Before long, various mysteries associated with the life of Christ were interspersed throughout these 150 "Ave Marias" to make absolutely certain that *Jesus* was the central focus of this Biblically-based meditation.

Many historians believe that the rosary developed slowly during a time span stretching from the 1100's A.D. until 1569 A.D. Finally, in 1569, a Dominican Pope named Pope Pius V fixed the form of the rosary as we know it today. The Pope's rosary had 15 decades. 15 decades x 10 "Hail Marys" per decade = 150 *(which is the number of Psalms contained in the Bible.)*

Is the rosary a "man-made invention?" The structure/format of the rosary was created by Christian men but all of the components that make up the rosary come from the Bible. Just as a modern-day preacher creatively assembles a sermon or a worship service with components found in the Bible, the rosary was composed by Christians who took various Bible verses and scriptural truths and "cut and pasted" them together.

Let us look at the heart and soul of the rosary: meditation upon the mysteries surrounding the life of Jesus Christ, our Lord and Savior.

Five Joyful Mysteries Surrounding the Life of Christ:

1. The angel Gabriel announces God's plan of salvation to Mary *(cf. Luke 1:26-38)*
2. Mary visits Elizabeth and tells her the good news of her Divine pregnancy *(cf. Luke 1:39-47)*
3. The birth of our Lord Jesus Christ — the Word becomes flesh and dwells among us *(cf. Luke 2:1-7)*

4. The presentation of the baby Jesus in the Temple by Mary and Joseph *(cf. Luke 2:22-32)*
5. The finding of twelve-year-old Jesus in the Temple by Mary and Joseph *(cf. Luke 2:41-52)*

Five Sorrowful Mysteries Surrounding the Life of Christ:

1. The agony of Jesus in the Garden *(cf. Mark 14:32-36)*
2. The scourging of Jesus at the pillar *(cf. John 18:28-38; John 19:1)*
3. Jesus is crowned with thorns *(cf. Mark 15:16-20)*
4. Jesus carries the cross *(cf. John 19:12-16)*
5. Jesus is crucified and dies *(cf. Luke 23:33-46)*

Five Glorious Mysteries Surrounding the Life of Christ:

1. The Resurrection of Jesus from the dead *(cf. Luke 24:1-6)*
2. The Ascension of Jesus into heaven *(cf. Luke 24:50-53)*
3. The descent of the Holy Spirit upon the Apostles at Pentecost *(cf. Acts 2:1-4)*
4. Because of the crucial role that she played in the life of our Savior Jesus Christ and because of her being conceived without the stain of original sin,[3] Mary was assumed into heaven, body and soul, by the power of God *(cf. Rev 11:19- 12:5; 1 Cor 11:2; 2 Thess 2:15; Matt 27:52; 2 Kings 2:11; Gen 5:24; Acts 8:39-40; Psalm 132:8; 1 Tim 3:15; cf. also Chapters 12 and 17 of this book).*
5. In reward for her life of unwavering faithfulness in cooperating with God's plan of salvation for the world (Luke 1:38), Mary was crowned "Queen of Heaven" by God. *(Cf. Rev 11:19 12:5; 1 Cor 11:2; 2 Thess 2:15; 1 Tim 3:15; cf. also Chapters 12 and 17 of this book)[4]*

The rosary is centered on the mysteries surrounding the life of Jesus Christ. The rosary invites us to look at Jesus through the eyes of the disciple who was closest to Him. Because Mary's life and Jesus' life were so closely interrelated, we remember a number of important events in her life that had a direct bearing on the life of her Divine Son.

We have already learned that the first part of the "Hail Mary" comes *directly* from Scripture (cf. Chapter 8 of this book.). The second Biblically-based part of the "Hail Mary" ("Holy Mary, Mother of God, pray for us sinners now and at the hour of our death") was composed in the 7th century to make the prayer one, not only of honor, but of petition also (cf. Chapter 8 of this book).

The other prayers that make up the rosary are the "Our Father" and the "Glory Be." The "Our Father" appears twice in the Bible (cf. Matt 6:9-13; Luke 11:2-4). The "Glory Be" prayer is found by combining the Biblical truths found in Matt 28:19 (God is Father, Son, and Holy Spirit) with Psalm 90:2 (God has existed ever since the beginning of time, He exists now, and He will exist forever.)

The prayer "O my Jesus, forgive us our sins, save us from the fires of hell, and lead all souls to heaven, especially those who have most need of Thy mercy" was revealed by Mary to the children at Fatima, Portugal in 1917. The truths contained in this prayer are certainly consistent with what the Scriptures present to us about the General Judgement (cf. Matt 25:31-46).

The word "rosary" comes from the Latin word *rosarium* (which means "rose garden.") Because the rose is a symbol of joy, it began to be associated with Mary.[5]

When we pray the rosary we are not praying *to* Mary but *through* Mary and *with* Mary *to* Jesus Christ our Savior. The rosary invites us to ponder the mysteries of our redemption in Christ over and over again.[6]

Common Objection #2

"Jesus clearly says in Scripture: 'In praying, *do not babble* like the pagans, who think that they will be heard because of their many words' (Matt 6:7). In praying the repetitive prayers of the rosary, you Catholics are 'babbling on like the pagans' and are going against Jesus' Biblical command."

A Catholic Response

In the Old Testament Book of 1st Kings we get an idea of what pagan prayer was like: "Taking the young bull that was turned over to them, they prepared it and called on Baal from morning to noon, saying, 'Answer us, Baal!' But there was no sound, and no one answering. And they hopped around the altar they had prepared" (1 Kings 18:26).

Let's compare the rosary to pagan prayer:

Pagan Prayer	The Rosary
Worship of numerous pagan gods (sun god, moon god, etc.).	Worship of Jesus Christ, the only Son of the one true God. Catholics often ask Jesus' mother, Mary, to pray along with us (cf. Acts 1:14) and to pray for us to her Son, Jesus (just as the saints in heaven are described doing in Sacred Scripture: cf. Rev 8:3-4; Rev 6:9-10).
The prayers to the pagan gods were rooted in superstition and myth.	The "Hail Mary," the "Our Father," and the "Glory Be" are all scripturally-based prayers (cf. Chapter 8 in this book).
Mindless repetition of empty phrases directed to non-existent pagan gods in hopes that they would somehow hear and respond (cf. 1 Kings 18:26).	Being persistent in prayer to the one true God as the Bible instructs us (cf. Luke 11:5-8; Luke 18:1-8; Rev 4:8; Matt 26:39-44; 1 Thess 3:10; 1 Thess 5:17; Psalm 136).

- In Psalm 136 the psalmist prays repetitively *26 times* in 26 verses: "God's love endures forever."
- St. Paul instructs the Christians in Thessalonica to *"pray without ceasing"* (1 Thess 5:17).
- St. Paul writes to the Thessalonians: *"Night and day* we pray beyond measure...to remedy the deficiencies of your faith" (1 Thess 3:10).
- In the Book of Revelation we read about a vision of heavenly worship in which the inhabitants of heaven *"...day and night did not stop exclaiming*: 'Holy, holy, holy is the Lord God almighty, who was, and who is, and who is to come'" (Rev 4:8).
- In Matt 26:39-44 we read that Jesus, in the garden of Gethsemane, sincerely prayed the exact same prayer to the Father *three times in a row.*

One can see from the *many* instances in Scripture where people are praying repetitively that the repetition, when done with a sincere heart and the proper motivation, is simply offering to the Lord a constant chorus of praise and responding to Jesus' command to be persistent in prayer. Note how, in the singing of Gospel songs and African-American spirituals, the refrain of the song is often repeated over and over again. This is done, not in mindless repetition, but to offer to the Lord a continual chorus of worship, keeping the singers easily-distracted human minds focused on heavenly Realities. [7]

The rosary is, indeed, "the New Testament on a string!" [8] Incorporating not only vocal prayer but mental prayer (meditation) as well, the rosary is a wonderful tool to help Catholics to express our Biblically-based Christian spirituality!

Endnotes

[515] Cf. Paul VI, *MC* 42; *SC* 103.
[1] Cf. *Catechism of the Catholic Church*, #2678.
[2] Jesus teaches Christians about the value of communal prayer in the Gospel of Matthew: "For where two or three are gathered

30

together in my name, there am I in the midst of them" (Matt 18:20).

3   Cf. Chapter 16 of this book.

4   Mark Miravalle writes, "A queen can be a 'female king' or independent ruler of a kingdom, or she can be the mother or spouse of the king. It is only in the second relative sense that Mary is rightly understood as Queen, as true Mother of Christ the 'King,' whose kingdom is the Mystical Body...This 'Queen Mother' guides and rules the members of her Son's kingdom in complete subordination and submission to Christ the King in the law and order of sanctifying grace." Cf. Mark Miravalle, *Introduction to Mary*, (Santa Barbara, CA: Queenship Publishing, Co., 1993), pp. 64-65. Mark Miravalle writes, "The Coronation of Mary foreshadows the heavenly crown that as St. Paul tells us, all children of God can expect upon running the race (1 Cor 9:24-25; 2 Tim 4:8). The last two (glorious mysteries of the rosary) then are a foretaste of what all Christians can expect in due measure when they remain faithful to the first thirteen mysteries of the Lord." Cf. *Introduction to Mary*, p. 95.

5   Mary says about herself in the Gospel of Luke: "...my spirit rejoices [finds joy] in God my savior" (Luke 1:47).

6   Scripture tells us that "...Mary kept all these things, reflecting [pondering] on them in her heart" (Luke 2:19).

7   The Revised Standard Version of the Bible states Jesus' intended meaning clearly when it says: "And in praying do not heap up *empty phrases* as the Gentiles do..." (Matt 6:7). Borrowing as heavily as it does from Sacred Scripture, the prayers of the rosary could hardly qualify as "empty phrases."

8   Pope Paul VI rightly referred to the rosary as "the compendium of the entire Gospel."

Chapter 10

"Have You Been Saved?"

What Does the Catholic Church Teach?

"Believing in Jesus Christ and in the One who sent him for our salvation is necessary for obtaining that salvation.[42] 'Since 'without faith it is impossible to please [God]' and to attain to the fellowship of his sons, therefore without faith no one has ever attained justification, nor will anyone obtain eternal life 'but he who endures to the end.'[43] ...Faith is an entirely free gift that God makes to man. We can lose this priceless gift, as St. Paul indicated to St. Timothy: 'Wage the good warfare, holding faith and a good conscience. By rejecting conscience, certain persons have made shipwreck of their faith.'[44] To live, grow, and persevere in the faith until the end we must nourish it with the word of God; we must beg the Lord to increase our faith;[45] it must be 'working through charity,' abounding in hope, and rooted in the faith of the Church[46]...Celebrated worthily in faith, the sacraments confer the grace that they signify.[48] They are *efficacious* because in them Christ himself is at work...The Church affirms that for believers the sacraments of the New Covenant are *necessary for salvation*."[51] (*Catechism of the Catholic Church*, #161, 162, 1127, 1129.)

Common Objection #1

"St. Paul clearly states: '...[I]f you confess with your mouth that Jesus is Lord and believe in your heart that God raised him from the dead, you will be saved' (Rom 10:9). Therefore, all that is necessary to obtain an absolute assurance of salvation in heaven is for a person to turn to Christ in faith and to simply accept Him as his 'personal Lord and Savior.' St. Paul also tells us that one cannot be saved through works: 'For by grace you have been saved through faith, and this is not from you; it is the gift of God; it is not from works, so no one may boast' (Eph 2:8-9). The Sacraments were invented by the Catholic Church as a means to 'work one's way to heaven.'"

A Catholic Response

A common Protestant understanding of justification holds that no one is ever really fully cleansed from sin. Rather, the "saved" Christian simply puts on the outer "cloak" of Jesus' righteousness — and thus enters into heaven at his death externally spotless. Since, in Protestant theology, Jesus' blood does not really cleanse our *entire being* but merely *covers* us so that we will be acceptable to the Father on Judgement Day, most Protestants hold that there is no need to be purged from personal post-baptismal sin — since Christ has accomplished all purging from sin upon the cross and has "coated" His disciples with His own righteousness/holiness. (The Protestant theology of justification is illustrated well in Martin Luther's statement that Christians are like "dunghills covered with snow." Luther believed that Christians are not [and could never be] inwardly spiritually pure but are only *externally "coated"* with the righteousness of Jesus Christ — which would make them "passable" before the Father on Judgment Day.)

On the other hand, the Catholic (and the Biblical) understanding of justification holds that Baptism into Christ cleanses the *entire person*, internally *and* externally, from all of the sins that he has at that present moment (cf. Acts 2:38) and makes him a "new creation" (cf. 2 Cor 5:17). Baptism into Christ makes us adopted sons and daughters of God and, therefore, adopted brothers and sisters of Jesus Christ (cf. 1 John 3:1-3; Rom 8:14-17). After being "clothed with Christ" in the waters of Baptism (cf. Gal 3:27-29), Christians become full-fledged members of God's family.

Consider the following analogy about the experience of being a member of a human family: After our birth into our human family we receive our family name and, when we are old enough, are given free will by our parents to go out and "play" in the neighborhood. In our adventures at the neighborhood playground we often fall down and "muddy" ourselves and have to return home daily for a good bath. After a thorough scrubbing by our parents, the beloved child is, once again, a sweet-smelling member of his family. If a sweaty, smelly child were to come into his parent's home and simply slip on some clean clothes and go and sit down at the supper table, his parent's noses would instantly detect the need for a good scrubbing and would quickly escort him off to the bathroom so that he could get properly cleaned up.

In a similar manner, after our baptismal birth into our heavenly family (cf. John 3:1-5, 22), our heavenly Father (God) gives us the free will to go out into the "playground" of the world. Just as a child in a human family often falls down and "muddies" himself in his adventures at the neighborhood playground, we often "muddy" ourselves spiritually and we commit sins throughout our life. Simply understood, the Sacraments are vehicles of grace (instituted by Jesus) to spiritually "scrub up" and to nourish our souls, on a regular basis throughout our life, in the Blood of the risen Christ so that we can maintain our internal *and* external baptismal cleanliness throughout our earthly life. Just as we human beings have to cleanse ourselves bodily on a wash-as-we-go basis throughout our life, Catholic Christians cleanse ourselves spiritually/Sacramentally on a wash-as-we-go basis in the Blood of the risen Jesus Christ.

The word "saved" (Greek: *sozo*) is certainly a Biblical concept (cf. Rom 10:9) but it must be understood within the context of the *entire* New Testament:

Past Tense	The Bible speaks about being "saved" (Greek: *sozo*) in the *past tense*: • Making reference to the *past event* of Jesus' saving death and resurrection that has redeemed humanity,[1] the writer of the Acts of the Apostles teaches: "There is no salvation through anyone else, nor is there any other name under heaven given to the human race by which we are to be saved [Greek: *sozo*]." (Acts 4:12, cf. also Eph 1:7)

169

Present Tense	Being "saved" (Greek: *sozo*) is also spoken about in Scripture in the *present tense*: • The Bible says that Christians who are baptized have been "clothed with Christ" and are able to share in the fruits of this past redemptive event performed by our Lord on Calvary: "[The experience of Noah and the flood recounted in the Old Testament]…prefigured baptism, which saves [Greek: *sozo*] you now…" (1 Pet 3:21; cf. also Gal 3:27; Rom 6:3-5) • "Whoever believes and is baptized will be saved [Greek: *sozo*]." (Mark 16:16) • "Through [the Gospel] you are also being saved [Greek: *sozo*], if you hold fast to the word I preached to you, unless you believed in vain." (1 Cor 15:2; cf. also Phil 2:12)
Future Tense	Being "saved" (Greek: *sozo*) is also described in the Bible as a *future event* that will be experienced only by those who are found faithful to Jesus Christ at the very end of their lives. *(Scripture teaches that salvation can be lost if a Christian is found unfaithful at the end of his life)*: • "…whoever endures to the end will be saved [Greek: *sozo*]." (Matt 10:22) • "…the one who perseveres to the end will be saved [Greek: *sozo*]." (Mark 13:13)

In the minds of some evangelical Christians, when they say that they are "saved" they usually mean that they have done what St. Paul asks us to do in Romans: "If you confess with your mouth that Jesus is Lord and believe in your heart that God raised him from the dead, you will be saved" (Rom 10:9). After praying a "sinner's prayer" that acknowledges their need for God and their faith in Jesus Christ, many fundamentalist Christians believe that they have a 100% absolute assurance of going to heaven at their death — whenever it may occur. Let's look at some key verses in the New Testament to see if being "saved" is as simple as that:

Biblical Elements of the Journey of Salvation:

- Professing personal faith in Jesus Christ as Lord and Savior and fully committing our lives to Him is the *first step* in an adult Christian's journey of salvation (cf. Rom 10:9).
- The Bible says that faith *alone* "is dead." After committing our lives to the Lord we are called to serve Him and do what He asks of us (cf. James 2:14, 17, 24; Rev 14:13; 19:8; 20:13).[2]
- The New Testament Scriptures point out the importance of being baptized into Jesus' family and, thus, inheriting our Lord's saving promise of eternal life in heaven (cf. John 3:1-5, 22; Titus 3:5; 1 Peter 3:18-21; Gal 3:27; Matt 28:19; Mark 16:16).[3]
- The New Testament teaches about the necessity of cooperating with God's free gift of grace each day *until the very end* of our life. The Bible says that those who do not persevere in their faith will not be "saved" (cf. Mark 13:13; Matt 10:22; Phil 2:12-13; Heb 3:14; 1 Cor 9:27; 10:12; 2 Tim 2:12; 1 Tim 1:18-19; Rom 11:22).
- The New Testament Bible talks about the importance of regularly confessing our sins and receiving God's forgiveness as the merits of Jesus' death and resurrection are applied to our post-baptismal sins (cf. John 20:21-23; Matt 9:1-8; Matt 16:18-19 and 2 Cor 5:10 for the Bible's instructions on how and to whom this confession of sins is to be made).[4]
- The New Testament Scriptures communicate to us Jesus' crucial command for Christians to regularly receive His Body and Blood in the Holy Eucharist and, thus, have the most intimate encounter with Christ possible here on this earth (cf. John 6:4, 53-54; Heb 10:23-31; Luke 22:19-20; 1 Cor 11:24-26).[5]

Alan Schreck writes about the *journey* of salvation:

"...The New Testament shows faith to be much more than an intellectual assent to the proposition that God exists or that Jesus Christ is Lord and Savior. This assent may be a first step, but it is not sufficient for salvation. Even evil spirits recognize and acknowledge Jesus' true identity. An unclean spirit cried out: 'I know who you are, the Holy One of God' (Mk 1:24). James declared, 'Even the demons believe — and shudder' (Jas 2:19)...

Many Christians today equate 'faith' with a 'decision for Christ' — a conscious, personal acceptance of Jesus Christ as the Lord and Savior of your life. This terminology is used mostly by evangelical Protestants, but Catholics agree that all mature Christians must make a conscious choice to accept Jesus Christ as their Lord and Savior and to commit themselves to follow him. Catholics make such a public recommitment every year when they renew their baptismal promises during the Easter liturgy...

It is also part of Catholic teaching to consider 'faith' as a *way of life* rather than as a major decision that happens once, twice, or a few times in one's life. Catholics realize the importance of the initial conversion and commitment to Christ, but they also emphasize the challenge of living out faith in Jesus Christ every day, by God's grace and with the guidance of the Holy Spirit."[6]

As I will point out in this chapter, the question "Are you saved?" (as understood by many evangelical Christians) does not speak accurately about the *journey* of salvation, in which we are required to cooperate with God's grace daily. The word "saved" can give the wrong impression that the journey or the process of salvation has already been completed (*e. g., the southern expression: "The dishes have been saved," or "Our money has been saved in the vault"*). [7] Our journey of salvation will be completed when we reach heaven. Only then can one say with 100% absolute assurance: "I am saved!"

Through His death and resurrection, Christ has *redeemed* us and *has made salvation possible* for all believers. *If* a person dies in the state of grace, *then* he will be saved. We all hope that we will be in a state of grace at death but we cannot forecast into the future. Remember the recent T. V. ministers who claimed that they were "saved" and then seriously strayed off of the path?

Some evangelical Christians confuse redemption *(a one moment event that happened when Jesus shed His Blood on Calvary)* [8] with salvation *(a life-long walk with Christ beginning at Baptism and ending when a person enters the kingdom of heaven).*

Was Judas "saved" when he left everything and became one of the twelve Apostles? He certainly accepted Jesus as his "Lord and Savior" when he joined the elite rank of the twelve. It appears that he did not, however, successfully cooperate with God's grace and, thus, faithfully complete the journey of salvation at the end of his life (cf. Acts 1:16-18).[9]

Writing to "saved" Christians in Corinth (cf. 1 Cor 1:1-3), St. Paul warns them, "Do you not know that the unjust will not inherit the kingdom of God? Do not be deceived; neither fornicators nor idolaters nor adulterers nor boy prostitutes nor sodomites nor thieves nor the greedy nor drunkards nor slanderers nor robbers will inherit the kingdom of God" (1 Cor 6:9-10). In other words, St. Paul is telling "saved" Christians that if they are engaged in activities such as these and don't repent and turn their lives around, they could very well lose their promise of everlasting life in heaven.

St. Paul says in Romans: "See, then, the kindness and severity of God: severity toward those who fell, but God's kindness to you, *provided you remain in his kindness; otherwise you too will be cut off*" (Rom 11:22).

St. Paul tells us in 1 Corinthians: "Therefore, whoever thinks he is standing secure should take care not to fall" (1 Cor 10:12). Here, again, we see the fact that "it's not over until it's over" when it comes to the journey of salvation.

Jesus speaks about the journey of faith in the Gospel of Mark: "...the one who perseveres *to the end* will be saved [Greek: *sozo*]" (Mark 13:13).

St. Paul writes to Timothy (a "saved" Christian): "I entrust this charge to you, Timothy, my child, in accordance with the prophetic words once spoken about you. Through them may you fight a good fight by having faith and a good conscience. *Some, by rejecting conscience, have made a shipwreck of their faith"* (1 Tim 1:18-19). We can see here that it is entirely possible for a Christian to seriously "backslide" in his faith journey and, thereby, make a "shipwreck" of his faith in Christ.

In a number of places in the New Testament we read about Baptism saving us. St. Paul writes to Titus about Baptism:"[Jesus] saved [Greek: *sozo*] us through the bath of rebirth…" (Titus 3:5).

St. Peter writes about being "saved" through the waters of Baptism: "This prefigured baptism, which saves [Greek: *sozo*] you now" (1 Pet 3:21).

Catholics are born the first time in the hospital and become children of their earthly parents. Catholics are "born again" and become children of God at the baptismal font.[10]

At Baptism our parents and godparents accepted Jesus on our behalf and promised God that they would form us spiritually so that we could come to know Jesus as we grew up and matured *(cf. Chapter 22 of this book to read about infant Baptism)*. Later on, at Confirmation, Catholics have the opportunity to stand up as young adults, in the midst of the faith community, and make a personal commitment to Christ ourselves *(cf. Chapter 21 of this book)*.

If you feel comfortable doing so and if you believe it with all your heart, please proclaim the following statement out loud: *"I accept Jesus Christ as my personal Lord and Savior and I ask Him to come into my heart and wash away all of my sins with the blood that He shed for me on Calvary."* According to many fundamentalists, you are now "saved." Did you do anything just now that you haven't done in the past? What many of us just said is, most likely, part of the *daily prayer* of *all* faithful Catholics. [11]

Faithful Catholics are just as "saved" as any Christian can be here on this earth. Unfortunately, some uninformed Catholics have left the Catholic Church because they (mistakenly) thought that another denomination could guarantee them that their salvation in heaven was 100% assured at death. In reality, there is no such absolute assurance here on earth. Catholic Christians have a *moral assurance* of salvation and trust totally in the Lord's promise of eternal life to be awarded to those found faithful at the very end of their lives (cf. Mark 13:13). Whether or not we will receive this heavenly gift from God, though, depends upon how we live out the remainder of our journey of salvation. [12]

Let's look at a visual picture of the Biblical understanding of the *journey* of salvation:[13]

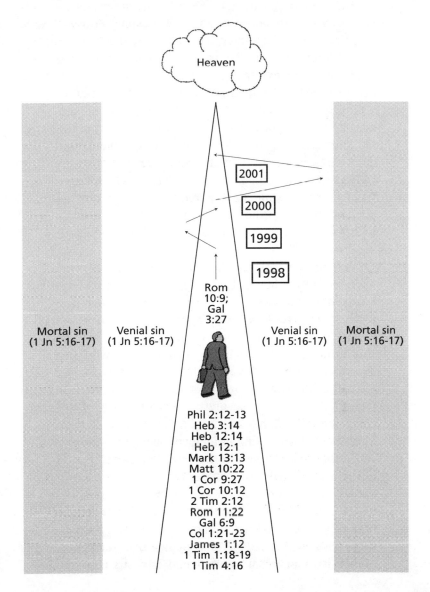

Catholic convert T. L. Frazier speaks about being "saved":

"All those truly saved wouldn't dream of missing Saturday evangelization, or 'witnessing' as we called it, lest the impression be given that one were back-sliding into apostasy. This may indicate one had never really been a Christian to begin with, despite all assurances given to the contrary at the altar-call that one was indeed forever saved. This is the idea that a Christian is 'once-saved-always-saved,' that one is eternally secure because one has received Christ by faith in an act of the will through sincerely praying a 'sinner's prayer.' According to this Fundamentalist dogma, no sin committed after getting 'saved,' no matter how heinous, will deny one access to heaven at death. Indeed, if one were truly saved, one would never commit such acts. A Christian might back-slide into sin, but he will ultimately repent. If he doesn't, he was never a Christian to begin with — even if he had been one's pastor or spiritual mentor all one's life.

Yet many 'born-again' Fundamentalists, people who have sincerely believed they were forever saved and had received solemn assurances of this effect from their pastor, have later been declared by the same pastor never to have been saved to begin with...! Really there is no way to distinguish between a 'backslidden' Christian and an absolute non-Christian in this sort of reasoning, even after the straying member returns to the fold. In fact, the highly personal and subjective nature of this concept of salvation leads most thoughtful Fundamentalists to decline passing judgement on whether the person sitting next to them in the pew, though perhaps an old friend, is really a 'Christian' or not. One never knows, that person may someday become a Catholic!

Nor is it even possible for one to be certain that he himself is actually saved. Not only is self-deception always possible, but people also change over the course of their lives and what a person may honestly and even fervently believe at one point may be doubted later on. A friend of mine who had been active in witnessing and daily Bible reading developed some personal problems in his life and gave up these practices. Lacking faith at that moment, he questioned whether he had really had genuine faith when he accepted Christ, and so was unable to decide whether he was backslidden or had ever been saved at all.

How ironic that a doctrine designed to give one eternal assurance can, during a difficult period of life when one especially needs his Christian Faith, leave one doubting whether he was ever a Christian to begin with! It's an assurance which assures the believer that the elect will assuredly go to heaven, but can't assure him that his 'born again' experience was authentic and thus that he's assuredly among the saved."[14]

The Bible reveals to us two different types of sins: "If anyone sees his brother sinning, if the sin is *not deadly*, he should pray to God and he will give him life... There is such a thing as a *deadly* sin about which I do not say that you should pray..." (cf. 1 John 5:16-17).

Sin

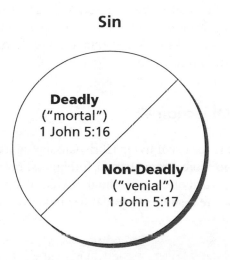

Deadly
("mortal")
1 John 5:16

Non-Deadly
("venial")
1 John 5:17

We can see here in Scripture the distinction between "deadly sin" (which the Church calls "mortal") and "non-deadly" (which the Church calls "venial.")[15] A deadly sin (if not repented from) "kills" a person's chances of going to heaven, while a non-deadly sin implies that reparation/atonement can be made for the sin in question.[16] In Rev 21:27 and Heb 12:14 we read that only the sinless and the holy can enter into heaven and, in 2 Cor 5:10, we read that we will *all* be held accountable for the sins that we commit in this life. (Refer to Chapter 11 of this book for a more in depth presentation on purgatory).

A Biblical answer that a Roman Catholic could give to the question "Have you been saved?" might be something like this:

- Yes, I *have been saved* when Jesus died on the cross for me 2,000 years ago on Calvary and, thus, redeemed all of humanity (cf. Acts 4:12; Eph 1:7).

- Yes, I *am being saved* as I strive, with the help of the Holy Spirit, to faithfully walk with Jesus Christ each and every day of my life (cf. Phil 2:12; Heb 3:14). My Baptism has configured me to Jesus Christ (cf. Rom 6:3-5; Gal 3:27).

- Yes, I *hope to be saved* when Jesus comes again at the end of time for the Final Judgement (cf. Matt 25:31-46; Rev 20:11-15). I pray that I persevere in my daily walk with the Lord and that I do not backslide unrepentantly into serious post-baptismal mortal sin (cf. 1 Cor 9:27; 1 Cor 10:12; 1 John 5:16-17; Mark 13:13).

Common Objection #2

"The Bible speaks of living Christians as 'saints': 'Now therefore ye are no more strangers and foreigners, but fellowcitizens with the saints, and of the household of God' (Eph 2:19). [17] Obviously, 'saints' are assured of eternal life in heaven with God."

A Catholic Response

In the Catholic Answers pamphlet *No "Assurance of Salvation"* we read:[18]

> "It is this kind of thinking that allows fundamentalists to conclude that the New Testament, when speaking of living people as saints, means not that they will *become* saints in heaven *if* they follow God's commandments (this is the way Catholics understand Paul to have written), but that they are already, right now, saints, just like the saints in heaven. They have no more chance of not being allowed into heaven than do heaven's present residents have of being thrown out...
>
> Catholics look at such verses as merely Paul's expectations for his disciples; fundamentalists look at them as his acknowledgment of their existing status. Ronald Knox, in *St. Paul's Gospel,* noted that there is no need 'to suppose that all these high-sounding phrases which St. Paul uses about the Church refer to a collection of Saints already made perfect. To be sure, he calls all Christian folk 'saints'; it is his way; he sees us not as we are but as we ought to be. These 'saints' had to be warned against fornication, against thieving, against bitter schisms; it is the Church we know." [p. 60][19]

What Did Jesus' Crucifixion and Resurrection Accomplish?

Fundamentalist Christian View:

In the Old Testament, the blood of animals was shed in Jewish Temple sacrifices to bring about reconciliation with God (cf. Lev 4). *("Substitutionary atonement" is the theological principle that, because of his sin, the sinner deserves death [cf. Gen 3.] Instead of the sinner himself dying, the sinner presents to God a substitute —*

an animal who is sacrificed and whose blood is shed in atonement for the sinner's personal transgressions.)

Also in the Old Testament, the faithful Israelites were "passed over" by God and no harm came to them (when the angel of death struck down all of the first-born in Egypt) if the doorposts of their homes were sprinkled with the blood of a male, unblemished lamb (cf. Exodus 12:1-13).

Blood was also sprinkled upon the faithful Israelites to ratify their life-giving covenant relationship with God (cf. Exodus 24:5-8).

For the Jew, blood, thus, meant (a) atonement with God, (b) protection from death, and (c) the bringing about of a new covenant with God.

Just as in the Old Testament, in the New Testament the shedding of the Blood of the Lamb of God — Jesus Christ (cf. John 1:29) has brought about (and continues to bring about) forgiveness and reconciliation with God the Father (cf. Heb 9:22).

The Christian faithful who have been spiritually "sprinkled" with the Blood of the unblemished Lamb of God, Jesus Christ (cf. 1 Pet 1:19), will be "passed over" on the Final Judgement Day (cf. Matt 25:31-46) and eternal death shall not come to them when Jesus returns to earth and strikes down the unfaithful who have turned their back on Him (cf. Rev 20:7-15; Rom 5:9).

Just as in the Old Testament, in the New Testament the Blood of Jesus shed on the cross ratifies our New Covenant (New Testament) relationship with God that was shattered by the sin of the first human beings (cf. Gen 3): "In Christ Jesus we who were far off [from the Father] have become near by the Blood of Christ" (Eph 2:13).

For the Christian, Jesus' Blood, thus, means (a) atonement with God, (b) protection from eternal death, and (c) the bringing about of a New Covenant with God.

Note that the type of branch used to sprinkle the blood of the Old Testament lamb (cf. Exodus 12:22) was the exact same branch used when Jesus, the New Testament Lamb (cf. 1 Cor 5:7; 1 Pet 1:18-19), was spiritually "sprinkling" His own Blood on all believers as He hung on the cross to bring about the redemption of all humanity (cf. John 19:29).

Catholic View

Same as above.

What Does Jesus' Crucifixion
and Resurrection Mean to Us as Christians?

Fundamentalist View

Once a person has accepted Jesus Christ as his "personal Lord and Savior" (cf. Romans 10:9), that person's past, present, and future sins are instantly "covered over" by the Blood of the Lamb of God — Jesus Christ (cf. 1 John 1:7; Heb 1:3). For the fundamentalist, Jesus' Blood shed on the cross is kind of like a "Teflon® coating" that covers them and causes their past, present and future sins not to "stick" to them (cf. Heb 10:17; Rom 4:8; Rev 7:14).[20] After praying a "sinner's prayer" and confessing faith in the Lord, they are "covered" with Jesus' righteousness — which they believe will "hide" their post-baptismal sins from God the Father on Judgement Day.

For all practical purposes, fundamentalists believe that they are immune from any and all personal responsibility and accountability for their sins and believe that they will pay no consequences for having committed them. After professing personal faith in Jesus as Lord and Savior, many fundamentalist Christians believe that they are, basically, on "cruise control" to heaven (provided they lead a reasonably holy life).

Because of the Blood of Jesus shed on the cross, fundamentalists believe that they will die totally cleansed from all their sins and, thus, will be totally fit to enter into heaven at the Final Judgement. Before the Final Judgement (which will take place at the end of time) some fundamentalists believe that the souls of the deceased are in a "state of sleep" (cf. 1 Thess 4:13-14) and, thus, are not capable of any type of interaction.[21] Holding this interpretation, it is easy to see why fundamentalists do not believe that the saints can intercede for us in heaven because, in their interpretation of 1 Thess 4:13-14, all deceased souls are in a state of sleep and cannot be communicated with. Fundamentalist theology, obviously, sees no need for purgatory, as it would only involve unnecessary additional purification.

For the fundamentalist there are two types of people: (a) those who have accepted Jesus Christ as their personal Lord and Savior and, as a result, have been totally cleansed of the guilt and consequences of all their past, present and future sins and are now simply waiting until the moment when they can enter directly into heaven at the Final Judgement and, (b) everyone else, who will be eternally damned to hell at the Final Judgement.

Catholic View

The Bible and the Catholic Church present the scriptural truth that salvation is not a one moment experience in a person's life but a *lifelong journey* in which we are called to cooperate daily with the grace of God until the very end of our lives (cf. Mark 13:13; Phil 2:12-13; Heb 3:14; 1 Cor 10:12; Rom 11:22, etc.). An adult Christian's journey of salvation *begins* when he accepts Jesus as his personal Lord and Savior (cf. Rom 10:9). Fundamentalists sometimes confuse justification *(a one moment experience when a person accepts Jesus as his personal Lord and Savior and is restored to a right relationship with God)* with salvation *(a lifelong journey of faithfulness to Jesus).*

Was St. Paul "saved?" He certainly accepted Jesus as his personal Lord and Savior. Why, then, in 1 Cor 9:27, was he so worried about not being able to be admitted into heaven? He was concerned that he might give in to sin and not faithfully complete his journey of faith throughout the remainder of his lifetime (cf. 1 Tim 1:15 where St. Paul calls himself "the foremost of sinners.")

Was the Apostle Judas Iscariot "saved?" He certainly accepted Jesus as his personal Lord and Savior in the beginning of his discipleship. It appears that he did not, however, remain faithful until the end — thus not successfully completing his journey of faith (cf. Luke 22:48). The story of the life of the Apostle Judas shows us that it is quite possible for a Christian to be lost — even after accepting Christ as his "personal Lord and Savior" at a certain point in his life. In the Gospel of Matthew, Jesus says: "Not everyone who says to me, 'Lord, Lord' will enter the Kingdom of heaven, but only the one who *does* the will of my Father in heaven..." (Matt 7:21). One can clearly see here the importance of remaining faithful to the journey of faith throughout one's life.

In 2 Cor 5:10, St. Paul (a "saved Christian") says to the "saved" Christians in Corinth that our sins in this life will have consequences in the next life and that we will *all* be held accountable for the sins that we commit (note that St. Paul doesn't say that the "saved" will not be held accountable for their sins.)[22]

Read about the importance of the Sacrament of Baptism in the journey of salvation (cf. John 3:1-5, 22; 1 Pet 3:18-21; Titus 3:5; Gal 3:27; Matt 28:19; Mark 16:16).

Read about the importance of the Sacrament of the Holy Eucharist in the journey of salvation (cf. John 6:4, 53-55; Heb 10:23-27; Luke 22:19-20).

Why did Jesus institute the Sacrament of Reconciliation (cf. John 20:21-23) if His Blood shed on the cross would be a "Teflon®" coating" that would automatically cover all of our sins and cause our past, present, and future sins not to "stick" to us?

In James 5:13-15 we read that Jesus forgives sins through the Sacrament of the Anointing of the Sick. Why would the early Christians celebrate this Sacrament if the Blood of Christ shed on the cross automatically forgave all past, present and future sins and gave Christians a "Teflon®" coating" that would not allow any sin to "stick" to them?

Jesus' Blood shed on the cross has allowed our sins to be *forgivable* (able to be forgiven after we personally appeal to the merits brought about by His crucifixion.) After sinning, the Christian must appeal to the "reservoir of forgiveness" that Jesus has brought about by the sprinkling of His Blood on Calvary.[23] Jesus' death on the cross has paid the debt for our sins but, after sinning, the Christian must avail himself of this "treasury" of forgiveness brought about by Jesus' crucifixion (cf. 1 John 1:8-10). It is in this light that we are to interpret Bible passages such as 1 John 1:7; Heb 1:3; Heb 10:17, and Rom 4:8. The Blood of Jesus shed on the cross has made the Sacraments of Reconciliation and Anointing of the Sick possible.

The Biblical doctrine of purgatory certainly does not make the statement that the Blood of Jesus was ineffectual in forgiving our sins. The Biblical doctrine of purgatory simply recognizes the Scriptural truth that (a) sin cannot enter heaven (cf. Rev 21:27), (b) we are all sinners (cf. 1 John 1:8-10), (c) that we will *all* be held accountable for the sins that we commit during our lifetime (cf. 2 Cor 5:10) and, (d) God is merciful (cf. Eph 2:4).

The Bible talks about the living making atonement for the sins of the deceased (cf. 2 Macc 12:38-46). This practice would make no sense at all if the deceased's soul were in heaven because he could not be aided by the prayers of those on earth (they have already reached the summit). This practice would make no sense at all if a deceased person's soul were in hell because those who go to hell will remain there forever (cf. Matt 25:41). If, however, a person's soul were in a temporary place of cleansing and was being held accountable (cf. 2 Cor 5:10) for its non-deadly (venial) sins (cf. 1 John 5:16-17) and was being readied to enter into heaven totally cleansed (cf. Rev 21:27), prayers from the living could indeed assist the deceased person's soul. What activity can a deceased person's soul have after the death of his body?: (Cf. Rev 6:9-10; Luke 16:19-31; Luke 9:28-36).

After he has first accepted Jesus as his personal Lord and Savior, the Blood of Jesus does not take away a Christian's accountability and his personal responsibility for his sins. What about the "saved" Christian who has "backslid" and sinned seriously and is not yet at the point of repentance when he tragically dies? Does the Blood of Jesus automatically forgive the sins of the person who was not yet at the point of being sorry for having committed them? Some fundamentalist denominations would say about backsliders: "the fallen away were fatally flawed from the first" *(meaning that they mistakenly thought that they were saved when, in fact, they really weren't.)* What kind of assurance is that if it is so easy to be drastically mistaken about your spiritual status? If, however one sees salvation as a lifelong journey, one who has backslid simply needs to sincerely repent and get himself back on track toward Jesus.

We read in 2 Samuel 12:13-18 about God forgiving David of the guilt of his sin but still making him pay the consequences for what he had done.

St. Paul says in Romans 8:1 "there is no condemnation for those who are in Christ Jesus." Purgatory is certainly *not* condemnation — it is purification and personal accountability for sins committed in this lifetime (cf. 2 Cor 5:10) before experiencing the *fullness of salvation* with God in heaven. Purgatory is, in effect, part of the *process* of being saved. (For a more in depth discussion about purgatory refer to Chapter 11 of this book.)

The heart of the salvation debate between Catholics and fundamentalists lies in the interpretation of Rev 21:27.[24] Catholics interpret Rev 21:27 to mean that the *total person* (internally *and* externally) must be free from sin in order to enter into heaven. A deceased sinner wearing an exterior "Teflon® shell" that he believes doesn't allow his sins to "stick" to them is not *internally* purified and he is, thus, not yet purified sufficiently to enter into heaven: "Who may go up the mountain of the Lord? Who can stand in his holy place? 'The clean of hand *and* pure of heart...'" (Psalm 24:3-4).

Catholics have a *moral assurance* of salvation in that we believe that God will be totally faithful to His promise of salvation to all of the faithful. The thing that we are not 100% sure about is the degree of our commitment to Christ at the moment of our death when we will be judged.

Consider the following Biblically-based timeline concerning events to occur in the afterlife:

10/3/98   6/16/2310[25]

Particular Judgement   **General Judgement**
at the moment of each person's death   at the end of time
(cf. Heb 9:27)   (cf. Matt 25)

3 Options: **2 Options:**
Totally fit = heaven immediately   *Totally fit* = heaven with the
Toally unfit = hell immediately   added glory of a glorified body.
God-oriented venial sinner = purgatory   *Toally unfit* = hell.
for a time until fully cleansed, then to
heaven immediately.

←———————— *Purgatory available for those souls* ————————→
requiring it before entering heaven.

It is not hard to see why fundamentalism is enjoying such wide-spread popularity. In adhering to selected passages from the Bible and ignoring others, it presents a very simplistic plan of salvation in which one is, effectively, on "cruise control" to heaven after he accepts Jesus Christ as his personal Lord and Savior (cf. Rom 10:9) (and leads a reasonably holy life). The fact is, if we look at the *whole* of the Scriptures, the *journey* of salvation is not nearly quite as simple as that. To quote the words of a well-known consumer advocate: "If something appears too good to be true — be careful — it probably is!"

Common Objection #3

"When the Holy Spirit descended upon the Apostles at Pentecost He bestowed upon them the gift of speaking in tongues (cf. Acts 2:4). After one is 'born again' and 'saved' he should possess the Holy Spirit's gift of speaking in tongues."

A Catholic Response

In Chapter 14 of his First Letter to the Corinthians St. Paul is, apparently, addressing a situation in the Christian community in Corinth in which some Christians were looking down on other Christians because they did not possess the gift of tongues. St. Paul puts the gift of tongues in its proper perspective: "Whoever speaks in a tongue builds himself up, but whoever prophesies builds up the church" (1 Cor 14:4); "...I would rather speak five words with my mind so as to instruct others also, than ten thousand words in a tongue" (1 Cor 14:19); "...tongues are a sign not for those who believe but for unbelievers, whereas prophecy is not for unbelievers but for those who believe" (1 Cor 14:22). Just because a Christian does not posses the particular gift of speaking in tongues does *not* mean that he is not filled with the Holy Spirit. The fact is that God may have given him many other spiritual gifts that the person who speaks in tongues doesn't have.

In Chapter 12 of his First Letter to the Corinthians St. Paul lists some of the gifts of the Holy Spirit: wisdom, the expression of knowledge, faith, healing, mighty deeds, prophecy, discernment, tongues, interpretation of tongues (cf. 1 Cor 12:4-10). St. Paul says that "To each individual the manifestation of the Spirit is given for some benefit" (1 Cor 12:7). In other words, the Holy Spirit has bestowed upon each individual Christian a unique combination of gifts that he is to use to build God's kingdom. The gift of tongues is *one* of the gifts of the Holy Spirit but, according to St. Paul, there are a *plethora* of other manifestations of the Spirit in the lives of faithful Christians.

May all Christians use our God-given gifts to compliment one another as we strive to build up the Body of Christ in unity!

Endnotes

42 Cf. *Mk* 16:16; *Jn* 3:36; 6:40 *et al.*
43 *Dei Filius* 3: DS 3012; cf. *Mt* 10:22; 24:13 and *Heb* 11:6; Council of Trent: DS 1532.
44 *1 Tim* 1:18-19.
45 Cf. *Mk* 9:24; *Lk* 17:5; 22:32.
46 *Gal* 5:6; *Rom* 15:13; cf. *Jas* 2:14-26.
48 Cf. Council of Trent (1547): DS 1605; DS 1606.
51 Cf. Council of Trent (1547): DS 1604.
1 "Redemption" can be defined as "to return to a person a possession that once belonged to him." Consider this simple illustration of redemption: Suppose that Tom made some bad financial decisions and was in need of some quick cash to pay his bills. To get the necessary money he takes his great grandfather's pocket watch and goes down to the pawn shop and pawns it for $50.00. Suppose that Tom's best friend, Steve, heard about what Tom had done and went to the pawn shop and paid the necessary price to re-gain *(redeem)* Tom's heirloom watch. Steve then leaves the pawn shop and goes over to Tom's house and returns to him, free of charge, his valuable possession. This is exactly what Jesus did on the cross for us: Jesus gave back to humanity the possession of eternal life that was forfeited by our first parents in the Garden of Eden (cf. Gen 3). The price of re-obtaining eternal life for humanity was His very life.

2 Cf. Chapter 4 of this book to read about the importance of an *alive* faith that is characterized by loving works of obedience to God (cf. Matt 25).

3 Cf. Chapter 21 of this book.

4 Cf. Chapter 18 of this book.

5 Cf. Chapter 5 of this book.

6 Alan Schreck, *Catholic and Christian*, (Ann Arbor, Michigan: Servant Books, 1984), pp. 22-23.

7 For the benefit of non-Southern readers, this saying means that the dishes are through being used and have been packed away safely in the kitchen cabinets.

8 Since the Mass is the re-presenting of Jesus' one sacrifice on the cross (cf. Chapter 6 of this book), the *Catechism of the Catholic Church* teaches: "Through the liturgy Christ, our redeemer and high priest, continues the work of our redemption in, with, and through his Church" (#1069).

9 The author of the Book of Hebrews speaks about the very real possibility of "backsliding" after being "saved": "For it is impossible in the case of those who have once been enlightened and tasted the heavenly gift...*and then have fallen away*, to bring them back to repentance again..." (Heb 6:4-6). Cf. also 2 Pet 3:17.

10 Matthew, Mark and Luke inform us that, at the very beginning of His public ministry, Jesus Himself is baptized in water and, afterwards, the Holy Spirit descends upon Him. In John's Gospel, when Nicodemus asks Jesus how a person could be "born again" once he is already a grown adult, Jesus replies "[through] *water* and Spirit" (a clear reference to the waters of Baptism.) Note that, after teaching about the importance of Baptism in John 3:1-5, Jesus goes out and administers Baptism to others Himself. (Cf. John 3:1-5, 22; cf. also Titus 3:5). Cf. Chapter 22 of this book to read about the early Church Fathers teaching about being "born again" in the waters of Baptism.

11 "This mystery [of faith], then, requires that the faithful believe in it, that they celebrate it, and that they *live from it in a vital and personal relationship with the living and true God.*" (*Catechism of the Catholic Church*, #2558).

[12] Can the captain of a cruise ship give each passenger on his boat a 100% absolute assurance of making it safe to their planned destination? Of course not. The Titanic didn't make it to its final destination, but many better-navigated ships, however, do. It depends upon the condition of the boat at the end of the journey as to whether or not it will arrive at its planned destination. The same thing holds true with Christians.

[13] In this diagram I have tried to graphically illustrate a Christian engaged in the *journey* toward heaven (which begins at Baptism when he is "clothed" with the saving merits of the death and resurrection of Jesus Christ — cf. Gal 3:27.) As he travels toward the Lord, most Christians will veer off of the road to heaven in minor ways (venial sins) and, sometimes, in major ways (mortal sins.) Jesus teaches us in verses such as Matt 10:22 that that we must be found faithful to Christ *at the end* of our journey in order to experience the fullness of salvation in heaven.

[14] Patrick Madrid (editor), *Surprised by Truth*, (San Diego, CA: Basilica Press, 1994), pp. 189-190.

[15] Cf. *Catechism of the Catholic Church*, #1854-1864.

[16] "For a sin to be mortal, three conditions must together be met: 'Mortal sin is sin whose object is grave matter and which is also committed with full knowledge and deliberate consent.'" *Catechism of the Catholic Church*, #1857.

[17] *King James Bible*, (Nashville, TN: Holman Bible Publishers, 1979), p. 127.

[18] *No "Assurance of Salvation" pamphlet*, (San Diego, CA: Catholic Answers)

[19] Suppose that a football coach had the habit of calling all of the players on his team "champ." Does that necessarily mean that they all would be members of the championship team that year? No, the coach is simply calling them by a name that invites them to live up to the wonderful possibility that lies before them. *If* the players on the football team practice hard and persist in their discipline, *then* they have the very good possibility of becoming the league champions in the future.

[20] "Teflon" is a registered trademark of E. I. Du Pont de Nemours and Company.

21 Protestant Christians differ *widely* in their teachings as to the disposition of a Christian's soul after the death of his body.

22 In 1 Corinthians St. Paul tells the "saved" Christians: "Do you not know that the unjust will not inherit the kingdom of God? Do not be deceived; neither fornicators...nor adulterers...nor thieves nor the greedy nor drunkards...will inherit the kingdom of God" (1 Cor 6:9-10).

23 The Sacraments are simply a means of applying the healing and life-giving merits of the death and resurrection of Christ to the souls of individual Christians throughout their lifetime.

24 "...nothing unclean will enter [heaven]..." (Rev 21:27).

25 Obviously, this date for the return of Christ is given for illustration purposes only for "that day and hour [when the world will end] no one knows, neither the angels of heaven, nor the Son, but the Father alone" (Matt 24:36).

Chapter 11

The Biblical Reality
of Purgatory

What Does the Catholic Church Teach?

"All who die in God's grace and friendship, but still imperfectly purified, are indeed assured of their eternal salvation; but after death they undergo purification, so as to achieve the holiness necessary to enter the joy of heaven... The Church gives the name *Purgatory* to this final purification of the elect, which is entirely different from the punishment of the damned...[604] The tradition of the Church, by reference to certain texts of Scripture, speaks of a cleansing fire.[605]

> As for certain lesser faults, we must believe that, before the Final Judgement, there is a purifying fire. He who is truth says that whoever utters blasphemy against the Holy Spirit will be pardoned neither in this age *nor in the age to come*. From this sentence we understand that certain offenses can be forgiven in this age, but certain others in the age to come.[606]

This teaching is also based on the practice of prayer for the dead, already mentioned in Sacred Scripture: 'Therefore [Judas Maccabeus] made atonement for the dead, that they might be delivered from their sin.'[607] From the beginning the Church has honored the memory of the dead and offered prayers in suffrage for them, above all the Eucharistic sacrifice, so that, thus purified, they may attain the beatific vision of God.[608] The Church also commends almsgiving, indulgences, and works of penance undertaken on behalf of the dead:

> Let us help and commemorate them. If Job's sons were purified by their father's sacrifice, why would we doubt that our offerings for the dead bring them some consolation? Let us not hesitate to help those who have died and to offer our prayers for them."[609]

(*Catechism of the Catholic Church*, #1030–1032.)

Common Objection #1

"The word 'purgatory' doesn't even appear in the Bible. It is a Catholic invention started so that the Church could make money off of people offering Masses for their deceased loved ones."

A Catholic Response

A common Protestant understanding of justification holds that nobody is ever really totally cleansed from sin. Rather, the Christian simply puts on the outer "cloak" of Jesus' righteousness — and thus enters into heaven at his death externally spotless. Since, in Protestant theology, Jesus' blood does not really cleanse our *entire being* but merely *covers* us so that we will be presentable to God the Father, most Protestants hold that there is no need to be purged from personal post-baptismal sin — since Christ has accomplished all purging from sin upon the cross and has "coated" His disciples with His own righteousness.

On the other hand, the Catholic (and the Biblical) understanding of justification holds that Baptism into Christ cleanses the *entire person*, internally *and* externally, from all of the sins that he has at that present moment (cf. Acts 2:38) and makes him a "new creation" (cf. 2 Cor 5:17). Baptism into Christ makes us adopted sons and daughters of God and, therefore, adopted brothers and sisters of Jesus Christ (cf. 1 John 3:1-3; Rom 8:14-17). After being "clothed with Christ" in the waters of Baptism (cf. Gal 3:27-29), Christians become full-fledged members of God's family.

Consider the following analogy about the experience of being a member of a human family: After our birth into our human family we receive our family name and, when we are old enough, are given free will by our parents to go out and "play" in the neighborhood. In our adventures at the neighborhood playground we often fall down and "muddy" ourselves and, thus, have to return home daily for a good bath. After a thorough scrubbing by our parents, the beloved child is, once again, a sweet-smelling member of his family. If a muddy, sweaty child were to come into his parent's home and simply slip on some clean clothes and go and sit at the supper table, his parent's noses would instantly detect the need for a good scrubbing and would quickly usher him off to the bathroom so that he could get properly cleaned up.

In a similar manner, after our baptismal birth into our heavenly family (cf. John 3:1-5, 22), our heavenly Father (God) gives us the free will to go out into the "playground" of the world. Just as a child in a human family often falls down and "muddies" himself in his adventures at the neighborhood playground, we often "muddy" ourselves spiritually and we commit sins. Just as we human beings have to cleanse ourselves bodily on a wash-as-we-go basis throughout our life, Catholic Christians cleanse ourselves spiritually/Sacramentally on a wash-as-we-go basis in the Blood of the risen Jesus Christ.

Simply put, the Catholic doctrine of "purgatory" can be defined as the process of the application of the saving merits of Jesus' death and resurrection to the soul of a deceased Christian who has died with non-deadly (cf. 1 John 5:16-17) post-baptismal sins on his soul. After this process of spiritual cleansing/purging the Christian's soul is, thus, prepared for total union with our all-holy God in heaven. The Sacraments, simply understood, are spiritual "baths" in the blood of the risen Christ that nourish and restore our soul to its original baptismal purity and allows us to be, once again, "sweet-smelling" members (internally *and* externally) of our heavenly family.

The *word* "purgatory" does not appear in the Bible, as such, but the *reality* of purgatory is solidly rooted in Scripture. The Church simply gave a name to the Biblical reality. To use an analogy: the reality of Haley's comet existed for a long time before an astronomer gave it a name in order to identify the existing reality. Other words that do not appear in the Bible are the words: "Bible," "Trinity," and "Incarnation." The realities of these things, however, are clearly contained in the Scriptures.

Consider these Scripture passages that, when pieced together, point to the reality of and the need for a "purgatory":

- For a soul to enter into heaven, the New Testament teaches that it must be totally spiritually cleansed and holy — both internally *and* externally:
  - "...nothing unclean will enter [heaven]..." (Rev 21:27).
  - "Blessed are the clean of heart, for they will see God" (Matt 5:8).
  - "Strive...for that holiness without which no one will see the Lord" (Heb 12:14).
  - "...be perfect, just as your heavenly Father is perfect" (Matt 5:48).

- The Bible teaches that there are two different types of sin: "If anyone sees his brother sinning, if the sin is *not deadly*, he should pray to God and he will give him life. This is only for those whose sin is *not deadly*. There is such a thing as a *deadly* sin, about which I do not say that you should pray. All wrongdoing is sin, but there is sin that is *not deadly*." (1 John 5:16-17) One can plainly see here that the Scriptures speak about two distinct kinds of sin, classified according to their severity and their consequences: (a) **deadly** *(which the Catholic Church refers to as "mortal") and* (b) **non-deadly** *(which the Catholic Church refers to as "venial").*[1] A "deadly" (mortal) sin does just what its name implies — if not repented from, it "kills" a person's chances of entering into heaven because the sinner has freely chosen, by his own actions, to totally turn his back on God.[2] A "non-deadly" (venial) sin does also what its name implies — a non-deadly (venial) sin is much less severe than a mortal sin and, thus, will not "kill" a person's chances of salvation. However, a venial sin still represents a rejection of God's Will to a lesser degree.

- In the Gospel of Matthew, Jesus speaks about the deadly (mortal) sin of sinning against the Holy Spirit: "And whoever speaks a word against the Son of Man will be forgiven; but whoever speaks against the Holy Spirit will not be forgiven, either in this age *or in the age to come*" (Matt 12:32). Why would Jesus, out of the blue, even bother to mention the possibility of forgiveness *in the age to come* if it were not possible for some less serious non-deadly (venial) sins? It appears that, from looking at this passage, that a Christian's conversion to Jesus does not cease at the death of his body.

- Including himself in his statement, St. Paul writes to the "saved" Christian community in Corinth (cf. 2 Cor 1:1-2): "For we must *all* appear before the judgement seat of Christ, so that each one may receive recompense, according to what he did in the body, whether good or evil" (2 Cor 5:10). What about the sincere God-oriented Christian who died and was not yet at the point of being able to forgive a person who had offended him in some grievous way? What recompense would this sincere Christian get from God for dying in the sin of unforgiveness?[3] According to Rev 21:27 and Heb 12:14 that person would not yet be ready to enter immediately into heaven. Would a merciful God condemn this God-oriented sinner to eternal punishment in hell? The Catholic Church, along with the early Church Fathers, would say "No" but recognizes that this person would not yet be spiritually ready to enter directly into heaven.

- Scripture speaks a number of times about the practice of the living praying for the deceased. In the New Testament, St. Paul prays for the soul of the deceased Onesiphorus: "May the Lord grant [Onesiphorus] to find mercy from the Lord..." (2 Tim 1:18). In the Old Testament we read: "...Turning in supplication, they prayed that the sinful deed[4] might be fully blotted out... Thus [Judas Maccabeus] made atonement for the dead that they might be freed from this sin" (2 Macc 12:38-46).[5] The word atonement can be broken down: at-one-ment (meaning that the prayer was aimed at helping to make the deceased sinner one with God again.) This practice of praying for the dead would make no sense at all if the person's soul were in heaven *(his soul would have reached its ultimate fulfillment)*. This practice would also make no sense at all if the person's soul were in hell *(St. Paul says in 2 Thess 1:9 that hell is eternal and that, once a soul enters, there is no getting out).* Praying for the dead would only make sense if a person died with non-deadly (venial) sins still left on his soul and was going through a temporary transitional period of purification before entering into heaven totally cleansed (cf. Rev 21:27). Numerous early Christian writings and ancient liturgies speak about the common practice of prayer for the dead *(refer to the end of this chapter).* Graffiti in the Christian catacombs graphically show the living faithful praying for their departed loved ones.[6] In the Book of Sirach we read: "Be generous to all the living, and withhold not your kindness from the dead" (Sirach 7:33).[7]

- After a person's body dies, his soul is in one of three places: (a) at death a soul goes to heaven if it is completely fit for heaven *(if it is completely sinless and totally God-oriented).* (b) at death a soul goes to hell if it is completely unfit for heaven *(if it is full of serious mortal sin and totally self-oriented).* (c) from Biblical evidence it appears that, at death, our merciful God allows a soul to go to a temporary place of cleansing ("purgatory") if that soul is basically God-oriented but still has some traces of venial sinfulness still left on the soul.[8] If a soul is in purgatory and is being readied for heaven, that soul can benefit from the prayers of the living on earth (cf. 2 Macc 12:38-46).

- St. Paul writes to Christians in Corinth: "If anyone builds [on the foundation of Christ] with gold, silver, precious stone, wood, hay, or straw, the work of each will come to light, for the Day will disclose it. It will be revealed with fire, and the fire [itself] will test the quality of each one's work. If the work stands that someone built upon the foundation, that person will receive a wage. But if someone's work is burned up, that one will suffer loss; the person will be saved, but only as through fire" (1 Cor 3:10-15). Patrick Madrid writes about this important passage from St. Paul:

> "This passage, more than any other in Scripture with the exception of 2 Maccabees 12, shows clearly the essential elements of the doctrine of purgatory. Notice several key aspects of St. Paul's teaching here.
> First, this process of disclosure takes place after death, at the moment the man stands before God and is

judged for his life's contents — 'It is appointed unto a man once to die, and then the judgement' (Heb 9:27).

Second, this judgement involves a purification that purges away all the dross that clings to his soul, what St. Paul describes as 'wood, hay, and straw.' These materials are burned away in this judgement. Conversely, that man's good works — 'gold, silver, and precious stones' — are refined and retained.

Third, this process of purification hurts; it involves suffering: 'If any man's work is burned up, he will suffer loss.' This means that this process described here is temporary, since the man in question is destined for heaven: 'He himself will be saved, but only as passing through fire.' This also indicates that this process of purification, 'as through fire,' takes place before that man enters heaven.

All this points to the fact that God, in His mercy, has prepared a way for those who die in the state of grace (cf. Rom 11:22) and friendship with Him to have the imperfections and temporal punishments due to sin purged away by the fire of His love before they enter into heavenly glory."[9]

Consider this visual diagram of the Biblical reality of purgatory:

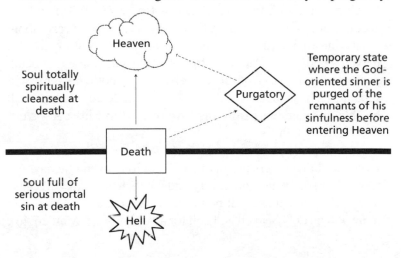

- Following the same theme of spiritual cleansing, in the Gospel of Mark, Jesus speaks about the necessary purification required of His followers: "Everyone will be salted with fire" (Mark 9:49). In the Psalms we read, "O Lord, our God, you answered them; you were a forgiving God, though you punished their offenses" (Psalm 99:8). This Scripture passage would certainly be consistent with the doctrine of purgatory, where Jesus promises salvation to the faithful but first requires them to let go of the remnants of their personal un-holiness before they see Him face-to-face.

- Between our *particular judgement*, which occurs at the moment of each person's death (cf. Heb 9:27) and the *General Judgement*, when Jesus comes again in glory at the end of the world and judges all people (cf. Matt 25:31-46), there is a period of time in which souls have the opportunity to be purified of their sinfulness so that they can enter into heaven totally cleansed (cf. Rev 21:27).[10]

- Spiritual contact with our loved ones does not cease at death (cf. 2 Macc 12:38-46). In Rev 6:9-10 we read about the martyrs in heaven (the saints) who cry out to God and ask Him to act on their behalf. In Rev. 8:3-4 we read about the saints in heaven constantly offering prayers to God (no doubt interceding with Him on behalf of others as they did so often on earth.)[11] Cf. the Parable of the rich man and Lazarus (Luke 16:19-31) and the account of Jesus' Transfiguration (Matt 17:1-8) and read about what kind of interaction a soul can have after the death of a person's body.[12] St. Paul tells the Christians in Rome that death does not separate us from Jesus or from one another: "What will separate us from the love of Christ? ...neither death, nor life...will be able to separate us from the love of God in Christ Jesus our Lord" (Rom 8:35-39).

- Every soul that enters purgatory will get to heaven one day. After the last soul leaves purgatory and enters heaven, it will cease to exist because there will be no more purpose for it. After that there will be only heaven and hell for all eternity (cf. Matt 26:46).

- Purgatory is a place of *hope*! In purgatory, our merciful God gives the God-oriented sinner the opportunity to enter heaven — even if he didn't die a perfect saint.

One can see, after putting all of these Scripture passages together, the reality of and the need for a transitional place of purification (i.e., "purgatory.")

One day I was teaching an 11th grade Confirmation class and I asked them, after their Confirmation, if they were planning to become more actively involved in the practice of their Catholic faith. One girl raised her hand and she said, "After Confirmation I think I want to join 'XYZ' church!" After I picked my jaw up off the floor I asked her why she wanted to do that. She said, "Because they don't believe in purgatory and I would much rather go straight to heaven when I die." I thought for a while and I responded to her, "Does denying a reality cause that reality to cease to exist? If I say that I don't believe that there is an Atlantic Ocean, does that make it evaporate?" Many Protestant churches deny the reality of purgatory but, in doing so, they are simply choosing to ignore an important truth rooted in the Scriptures. Not acknowledging a truth does not cause that truth to change.

Common Objection #2

"The merits of Jesus' death and resurrection have brought about the total remission of sin. Purgatory, therefore, is simply unnecessary."

A Catholic Response

Alan Schreck, in his book *Catholic and Christian* answers this often-heard objection:

"[A]ll sin is totally forgiven and removed through the passion, death, and resurrection of Jesus Christ. Catholic Christians understand purgatory as a way that this salvation in Jesus actually 'happens' or is applied to individual persons. If a person dies in some bondage to sin, or has been crippled by sin's effects, this sin and its effects must be removed, forgiven, and purged before the person sees God face-to-face. Why? Because of God's holiness. Sin and God are diametrically opposed. God is so pure, so holy, that nothing impure or sinful can enter into his presence (see Rv 21:27). Sin is burned away by God's holiness, by his anger against sin, and by his love of the repentant sinner, "for our God is a consuming fire" (Heb 12:29)...

The prophet Isaiah had a vision of God upon a throne with the angels surrounding him crying, 'Holy, holy, holy, is the Lord of hosts' (Is 6:1-3). Isaiah's immediate response was: 'Woe is me! For I am a man of unclean lips...yet my eyes have seen...the Lord of hosts!' (Is 6:5). But the Lord sent an angel to purify Isaiah's lips with a burning coal from the altar of God. 'And he touched my mouth and said, 'Behold, this has touched your lips; your guilt is taken away and your sins forgiven' (Is 6:7). Only then was Isaiah able to speak the Word of God to the people."[13]

Patrick Madrid writes about purgatory:

"Purgatory actually has nothing whatsoever to do with salvation. It is a temporary phase of purification that only the saved can go through... [Purgatory] has to do with cleansing the saved and preparing them for the eternal joys of heaven. Purgatory deals with the temporal effects due to sin; it does not deal with the eternal penalties merited by sin. Only Christ, through His death on the Cross, is capable of eradicating the eternal penalty due to sin. However, there are numerous effects of our sins that remain.

Christ's death on the cross did not eliminate the effects of sin in the temporal order. For example, two central consequences of the Original Sin (cf. Gen 2:15-17; 3:1-19) (i.e., the 'temporal punishments due to sin') are sickness and death. Now, when Christ died on the cross,

He redeemed us from the eternal penalty due to that sin (as well as all of our personal, actual sins), but He did not thereby eliminate the temporal effects that were caused by that sin: primarily sickness and death. The temporal effects due to sin extend, sadly, far beyond just physical illness and death (In 1 Corinthians 11:27-32 Paul mentions that certain sins have lethal side effects.) They include the spiritual impurities and weaknesses that cling to the soul."[14]

Common Objection #3

"The doctrine of purgatory, in effect, is a 'Catholic license to sin.' It is a safety net which allows a Catholic to live any way that he wants to and still make it to heaven one day."

A Catholic Response

This has never been the teaching or the understanding of the Catholic Church concerning the doctrine of purgatory and any Catholic who believes this may very well have an eternal disappointment coming to him. In the words of Jesus, "How narrow the gate and constricted the road that leads to life. And those who find it are few" (Matt 7:13-14). Purgatory is for the sincere Christian who has striven, to the very best of his ability, to walk the constricted road and to enter the narrow gate but fell short of spiritual perfection. In God's tremendous mercy, through the merits of the death and resurrection of His Son, He cleanses and prepares them spiritually before they enter eternal life with Him in heaven.

Did the Early Christians Believe That Earthly Prayer Benefited the Souls of the Faithful Departed and, Therefore, Implicitly Believe in the Existence of a Transitional Place of Spiritual Purification After Death (i.e., "Purgatory")?

- "The citizen of a prominent city, I erected this while I lived, that I might have a resting place for my body. Abercius is my name, a disciple of the chaste shepherd who feeds his sheep on the mountains and in the fields, who has great eyes surveying everywhere, who taught me the faithful writings of life. Standing by, I, Abercius, ordered this to be inscribed; truly I was in my seventy-second year. May everyone who is in accord with this and who understands it pray for Abercius." Abercius in his *Epitaph* (circa 180 A.D.)[15]

- "We offer sacrifices for the dead on their birthday anniversaries." Tertullian in his *The Crown* (circa 211 A.D.)[16]

- "A woman, after the death of her husband...prays for his soul and asks that he may, while waiting, find rest; and that he may share in the first resurrection. And each year, on the anniversary of his death, she offers the sacrifice." Tertullian in his *Monogamy* (circa 213 A.D.)[17]

- "But also, when God will judge the just, it is likewise in fire that he will try them. At that time, they whose sins are uppermost, either because of their gravity or their number, will be drawn together by the fire and will be burned. Those, however, who have been imbued with full justice and maturity of virtue, will not feel that fire; for they have something of God in them which will repel and turn back the strength of the flame." Lactantius in his *The Divine Institutions* (circa 307 A.D.)[18]

- "I pray you, O light of the dying, that mother may rest well." *Epitaph of Pectorius* (circa 350 A.D.)[19]

- "If a soul departs from this world with sins, what does it profit it to be remembered in prayer? Well, if a king were to banish certain persons who had offended him, and those intervening for them were to plait a crown and offer it to him on behalf of the ones being punished, would he not grant a remission of their penalties? In the same way we too offer prayers to Him for those who have fallen asleep, though they be sinners. We do not plait a crown, but offer up Christ who has been sacrificed for our sins; and we thereby propitiate the benevolent God for them as well as for ourselves." St. Cyril of Jerusalem in his *Catechetical Lectures* (circa 350 A.D.)[20]

- "...Do not bury me with perfumes. Give them not to me, but to God. Me, conceived in sorrows, bury with lamentations, and instead of perfumes assist me with your prayers; for the dead are benefited by the prayers of living Saints." St. Ephrem (d. 373 A.D.)[21]

- "We commemorate the Holy Fathers, and Bishops, and all who have fallen asleep from amongst us, believing that the supplications which we present will be of great assistance to their souls, while the holy and tremendous Sacrifice is offered up... So we, in offering up a crown of prayers in behalf of those who have fallen asleep, will obtain for them forgiveness through the merits of Christ." St. Cyril of Jerusalem (d. 386 A.D.)[22]

- Upon the death of the Emperor Theodosius, St. Ambrose prays: "Give perfect rest to Thy servant Theodosius, that rest which Thou hast prepared for Thy Saints. May his soul return thither whence it descended, where it cannot feel the sting of death... I loved him and therefore will I follow him, even unto the land of the living. Nor will I leave him until, by tears and prayers, I shall lead him...unto the holy mountain of the Lord..." St. Ambrose (d. 397 A.D.)[23]

- "I therefore, O God of my heart, do now beseech Thee for the sins of my mother. Hear me through the medicine of the wounds that hung upon the wood... May she, then, be in peace with her husband... And inspire, my Lord,... Thy servants, my brethren, whom with voice and heart and pen I serve, that as many as shall read these words may remember at Thy altar, Monica, Thy servant..." St. Augustine in his *Confessions* (circa 400 A.D.)[24]

- "Let us pray also for the repose of the souls of the departed servants of God and for the forgiveness of their every transgression, deliberate and indeliberate..." The Liturgy of St. John Chrysostom (d. 407 A.D.)[25]

- "It was not without good reason *ordained by the Apostles* that mention should be made of the dead in the tremendous mysteries, because they knew well that they would receive great benefit from it." St. John Chrysostom (d. 407 A.D.)[26]

Endnotes

[604] Cf. Council of Florence (1439): DS 1304; Council of Trent (1563): DS 1820; (1547): 1580; see also Benedict XII, *Benedictus Deus* (1336): DS 1000.

[605] Cf. *1 Cor* 3:15; *1 Pet* 1:7.

[606] St. Gregory the Great, *Dial.* 4, 39: PL 77, 396; cf. *Mt* 12:31.

[607] *2 Macc* 12:46.

[608] Cf. Council of Lyons II (1274): DS 856.

[609] St. John Chrysostom, *Hom. in 1 Cor.* 41, 5: PG 61, 361; cf. *Job* 1:5.

[1] Cf. *Catechism of the Catholic Church*, #1854.

[2] St. Paul writes to the "saved" Christian community in Corinth (cf. 1 Cor 1:1-3): "Do not be deceived; neither fornicators nor idolaters nor adulterers nor boy prostitutes nor sodomites nor thieves nor drunkards nor slanderers nor robbers will inherit the kingdom of God" (1 Cor 6:9-10). To say that people who commit these types of sins "will not inherit the kingdom of God" clearly points to the fact that they are among the "deadly" (mortal) sins alluded to in 1 John 5:16-17. Note that Webster's Dictionary defines "fornication" as "human sexual intercourse other than between a man and his wife." "Fornication," therefore, would include the acts of pre-marital sex, extra-marital sex, homosexual sex, incest, etc. These acts, according to Scripture, are mortally sinful and, unless repented of, could very well cause the damnation of a person's soul.

[3] In the Gospel of Matthew, Jesus concludes His parable about the unforgiving servant: "...Then in anger his master handed him over to the torturers until he should pay back the whole debt. So will my heavenly Father do to you unless each of you forgives his brother from his heart" (Matt 18:34-35). From Jesus' words it is obvious that a person who dies in unforgiveness is not ready to enter instantly into the kingdom of heaven.

4   Some of the deceased Jewish soldiers (who were apparently otherwise faithful in the practice of their faith) died while wearing jewelry that was associated with pagan gods.

5   Note that nowhere in the New Testament does Jesus condemn or even criticize the prevailing Jewish practice of praying for the souls of the dead. If the Jews were wrong on such a crucial theological matter such as this, our Lord certainly would have immediately set them straight.

6   Note that, in 2 Macc 12:43, money is collected to send to the Jewish Temple to have religious services offered for the souls of the dead who died in non-deadly (venial) sin. We can see how Catholics offering Masses for the souls of the deceased parallels this ancient practice documented in Scripture.

    Albert Nevins writes: "Just as St. Paul added his sufferings (Col 1:24) to the sufferings of Christ for the sake of the Church, so we too can add our sufferings and prayers for the good of its members." Cf. Albert Nevins, M.M., *Answering A Fundamentalist*, (Huntington, IN: Our Sunday Visitor, Inc., 1990), pp. 91-92.

7   Catholic convert David Currie writes: "Although the exact meaning of 1 Corinthians 15:29 is hotly debated, one fact is quite clear. Living Christians can do something to benefit those souls already dead: 'Now if there is no resurrection, what will those do who are baptized for the dead? If the dead are not raised at all, why are people baptized for them?' This verse makes absolutely no sense within the Evangelical concept of heaven and hell. Without purgatory, what could possibly be gained by doing anything for the dead? Their destiny is unalterable. The uninterrupted teaching of the Church has been that our prayers do benefit dead Christians." David B. Currie, *Born Fundamentalist Born Again Catholic*, (San Francisco, CA: Ignatius Press, 1996), p. 133.

8   Cf. 1 Pet 3:18-19 and note that there exists a place of waiting for the fullness of salvation to come about.

9   Patrick Madrid, *Any Friend of God is a Friend of Mine*, (San Diego, CA: Basilica Press, 1996), pp. 68-70.

10   Obviously, the deceased are no longer on "calendar time" as are the living. The time frame that I am speaking about is the

time between a particular person's death and the Second Coming of Christ at the end of the world.

11 Cf. Rom 10:1, Col 1:9-11.

12 James Cardinal Gibbons writes, "If, then, it is profitable for you to pray for your brother in the flesh, why should it be useless for you to pray for him out of the flesh? For while he was living you prayed not for his body, but for his soul." Cf. James Cardinal Gibbons, *The Faith of Our Fathers*, (Rockford, IL: TAN Books and Publishers, Inc., 1980), p. 183.

13 Alan Schreck, *Catholic and Christian*, (Ann Arbor, Michigan: Servant Books, 1984), pp. 195-196. Cf. also Chapter 10 of this book.

14 Patrick Madrid, *Any Friend of God is a Friend of Mine*, pp. 66-68.

15 Karl Keating (editor), *This Rock* Magazine "The Father's Know Best," (San Diego, CA: Catholic Answers, Inc., May/June 1992, pp. 47-49.

16 William A. Jurgens (editor and translator), *The Faith of the Early Fathers (Volume 1)*, (Collegeville, MN: The Liturgical Press, 1970), p. 151.

17 *Ibid.*, p. 158.

18 Karl Keating (editor), *This Rock* Magazine "The Father's Know Best," (San Diego, CA: Catholic Answers, Inc., May/June 1992, pp. 47-49.

19 William A. Jurgens (editor and translator), *The Faith of the Early Fathers (Volume 1)*, p. 79.

20 *Ibid.*, p. 363.

21 *The Faith of Our Fathers*, p. 177.

22 *Ibid.*, pp. 176-177.

23 *Ibid.*, p. 177.

24 *Ibid.*, p. 178.

25 *Catholic and Christian*, p. 198.

26 *The Faith of Our Fathers*, p. 178.

Chapter 12

"...Hold Fast to the Traditions, Just as I Handed Them on to You":[1] The Importance of Sacred Scripture AND Sacred Apostolic Tradition

What Does the Catholic Church Teach?

"'And such is the force and power of the Word of God that it can serve the Church as her support and vigor and the children of the Church as strength for their faith, food for the soul, and a pure and lasting font of spiritual life.'[109] Hence, 'access to Sacred Scripture ought to be open wide to the Christian faithful.'[110] ... The Church 'forcefully and specifically exhorts all the Christian faithful...to learn 'the surpassing knowledge of Jesus Christ,' by frequent reading of the divine Scriptures. 'Ignorance of the Scriptures is ignorance of Christ.'[112]...*Sacred Scripture* is the speech of God as it is put down in writing under the breath of the Holy Spirit.'[42]... 'And [Holy] *Tradition* transmits in its entirety the Word of God which has been entrusted to the apostles by Christ the Lord and the Holy Spirit...[43] As a result the Church, to whom the transmission and interpretation of Revelation is entrusted, 'does not derive her certainty about all revealed truths from the holy Scriptures alone. Both

Scripture and Tradition must be accepted and honored with equal sentiments of devotion and reverence...'[44] ...[T]he task of interpretation has been entrusted to the bishops in communion with the successor of Peter, the Bishop of Rome...' Yet this Magisterium is not superior to the Word of God, but is its servant. It teaches only what has been handed on to it...'"[48] (*Catechism of the Catholic Church*, #131, 133, 81, 82, 85, 86.)

Common Objection #1

"Jesus speaks out strongly in the Bible against following tradition: 'You disregard God's commandment but cling to human tradition.' '...How well you have set aside the commandment of God in order to uphold your tradition'" (Mark 7:8-9)![2] In the face of such a strong scriptural command as this, how can you Catholics possibly teach that Scripture and tradition must be accepted and honored with 'equal sentiments of devotion and reverence'?"

A Catholic Response

When the Catholic Church speaks about the importance of Tradition *(capital "T")*, we don't mean "man-made customs." *(In Mark 7:8-9 cited above, Jesus warned the often-hypocritical Pharisees and Scribes about blindly following their Jewish man-made customs and traditions to the "T" and ignoring what was most important — their relationship with God and their compassion for other people.)* When the Catholic Church says that Scripture[3] and Tradition are both sources of God's revelation, we are speaking about the living Sacred Faith Tradition of the Apostles that existed long before any New Testament book was written and centuries before the New Testament canon was decided upon.

In Mark 7:8-9 Jesus warns the Pharisees and Scribes about following corrupt *traditions* (Greek: *paradosis*) of men that nullify the Word of God. In contrast to this warning about following false man-made traditions that nullify the Word of God, in numerous other places in the New Testament, Christians are urged to closely adhere to the sacred *Traditions* (Greek: *paradosis*) handed down by the Apostles.

- St. Paul refers to this Sacred Apostolic Tradition when he writes: "I praise you because you remember me in everything and hold fast to the *traditions* [Greek: *paradosis*], just as I handed them on to you" (1 Cor 11:2).[4]

- St. Paul again refers to this Sacred Apostolic Tradition: "Therefore, brothers, stand firm and hold fast to the *traditions* [Greek: *paradosis*] that you were taught, either by an oral statement or by a letter of ours" (2 Thess 2:15).[5]

- One reads in Paul's Second Letter to Timothy about the *oral* passing on of Apostolic teaching: "And *what you heard from me* through many witnesses entrust to faithful people who will have the ability to teach others as well" (2 Tim 2:2).

- In his First Letter to the Corinthians St. Paul again talks about the *oral* passing on of the teaching of the Apostles: "Now I am reminding you, brothers, of the gospel *I preached to you...* Through it you are also being saved, if you hold fast to the word *I preached to you...*" (1 Cor 15:1-2).

Martin Luther's doctrine of *sola scriptura* (meaning that the Bible *alone* is designed to be the sole infallible guide for Christian belief and practice) is not found anywhere in the Bible. A few times in the Bible one does read about some of the qualities of and the uses for Scripture: "All scripture is inspired by God and is useful for teaching, for refutation, for correction, and for training in righteousness, so that one who belongs to God may be competent, equipped for every good work" (2 Tim 3:16-17). Notice that this passage does not say anywhere that God's complete revelation concerning Christian belief and practice is to be found *only* in the written Bible. In the Old Testament Book of Malachi we read: "For the lips of the priest are to keep knowledge, and instruction is to be sought from his mouth, because he is the messenger of the Lord of hosts" (Mal 2:7).[6]

Catholic convert Bob Sungenis writes:

> "[Protestant scholars and pastors] pointed to verses that spoke of the veracity and inerrancy of the Bible,

but could show none that explicitly taught that Scripture is our sole, formally sufficient authority. Interestingly, some of these Protestants were candid enough to admit that the Bible nowhere taught *sola scriptura*, but they compensated for this curious lacuna by saying the Bible doesn't have to teach *sola scriptura* in order for the doctrine to be true. But I could see that this position was utterly untenable. For if *sola scriptura* — the idea that the Bible is formally sufficient for Christians — is not taught in the Bible, *sola scriptura* is a false and self-refuting proposition.

As I studied Scripture in the light of the Catholic materials I had been sent, I began to see that the Bible in fact points to the Church as being the final arbiter of truth in all spiritual matters (cf. 1 Timothy 3:15; Matthew 16:18-19; 18:18; Luke 10:16).

This made sense, especially on a practical level. Since only an entity with the ability to observe and correctly interpret information can act as an authority, I saw that the Bible, though it contains God-breathed revelation, cannot act as a final 'authority' since it is dependent on thinking personalities to observe what it says and, more importantly, interpret what it means. I also saw that the Bible warns us that it contains difficult and confusing information which is capable (if not prone) to being twisted into all sorts of fanciful and false interpretations (2 Peter 3:16)."[7]

Numerous times in Scripture the reader is given the disclaimer that not every important theological and spiritual truth appears in written form in the Bible:

- "Now Jesus did many other signs in the presence of [his] disciples that are not written in this book" (John 20:30).

- "There are also many other things that Jesus did, but if these were to be described individually, I do not think the whole world would contain the books that would be written" (John 21:25).

- "I have much more to tell you, but you cannot bear it now. But when he comes, the Spirit of truth, he will guide you to all truth..." (John 16:12-13).

- "Although I have much to write to you, I do not intend to use paper and ink. Instead, I hope to visit you and to speak face to face so that our joy may be complete" (2 John 1:12).

- "I have much to write to you, but I do not wish to write with pen and ink. Instead, I hope to see you soon, when we can talk face to face" (3 John 1:13).

Here we clearly see that the Bible says that not all of Jesus' teachings were reduced to writing.[8]

David Currie writes:

"The fact that there was a tremendous amount of Jesus' life and teaching that was never written down cannot be denied...

Simply because something was not chosen for inclusion in a book did not mean it was no longer true, or that it was not actively taught by the apostles in the first century. In fact, in the case of the epistles, the reverse would seem to be more plausible. Many of the most common and well-known practices and teachings of the early Church would be the least likely to be included in any of the writings of the early Church for the simple reason that they would be least likely to be misunderstood or called into question and thus require a written reinforcement or correction. This has been called the 'occasional nature' of the New Testament."[9]

When the phrase "the word of God" or "the word of the Lord" appears in the Bible it does not refer only to written Scripture. The "word of God/Lord" often refers to verbally transmitted Divine revelation (cf. Gen 15:4), verbally given Divine instruction (cf. Num 15:31), verbally communicated Divine commands (cf. Deut 18:18), preached Divine proclamations (cf. 2 Kings 7:1), and, finally, the "Word of God" refers to Divine Flesh and Blood — the Incarnation (cf. John 1:1, 14). One can see how the "word of God" was being received by God's people *long before* the written Bible took shape.

St. Peter tell us: "...speaking of these things as he does in all his letters. In them there are some things hard to understand that the ignorant and unstable distort to their own destruction, just as they do the other scriptures" (2 Pet 3:16). Here we see that individuals, *by themselves*, can easily distort the true meaning of the Scriptures. Because the Catholic Church is the author of the New Testament Bible, St. Paul calls the Church "the pillar and foundation of the truth" (1 Tim 3:15). Therefore, it is only fitting that St. Peter should write: "...no one can explain *by himself* a prophecy in the Scriptures" (2 Pet 1:20).[10] The Bible says that *the Church* is the possessor of the correct interpretation of Scripture.

In the Acts of the Apostles we read: "Philip ran up and heard him reading Isaiah the prophet and said, 'Do you understand what you are reading?' He replied, 'How can I, *unless someone instructs me?*' So he invited Philip to get in and sit with him" (Acts 8:30-31). Here we see that an individual should look to *the Church* for the authentic interpretation of the Scriptures.[11] Cf. Luke 24:27.

In the Book of Nehemiah we read about the priest Ezra having to interpret the Scriptures after he read them aloud to the people so that the individual listeners could grasp their correct meaning (cf. Neh 8:8-9).

Note well that the Bible is not self-interpreting.[12] Consider these apparently contradictory passages:

- Jesus says, "Call no one on earth your father..." (Matt 23:9), while St. Paul says, "...I became your father in Christ Jesus through the gospel. Therefore, I urge you, be imitators of me..." (1 Cor 4:15-16).[13]
- St. Paul says, "For we consider that a person is justified by faith apart from works of the law" (Rom 3:28), while St. James says, "See how a person is justified by works and not by faith alone" (James 2:24).[14]
- St. Peter tells us: "...baptism,...saves [us] now" (1 Pet 3:21), while St. Paul says, "...for, if you confess with your mouth that Jesus is

Lord and believe in your heart that God raised him from the dead, you will be saved" (Rom 10:9).[15]

Former Protestant minister *(now Catholic convert)* Marcus Grodi writes:

"Every Sunday I would stand in my pulpit and interpret Scripture for my flock, knowing that within a fifteen mile radius of my church there were dozens of other Protestant pastors — all of whom believed that the Bible alone is the sole authority for doctrine and practice — but each was teaching something different from what I was teaching. 'Is my interpretation of Scripture the right one or not?' I'd wonder. 'Maybe one of those other pastors is right, and I'm misleading these people who trust me.'"[16]

Rev. John A. O'Brien writes about the big promoter of the doctrine of *"sola scriptura,"* Martin Luther:

"[In] the first years of his separation from the Church, Luther declared that the Bible could be interpreted by everyone, 'even by the humble miller's maid, nay a child of nine.' Later on, however, when the Anabaptists, the Zwinglians and others contradicted his views, the Bible became 'a heresy book,' most obscure and difficult to understand. He lived to see numerous heretical sects rise up and spread through Christendom, all claiming to be based upon the Bible.

Thus, in 1525 he sadly deplored the religious anarchy to which his own principle of the private interpretation of Scripture had given rise: 'There are as many sects and beliefs as there are heads. This fellow will have nothing to do with Baptism: another denies the Sacrament; a third believes that there is another world between this and the Last Day. Some teach that Christ is not God; some say this, some say that. There is no rustic so rude but that, if he dreams or fancies anything, it

213

must be the whisper of the Holy Spirit, and he himself a prophet." [17]

How do we know which Traditions are authentic and which are not? In Matt 16:18 Jesus promises that the gates of hell would not prevail against His Church. In other words, the teachings of the Church are protected from error by Christ. [18] Which Church did Christ set up and who has the unbroken line descending from Him? (cf. Chapter 3 of this book.)

Al Kresta writes:

> "...[T]he late apologist and evangelist, Francis Schaeffer, used to say that the Reformation showed us the importance of the man of God alone (cf. 2 Tim 3:17), with the Bible alone, guided by the Spirit alone. But as I studied Scripture that's not what I saw. The man of God is never depicted as (nor expected to be) using the Bible alone; he is called by Christ to function with authority in his teaching ministry, but only within the larger context of the doctrinal unity of the magisterium of the teaching Church.[19]
>
> Christians are never depicted in Scripture as being 'lone rangers,' left to decide for themselves what they think Scripture means (cf. 2 Pet 1:20-21). Without the teaching guidance of the Church, all sorts of fanciful and erroneous interpretations of Scripture can spring up (2 Pet 3:15). That's why Paul admonished the early Christians to always hold fast to the unity of doctrine (cf. 1 Cor 1:10)...
>
> Reformation Protestantism claimed the Bible alone is the only infallible rule of faith and practice. But, ironically, it was the emphasis on the Bible alone that caused all the confusion and division within Protestantism."[20]

James Akin writes:

> "The Protestant doctrine of *sola scriptura* also began to trouble me as I wondered how it is that we can

know for certain which books belong in the Bible. Certain books of the New Testament, such as the synoptic gospels, we can show to be reliable historical accounts of Jesus' life, but there were a number of New Testament books (e. g., Hebrews, James, 2 Peter, 2 and 3 John, Jude, and Revelation) whose authorship and canonical status were debated in their favor and included in the canon of inspired books, but I saw that I, a person two thousand years removed from their writing, had no possibility of *proving* these works were genuinely apostolic. I simply had to take the Catholic Church's word on it.

...[T]here was no way to show from within Scripture itself exactly what the books of the Bible should be. But I realized that by looking to the Church as an authentic and reliable Witness to the canon, I was violating the principle of *sola scriptura*. The "Bible only" theory turned out to be self-refuting, since it cannot tell us which books belong in it and which don't.

What was more, my studies in Church history showed that the canon of the Bible was not finally settled until about three hundred years after the last apostle died. If I was going to claim that the Church had done its job and picked exactly the right books of the Bible, this meant that the Church had made an infallible decision three hundred years *after* the apostolic age, a realization which made it believable that the Church could make even later infallible decisions, and that the Church could make such decisions even today."[21]

Catholic convert Tim Staples says:

"...Since [my Catholic friend] knew of my plans to be a Protestant minister, he asked me whether I believed my interpretations of Scripture would be infallible. Of course not.' I responded. 'I'm a fallible, sinful human being. The only infallible authority we have is the Bible.'

'If that's so,' he countered, 'how can your interpretation of Scripture be binding on the consciences of the members of your congregation? If you have no guarantee that your interpretations are correct, why should they trust you? And if your interpretations are purely human in nature and origin, aren't they then merely traditions of men? Jesus condemned traditions of men which nullify the Word of God. If it's possible, as you admit, that your interpretations may be wrong — you have no infallible way of knowing for sure — then it's possible that they are nullifying the Word of God."[22]

Common Objection #2

"Name one Tradition that is necessary for my salvation that is not contained in the Bible."

A Catholic Response

I'll name two.

1) The declaration of which books belong in the Bible and which do not. Since the Bible does not have an inspired table of contents, it was the Catholic Church in the 4th and 5th centuries who decided, under the guidance of the Holy Spirit, which writings conveyed Apostolic truth and were inspired by God and which were not.[23] This is part of the Apostolic Tradition of the early Church that is not contained in the written Bible.

2) The authentic and true interpretation of the various passages contained in the written Bible. Since the Bible is not self-interpreting, we look to the Tradition of the Apostles — communicated in the writings of the early Church Fathers and present in the teachings of the Church's Magisterium throughout the course of history, for the correct interpretation of crucial Biblical texts in order to formulate doctrine.

Common Objection #3

"In Acts 17:11 we read about the Bereans who searched the Scriptures before they accepted the things being preached to them. Clearly, they were following the practice of *sola scriptura*."

A Catholic Response

At the Internet web site *The Beggar King Homepage* we read the following about St. Paul's visit to Beroea recounted in Acts 17:

> "Everyone loves the Bereans, and we all like to fancy ourselves as equally "noble." It is one of the favorite proof-texts of *"Sola Scriptura"* adherents.
>
> In Acts 17:11 we read, *"Now the Bereans were of more noble character than the Thessalonians, for they received the message with great eagerness and examined the Scriptures every day to see if what Paul said was true."*
>
> Many Protestants see in this a kind of trump card in which Scripture overrules oral teaching. So the question is, "Are the Bereans an example of *Sola Scriptura* in action? And are present-day Protestants behaving as the Bereans do in Acts?"
>
> It is important to take a careful look at how the Bereans behave and to compare it to the similar passages in Scripture. When we do this we may see a pattern develop.
>
> Acts 17 gives an account of how Paul arrived in Thessalonika: *"Passing through Amphipolis and Apollonia, they [Paul and Silas] eventually reached Thessalonika, where there was a Jewish synagogue. Paul as usual introduced himself and for three consecutive Sabbaths developed the arguments from scripture for them, explaining and proving how the Christ should suffer and rise from the dead. 'And the Christ', he said, 'is this Jesus who I am proclaiming to you'."* [Acts 17:1-3, Jerusalem version]
>
> In Paul's mission to the Thessalonians, he behaves as a traveling rabbi. When he gets to town he introduces himself to the synagogue officials. When Acts says "as usual" here it refers to the Jewish custom, not only to Paul's individual habits. As a visiting rabbi Paul would have license to preach and to discuss the Torah. The

important part here is that Paul is not preaching to pagans, but to the Jews of the synagogue; in other words to people who KNOW scripture.

From their Scriptures Paul "developed the arguments..." Literally in the Greek he "opened, unfolded, unlocked" the Scriptures, explaining and proving" points about the expected Messiah. But then comes the jump, he turns from scripture to his own testimony: "And the Christ is this Jesus who I am proclaiming!"

We clearly see two elements at work here: the Scriptures AND the oral teaching. Paul uses BOTH elements together to bring the Good News to the Thessalonians.

The results are mixed: *"Some of them were convinced and joined Paul and Silas, and so did a great many God-fearing people and Greeks, as well as a number of rich women."* [Acts 17:4] But not everybody was convinced: "The Jews, full of resentment, enlisted the help of a gang from the marketplace [and] stirred up the crowd" against Paul and he was forced to leave for Beroea.

So we have two groups: the Jews and Judaized Greeks [the "God-fearing"] who "were convinced" by Paul, and the other Jews, the unconvinced. In fact, in the Greek they are described as opposites. The first group is described as *peitho* [which is translated here as "convinced"] and the second, the Jews who were "full of resentment" is described as *apeitheo*.

The word *peitho* in Greek means more than to be "convinced by." It means to "believe, to trust in, yield to and to be obedient to."

BOTH groups believed in Scripture. The difference is that the group who was convinced trusted in Paul's testimony and even was obedient to his authority to preach the truth!

Now let's follow Paul to Beroea... *"When it was dark the brothers immediately sent Paul and Silas away to Beroea, where they visited the Jewish synagogue as soon as they arrived."* [Acts 17:10] So we have a parallel situation to the visit to Thessalonika. Again Paul goes to the synagogue to meet the leaders as was the custom.

But this time things go better: *"Here the Jews were more noble than those in Thessalonika, and they welcomed the word very readily; every day they studied the Scriptures to check whether it was true. And many Jews became believers, so did many Greek women from the upper classes and a number of men."* [Acts 17:11-12]

Now what is the difference that accounts for the better results in Beroea? Most Protestants would say that it is the Berean's reliance on Scripture alone as the sole rule of faith. Can that be true?

In both cities Paul preached in the synagogue to Jews and Judaized Greeks. We may well assume that in Beroea he "developed the arguments from scripture for them, explaining and proving how the Christ should suffer and rise from the dead" just as he did in Thessalonika. So there is no way around the conclusion that both cities had a profound knowledge of Scripture. Discourse and debate on the meaning of Scripture was commonplace in their synagogues.

The REAL difference is that the Jews in Beroea "welcomed the word very readily." Which word? The oral testimony. Their hearts were open to Paul's proclamation. The Thessalonians on the other hand rejected Paul's interpretation of Scripture AND his testimony that Jesus is the Messiah.

Had the Bereans applied Scripture in the way that *Sola Scriptura* proponents imagine they did, they would have ended up like the majority in Thessalonika. While many of the statements which Paul made about the prophecies regarding the Messiah would be easily backed up by checking the text there was one fact which they would not find in those texts: That "the Christ is this Jesus whom I am proclaiming!" That central fact stood or fell on their willingness to accept Paul's teaching. Scripture would support Paul's witness, but a straightforward reading of the text could not verify such a doctrine.

"Searching the Scriptures" is not enough by itself for the Bereans. They were different in that they "welcomed the word very readily." A people with a hardened heart would search Scripture from beginning to end and never have a willingness to receive the word Paul brought. As Paul wrote to the Galatians: *"Let me ask you one question: was it because you practiced the Law [literally: the Torah] that you received the Spirit, or because you believed what was preached to you?"* [Galatians 3:2] A good question for the Bereans also. A good question for us!

Jesus met similar problems. In Jerusalem for a festival Jesus healed a man on the Sabbath. When he was opposed by some of the men at the temple he told them, "You search the Scriptures because you believe that in them you have eternal life; now these same Scriptures testify to me, and yet you refuse to come to me for life!" [John 5:39]

Even the disciples studied Scripture but lacked understanding! After his resurrection Jesus met two disciples on the road to Emmaus. *"Then, starting with Moses and the prophets, he explained to them the passages throughout the Scriptures that were about him."* [Luke 24:27]

What the Jews to whom Jesus spoke were missing wasn't knowledge of Scripture. They had that. But they didn't have that understanding which Jesus can give. This understanding is what Paul, acting under Jesus' authority, offered the Bereans and Thessalonians. Only the Bereans were noble enough to "welcome the word very readily."

This combination of Scripture and Witness, of the oral and written transmission of the Good News, is found everywhere throughout the Bible.

In Acts 2 we see the first harvest of the new-born Church. Anointed by the Spirit in Pentecost, Peter addresses the assembled crowd of Jews and tells them he is not drunk but *"on the contrary, this is what the prophet spoke of. 'In the days to come, it is the Lord who speaks, I will pour out my spirit on all mankind.'* [Acts 2:17] So we see here Peter referring to Scripture. Then he continues: *"Men of Israel, listen to what I say; Jesus of Nazareth was a man commended to you by God..."* [Acts 2:22] Now we see Peter turning to testimony. He takes the Scriptures with which the Jews were surely familiar and interprets them, through the power he receives from Jesus and the Holy Spirit. The two work together, never separately. In Peter's address this pattern is followed three times!

Later Philip is sent to bring the Good News to a eunuch on the Gaza road. *"When Philip ran up he heard the man reading Isaiah the prophet and asked, 'Do you understand what you are reading?' 'How can I,' he replied, 'UNLESS I have someone to guide me?'"* [Acts 8:30-31] It was not for lack of searching Scripture that the man lacked salvation, but it was the lack of an authority to guide him! Again, Scripture and the authoritative oral teaching go together.

Paul commends Timothy for his faith this way: *"But as for you [Timothy], continue in what you have learned and become convinced BECAUSE you know those from whom you have learned it, and how from infancy you have known the Holy Scriptures which are able to make you wise for salvation in Christ Jesus."* [2 Timothy 3:14-15] Note again the same pattern we have seen. Timothy received the faith in Christ through the teaching of men whom he knew and trusted, not from Scripture. But his knowledge of Scripture had made him grow in wisdom so as to receive this faith. The same two elements are there, the Tradition in both oral and written form, in harmony. No where does Paul say that Scripture itself is wholly sufficient for Timothy.

In his second letter to the Thessalonians Paul again stresses the two elements on which our Faith rests: *"Stand firm, brothers, and keep the traditions that we have taught you, whether by word of mouth or by letter.*" [2 Thess 2:15]

The Bereans were not "noble" merely because they searched Scripture. They had that something extra; "they welcomed the word very readily." They accepted Paul's testimony! They were unwilling to be misguided [they tested Paul's word by Scripture] but they WERE willing to be guided [they accepted his authority to reveal what Scripture means].

The Bereans were not *Sola Scriptura* adherents. If they had been they would have rejected Paul's testimony that "the Christ is this Jesus who I am proclaiming!" The doctrine Paul came to preach was not to be found in Scripture, yet it was in harmony with it. Rather, like the disciples on the road to Emmaus, like the eunuch who met Philip, like Timothy, they accepted the Good News on the basis of Scripture AND the authoritative teaching and interpretation which comes from Jesus through the Church."[24]

What Did the Early Christians Believe About the Importance of Sacred Scripture AND the Sacred Tradition of the Apostles?

- "As I said before, the Church, having received this preaching and this faith, although she is disseminated throughout the whole world, yet guarded it, as if she occupied but one house... For, while the languages of the world are diverse, nevertheless, the authority of the tradition is one and the same." St. Irenaeus in his *Against Heresies* (circa 180 A.D.) [25]

- "What if the Apostles had not in fact left writings to us? Would it not be necessary to follow the order of tradition, which was handed down to those to whom they entrusted the Churches?" St. Irenaeus in his *Against Heresies* (circa 180 A.D.) [26]

- "The path of those, however, who belong to the Church, goes around the whole world; for it has the firm tradition of the

Apostles, enabling us to see that the faith of all is one and the same." St. Irenaeus in his *Against Heresies* (circa 180 A.D.) [27]

- "Let us believe, then, dear brethren, according to the tradition of the Apostles." St. Hippolytus of Rome in his *Against the Heresy of a Certain Noetus* (circa 200 A.D.) [28]

- "The teaching of the Church has indeed been handed down through an order of succession from the Apostles, and remains in the Churches even to the present time. That alone is to be believed as the truth which is in no way at variance with ecclesiastical and apostolic tradition." Origen in his *The Fundamental Doctrines* (circa 220 A.D.) [29]

Endnotes

[1]   The words of St. Paul to the Christians at Corinth instructing them to firmly adhere to the oral faith Tradition handed down to them from the Apostles (cf. 1 Cor 11:2).

[109] *DV* 21.

[110] *DV* 22.

[112] *DV* 25; cf. *Phil* 3:8 and St. Jerome, *Commentariorum in Isaiam libri* xviii prol.: PL 24, 17b.

[42]   *DV* 9.

[43]   *DV* 9.

[44]   *DV* 9.

[48]   *DV* 10 paragraph 2.

[2]   Cf. also Matt 15:3-9 and Col 2:22 where following *corrupt* human traditions that nullify the Word of God are condemned by Jesus.

[3]   Fr. Peter Stravinskas reminds us, "If a Catholic were to read no Scripture beyond the texts used for Sunday Mass over the three-year period that person would have been exposed to more than seven thousand verses of the Bible..." Cf. Rev. Peter M. J. Stravinskas, *The Bible and the Mass*, (Ann Arbor, Michigan: Servant Publications, 1989), p. 48.

[4]   Note that the Bible does not record a single instance where Jesus Himself ever wrote down one line of Scripture (except, possi-

bly, when He bent down and mysteriously wrote on the ground in the account of the woman caught in adultery — Cf. John 8:6). With the exception of the Book of Revelation (cf. Rev 1:1-2), nowhere in the Bible does Jesus ever command any of His followers to write anything down. When Jesus gives His Apostles and disciples the "great commission" He tells them, not to go and write a New Testament Bible so that each Christian could discern for himself what God is calling him to do, but to "...*[teach]* them to observe all that I have commanded you..." (Matt 28:20), "Go into the whole world and *proclaim* the gospel to every creature..." (Mark 16:15), and "Whoever *listens* to you listens to me..." (Luke 10:16). James Cardinal Gibbons reminds us, "The most perfect Christians lived and died and went to heaven before the most important parts of the Scriptures were written. And what would have become of them if the Bible alone had been their guide? The art of printing was not invented till the fifteenth century [1440]. How utterly impossible it was to supply everyone with a copy of the Scriptures *from the fourth to the fifteenth century*." Cf. James Cardinal Gibbons, *The Faith of Our Fathers*, (Rockford, IL: TAN Books and Publishers, Inc., 1980), p. 66, 69.

5   Cf. the diagram in Chapter 3 of this book to see that the written Bible came from the Sacred Faith Tradition of the Apostles that existed orally for many years before any writing was committed to paper.

6   Note that the prophet Malachi doesn't tell the Jews to go to the written Torah by themselves and try to discern, on their own, what God is trying to teach them. Malachi asks the Jews to go to the *Church* for the correct interpretation of the Scriptures. Cf. also Deut 17:8-10.

7   Patrick Madrid (editor), *Surprised by Truth*, (San Diego, CA: Basilica Press, 1994), p. 118.

8   Catholic apologist Scott Hahn states: "What family do you know in which everything that the kids are expected to do is written down? We'd have fifty volumes in my family and still would have to write more just to interpret the fifty volumes. What country do you know that writes a constitution and then says, 'O.K. every citizen to himself! You're free to interpret and ap-

ply it on your own. May the spirit of Washington go with you!'
We have a constitution but we also have a government ... to
apply it in a dynamic ongoing way..." Cf. Scott Hahn, *Eucharistic Day at Marytown Audio Cassette*, (West Covina, CA: St.
Joseph Communications, Inc.).

9   David B. Currie, *Born Fundamentalist Born Again Catholic*,
(San Francisco, CA: Ignatius Press, 1996), p. 54.

10 *Good News Bible: Today's English Version*, (New York, NY:
American Bible Society, 1976), pp. 321-322.

11 In Matt 18:15-17 Jesus says that the *Church* is to serve as the
final court of appeal when questions and conflicts concerning
life in the Christian community arise. Jesus says that if a person
refuses to listen *"even to the Church,"* he should be treated as
an outcast.

12 If the Bible were self-interpreting there would not be thousands
of different Christian denominations all claiming to be "led by
the Holy Spirit" and all claiming to adhere to the "plain meaning of Scripture" teaching *very* different doctrines. If the Bible
were self-interpreting there wouldn't be any need for sermons,
Bible commentaries, or Sunday school. Note that every preacher
or teacher puts his/her denomination's "spin" (interpretation)
on the Biblical text. The tremendous value of the writings of
the early Church Fathers is that they show us what was the
early Church's interpretation of crucial Scriptural texts. Please
refer to these writings cited at the end of each chapter throughout this book.

13 Cf. Chapter 1 of this book.

14 Cf. Chapter 4 of this book.

15 Some evangelical Christians will speak out against the authority of the Pope but, what they don't realize is that, their pastor
is acting as the "pope" of their own church because he/she is
teaching his/her *interpretation* of what various Bible passages
mean. The fundamental question at issue is this: To whom do
you give the authority to interpret the Bible for you? Is it your
"non-denominational" pastor, yourself, or the 2,000-year-old
Catholic Church founded by Jesus Christ that was promised
eternal Divine guidance and protection (cf. Matt 28:20)? Remember that the Bible itself warns that it is very easy for the

uninformed reader, by himself, to come up with erroneous interpretations of Scripture (cf. 2 Pet 3:16; 1:20).

[16] *Surprised by Truth*, p. 38.

[17] Rev. John A. O'Brien, *The Faith of Millions*, (Huntington, IN: Our Sunday Visitor, Inc., 1963, 1974), p. 136.

[18] Cf. Chapter 14 of this book.

[19] Cf. Matt 18:15-17; Phil 1:27-28, 2:2; 1 Tim 3:15; 4:11-16, 6:2-3; 2 Tim 4:1-5; Titus 1:7-11, 13-14; 2:15; 3:8-10.

[20] *Surprised by Truth*, p. 265, 268.

[21] *Ibid.*, pp. 66-67.

[22] *Ibid.*, pp. 216-218.

[23] Cf. Chapter 2 of this book.

[24] Cf. *The Beggar King Homepage* at <http://webusers.anet-stl.com/~nosmo/bereans.htm> Cf. also Catholic apologist Steve Ray's web site at http://www.catholic-convert.com.

[25] William A. Jurgens (editor and translator), *The Faith of the Early Fathers (Volume 1)*, (Collegeville, MN: The Liturgical Press, 1970), p. 85.

[26] *Ibid.*, pp. 90-91.

[27] *Ibid.*, p. 101.

[28] *Ibid.*, p. 165.

[29] *Ibid.*, p. 190.

Chapter 13

"Upon This Rock I Will Build My Church":[1] The Authority of the Pope

What Does the Catholic Church Teach?

"The Lord Jesus endowed His community with a structure that will remain until the Kingdom is fully achieved. Before all else there is the choice of the Twelve with Peter as their head[168]... 'When the work which the Father gave the Son to do on earth was accomplished, the Holy Spirit was sent on the day of Pentecost in order that He might continually sanctify the Church.'[174] ...Particular Churches are fully catholic through their communion with one of them, the Church of Rome 'which presides in charity.'[315] 'For with this church, by reason of its pre-eminence, the whole Church, that is the faithful everywhere, must necessarily be in accord.'[316] Indeed, 'from the incarnate Word's descent to us, all Christian churches everywhere have held and hold the great Church that is here [at Rome] to be their only basis and foundation since, according to the Savior's promise, the gates of hell have never prevailed against her.'[317] 'The Church knows that she is joined in many ways to the baptized who are honored by the name of Christian, but do not profess the Catholic faith in its entirety or have not preserved unity or communion under the successor of Peter.'"[322] (*Catechism of the Catholic Church*, #765, 767, 834, 838.)

Common Objection #1

"In the original Greek language of the New Testament, Jesus says to Peter in the Gospel of Matthew: 'And so I say to you, you are *[Petros]* and upon this *[petra]* I will build my Church...' (Matt 16:18). In Greek, Peter's name (*Petros*) means "little stone" while the word for "rock" in Greek (*petra*) means "big boulder." Hence, what Jesus was saying to Peter in Matt 16:18 was actually: 'And so I say to you, you are a *[little stone]* and upon this *[big boulder]* I will build my church...'" What Jesus was really telling Peter was that His Church was to be built upon his confession of faith in Him as Messiah (cf. Matt 16:16) and that *He Himself* was to be the massive rock foundation of the Church."

A Catholic Response

In Greek, Matt 16:18 is, indeed, rendered: "And so I say to you, you are *[Petros]* and upon this *[petra]* I will build my church..." Without understanding the reason behind the discrepancy in the Greek words for "Peter" and "rock," some Christian denominations claim that Jesus was not referring to the Apostle Peter when He used the word "rock" but was referring, instead, to Himself.

Although the New Testament was written in Greek, Jesus did not speak the Greek language. Scholars tell us that Jesus spoke Aramaic (and probably Hebrew).[2] The New Testament writers were, therefore, faced with the task of translating Jesus' Aramaic statements into Greek. In Jesus' native language of Aramaic He said to Peter in Matt 16:18: "And so I say to you, you are *[Kepha]* and upon this *[kepha]* I will build my Church..." (*Cf. John 1:42 where Peter is referred to by his Aramaic name "Kephas."*) When the New Testament writers went to translate Jesus' Aramaic word *"kepha"* (meaning "rock") into Greek, they encountered a grammatical problem with masculine and feminine word forms. The Greek translators had no problem referring to an inanimate rock (*kepha* in Aramaic) with the Greek feminine noun *petra*. The problem arose when the Greek translators had to use the Greek feminine word *"petra"* to refer to a man named "Kepha."[3] To solve the problem the translators used the masculine name *Petros*, which is derived from the feminine Greek noun *petra*. As one can clearly see, the discrepancy in the Greek words found in Matt 16:18 was the result of a grammatical difficulty encountered in translation. Once one understands the reason for the variation in Greek words found in Matt 16:18, it becomes clear that the Apostle "Peter" and the "rock" on which Jesus would build His Church are one and the same.[4]

James Akin writes about Jesus' words to St. Peter recounted in Matt 16:17-19:

> "The second statement to Peter would be something which minimized or diminished him, pointing out his insignificance, with the result that Jesus would be saying, 'Blessed are you, Simon Bar-Jonah! You are an insignificant little pebble. Here are the keys to the kingdom of heaven!' Such an incongruous sequence of statements would have been not merely odd, but inexplicable."[5]

T. L. Frazier writes about Peter:

> "Actually, if the Evangelist had intended to contrast Peter the 'stone' with Jesus the 'Rock,' the obvious word to use for Simon Peter would have been *lithos*, the more common Greek word for stone or small rock. This would also have eliminated any possible confusion between Peter and Jesus. On the other hand, the deliberate use of *petros* and *petra* points to an attempt to translate an Aramaic pun into Greek, which of course is what Catholics contend. Interestingly, Jesus himself is called *lithos* (e. g., Matt 21:42, 44) four times more often than he's called *petra* (12 times to 3), a fact which doesn't dissuade Peter from characterizing all believers as 'stones' *(lithoi)* in 1 Peter 2:5."[6]

Let's examine a few passages from the New Testament and see how St. Peter enjoyed a relationship with Jesus that was not shared by any other follower:

- In Matt 16:19, Peter is the only disciple in Scripture to receive the "keys to the kingdom of heaven" from Jesus. [7] *(Note that keys are an ancient symbol of power and authority alluded to a number of times in Scripture — cf. Rev 1:18; Rev 20:1; Isaiah 22:22.)* [8] Note that Peter received the "keys" and his "binding and "loosing" authority separately from and prior to the rest of the disciples (cf. Matt 16:18; 18:18). If Peter was not the "rock" on which the Church was to be built, why did Jesus entrust the "keys to the kingdom of heaven" to him?

- In Matt 16:18, Peter is the only disciple in Scripture to be called "rock" by Jesus. *(Note that the name "rock" is used many times in Scripture to refer to God — cf. Deut 32:31; Psalm 89:27.)* In having his name changed to *"Kepha"* (meaning "rock"), the human Peter certainly did not become Divine but was promised Divine assistance at every moment as he undertook the ministry of pastoring the Christian community in Jesus' physical absence.[9]

- In John 1:42, Peter has his name changed by Jesus. *(Note that a change of name in the Bible meant a change of vocation. God changed Abram's name to "Abraham" in Gen 17:5 and he became the father of the Jewish faith. Along the same lines, God changed Jacob's name to "Israel" in Gen 35:10 and the tribes of Israel, which made up God's Chosen People, were named after his twelve sons — cf. Gen 35:22-26; Num 1:1-54.)* Again, if Peter was not the "rock" on which Jesus intended to build His Church, why did Jesus change his name and, thus, signify a new calling for him?

- Although the Gospel of John tells us that Peter was not the first to be called by Jesus (cf. John 1:35-42), Peter's name appears first in every scriptural listing of the names of the Twelve Apostles (cf. Matt 10:2-4; Mark 3:16-19; Luke 6:12-19; Acts 1:13.)[10]

- We read the following listing of the Apostles in Matt 10:2-4: "The names of the twelve apostles are these: first [Greek: *protos*], Simon called Peter, and his brother Andrew; James, the son of Zebedee, and his brother John; Philip and Bartholomew, Thomas and Matthew the tax collector; James, the son of Alphaeus, and Thaddeus; Simon the Cananean, and Judas Iscariot who betrayed him." The Greek word *protos* means "foremost," "best," or "chief." Note that "second," "third," "fourth," etc... are not assigned to the other Apostles after St. Peter is identified as "first." This gives a clear indication that "first" (Greek: *protos*) is not intended to be a mere numerical listing but a designation of pre-eminence (e. g., the "First Lady" of the United States.)

- At many crucial moments, Peter often served as spokesman for the rest of the Apostles (cf. Mark 8:29; John 6:68-69; Acts 2:14-41, etc.).

- Peter is mentioned by name in the New Testament more than any other Apostle or disciple (182 times.) The Apostle with the next most mentions of his name is John (34 times.)[11] In the Book of Acts alone *(the Biblical account of the beginning years of the early Christian Church),* Peter's name is mentioned 56 times.

- In John 21:15-17, Peter is the only Apostle in Scripture to be told by Jesus to "Feed [His] lambs... Tend [His] sheep... Feed [His] sheep." Thus, Peter received personally the pastoral charge from Christ to spiritually nourish and care for His *entire* flock.[12]

- In Luke 22:31-32, Peter is the only Apostle to be personally prayed for by Christ so that his "own faith may not fail." After praying for Peter specifically by name, Jesus gives him the commission: "you must strengthen your brothers" (meaning to spiritually feed and guide them.)

- Out of all the boats available, Jesus chooses Peter's boat to preach from and to work a miracle from (cf. Luke 5:3). The Catholic Church is sometimes called "the Bark of Peter." A "bark" is a small sailing ship. Peter was chosen to be the "first mate," if you will, of Jesus' "Boat" — His Church. The sailing ship is an ancient symbol of the Church because all Christians are engaged in a pilgrimage toward heaven. The "wind" that fills the Church's sails and propels the Church as we journey toward Jesus and His Father in heaven is the "breath" of the Holy Spirit.

- In Acts 2:14-41, after the Holy Spirit descended upon the Apostles at Pentecost, Peter immediately stands up and, without any opposition at all from the other Apostles in attendance, delivers the first sermon to the Church — which results in the Baptism of nearly three thousand new converts.

- In Acts 3:1-10, Peter is the first Apostle to perform a miracle in Jesus' Name after Pentecost and, in Acts 4, he is the one who defends the Christian faith before the Jewish Sanhedrin.

- In Acts 1:15-26, Peter is the one who personally supervised — without any opposition at all from the other Apostles in attendance — the extremely important election of the Apostle Judas Iscariot's replacement after he committed suicide.

- In Acts 10:9-49, Peter receives the crucial revelation from God to open the Christian Church to non-Jews (Gentiles).

- In Acts 15:1-12, Peter is the one who stands up and definitively declares to the assembled Church leaders at the Council of Jerusalem the teaching that non-Jewish (Gentile) Christians need not follow the Old Testament Mosaic Law to be saved.

- In John 20:1-10 we read that, even though the Apostle John got to the empty tomb first on Easter morning, he waits for Peter to arrive before he goes in to examine things. (Cf. also Luke 24:12 in which Peter was the first Apostle to enter the empty tomb on Easter morning.)

- Luke 24:34 and 1 Cor 15:5 tell us that Peter was the first Apostle to whom the risen Jesus appears after His Easter resurrection.

- In Matt 16:15-16, Mark 8:29 and Luke 9:20 Peter gave the answer *(on behalf of the rest of the disciples)* to Jesus' crucial question concerning His identity: "Who do you say that I am?"

- In Gal 1:18, St. Paul makes it his business to travel to Jerusalem to consult and confer with Peter after his conversion experience.

- In 1 Peter 5:13, Peter refers to himself as *"the chosen one* at Babylon." (Note that "Babylon" was a Biblical code name for the city of Rome because many of the city's inhabitants were non-believing pagans leading immoral lives.)

- In Luke 10:16, Jesus tells His 72 disciples: "Whoever listens to you listens to me. Whoever rejects you rejects me..." If that holds true for an ordinary Christian disciple who was not called "rock" and who was not personally given the "keys" of authority by Christ, how much more true would it be of St. Peter who received these honors/responsibilities directly from our Lord!

Historically, in an unbroken line, the current Pope of the Roman Catholic Church is the direct successor to St. Peter, the first Bishop of Rome (cf. Chapter 3 of this book). The Pope's authority is derived from the authority that Christ gave to St. Peter (whom He declared to be "rock" in Matt 16:18).

In the King James Bible we read in Acts 1:20 about Matthias taking the place of (succeeding) the Apostle Judas: "...and his bishopric [Greek: *episkopēn*] let another take."[13] One can clearly see here how the Apostles felt the need to maintain an Apostolic presence among the Christian people.

The governments of numerous countries throughout the world are set up using a system of "ministers" (e. g., the minister of defense, the minister of commerce, the minister of agriculture, etc.). Above all of these individual ministers is a person who is known as the "prime minister." The prime minister, in turn, reports directly to the king of the country and often represents him in various capacities. Consider the following diagram:[14]

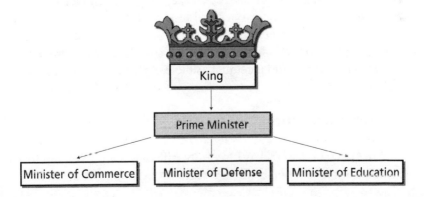

Just as the king is head of a particular country, Jesus is the head of the Catholic Church: "He is head of the body, the church..." (Col 1:18). Catholics look to St. Peter, not as "king" of the Church, but as the "prime minister" who was chosen by Christ to be above the other ministers (the other eleven Apostles) and to represent Him physically in His absence.[15] *(Refer to Matt 16:18-19 and see where Jesus gives to Peter, the Prime Minister, the "keys" of authority. Cf. also Isaiah 22:20-22 where Eliakim is given the keys of authority and chosen to be "prime minister" for his people.)*

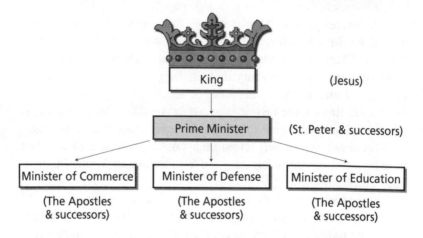

Why are we called *Roman* Catholics if Jesus never even visited Rome in His lifetime? Because Peter, the "rock" on which Jesus said His Church would be built (cf. Matt 16:18) was martyred and buried in Rome.[16] The fact is that the main altar of St. Peter's Basilica at the Vatican is positioned right on top of the tomb of St. Peter — the "rock" foundation set up by our Lord Jesus Christ Himself!

Roman Catholics certainly do not *worship* the Pope because worship is due to God alone. Catholics look to the Pope for spiritual leadership and guidance, just as the early Christians looked to St. Peter.

Common Objection #2

"In Gal 2:11-14 Peter is forcefully called down by St. Paul for trying to impose Jewish dietary regulations upon the Christian

Church. Certainly if he were seen as the supreme leader of the Church, this would never have happened."

A Catholic Response:

In Gal 2:11-14, Peter finds himself dining in the midst of a mixed group of Jewish and non-Jewish Christians at Antioch. St. Peter (born a Jew) had been eating with the non-Jewish Christians at the beginning of the meal but, when a group of newly-converted Jewish Christians arrived from Jerusalem, he temporarily reverted back to the Jewish custom of Jews only dining with Jews (cf. Acts 10:28). In Gal 2:11-14 we read about an instance of Paul disagreeing with Peter, not over a matter of religious faith or morals, but over a matter of *pastoral practice.*

In his Letter to the Romans, St. Paul speaks about the concern that Christians should have not to offend newly-converted Christians who are still immature in their faith: "it is good not to eat meat or drink wine or do anything that causes your brother to stumble" (Rom 14:21, cf. also Rom 15:12).[17] Might the reason that Peter temporarily reverted back to the Jewish custom of Jews eating by themselves be that he wanted to be pastorally sensitive to the newly-converted Jewish Christians? Might the reason that Peter temporarily reverted back to the old Jewish custom be that he wished to avoid possibly alienating the newly-converted Jewish Christian visitors with this strange new Christian dining practice?[18]

Peter certainly knew that it was perfectly O.K. for Jews to eat with non-Jews. He plainly says in the Acts of the Apostles: "You know that it is unlawful for a Jewish man to associate with, or visit, a Gentile, but God has shown me that I should not call any person profane or unclean" (Acts 10:28).

What could very well be the case in Gal 2:11-14 is that Peter's attempt to be pastorally sensitive and accommodating to the visiting newly-converted Jewish Christians was misunderstood or either was poorly implemented by him (cf. Acts 21:15-26 where, in Jerusalem, St. Paul follows Jewish customs to also be sensitive to newly-converted Jewish Christians).[19]

James Cardinal Gibbons writes about Gal 2:11-14:

"Cannot our Governor animadvert upon the President's conduct without impairing the President's jurisdiction? ...

St. Paul mentions it as a fact worthy of record that he actually *withstood Peter to his face*. Do you think it would be worth recording if Paul had rebuked James or John or Barnabas? By no means. If one brother rebukes another, the matter excites no special attention. But if a son rebukes his father, or if a Priest rebukes his Bishop to his face, we understand why he would consider it a fact worth relating. Hence, when St. Paul goes to the trouble of telling us that he took exception to Peter's conduct, he mentions it as an extraordinary exercise of Apostolic freedom, and leaves on our mind the obvious inference that Peter was his superior."[20]

Common Objection #3

"In the New Testament, 'Babylon' is a code name for the sinful city of Rome. Also, the writer of the Book of Revelation calls Rome 'the mother of harlots' (Rev 17:5). This, obviously, means that the "harlot" spoken about is the *Roman* Catholic Church."

A Catholic Response

John McKenzie, S.J. in his book, *Dictionary of the Bible*, says: "There can be no doubt that Rome is meant by Babylon in [Rev] 14:8, 16:19, 17:5, 18:2, 10, 21. The hostility of these passages is in contrast to the favorable [cf. Rom 1:7-8] or at least neutral attitude toward Rome expressed elsewhere in the NT, and it is probably a reflection of the hostility toward Christians shown by [the Emperor] Nero and in particular Domitian, whose reign is closer to the composition of [the Book of Revelation]."[21]

Obviously, prior to the Emperor Constantine's 313 A.D. decree that allowed Christianity to be practiced openly in public, there were no publicly advertised "Church buildings" to be found anywhere in the Roman empire. Therefore, Christians living within the boundaries of the city of Rome (or anywhere else in the Roman

Empire) gathered for worship in each other's homes and in the underground catacombs in order to escape the deadly persecutions being waged upon them by the pagan Roman authorities. In an effort to stamp out the Christian Church, Christians were often dragged into Roman sports arenas (e. g., the Emperor Nero's "Circus") and were forced to fight to death for the entertainment of the pagan Roman officials and citizens.[22]

Because of the fierce persecutions of the Christian Church by the authorities and citizens of the pagan Roman empire (cf. Acts 28:17-18), "Babylon" was used by some Biblical writers as a secret code name for the city of Rome so that, if their writings were ever discovered, the Roman officials would not know where to locate the various communities of Christians.[23]

The modern-day Vatican occupies 109 acres in the 582 square mile contemporary city of Rome, Italy.[24] When the Bible calls the city of Rome "the mother of harlots," it is speaking about the *pagan citizens* living within the boundaries of the ancient city of Rome and the Roman Empire who failed to put their faith in Christ, who led sinful immoral lives, and who persecuted our Lord's Church so bitterly.

Common Objection #4

"But Peter denied Jesus three times (cf. Luke 22:54-62) and fell asleep on Him in the Garden of Gethsamanae at the time when He needed him most (cf. Luke 22:39-45)! How could he possibly be seen as the supreme leader of the Christian community?"

A Catholic Response

The Old and New Testaments are *filled* with accounts of God commissioning weak and sinful human beings to assume leadership roles among His Chosen People: (cf. Moses in Deut 32:51-52; David in 2 Sam 11; Solomon in 1 Kings 11; Judas in Luke 22:47; "Saul" in Acts 9:1-2; Peter, James, and John in Luke 22:39-46.) In the midst of their own personal weakness and sinfulness, God uses these "earthen vessels" in a beautiful way to carry on His work of building the Kingdom.[25] Peter's three heart-felt expressions of love for Jesus recounted in John's Gospel (cf. John 21:15-17) are interpreted by many Christians as his repenting and his making reparation for the sin of his three earlier denials (cf. John 18:17, 25-27).

What Did the Early Christians Believe About the Primacy of St. Peter and His Successors?

- "Our Apostles knew through our Lord Jesus Christ that there would be strife for the office of bishop. For this reason, therefore, having received perfect foreknowledge, they appointed those who have already been mentioned, and afterwards added the further provision that, if they should die, other approved men should succeed to their ministry." St. Clement of Rome in his *Letter to the Corinthians* (circa 80 A.D.)[26]

- "...[W]e are in a position to enumerate those who were instituted bishops by the Apostles, and their successors to our own times." St. Irenaeus in his *Against Heresies* (circa 180 A.D.)[27]

- "...[T]he successions of the bishops of the greatest and most ancient Church known to all, founded and organized at Rome by the two most glorious Apostles, Peter and Paul, that Church which has the tradition and the faith which comes down to us after having been announced to men by the Apostles. For with this Church, because of its superior origin, all Churches must agree, that is, all the faithful in the whole world; and it is in her that the faithful everywhere have maintained the Apostolic tradition." St. Irenaeus in his *Against Heresies* (circa 180 A.D.)[28]

- "The blessed Apostles [Peter and Paul], having founded and built up the Church [of Rome], they handed over the office of the episcopate to Linus. Paul makes mention of this Linus in the Epistle to Timothy. To him succeeded Anencletus; and after him, in the third place from the Apostles, Clement was chosen for the episcopate. He had seen the blessed Apostles and was acquainted with them. It might be said that he still heard the echoes of the preaching of the Apostles, and had their traditions before his eyes... To this Clement, Evaristus succeeded; and Alexander succeeded Evaristus. Then, sixth after the Apostles, Sixtus was appointed; after him, Telesphorus, who also was gloriously martyred. Then Hyginus; after him, Pius; and after him, Anicetus. Soter succeeded Anicetus, and now, in the twelfth place after the Apostles, the lot of the episcopate has fallen to Eleutherus. In this order, and by the teaching of the Apostles handed down in the Church, the preaching of the truth has come down to us." St. Irenaeus in his *Against Heresies* (circa 180 A.D.)[29]

- "It is necessary to obey those who are the presbyters in the Church, those who, as we have shown, have succession from the Apostles; those who have received, with the succession of the episcopate, the sure charism of truth according to the good pleasure of the Father. But the rest, who have no part in the primitive succession and assemble wheresoever they will, must be held in suspicion." St. Irenaeus in his *Against Heresies* (circa 180 A.D.)[30]

- "The true gnosis is the doctrine of the Apostles, and the ancient organization of the Church throughout the world, and the manifestation of the body of Christ according to the successions of the bishops, by which successions the bishops have handed down the Church which is found everywhere; and the very complete tradition of the Scriptures." St. Irenaeus in his *Against Heresies* (circa 180 A.D.)[31]

- "On hearing these words, the blessed Peter, the chosen, the pre-eminent, the first among the disciples, for whom alone with Himself the Savior paid tribute, quickly grasped and understood their meaning. And what does he say? 'Behold, we have left all and have followed you." St. Clement of Alexandria in his *Who is the Rich Man That is Saved?* (circa 190 A.D.)[32]

- "I can point out the trophies of the Apostles [Peter and Paul]. For if you are willing to go to the Vatican or to the Ostian Way, you will find the trophies of those who founded this Church." *Fragment in Eusebius* (circa 198 A.D.)[33]

- "When I had come to Rome, I made a succession up to Anicetus, whose deacon was Eleutherus. And after Anicetus, Soter succeeded; and after him Eleutherus. In each succession and in each city there is a continuance of that which is proclaimed by the Law, the Prophets, and the Lord." *Fragment in Eusebius* (circa 198 A.D.)[34]

- "...[L]ike the Church of the Romans where Clement was ordained by Peter... Therefore, they will be challenged to meet this test even by those Churches which are of much later date — for they are being established daily — and whose founder is not from among the Apostles nor from among the apostolic men." Tertullian in his *The Demurrer Against the Heretics* (circa 200 A.D.)[35]

- "Look at the great foundation of the Church, that most solid of rocks, upon whom Christ built the Church!" Origen in his *Homilies on Exodus* (circa 244 A.D.)[36]

- "Our Lord, whose commands we ought to fear and observe, says in the Gospel, by way of assigning the episcopal dignity and settling the plan of His Church: 'I say to you that you are Peter, and upon this rock I will build my Church, and the gates of hell will not overcome it. And to you I will give the keys of the Kingdom of heaven: and whatever things you bind on earth will be bound also in heaven, and whatever you loose on earth, they will be loosed also in heaven. From that time the ordination of bishops and the plan of the Church flows on through the changes of times and successions." St. Cyprian of Carthage in his *Letter to the Lapsed* (circa 250 A.D.)[37]

- "...[B]ut a primacy is given to Peter, whereby it is made clear that there is but one Church and one chair... If someone does not hold fast to this unity of Peter, can he imagine that he still holds the faith? If he desert the chair of Peter upon whom the Church was built, can he still be confident that he is in the Church?" St. Cyprian of Carthage in his *The Unity of the Catholic Church* (circa 251 A.D.)[38]

- "There is one God and one Christ, and one Church, and one Chair founded on Peter by the Word of the Lord. It is not possible to set up another altar or for there to be another priesthood besides that one altar and that one priesthood. Who ever has gathered elsewhere is scattering." St. Cyprian of Carthage in his *Letter to All His People* (circa 251 A.D.) [39]

- "Cornelius was made bishop by the decision of God and of His Christ, by the testimony of almost all the clergy, by the applause of the people then present, by the college of venerable priests and good men, at a time when no one had been made before him — when the place of Fabian, which is the place of Peter, the dignity of the sacerdotal chair, was vacant." St. Cyprian of Carthage in his *Letter to Antonianus, A Bishop in Numidia* (circa 251 A.D.)[40] [41]

What Did the Early Christians Believe About the Primacy of the Church in Rome?

- "[T]o the Church also which holds the presidency in the place of the country of the Romans, worthy of God, worthy of honor, worthy of blessing, worthy of praise, worthy of success, worthy of sanctification, and, because you hold the presidency of love, named after Christ and named after the Father: her therefore do I salute in the name of Jesus Christ, the Son of the Father." St. Ignatius of Antioch in his *Letter to the Romans* (circa 110 A.D.)[42]

- "You have also, by your very admonition, brought together the planting that was made by Peter and Paul at Rome and at Corinth; for both of them alike planted in our Corinth and taught us; and both alike, teaching similarly in Italy, suffered martyrdom at the same time." *Fragment in Eusebius* (circa 198 A.D.)[43]

- "But if you are near to Italy, you have Rome, whence also our authority derives. How happy is that Church, on which Apostles poured out their whole doctrine along with their blood, where Peter endured a passion like that of the Lord, where Paul was crowned in a death like John's." Tertullian in his *The Demurrer Against the Heretics* (circa 200 A.D.)[44]

- "Peter was girded about by another when he was made fast to the cross. Paul obtained a birth suited to Roman citizenship, when in that city he was given re-birth by an ennobling martyrdom." Tertullian in his *Antidote Against the Scorpion* (circa 211 A.D.)[45]

Endnotes

[1] Jesus' words to the Apostle Peter found in Matt 16:18-19.

[168] Cf. Mk 3:14-15.

[174] *LG* 4; cf. *Jn* 17:4.

[315] St. Ignatius of Antioch, *Ad Rom.* 1, 1: *Apostolic Fathers*, II/2, 192; cf. LG 13.

[316] St. Irenaeus, *Adv. haeres.* 3, 3, 2: PG 7/1, 849; cf. Vatican Council I: DS 3057.

[317] St. Maximus the Confessor, *Opuscula theo.*: PG 91: 137-140.

[322] *LG* 15.

[2] Bruce M. Metzger and Michael D. Coogan (editors), *The Oxford Companion to the Bible*, (New York, NY: Oxford University Press, 1993), p. 46. Note that, when Jesus spoke *"Eli, Eli, lema sabachthani"* from the cross (cf. Matt 27:46), He was speaking, not in Greek, but in His native tongue of Aramaic.

[3] Suppose that the Greek word for "rock" was "Georgette." If one wanted to call a man a "rock" in Greek, he would not use the word "Georgette" but would masculine-ize the word to "George."

[4] St. Paul writes to the Ephesians: "...you are fellow citizens with the holy ones and members of the household of God, *built upon the foundation of the apostles* and prophets, with Christ Jesus himself as the capstone" (Eph 2:19-20). One can see here the scriptural truth that the Church is built upon *the foundation of the apostles*. Jesus designates St. Peter to be the "rock" foundation on which His Church was to be built while He Himself serves as the "capstone" of the structure. (Cf. Eph 1:22-23 where St. Paul calls Jesus the "head" of the "body" of the Church.)

[5] Patrick Madrid (editor), *Surprised by Truth*, (San Diego, CA: Basilica Press, 1994), pp. 68-69.

[6] *Surprised by Truth*, pp. 200-201.

7   "As the steward of Jesus Christ on earth, St. Peter is the first of many who will govern the Church of Christ from the Chair of St. Peter. The keys are symbolic of the sovereign's power and authority as they are entrusted to his prime minister for a period of time to act for the sovereign in fulfilling the sovereign's wishes. The sovereign, or king, never relinquishes his authority during this period of delegation. At the end of the period of delegation, the king reassumes his total command and authority over the kingdom. Jesus Christ, while still retaining his sovereignty, entrusted the keys to the kingdom of heaven to Peter (and his successors) on earth until the end of time." Scott Butler, Norman Dahlgren, David Hess, *Jesus, Peter & The Keys*, (Santa Barbara, CA: Queenship Publishing Co., 1996), p. 39.

8   Note that the familiar jokes that we sometimes hear about a person dying and going to heaven but first being greeted by St. Peter at the heavenly gates is a reference to his Christ-given role as "key-holder" of the gates of heaven (cf. Matt 16:18-19).

9   Catholic convert T.L. Frazier writes, "...Abraham is called the rock from which the Old Covenant people of God were hewn in Isaiah 51:1-2. I found the comparison between Abraham, the rock whose name was also changed by God (Gen 17:5), and Simon Peter, the rock on which the new, spiritual Israel is to be built, to be intriguing. It suggested that Jesus might be deliberately echoing this idea from Isaiah and making Peter the new Patriarch of the New Covenant people of God." Cf. *Surprised by Truth*, p. 199.

10 Note that, when a speaker addresses an audience, doesn't he normally begin by addressing the dignitaries in attendance in order of their rank (i.e., "Mr. President, members of Congress, public officials, citizens of the United States...")?

11 Msgr. Bob Guste, *The Gift of the Church*, (Santa Barbara, CA: Queenship Publishing Co., 1993), p. 64.

12 James Cardinal Gibbons writes about St. Peter: "The whole sheepfold is confided to him, without any exception or limitation. Peter has jurisdiction not only over the lambs — the weak and tender portion of the flock — by which are understood the faithful; but also over the sheep, *i.e.*, the pastors themselves, who hold the same relations to their congregations that the sheep

hold to the lambs, because they bring forth unto Jesus Christ, and nourish the spiritual lambs of the fold. To other Pastors a certain portion of the flock is assigned; to Peter the entire fold; for, never did Jesus say to any other Apostles or Bishop what He said to Peter: Feed My whole flock." Cf. James Cardinal Gibbons, *The Faith of Our Fathers*, (Rockford, IL: TAN Books and Publishers, Inc., 1980), p. 83.

[13] *King James Bible*, (Nashville, TN: Holman Bible Publishers, 1979), p. 78.

[14] Scott Hahn, *Answering Common Objections Audio Tape*, (West Covina, CA: St. Joseph Communications, Inc., (818) 331-3549)

[15] Note that there is only one king of England but that fact does not deny the existence of officials to whom royal authority has been delegated. If twenty-five officials act in the king's name, that does not mean that there are twenty-five kings. Cf. Fathers Rumble and Carty, *Radio Replies (First Volume)*, (Rockford, IL: TAN Books and Publishers, Inc., 1979), p. 86.

[16] Cf. the writings of the early Church Fathers at the end of this chapter.

[17] St. Paul writes about the importance of Christians accepting other people where they are at as they begin to evangelize them with the Gospel: "Although I am free in regard to all, I have made myself a slave to all so as to win over as many as possible. To the Jews I became like a Jew to win over Jews; to those under the law I became like one under the law — though I myself am not under the law — to win over those under the law" (1 Cor 9:19-20). In Gal 2:11-14 St. Peter, like St. Paul, "became like a Jew to win over Jews."

[18] Cf. James Cardinal Gibbons, *The Faith of Our Fathers*, (Rockford, IL: TAN Books and Publishers, Inc., 1980), p. 85.

[19] *Jesus, Peter & The Keys*, pp. 204-207.

[20] *The Faith of Our Fathers*, p. 86.

[21] John L. McKenzie, S.J., *Dictionary of the Bible*, (New York, NY: Collier Books Macmillan Publishing Co., 1965), p. 749.

[22] Note that it is on top of the ruins of "Nero's Circus" (and the adjoining cemetery in which the tomb of St. Peter was discovered) that the headquarters of the Catholic Church ("the Vatican") stands today. Recall Jesus' words to St. Peter: "And

so I say to you, you are Peter, and upon this rock I will build my church..." (Matt 16:18-19).

23 In Acts of the Apostles (written circa 63 A.D.), Luke does not give Peter's whereabouts because the emperor Nero was in power in Rome at the time and the Christian community didn't want to give the Roman authorities written directions as to the whereabouts of their members.

24 Cf. *Encyclopedia Americana* (Volume 27), (Danbury, CT: Grolier, Inc., 1995), p. 910. and (Volume 23), p. 686.

25 Remember the words of St. Paul: "...I will rather boast most gladly of my weaknesses, in order that the power of Christ may dwell with me" (2 Cor 12:9).

26 William A. Jurgens (editor and translator), *The Faith of the Early Fathers (Volume 1)*, (Collegeville, MN: The Liturgical Press, 1970), p. 10.

27 *Ibid.*, p. 89.

28 *Ibid.*, p. 90.

29 *Ibid.*, p. 90.

30 *Ibid.*, p. 96.

31 *Ibid.*, p. 97.

32 *Ibid.*, p. 187.

33 *Ibid.*, p. 44.

34 *Ibid.*, p. 80.

35 *Ibid.*, p. 122.

36 *Ibid.*, p. 205.

37 *Ibid.*, p. 229.

38 *Ibid.*, p. 220.

39 *Ibid.*, p. 229.

40 *Ibid.*, p. 230.

41 St. Ambrose (circa 380 A.D.) summed it up nicely when he said: *"Ubi Petrus, ibi Ecclesia."* ("Where Peter is, there is the Church.")

42 *The Faith of the Early Fathers (Volume 1)*, p. 21.

43 *Ibid.*, p. 45.

44 *Ibid.*, p. 122.

45 *Ibid.*, p. 152.

Chapter 14

"Simon ... I Have Prayed That Your Own Faith May Not Fail":[1] The Infallibility of the Pope

What Does the Catholic Church Teach?

"...It is this Magisterium's task to preserve God's people from deviations and defections and to guarantee them the objective possibility of professing the true faith without error... To fulfill this service, Christ endowed the Church's shepherds with the charism of infallibility in matters of faith and morals. The exercise of this charism takes several forms: '...The Roman Pontiff, head of the college of bishops, enjoys this infallibility in virtue of his office, as supreme pastor and teacher of all the faithful — who confirms his brethren in the faith — he proclaims by a definitive act a doctrine pertaining to faith or morals... The infallibility promised to the Church is also present in the body of bishops when, together with Peter's successor, they exercise the supreme Magisterium,' above all in an Ecumenical Council.[418] When the Church through its supreme Magisterium proposes a doctrine 'for belief as being divinely revealed,'[419] and as the teaching of Christ, the definitions 'must be adhered to with the obedience of faith.'[420] This infallibility extends as far as the deposit of divine Revelation itself."[421] (*Catechism of the Catholic Church*, #890–891.)

Common Objection #1

"How can the Pope possibly be infallible? He is a human being and makes mistakes just like the rest of us."

A Catholic Response

- In the Gospel of Matthew, Jesus tells the Apostle Peter: "And so I say to you, you are Peter, and upon this rock I will build my church, and the gates of the netherworld shall not prevail against it. I will give you the keys to the kingdom of heaven. Whatever you bind on earth shall be bound in heaven; and whatever you loose on earth shall be loosed in heaven" (Matt 16: 18-19). How strong and stable would this "rock foundation" be if the person holding the office of Peter were susceptible to error in essential matters of religious faith or morals? If Jesus was to respond to Peter's decisions with an identical "binding" and "loosing" in heaven, how could Christ possibly ratify error?

- In the Gospel of Luke, Jesus says to Peter: "I have prayed that your own faith may not fail; and once you have turned back, you must strengthen your brothers" (Luke 22: 31-32). Because Jesus commissioned Peter to "strengthen his brothers" in their Christian faith, we Catholics believe that the Holy Spirit will not allow the person holding the office of Peter to err in matters of religious faith and morals.

- In the Gospel of John, Jesus says, "And I will ask the Father, and he will give you another Advocate to be with you always, the Spirit of truth...you know it, because it remains in you, and will be in you. I will not leave you orphans..." (John 14: 16-18).

- In the Gospel of Matthew, Jesus gives His disciples the "great commission": "Go, therefore, and make disciples of all nations, baptizing them..., [and] teaching them to observe all that I have commanded you. And behold, I am with you always, until the end of the age" (Matt 28: 19-20). In this important Scripture passage, Jesus commissions His disciples to teach and gives them the promise that He would protect them from religious and moral error until He comes again. We can see here that the Church is infallible because the Ones who promised that they would guide it (Jesus and the Holy Spirit) are infallible.

- In the Gospel of John, Jesus says, "I have much more to tell you, but you cannot bear it now. But when he comes, the Spirit of truth, he will guide you to all truth" (John 16: 12-13). Jesus promised that the Holy Spirit would keep constant watch over His Church and not allow it to go astray in essential matters of faith or morals.

- In the Gospel of Luke, Jesus tells His 72 disciples: "Whoever listens to you listens to me. Whoever rejects you rejects me" (Luke 10: 16). If this is true about Jesus' 72 disciples how much more would this be true of the "prime minister" chosen by our Lord Himself, St. Peter (cf. Matt 16: 18-19)!

- St. Paul writes that the Church is "the pillar and foundation of the truth" (1 Tim 3: 15). Could the "prime minister" of the Roman Catholic Church (the Pope) be capable of making an error in essential matters of faith or morals and the Church still be considered to be "the pillar and foundation of the truth?" Hardly.[2]

Bob Sungenis writes:[3]

"I found an indisputable example of the infallibility of the Catholic Church when I began to reflect on the question of the canon of Scripture — how the books of the Bible were determined, an issue often ignored by Protestants. There is no 'inspired table of contents' anywhere in Scripture. The decision as to which books should be included in the Bible and which books should not, was made by the Catholic Church in the councils of Hippo (A.D. 393), and Carthage (A.D. 397, and 419). These decisions were later ratified and solemnly defined by the ecumenical councils of Second Nicea (787), Florence (1440), and Trent (1525 46)... Since the Bible does not indicate which books belong within it, and since Protestants do not believe the Church has any authority to infallibly determine which books belong and which books don't, Protestants are left with an epistemological dilemma. Hence they are forced to the logical but heretical conclusion that there may be inspired books that should be in the Bible but were left out in error, and that there may be uninspired books in the Bible that have no business being there, but were added in error...

In holding the 'fallible canon' theory, Protestants cannot be infallibly certain that the Bible they hold in their hands is in fact the Bible... For if one cannot be certain which books belong in the Bible, how can one presume to use it 'alone' as a reliable guide to saving faith in God? The irony is that while Protestants use the theory of *sola scriptura* to advance their attacks on the Catholic Church, they have no infallible way of knowing what comprises Scripture in the first place...

In seminary we were taught a variation on the 'fallible canon' theory. The Bible was said to be 'self-authenticating,' in other words, the Bible, by its very nature, simply compelled one to accept its books as inspired. That may be a comforting thought for Protestants, but it is no different from the Mormon's claim that he just knows the Book of Mormon is the inspired Word of God, because the Book of Mormon feels true to him. This is hardly a reliable way of ascertaining which books belong in the Bible. And don't forget, there are a number of books in the Bible, such as Philemon, 3 John, and others, that don't jump out at the reader as being particularly inspired (read them sometime, and see what you think)...

The truth is, Protestants are living off the borrowed capital of the Catholic Church, for it was the Catholic Church that infallibly recognized, under the divine guidance of the Holy Spirit, the canon of Scripture. Each time Protestants quote from the Bible they unwittingly acknowledge their trust in the infallible divine guidance given to the Catholic Church by Christ. Many Evangelicals and Fundamentalists argue that the Catholic Church did not give us the canon, the Holy Spirit did. But there is no argument between Catholics and Protestants here. Of course the Holy Spirit gave the canon of the Bible, say Catholics. The real question is how he gave it. How did the Holy Spirit communicate the knowledge of the canon to the Church? By asserting that the Holy Spirit gave the canon to the Church, the Protestant must admit that the Holy Spirit guided the Church into an infallible decision. The only way out of this dilemma is the so-called 'fallible canon' theory..."[4]

Catholic apologist Scott Hahn reminds us that St. Peter was certainly infallible on at least two occasions — when he wrote the First Letter of Peter and the Second Letter of Peter. [5] If God could watch over him and protect him from error in matters of faith and morals during the time when he wrote those letters, could it also be conceivable that God could also have been with him throughout his ministry and with the successors that followed him so that the fullness of religious faith and morals could be passed on intact to each successive new generation of Christian believers? [6] Cf. Chapter 13 of this book to read more about the authority of the successor of St. Peter (the Pope).

As is stated in the *Catechism of the Catholic Church* quoted at the beginning of this chapter, not every statement uttered by the Pope is infallible. For the Pope to declare a teaching to be infallible it must meet certain requirements:

- The teaching must involve matters of religious faith or morals (it cannot be a personal opinion in some other realm or field.)
- The teaching must be definitively proclaimed by the Pope to be Divinely revealed and, therefore, binding upon all of the faithful.
- The proclamation of the infallible teaching is done *ex cathedra* and appeals to the Pope's Apostolic authority.

Note that "infallibility" does not mean "impeccability" (the inability to sin). As a matter of fact, our current Pope celebrates the Sacrament of Penance on a regular basis to receive God's forgiveness for his own personal failings and shortcomings (as should we all!)

The *Catechism of the Catholic Church* goes on to teach about the acceptance by the Catholic faithful of non-infallible teachings proposed by the ordinary Magisterium: "To this ordinary teaching the faithful 'are to adhere to it with religious assent' which, though distinct from the assent of faith, is nonetheless an extension of it" (#893).

Rev. John A. O'Brien writes about former Popes of the Catholic Church:

> "As a matter of fact, the popes have been, with few exceptions, men of virtuous lives. Twenty-nine out of the first thirty pontiffs died as martyrs for the faith. Out of the total who have sat upon the Chair of Peter, seventy-seven are invoked upon our altars as saints of God because of their eminent holiness. Only about half a dozen [out of two hundred sixty four] have been charged with serious moral lapses. This is a strikingly small proportion when it is remembered that one out of the twelve chosen by Christ Himself was unworthy — Judas Iscariot. ...[A] judge is clothed by the laws of our country with certain legal power and authority. If in his private life he were guilty of some moral indiscretions, this circumstance would not rob his decisions of their validity. His authority in court is not dependent upon the character of his private life; it is conferred upon him by virtue of the office he holds."[7]

What Did the Early Christians Believe About the Infallibility of the Pope in Matters of Faith and Morals?

- "For the Apostles, like a rich man in a bank, deposited with her most copiously everything which pertains to the truth; and everyone whosoever wishes draws from her the drink of life... If there should be a dispute over some kind of question, ought we not to have recourse to the most ancient Churches in which the Apostles were familiar, and draw from them what is clear and certain in regard to that question?" St. Irenaeus in his *Against Heresies* (circa 180 A.D.)[8]

- "Grant, then, that all have erred; that the Apostle was mistaken in bearing witness; that the Holy Spirit had no such consideration for any one Church as to lead it into truth, although He was sent for that purpose by Christ, who had asked the Father to make Him the Teacher of truth; that the Steward of God and Vicar of Christ neglected His office, and permitted the Churches for a time to understand otherwise and to believe otherwise than He Himself had preached through the Apostles: now, is it likely that so many and such great Churches should have gone astray into a unity of faith?" Tertullian in his *The Demurrer Against the Heretics* (circa 200 A.D.)[9]

Endnotes

[1]   Jesus' words to St. Peter found in Luke 22: 31-32.

[418] LG 25; cf. Vatican Council I: DS 3074.

[419] DV 10 paragraph 2.

[420] LG 25 paragraph 2.

[421] Cf. LG 25.

[2]   Catholic convert Julie Swenson writes: "Is Protestantism the pillar and foundation of truth? ...How could it be that the thousands of competing and conflicting Protestant denominations were somehow corporately a stable 'pillar and foundation' for the truth? After all, no one of them agreed totally with any of the others as to what the truth is. Which one had the truth? I closed the Bible in disappointment, unable to accept the implications of this verse, which portrayed a unified, stable, and visible Church." Cf. Patrick Madrid (editor), *Surprised by Truth*, (San Diego, CA: Basilica Press, 1994), p. 138.

[3]   Patrick Madrid (editor), *Surprised by Truth*, (San Diego, CA: Basilica Press, 1994), pp. 122-126.

[4] Note that the most accurate arrow in the world is of no use if one does not possess the most accurate bow in the world to deliver the arrow flawlessly to its intended target. In the same way, the infallible Bible is of no use unless there is an infallible interpreter to deliver its true message to believers. Because Protestant Christians do not believe that there is an infallible interpreter of the Bible, there are as many interpretations of the Bible as there are Protestant denominations.

[5] Scott and Kimberly Hahn, *Rome Sweet Home: Our Journey to Catholicism*, (San Francisco, CA: Ignatius Press, 1993), p. 75.

[6] "An infallible authority, far from limiting our freedom, can give us greater freedom. Christ says of his teaching, 'You will know the truth and the truth will make you free' (John 8: 32). Knowing the truth about anything frees us from ignorance, doubt, insecurity — if we know our watch is correct, we are freed from uncertainty about the time. The more truths science discovers about man and the universe, the greater freedom we can have from disease and calamities." Anthony Wilhelm, *Christ Among Us*, (Ramsey, NJ: Paulist Press, 1967, 1973, 1975, 1981), pp. 154-155.

[7] Rev. John A. O'Brien, *The Faith of Millions*, (Huntington, Indiana: Our Sunday Visitor, Inc., 1963, 1974), p. 109.

[8] William A. Jurgens (editor and translator), *The Faith of the Early Church Fathers (Volume 1)*, (Collegeville, MN: The Liturgical Press, 1970), pp. 90-91.

[9] *Ibid.*, p. 121.

Chapter 15

Did Mary Have Other Children Besides Jesus?

What Does the Catholic Church Teach

"Against this doctrine the objection is sometimes raised that the Bible mentions brothers and sisters of Jesus.[157] The Church has always understood these passages as not referring to other children of the Virgin Mary. In fact James and Joseph, 'brothers of Jesus,' are the sons of another Mary, a disciple of Christ, whom St. Matthew significantly calls 'the other Mary.'[158] They are close relations of Jesus, according to an Old Testament expression."[159] (*Catechism of the Catholic Church*, #500.)

Common Objection #1

"Scripture talks about Jesus being Mary's "firstborn son" (cf. Luke 2:7). We can conclude from this statement that she, at least, had a second-born son and maybe even more children."

A Catholic Response

In the Book of Exodus God commands the Jews to "Consecrate to me every first-born that opens the womb..." (Exod 13:2). Obviously, Jewish parents did not have to wait to see if they would have other children before they could call their first child their "first-born." In fact, many Jewish families consecrated their "first-born" to the Lord and then had no successive children.

Luke 2:7 simply states that the first child that Mary gave birth to was a boy named Jesus. In the Scriptures the term "first-born son" was a common one and was used to designate the person who had inheritance rights (cf. Deut 21:15-17). The term "first born son" made no statement at all about any successive children of a couple.

Common Objection #2

"The Bible clearly states that Jesus' 'brothers' were named 'James, Joses, Judas, and Simon' (cf. Mark 6:3). What more proof do you need than that to believe that Mary and Joseph had other children besides Jesus?"

A Catholic Response

The word "brother" that appears in Mark 6:3 (Greek: *adelphos*) is used in the New Testament to refer both to blood brothers (cf. Matt 4:21-22) as well as kinsmen/associates (cf. Acts 9:17). Since *adelphos* is used both to refer to blood brothers *and* associates/kinfolk, how do we know how to correctly interpret the statement that James, Joses, Judas, and Simon were "brothers [*adelphos*]" of Jesus?

- After Mark the evangelist tells us that Jesus is *the* son of Mary, we read: "[Is He not] the *brother* [Greek: *adelphos*] of James and Joses and Judas and Simon?..." (Mark 6:3).[1]

- In the Gospel of Mark, Jesus uses the term "brothers and sisters," not in the literal sense of blood brothers and sisters, but in a broad, spiritual sense: "[Jesus] said to them in reply, 'Who are my mother and my brothers?' And looking around at those seated in the circle he said, 'Here are my mother and my brothers. For whoever does the will of God is my *brother* [Greek: *adelphos*] and sister and mother'" (Mark 3:31-35). The terms "brother" and "sister" are commonly used by many people today in the same manner (e.g., "my brother/sister in Christ").

- A number of times in the King James Bible, people are called each other's "brother" when, in fact, they were not blood brothers at all but were merely "kinsmen": "And they took Lot, Abram's brother's son, who dwelt in Sodom... And he brought back all the goods, and also brought again his *brother* Lot..." (Gen 14:12, 16). We also read in the King James Bible: "And it came to pass, when Jacob saw Rachel the daughter of Laban his mother's brother... And Laban said unto Jacob, Because thou art my *brother*..." (Gen 29:10, 15). (Note that Lot was actually Abraham's *nephew* and Laban was Jacob's *uncle*, yet the King James Bible calls them "brothers.")[2]

- St. Paul tells us that Jesus appeared "to more than five hundred *brothers* [Greek: *adelphos*] at once..." (1 Cor 15:6). If all of those men were blood brothers, I'd sure like to meet that mother! Obviously, the term "brother" in this case means "spiritual brothers" in a broad sense.

- In the account of the finding of the twelve-year-old Jesus in the Temple (cf. Luke 2:41-52), the reader certainly gets the impression that the lost Jesus is Mary and Joseph's *only* child, as the story makes no mention at all about the existence of any other blood brothers or sisters among the travelers.

- Probably the biggest Scriptural argument that Mary did not have any other natural-born children can be found in the Gospel of John when Jesus, from the cross, gives His mother to the Apostle John: "When Jesus saw his mother and the disciple there whom he loved, he said to his mother, 'Woman, behold, your son.' Then he said to the disciple, 'Behold, your mother.' And from that hour the disciple took her into his home" (John 19:26-27). This action of Jesus would have made no sense at all if He had other blood brothers and sisters (especially in the very close-knit family unit of the Jewish people at the time of Jesus). Since Mary had no other natural-born children to care for her, Jesus entrusts her to the care of the Apostle John.

In Jesus' native language of Aramaic there was no word for "cousin." If a person wanted to refer to someone as his "cousin" he could not do it in a direct manner and had to resort to a lengthy description of his relationship to that person (e.g. a cousin may have been described as "the son of the sister of my father"). Since this was a very awkward way of speaking, the word for "brother" was sometimes used as a short cut to refer to a kinsman.

David Currie writes about Mary: "...[W]hen the Bible uses the word 'brother' for a relative for Jesus, it could not possibly mean that literally. No one could have the same father as Jesus did, so the word 'brother' cannot be taken at face value. All Evangelicals should agree that the closest sibling possible to Jesus would be a half-brother."[3]

Catholic convert Tim Staples speaks about the perpetual virginity of Mary:

> "...Luke 6:15-16 reveals that James and Joses, though elsewhere called 'brothers' of Jesus, are here shown to be the sons of Alphaeus (cf. Matt 10:3, 27:56) whose wife Mary was actually the blessed Virgin Mary's sister, or perhaps her cousin (cf. John 19:25). These 'brothers' were actually Jesus' cousins...
>
> But even if those men were Jesus' cousins, I thought, Scripture says that Jesus was Mary's 'firstborn," implying she had other children afterwards (Matt 1:25). [My friend] Matt reminded me that the text did not say they had marital relations — that was simply my interpretation. And 'firstborn' is a ceremonial title give to the firstborn male child who inherited a unique birthright from his father (cf. Gen 25:33). An only child could have this title just as validly as the firstborn of many brothers."[4]

Mark Miravalle writes about Mary's perpetual virginity: "[T]he virginal womb of Mary is the shrine of the Holy Spirit, and a human conception following the miraculous conception by the Holy Spirit would not respect its sacred and unique seed of precedence."[5]

Consider this analogy: Many sports teams will retire the jersey of older sports greats because they know that any other player wearing that particular jersey would not stand a chance at even coming close to accomplishing the tremendous feats that the previous player did. In a similar way, after the birth of Jesus the God-man, Mary's womb was "retired" by God because any mere human birth that would have followed would have diminished the unique and unrepeatable importance of the Divine first-born. The doctrine of Mary's perpetual virginity certainly is not intended to cast a negative light on the exercise of the conjugal act within the vocation of marriage. It simply makes a statement about the profound uniqueness of her calling and the supreme holiness of the God-man that dwelt within her body. I wonder if the prophet Ezekiel had any idea of how profoundly his prophecy was to be fulfilled in Mary when he wrote: "...This gate is to remain closed; it is not to be opened for anyone to enter by it; since the Lord, the God of Israel, has entered by it, it shall remain closed" (Ezek 44:2).

The key to determining what the word "brother" or "sister" means when it appears in the Bible is to look at the context in which it appears and to look at the *whole* of the Bible to see if the interpretation is consistent with other passages.

Common Objection #3

"The Bible says that '[Joseph] had no relations with [Mary] *until* she bore a son, and he named him Jesus' (Matt 1:25). We can, therefore, surely conclude from this that Mary had marital relations with Joseph after she bore Jesus."

A Catholic Response

The Greek word translated as "until" in Matt 1:25 is *heos*. The *New Strong's Exhaustive Concordance of the Bible* states that the word "until" (Greek: *heos*) can simply mean "hither to" or "up to" (which would make no statement at all about any future activity).[6]

In 1 Cor 15:25 St. Paul writes that "...[Jesus] must reign *until* [Greek: *heos*] he has put all his enemies under his feet." Does this mean that, after all of Jesus' enemies are conquered and put under His feet, He will stop reigning? Of course not (cf. Luke 1:33)! We can clearly see here how the word "until" (Greek: *heos*) does not necessarily mean that, after a certain point, a different action occurred.

Note that, in the Book of Genesis, Noah sends out a raven from the ark as a way to find out if the flood waters had subsided *(if the raven did not come back, Noah would assume that it found some place to land and that the flood waters were beginning to go down.)* In Gen 8:7 we read about the bird: "...It flew back and forth *until* the waters dried off from the earth." Does that mean that the raven came back to the ark *after* the flood waters subsided? The fact is that the bird *never* came back because he found a place to land because the flood waters had resided. The word "until" in this case simply means that the bird didn't come back up to a certain point in time. It makes no statement about what the bird did after that time.

Thus, the word "until" can simply mean that some action did not happen up to a certain point (e.g., "You cannot use the car *until* 3:00pm.") Can one necessarily conclude from this statement that, after 3:00pm, the car was definitely used? No. Maybe the person found another car to borrow or maybe the person changed his plans and didn't need the car. The only thing that we can gather from Matt 1:25 was that Mary and Joseph did not have marital relations before Jesus was born. The Scripture passage makes no statement about what they did after the birth of Jesus.

Fr. Peter Stravinskas, in his book *The Catholic Answer Book,* writes about the perpetual virginity of Mary:

"The Church has always taught that Mary was a perpetual virgin. This information can be gleaned from many sources, but especially from the earliest liturgical prayers in which reference is made to 'the Virgin.' If Mary had not remained a virgin until her death, why speak of her after the birth of Christ as such? If one has an uncle who is a bachelor, he is rightly referred to as one's 'bachelor uncle.' If he marries and thus ceases to be a bachelor, calling him a 'bachelor uncle' would be senseless. In the same way, the early Church spoke of Mary 'the Virgin' precisely because of the belief that she lived and died a virgin. When this teaching was questioned in later centuries, we find the addition of the adverb 'ever.' Thus do the Creed of Epiphanius (circa A.D.

374), the Second Council of Constantinople (A.D. 553), and the Lateran Council (A.D. 649) all speak of the 'ever-Virgin Mary.' St. Augustine, St. Jerome, and St. Cyril of Alexandria followed the same usage, as did the Protestant reformers Luther, Calvin, and Zwingli."[7]

What Did the Early Christians Believe About Jesus Having Other Blood Brothers and Sisters?

- The Creed of Epiphanius (circa 374 A.D.), the Second Council of Constantinople (553 A.D.), the Lateran Council (649 A.D.) all speak of Mary as "ever-Virgin."

- "Let those, therefore, who deny that the Son is by nature from the Father and proper to His essence, deny also that He took true human flesh from the ever-virgin Mary." St. Athanasius in his *Discourses Against the Arians* (circa 358 A.D.)[8]

- "Mary's life should be for you a pictorial image of virginity. Her life is like a mirror reflecting the face of chastity and the form of virtue. Therein you may find a model for your own life...showing what to improve, what to imitate, what to hold fast to." St. Ambrose in his *The Virgins* (circa 377 A.D.)[9]

- "The friends of Christ do not tolerate hearing that the Mother of God ever ceased to be a virgin." St. Basil the Great (d. 379 A.D.) in his *Hom. in S. Christi Generationem*[10]

Endnotes

[157] Cf. *Mk* 3:31-35; 6:3; *1 Cor* 9:5; *Gal* 1:19.

[158] *Mt* 13:55; 28:1; cf. *Mt* 27:56.

[159] Cf. *Gen* 13:8; 14:16; 29:15, etc.

[1] Scripture scholar Joseph Fitzmyer, S.J., writes about the identity of Jesus' "brothers" James and Joses: "Mark 15:40 supplies a reason for raising the question about the meaning of *adelphos*. It lists three women standing at a distance from the

cross and looking at the crucified Jesus: Mary Magdalene, Mary the mother of James the younger and of Joses, and Salome. It is hardly likely that the evangelist would be using such a circumlocution as 'Mary the mother of James and Joses' to designate the mother of the person hanging on the cross. He would have almost certainly said 'his mother' or 'the mother of Jesus.' Moreover, it is only in the Johannine tradition that it is said that 'his mother' was standing by the cross (19:25). The Synoptic tradition knows nothing of this. But since the sons James and Joses are two of the *adelphoi* mentioned in Mark 6:3, the question is then raised: In what sense is *adelphos* used there? If it means 'blood brother,' then it would imply that Mark was using a strange circumlocution to say that Mary, the mother of Jesus, was standing at a distance from the cross. But if the phrase in 15:40 does not refer to the mother of the crucified Jesus, then Mark 15:40 would seem to suggest that *adelphos* in 6:3 is to be understood in a sense other than 'blood brother,' e.g., 'relative, kinsman.'" Cf. Joseph Fitzmyer, S.J., *A Christological Catechism*, (New York, NY: Paulist Press, 1982), pp. 72-73. (Please note that these "brothers" and "sisters" of Jesus mentioned in Mark 6:3 are never once called the "sons/daughters" of Mary.)

2   *King James Bible*, (Nashville, TN: Holman Bible Publishers, 1979), pp. 8, 18.

3   David B. Currie, *Born Fundamentalist Born Again Catholic*, (San Francisco, CA: Ignatius Press, 1996), p. 156.

4   Patrick Madrid (editor), *Surprised by Truth*, (San Diego, CA: Basilica Press, 1994), p. 214.

5   Mark Miravalle, *Introduction to Mary*, (Santa Barbara, CA: Queenship Publishing Co., 1993), p. 49.

6   James Strong, LL.D, S.T.D., *The New Strong's Exhaustive Concordance of the Bible*, (Nashville, TN: Thomas Nelson Publishers, 1990), p. 34.

7   Rev. Peter Stravinskas, *The Catholic Answer Book*, (Huntington, IN: Our Sunday Visitor, Inc., 1990), p. 41.

8   William A. Jurgens (editor and translator), *Faith of the Early Fathers (Volume 1)*, (Collegeville, MN: The Liturgical Press, 1970), p. 330.

9   Karl Keating (editor), *This Rock Magazine*, "The Fathers Know Best" (San Diego, CA: Catholic Answers, Inc., "Mary's Privileges", pp. 36-38.

10 Anthony Wilhelm, *Christ Among Us (Third Revised Edition)*, (New York, NY: Paulist Press, 1967, 1973, 1975, 1981), p. 70.

Chapter 16

God Prepares a Spotless Mother to Bear a Spotless Lamb:[1] The Immaculate Conception of Mary in Her Mother's Womb Without Original Sin

What Does the Catholic Church Teach?

"To become the mother of the Savior, Mary 'was enriched by God with gifts appropriate to such a role.'[132] The angel Gabriel at the moment of the annunciation salutes her as 'full of grace.'[133] In fact, in order for Mary to be able to give the free assent of her faith to the announcement of her vocation, it was necessary that she be wholly borne by God's grace... Through the centuries the Church has become ever more aware that Mary, 'full of grace' through God,[134] was redeemed from the moment of her conception. That is what the dogma of the Immaculate Conception confesses, as Pope Pius IX proclaimed in 1854:

> The most Blessed Virgin Mary was, from the first moment of her conception, by a singular grace and privi-

lege of almighty God and by virtue of the merits of Jesus Christ, Savior of the human race, preserved immune from all stain of original sin. [135]

...The 'splendor of an entirely unique holiness' by which Mary is 'enriched from the first instant of her conception' comes wholly from Christ: she is 'redeemed, in a more exalted fashion, by reason of the merits of her Son.' [136] The Father blessed Mary more than any other created person 'in Christ with every spiritual blessing in the heavenly places' and chose her 'in Christ before the foundation of the world, to be holy and blameless before him in love.' [137] ...The Fathers of the Eastern tradition call the Mother of God 'the All-Holy' *(Panagia)* and celebrate her as 'free from any stain of sin, as though fashioned by the Holy Spirit and formed as a new creature.' [138] By the grace of God Mary remained free of every personal sin her whole life long." (*Catechism of the Catholic Church,* #490–493.)

Common Objection #1

"In the Gospel of Luke, Mary says, '...my spirit rejoices in God my *savior*' (Luke 1:46). Since only sinners need a Savior, we can rightly conclude that Mary was a sinner just like the rest of us."

A Catholic Response

The doctrine of the Immaculate Conception is sometimes confused with the doctrine of the virgin birth of Jesus Christ by the power of the Holy Spirit (cf. Luke 1:26-35). It does *not* refer to this. The doctrine of the Immaculate Conception states that Mary, unlike the rest of humanity, was conceived in her mother's womb without the stain of original sin so that she could be the spotless vessel to bring the spotless and sinless Lamb of God (Jesus Christ) into the world.[2]

In the Book of Genesis, God addresses "the serpent" (Satan) after he tempted our first parents to sin: "I will put enmity *[meaning: "complete and total opposition"]* between you and the woman, and between your offspring and hers, He will strike at your head while you strike at his heel" (Gen 3:15).

We can see here in Scripture that God put complete and total opposition not only between the original "woman" (Eve) and the original "serpent" (Satan) but also between a certain future "woman" (along with her future offspring) and the future "offspring" of the devil. Many of the early Church Fathers saw the future offspring of a woman who would be in totally opposition to evil and crush the head of Satan as Jesus Christ: "...[The] Son of God was revealed to destroy the works of the devil" (1 John 3:8).

As a result, the future "woman" mentioned in Gen 3:15 (who the Church sees as a foreshadowing of Mary) began life sinless in her mother's womb and, thus, remained in total enmity (complete and total opposition to evil) in order to be the spiritually pure vessel that would be used by God to bear the sinless Conqueror of Satan, Jesus Christ.

Mark Miravalle writes about the sinlessness of Mary:

> "The early Church fathers also compared Mary's sinless state as being identical to Eve's state before the participation of Eve in Original Sin. Mary as the 'New Eve' was seen to be in the same state of original grace and justice that Eve was in when she was created by God. Since Eve was obviously conceived in grace, without the fallen nature that we receive due to Original Sin, the parallel made by the Church Fathers between Mary and Eve before the fall illustrates their understanding of Mary's likewise immaculate nature.
>
> In the words of St. Ephraem (d. 373): 'Those two innocent...women, Mary and Eve, had been [created] utterly equal, but afterwards one became the cause of our death, the other the cause of our life.'
>
> ...Belief in Mary's Immaculate Conception is not difficult, if we remember that it was God's original intention that all humans be conceived in sanctifying grace. God's original plan was for all humans to begin their existence in the family of God in the state of sanctifying grace. Mary, rather than being the exception, ful-

fills in a real sense the original intention of what God wanted for all His human children: to be members of His family from the first moment of their existence."[3]

In the Gospel of John we read about the Second Person of the Blessed Trinity before the Incarnation: "In the beginning was the Word, and the Word was with God, and the Word was God... All things came to be through him, and without him nothing came to be" (John 1:1-3). Jesus is the only Son who had the ability to create His own mother! If you had the opportunity to create your own mother would you create her spiritually defiled and destined for eternal death, or would you create her spiritually pure and spotless? I don't think that any of us would choose the former option — and neither did Jesus. He wanted to create the mother that would be best suited spiritually to give birth to Him and to raise Him to fully carry out His Father's mission.[4]

In the Gospel of Luke the Angel Gabriel says to Mary: "Hail, full of grace..." (Luke 1:28).[5] Since God's grace displaces sin, for Mary to be called "*full of grace*" would mean that the over-abundant grace that was bestowed upon her by God left no room for sin of any kind to dwell within her.[6]

Also, in the Gospel of Luke Elizabeth tells Mary: "Most blessed are you among women..." (Luke 1:42). This verse refers to Mary's blessedness from the instant of her conception in her mother's womb.[7]

Again in the Gospel of Luke, Mary says about herself: "...from now on will all ages call me blessed" (Luke 1:48). This is yet another Scripture passage that speaks about Mary's blessedness from the first instant of her conception in her mother's womb.

In the Book of Revelation we read about a "woman" who was, "clothed with the sun, with the moon under her feet, and on her head a crown of twelve stars... She gave birth to a son, a male child, destined to rule all the nations with an iron rod. Her child was caught up to God and his throne... But the woman was given the two wings of the great eagle, so that she could fly to her place in the desert, where, far from the serpent, she was taken care of..." (Rev 12:1, 5, 14). A number of Catholic Scripture scholars have observed how this passage from Revelation is beautifully fulfilled by the doctrine of the Immaculate Conception as this "woman" is a vision of the Virgin Mary[8] and her "flight into the desert far from the serpent" speaks about God protecting her from any and all diabolical influence (i.e., she was immaculately conceived without original sin in her mother's womb and never sinned during her lifetime.)[9]

Note that Adam and Eve were immaculately "conceived" without the stain of original sin. Note that Jesus was immaculately conceived without original sin. If God did it three times in history, is it possible for Him to do it a fourth time? The Catholic Church and Sacred Apostolic Tradition say "Yes!"[10]

Original sin is passed on from one generation to the next.[11] Jesus took on His human nature through His human mother. Therefore, if Mary had been tarnished by original sin, she would have passed that on to her Son. Because of her special role in salvation history, Mary was preserved from original sin so that she would be a spotless vessel to receive the Second Person of the Blessed Trinity.[12]

The merits of Jesus' death and resurrection were applied to Mary before her conception *(preservative redemption)* so that she could be a pure channel for Christ to come into our world. Some fundamentalist Christians point out that, in Luke 1.46, Mary calls God her "Savior" and reason that she was necessarily a sinner because only sinners need a Savior.

Consider this analogy that is sometimes used by Catholic apologist Karl Keating that illustrates "preservative redemption": Suppose that a woman is walking along a jungle path and, in the middle of the path, carefully camouflaged by branches and leaves, is a deep pit. The woman doesn't notice the pit and falls down into it. A passerby, seeing the woman caught in the pit, pulls her out. The passerby is the woman's "savior" because he saved her from being trapped in the pit and from eventually dying. Suppose that another woman is walking along the same path in the jungle and she is approaching the same pit in the middle of the road. Just as she is about to tumble into it, an observer reaches out, grabs her by the arm, and yanks her back. She too is saved from the pit, but in anticipation — before falling in — rather than after the fact. Both women are saved from the pit *(original sin)* and both women have a Savior *(Jesus Christ).*[13]

Tim Staples writes:

> "If the Old Testament ark had to be pure,[14] how much more the New Testament ark [cf. Luke 1:43; 2 Samuel 6:9]. If John the Baptist was 'filled with the Holy Ghost, even from his mother's womb' (Luke 1:15) to prepare the way of the Lord, how much more would Mary need grace to prepare her body and soul for the august task of carrying God himself within her! Not only does the reference to her being the ark of God imply her sinlessness, but the angel Gabriel names her 'one who has been perfected in grace' (Luke 1:28)."[14]

This long-held belief that is part of Apostolic Tradition (cf. 1 Cor 11:2, 2 Thess 2:15) was finally officially defined by the Church, which the Bible calls "the pillar and foundation of the truth" (1 Tim 3:15) in 1854.[15]

Common Objection #2

"St. Paul clearly says in his Letter to the Romans: *'all* have sinned and are deprived of the glory of God'" (Rom 3:23). Since Mary is a member of the human race, she is included in St. Paul's statement and could not possibly have been born without the stain of original sin on her soul."

A Catholic Response

The Greek word for "all" that is used in Romans 3:23 is *pas*. There are numerous examples in the New Testament where "all" (Greek: *pas*) does not mean "each and every single person without exception." [16] Consider the following passages:

- "For just as in Adam *all* [Greek: *pas*] die, so too in Christ shall *all* [Greek: *pas*] be brought to life..." (1 Cor 15:22). The Bible tells us that Enoch and Elijah did not die but were assumed into heaven while still alive (cf. Gen 5:24; Heb 11:5; 2 Kings 2:11). The second part of this verse states that in Christ "all" will be brought to life. The fact is that some people, unfortunately, will not choose Jesus Christ or God and, thus, freely choose eternal death for themselves.

- "At that time Jerusalem, *all* [Greek: *pas*] Judea, and the whole region around the Jordan were going out to [John] and were being baptized by him in the Jordan River..." (Matt 3:5-6). We know that each and every person in Judea was not baptized by John in the Jordan River.

- "I myself am convinced about you, my brothers, that you yourselves are full of goodness, filled with *all* [Greek: *pas*] knowledge, and able to admonish one another" (Rom 15:14). The only one that has "all" knowledge is God. Human beings have partial knowledge of some things.

Mark Miravalle writes about St. Paul's words recounted in Rom 3:23 that "all have sinned.":

> "...[T]he Church rightfully interprets this passage as a divinely revealed truth about the general masses that make up humanity. But since the teachings of St. Paul were primarily directed to spreading the Good News which had to precede an accurate understanding of Marian doctrine (Mary is who she is because of her Son), then clearly it would be inappropriate for St. Paul to make an explicit, exceptional clause about the Mother of Jesus in his teaching of the universal need for Redemption. This would be inappropriate before the people of the time had fundamental, doctrinal clarity about the basic message of the Gospel.
>
> Clearly, St. Paul's intention in this passage of Romans was not a teaching on Marian doctrine, but a general instruction on the universal sin of humanity, and thereby the universal need for a redeemer."[17]

In Romans 3:23, St. Paul refers to all people who are born with original sin and are, thus, under the dominion of Satan (i.e., you and I). Since God preserved Mary from any and all sin at her conception in her mother's womb, she was/is completely out of the devil's domain.

What Did the Early Christians Believe About the Immaculate Conception of Mary in Her Mother's Womb Without the Stain of Original Sin?

• "You alone and your Mother are more beautiful than any others; For there is no blemish in you, nor any stains upon your Mother. Who of my children can compare in beauty to these?" St. Ephraim in his *The Nisibene Hymns* (circa 350 A.D.)[18]

• St. Ambrose (d. 379 A.D.) refers to Mary as "free from all stain of sin."[19]

• "Having excepted the holy Virgin Mary, concerning whom, on account of the honor of the Lord, I wish to have absolutely no question when treating of sins — for how do we know what abundance of grace for the total overcoming of sin was conferred upon her, who merited to conceive and bear him in whom there was no sin? — so, I say, with the exception of the Virgin, if we could have gathered together all those holy men and women, when they were living here, and had asked them whether they were without sin, what do we suppose would have been their answer? Would it be what Pelagius says, or would it be what the apostle John says? I ask you, however excellent might their holiness have been when in the body, if they had been so questioned, would they not have declared in a single voice: 'If we say we have no sin, we deceive ourselves, and the truth is not in us! (1 John 1:18)?" St. Augustine in his *On Nature and Grace* (circa 415 A.D.)[20]

Endnotes

[1] St. Peter speaks of the sinless Jesus as a "spotless unblemished lamb" (1 Pet 1:19, cf. also Exod 12:5-13).
[132] *LG* 56.
[133] *Lk* 1:28.
[134] *Lk* 1:28.
[135] Pius IX, *Ineffabilis Deus*, 1854: DS 2803.
[136] *LG* 53, 56.

137 Cf. *Eph* 1:3-4.

138 *LG* 56.

2 James Cardinal Gibbons reminds us that whenever God chooses a person for some important work, He bestows upon that person the gifts and graces necessary for faithfully discharging the mission (e. g., When God called Moses, He gave him the assurance that He would help him to overcome his speech impediment — Exod 4:12; When God called Jeremiah He assured him that from the womb He had been preparing Him for his mission — Jer 1:5; Elizabeth was filled with the Holy Spirit so that she could faithfully carry our her mission of bringing John the Baptist into the world — Luke 1:41; The Apostles were each filled with the gifts and graces necessary to carry out their mission — 2 Cor 3:6, etc...). Of all who participated in the ministry of redemption, there is none who held a role so important as the Blessed Virgin Mary. Consequently, she needed the *highest* degree of holiness and grace possible...If God said to His Old Testament priests 'Purify yourselves, you who carry the vessels of the Lord [cf. Isaiah 52:11], how clean would Mary, the one who bore *the* vessel of God have had to been? (Cf. James Cardinal Gibbons, *The Faith of Our Fathers*, Rockford, IL: TAN Books and Publishers, Inc., 1980), pp. 135-137.

3 Mark Miravalle, *Introduction to Mary*, (Santa Barbara, CA: Queenship Publishing Co., 1993), pp. 39-40, 42.

4 F. J. Sheed, *Theology for Beginners*, (Ann Arbor, Michigan: Servant Books, 1981), p. 128.

5 *Douay-Rheims Bible*, (Rockford, IL: TAN Books and Publishers, Inc., 1971), p. 65.

6 Mark Miravalle writes about the Angel Gabriel's words to Mary recounted in Luke 1:28: "In the Greek text of Luke 1:28, we have additional implicit reference to Mary's Immaculate Conception taking place before the announcement of the Angel. The Greek word *kekaritomene*, is a perfect participle, and so we translate Luke 1:28 most accurately in this way, 'Hail, you who *have been* graced.' The Greek translation of the angel's greeting refers to an event of profound grace experienced by Mary that was already completed in the past." Cf. *An Introduction to Mary*, p. 39.

⁷ Note that Mary was the first Christian to receive "Holy Communion." Jesus Christ — Body, Blood, Soul, and Divinity — dwelt in her womb for nine full months. To paraphrase Luke 1:31 the Angel Gabriel says to Mary, "The Body of Christ." To paraphrase Luke 1:38 Mary's response to the angel was a wholehearted, "Amen!" The Immaculate Conception was God's preparation of Mary to carry the Holiest of Communions in her womb. *"...Purify yourselves, you who carry the vessels of the Lord.* (Isaiah 52:11)

⁸ Cf. *Catechism of the Catholic Church*, #1137-1138.

⁹ Scott Hahn, *The End: A Study of the Book of Revelation Audio Cassette*, (West Covina, CA: St. Joseph Communications, Inc. (818) 331-3549).

¹⁰ To Sarah's doubting God responds: "Is anything too marvelous for the Lord to do..." (Gen 18:14)?

¹¹ Cf. Psalm 51:7, Job 14:4, Rom 5:12-14, Jer 14:20, Gen 8:21. Note that drug-addicted mothers give birth to drug-addicted children. Sin-addicted mothers do the same. Would anyone place a germ-free object on a germ-infested object? No, because one would instantly contaminate the other. If Mary had been conceived with the stain of original sin on her soul, she would have spiritually "contaminated" the soul of her Divine offspring, Jesus.

¹² Alan Schreck writes: "...[I]t seemed impossible to Christians that the all-holy God, whose very nature is opposed to sin, could have been born to someone bound by the sin and rebellion of the fallen human condition. How could Mary have been a sinner, and still have carried the fullness of the all-holy God in her womb?...The doctrine of the Immaculate Conception is more of a statement about Jesus than about Mary. It proclaims that Jesus was someone so unique and holy that God would even prepare his mother for his birth by preserving her from sin." Cf. Alan Schreck, *Catholic and Christian*, (Ann Arbor, Michigan: Servant Books, 1984), pp. 176-177.

¹³ Karl Keating, *What Catholics Really Believe*, (Ann Arbor, Michigan: Servant Publications, 1992), p. 72.

[14] In the Old Testament, God tells Moses: "You shall make an ark of acacia wood...*Plate it inside and out with pure gold*, and put a molding of gold around the top of it" (Exod 25:10-11).

[14] Patrick Madrid (editor), *Surprised by Truth*, (San Diego, CA: Basilica Press, 1994), p. 232.

[15] John Henry Cardinal Newman said about the Immaculate Conception of Mary: "[Catholics] do not believe in it because it is defined [as being infallible], but it was defined [as infallible] because we believed in it." Many Catholics believe that the truth of the doctrine of the Immaculate Conception was confirmed in 1858 when, at Lourdes, France, the Blessed Virgin Mary appeared to a simple peasant girl named Bernadette Soubirous *(who had no knowledge at all that the Church had officially defined the doctrine of the Immaculate Conception)* and announced to her, "I am the Immaculate Conception."

[16] John Hellmann, *Mary and Romans 3:23*, http://members.aol.com/johnprh/all.html.

[17] *Introduction to Mary*, pp. 161-162. (Author's note: Would it be wise for a high school chemistry teacher, on the first day of classes when he should be trying to communicate to his class some of the basic principles of chemistry, to begin class by listing all of the exceptions and the variables that, when introduced, would change the normal course of events? No, the wise chemistry teacher would want to deal extensively with the basics first and then, when his students got a firm grasp of the fundamentals, would present the exceptions to the basic rules. St. Paul, in writing that "all have sinned," was instructing the Christian community in Rome [circa 57 A.D. — before any of the Gospels were composed] that humanity needed a Savior. Since the theology of the "preservative redemption" of Mary by God had not yet been fully articulated at this early date, St. Paul was simply trying to school the Roman Christians on the basics of the Gospel message before dealing with any possible extraordinary exceptions.)

[18] William A. Jurgens (editor and translator), *The Faith of the Early Fathers (Volume 1)*, (Collegeville, MN: The Liturgical Press, 1970), p. 313.

[19] *Introduction to Mary*, p. 40.

[20] Karl Keating (editor), *This Rock Magazine*, "The Father's Know Best," (San Diego, CA: Catholic Answers, Inc.), "Mary's Privileges," pp. 36-38.

Chapter 17

"A Woman Clothed With the Sun":[1] The Assumption of Mary Into Heaven, Body and Soul, by the Power of God

What Does the Catholic Church Teach?

"'Finally the Immaculate Virgin, preserved free from all stain of original sin, when the course of her earthly life was finished, was taken up body and soul into heavenly glory, and exalted by the Lord as Queen over all things, so that she might be more fully conformed to her Son, the Lord of lords and conqueror of sin and death.'[506] The Assumption of the Blessed Virgin is a singular participation in her Son's Resurrection and an anticipation of the resurrection of other Christians..." (*Catechism of the Catholic Church*, #966.)

Common Objection #1

"The New Testament gives no account of Mary being assumed body and soul into heaven. Where did the Catholic Church get this idea?"

A Catholic Response

- The New Testament clearly shows us that it is possible for the faithful to experience bodily resurrection before the Second Coming of Christ. After Jesus is crucified we read in Matthew's Gospel: "[T]ombs were opened, and the bodies of many saints who had fallen asleep were raised..." (Matt 27:52-53).

- In the Second Book of Kings we read that the Prophet Elijah was taken up (assumed) into heaven body and soul: "As they walked on conversing, a flaming chariot and flaming horses came between them, and Elijah went up to heaven in a whirlwind" (2 Kings 2:11).

- In the Book of Genesis we read that Enoch was taken up (assumed) into heaven body and soul: "Then Enoch walked with God, and he was no longer here, for God took him" (Gen 5:24).

- In the Acts of the Apostles, we read about God transporting the Apostle Philip, body and soul, from one place to another: "When they came out of the water, the Spirit of the Lord snatched Philip away, and the eunuch saw him no more, but continued on his way rejoicing. Philip came to Azotus, and went about proclaiming the good news to all the towns until he reached Caesarea" (Acts 8:39-40).

- In the Book of Revelation we read about St. John's description of a vision that he had of heaven[2] : "Then God's temple in heaven was opened, and the ark of his covenant could be seen...A great sign appeared in the sky, a woman clothed with the sun, with the moon under her feet, and on her head a crown of twelve stars....She gave birth to a son, a male child, destined to rule all the nations with an iron rod..." (Rev 11:19 — 12:5).[3] Concerning "the woman" spoken about in Rev 12, we read in the *Navarre Bible Commentary*:

  "The woman can stand for the people of Israel, for it is from that people that the Messiah comes... She can also stand for the [Christian] Church, whose children strive to overcome evil and bear witness to Jesus Christ... The passage can also refer to the Virgin Mary because it was she who truly and historically gave birth to the Messiah, Jesus Christ our Lord [cf. Rev 12:5]. St. Bernard comments: 'The sun contains permanent colour and splendor; whereas the moon's brightness is unpredictable and changeable, for it never stays the same. It is quite right, then, for Mary to be depicted as clothed with the sun, for she entered the profundity of divine wisdom much further than one can possibly conceive (DeB. Virgine, 2)...the inspired text of the Apocalypse is open to interpreting this woman as a direct reference to the Blessed Virgin who, as mother, shares in the pain of Calvary [cf. Lk 2:35] and who was prophesied in Isaiah 7:14 as a 'sign' [cf. Mt 1:22-23]."[4]

We can see here that "the woman" described in Rev 12 can, indeed, refer to the Blessed Virgin Mary, assumed into heaven body and soul, who can, at the same time, embody a collective group of people (the people of Israel and/or the Christian Church).[5] Early Christians such as St. Epiphanius of Salamis (circa 375 A.D.),[6] Quodvultdeus (circa 450 A.D.), and Andrew of Caesarea (circa 550 A.D.) saw this "woman" in heaven as the Blessed Virgin Mary, assumed into heaven body and soul, with her Son, Jesus.

The Church's Magisterium has made numerous statements about the identity of "the woman" depicted in Revelation 12. In 1904, Pope Pius X in his encyclical on the Immaculate Conception *Ad Diem Illum Laetissimum* writes the following about Mary:

"...[W]ho can contemplate the Immaculate Virgin without feeling moved to fulfill that precept which Christ called peculiarly his own namely, that of loving one another as he loved us. 'A great sign,' thus the Apostle St. John describes a vision divinely sent him appears in the heavens, 'A woman clothed with the sun and with the moon under her feet and a crown of twelve stars upon her head.' (Apoc. xii, 1) *Everyone knows that this woman signified the Virgin Mary,* the stainless one who brought forth our Head. The Apostle continues: 'And, being with child, she cried travailing in birth, and was in pain to be delivered' (Apoc. xii., 2) John therefore saw the Most Holy Mother of God already in eternal happiness..."[7]

In addition, Pope John Paul II, in his encyclical *Redemptoris Mater*, writes about the Blessed Virgin Mary:

"Thanks to this special bond linking the Mother of Christ with the Church, there is further clarified the mystery of that 'woman' who, from the first chapters of the Book of Genesis until the Book of Revelation, accompanies the revelation of God's salvific plan for humanity. For Mary, present in the Church as the Mother of the Redeemer, takes part, as a mother, in the 'monumental struggle against the powers of darkness' which continues throughout human history. *And by her ecclesial identification as the 'woman clothed with the sun' [Rev 12:1], it can be said that 'in the Most Holy Virgin the Church has already reached that perfection whereby she exists without spot or wrinkle.*"[8]

In the *Catechism of the Catholic Church* we read about the identity of "the woman" spoken about in Revelation 12:

"The book of Revelation of St. John, read in the Church's liturgy,...reveals to us...the ones who take part in the service of the praise of God and the fulfillment of his plan: the heavenly powers, all creation..., the servants of the Old and New Covenants...the new People of God...and the all-holy Mother of God (the Woman)..."[9]

Because of her Immaculate Conception in her mother's womb without the stain of original sin *(cf. Chapter 16 of this book)* and because of the integral role that she played in salvation history,

God allowed Mary to experience the fullness of salvation in heaven, body and soul.[10]

Negative proof of the Assumption is the fact that we have no record of any grave containing Mary's bones *(which would have been highly venerated by the early Christians.)*[11]

Mary is the model for all Christians because she is now what all faithful disciples hope to be in the future ... assumed into heaven with God, body and soul, at the General Judgement (cf. 1 Thess 4:13-18; Matt 25:31-46).[12] The long-held belief of the Assumption of Mary into heaven was finally officially defined by the Church (whom the Bible calls "the pillar and foundation of the truth" [1 Tim 3:15]) in 1950.[13] Please refer to Chapter 11 of this book to read about the importance of Sacred Scripture *and* Sacred Tradition (cf. 1 Cor 11:2; 2 Thess 2:15).

What Did the Early Christians Believe Concerning the Assumption of Mary Into Heaven, Body and Soul, by the Power of God?

- "The course of this life having been completed by Blessed Mary, when now she would be called from the world, all the Apostles came together from their various regions to her house. And when they had heard that she was about to be taken from the world, they kept watch together with her. And behold, the Lord Jesus came with His angels, and taking her soul, He gave it over to the Angel Michael and withdrew. At daybreak, however, the Apostles took up her body on a bier and placed it in a tomb; and they guarded it, expecting the Lord to come. And behold, again the Lord stood by them; and the holy body having been received, He commanded that it be taken in a cloud into paradise: where now, rejoined to the soul, [Mary] rejoices with the Lord's chosen ones, and is in the enjoyment of the good of an eternity that will never end." St. Gregory of Tours in his *Eight Books of Miracles* (circa 580 A.D.)[14]

- "The Lord commanded the holy body [of Mary] to be borne on a cloud to Paradise where, reunited to its soul and exalting with the elect, it enjoys the everlasting bliss of eternity." St. Gregory of Tours (d. 593)[15]

- "In the Holy and divinely-inspired Scripture no mention is made of anything concerning the end of Mary the Holy Mother of God; but we have received from ancient and most truthful tradition that at the time of her glorious repose, all the Holy Apostles, who then were dispersed abroad in the world for the salvation of the nations, were in but a moment of time transported through the air to Jerusalem; and when they were there an angelic vision appeared to them, and the divine chanting of the supernal powers was heard. And thus in divine and heavenly glory her holy soul was delivered in a way that no word can describe into the hands of God. And her body, which had been the Tabernacle of God, after the chanting of the angels and of the Apostles was finished and last respects were paid, was placed in a coffin in Gethsemani. In that place the chanting and choral singing of the angels continued without cease for three days. After the third day the angelic chanting ceased. The Apostles were present there when Thomas, the only one who had been absent, after the third day; and since he wanted to worship the body that had been the Tabernacle of God, they opened the coffin. And they were unable anywhere to find her most lauded body. When they found only her grave wrappings there, and the indescribable perfume which was born aloft from them, they sealed the coffin. Struck by the wonder of the mystery they could only think that He who had been pleased to become incarnate from her in His own Person and to become Man and to be born in the flesh, God the Word, the Lord of Glory, who preserved her virginity intact after her parturition, — He was pleased even after her departure from life to honor her immaculate and undefiled body with incorruption and with translation prior to the common and universal resurrection." St. John Damascene in his *Second Homily on the Dormition of Mary* (circa 745 A.D.)[16]

Endnotes

[1] Cf. the heavenly vision recounted by St. John in Rev 11:19- 12:5.
[506] *LG* 59; cf. Pius XII, *Munificentissimus Deus* (1950): DS 3903; cf. *Rev* 19:16.

2   Recall that St. John was the Apostle who cared for Mary after Jesus' death (cf. John 19:26-27).

3   Scripture scholar George Montague, S.M. writes about Rev 12:1-5: "The child [that 'the woman'] delivers is 'destined to rule all the nations with an iron rod' (12:5), a clear allusion to the messianic Psalm 2:9 [cf. also Rev 19:5]. We think at once of Jesus' birth through Mary. In the complex overlying imagery of John, it would be rash to exclude that meaning." Cf. George T. Montague, S.M., *The Apocalypse*, (Ann Arbor, Michigan: Charis/Servant Books, 1992), p. 146.

4   James Gavigan, Brian McCarthy, Thomas McGovern (editors), *The Navarre Bible: The Book of Revelation*, (Dublin, Ireland: Four Courts Press, 1992), p. 97.

5   In Heb 9:3-4, we read that the Old Testament Ark of the Covenant contained manna, the staff of the priest Aaron, and the Ten Commandments. Mary's womb, the "Ark of the New Covenant" contained the Bread of Life (cf. John 6:33), the eternal High Priest (cf. Heb 7:24) and the Word of God (cf. John 1:14).

6   Cf. *Panarion*, Book 78, part II.

7   Claudia Carlen Ihm, *The Papal Encyclicals (1903-1939)*, (Consortium Books/McGrath Publishing Co., 1981), p. 16.

8   Pope John Paul II, Encyclical Letter *Redemptoris Mater*, (Washington, D.C.: Office of Publishing and Promotion Services United States Catholic Conference, 1987), p. 103.

9   Cf. *Catechism of the Catholic Church*, #1137 — 1139.

10   Mark Miravalle writes about Mary: "According to St. Paul (cf. Rom 5-8; Hebrews 2), the consequences of Satan's seed, evil, are twofold: sin and death (or bodily corruption). Therefore, Mary, who shared in her Son's victory over Satan and his seed (cf. Gen 3:15), would have to be saved from both sin and death or corruption. Mary did triumph over sin in her Immaculate Conception and triumphed over death (specifically corruption of the body) in her glorious Assumption at the end of her earthly life." Mark Miravalle, *An Introduction to Mary*, (Santa Barbara, CA: Queenship Publishing Co., 1993), pp. 51-52.

11   The Church has never officially defined whether or not, at the end of her life, Mary experienced some momentary separation of her body and soul before being assumed into heaven. Pope

Pius XII purposely avoided any direct statement concerning Mary's death by using the general expression, "at the end of her earthly life." The majority of theologians believe that Mary did experience some sort of momentary separation of her body and soul. What is certain, though, is that Mary did not experience any corruption of her body which is a result of original sin. Cf. *Introduction to Mary*, pp. 54-55.

12 I wonder if the author of Psalm 132 had any inkling how profoundly his words were to be fulfilled by the Ascension of Jesus and the Assumption of His mother, Mary, into heaven when he wrote: "Arise, Lord, come to your resting place, you and your *majestic ark*" (Psalm 132:8).

13 John Henry Cardinal Newman's words about the Immaculate Conception of Mary apply also to her Assumption: "[Catholics] do not believe in it because it is defined [as being infallible], but it was defined [as infallible] because we believed in it."

14 William A. Jurgens (editor and translator), *The Faith of the Early Fathers (Volume 3)*, (Collegeville, MN: The Liturgical Press, 1979), p. 306.

15 *Introduction to Mary*, p. 52.

16 *The Faith of the Early Fathers (Volume 3)*, p. 350.

Chapter 18

"Whatever You Loose on Earth Shall be Loosed in Heaven":[1] Receiving God's Forgiveness Through the Ministry of a Priest

What Does the Catholic Church Teach?

"Christ instituted the sacrament of Penance for all sinful members of his Church: above all for those who, since Baptism, have fallen into grave sin, and have thus lost their baptismal grace and wounded ecclesial communion... Over the centuries the concrete form in which the Church has exercised this power received from the Lord has varied considerably. During the first centuries the reconciliation of Christians who had committed particularly grave sins after their Baptism (for example, idolatry, murder, or adultery) was tied to a very rigorous discipline, according to which penitents had to do public penance for their sins, often for years, before receiving reconciliation. To this 'order of penitents' (which concerned only certain grave sins), one was only rarely admitted and in certain regions only once in a lifetime. During the seventh century Irish missionaries, inspired by the Eastern monastic tradition, took to continental Europe the 'private' practice of penance, which does not require public and prolonged completion of penitential works before reconciliation with the Church. From that time on, the sacrament has been performed in secret between penitent and priest. This new practice envisioned the possibility of repetition and so opened the way to a regular frequenting of this sacrament. It allowed the forgiveness of grave sins and venial sins to be integrated into one sacramental celebration. In its main lines this is the form of penance that the Church has practiced down to our day." (*Catechism of the Catholic Church*, #1446–1447.)

Common Objection #1

"In the Gospel of Mark we read, 'Who but *God alone* can forgive sins' (Mark 2:7)? In the Gospel of Luke, Jesus teaches Christians to pray, '*Father*, hallowed be your name...*forgive us our sins...*' (Luke 11:2, 4). Why, then, do you Catholics believe that priests have the power to forgive sins? Priests are mere human beings and sinners just like the rest of us!"

A Catholic Response

• In the Gospel of John, Jesus speaks to His twelve special disciples — the Apostles (who were mere sinful human beings)[2]: "...As the Father has sent *me*, so I send *you*. And when he had said this, he breathed on them and said to them, 'Receive the Holy Spirit. Whose sins *you* forgive are forgiven them, and whose sins *you* retain are retained'" (John 20:21-23). Before leaving earth and ascending into heaven, Christ endows His Apostles with the Holy Spirit and commissions them to be the human instruments of His forgiveness after His death. From the plain and straight-forward words of our Lord to His Apostles recounted in John 20, it is apparent that He desired for them and their successors to be ministers of the "Sacrament of Penance." Just as the Father had sent Jesus to carry out His ministry of reconciliation and healing here on earth, Jesus authorizes His Apostles to continue His ministry of reconciliation and healing, in His Name, here on earth.[3] Jesus' words in John 20 presume a verbal confession to the Divinely-appointed Apostle in order for him to be able to make a judgement as to whether to forgive or retain the sins in question.

- In the Gospel of Matthew, Jesus singles out Peter, by himself, (a mere sinful human being who was also the first Bishop of Rome and the first "Pope" of the Roman Catholic Church)[4] and tells him: "...whatever *you* bind on earth shall be bound in heaven; and whatever *you* loose on earth shall be loosed in heaven" (Matt 16:18-19).

- Again, in the Gospel of Matthew, after delegating the ministry of reconciliation to St. Peter, by himself, Jesus tells His other appointed ministers (who were mere sinful human beings), "...whatever *you* bind on earth shall be bound in heaven, and whatever *you* loose on earth shall be loosed in heaven" (Matt 18:18).

- In the Book of James we can see how God chooses to forgive sin through the ministry of (mere sinful) human beings: "Is anyone among you sick? He should summon the presbyters[5] of the church, and they should pray over him and anoint him with oil in the name of the Lord, and the prayer of faith will save the sick person, and the Lord will raise them up. *If he has committed any sins, he will be forgiven.* Therefore, *confess your sins to one another* and pray for one another, that you may be healed" (James 5:14-16).

- In Matt 9:1-7 Jesus heals a paralytic's physical body and forgives his sins and then we read: "When the crowds saw this they were struck with awe and glorified God who had given such authority *to human beings*" (Matt 9:8). [6] We see plainly in the Scriptures that Jesus gave human beings the authority to heal physical ailments and to forgive sins — in His name, of course!

- St. Paul speaks about the "ministry of reconciliation" that Jesus bestowed upon him and the rest of the Apostles: "And all this is from God, who has reconciled us to himself through Christ and *given us the ministry of reconciliation...*" (2 Cor 5:17-20).[7]

- St. Paul speaks about his ministry of the forgiveness of sins to the Christian leaders in Corinth: "Whomever you forgive anything, so do I. For indeed what I have forgiven, if I have forgiven anything, has been for you in the presence of Christ, so that we might not be taken advantage of by Satan..." (2 Cor 2:10-11).

- In Luke's Gospel Jesus sends His disciples out into the world to do ministry. As they leave He authorizes and empowers them to speak on His behalf: "Whoever listens to you listens to me. Whoever rejects you rejects me..." (Luke 10:16). In the Sacrament of Penance the Roman Catholic priest *(whose ordination can be traced back in an unbroken line to the Apostles)* acts as the "mouthpiece of Jesus" when he says to the penitent: "I absolve you of your sins *in the name of the Father and of the Son and of the Holy Spirit. Amen."*

- In the Gospel of Matthew we read that, as people came forward to be baptized by John the Baptist, they "acknowledged their sins" (Matt 3:6). The only way for Matthew to be able to write that the baptismal candidates were "acknowledging their sins" would be if they were audibly acknowledged in some manner or another. If their acknowledgment of sins was merely a silent internal conversation between God and the person being baptized, Matthew would certainly have not been aware that any kind of acknowledgment was being made.

- In the Acts of the Apostles we read that when certain new converts converted over to the Christian faith they "...came forward and openly acknowledged their former sinful practices" (Acts 19:18).[8]

- Note how, in the parable of the Prodigal Son (cf. Luke 15:11-32), all of the elements of the Sacrament of Penance are contained: (1) the sinner repents, (2) he makes a verbal "confession," (3) as an outward symbol of his interior resolve to lead a holier life, he is willing to perform "penance" and, (4) he joyfully experiences reconciliation with his father.

Historically, the Roman Catholic Bishops are the descendants, in an unbroken line, to the Apostles (refer to Chapter 3 of this book). Because the Bishops can't be everywhere, priests are ordained to represent the Bishops in the local Church parishes. The priest's authority to forgive sins in Jesus' name is derived from the Bishops — whose authority is derived from the Apostles — whose authority is derived from Jesus Christ Himself.

Indeed, only God can forgive sins. The priests are the human instruments of *God's forgiveness* and Scripture tells us that they have the power to "bind" and to "loose" people's sins in Jesus' name.

Common Objection #2

"I go to Jesus directly for the forgiveness of my sins. I don't need some priest (who is probably just as big a sinner as I) to serve as a mediator between Christ and me."

A Catholic Response

Dr. Scott Hahn, a former Presbyterian minister and convert to the Catholic faith, says that he commonly answers this objection in this way: "I go directly to Jesus also and He tells me every time, 'Hey Scott, check out my 2,000-year-old confession instructions that I have already conveniently written down for you in John 20:21-23; Matt 16:18-19; Matt 18:18; 2 Cor 5:17-21, etc...!'"

Let me try to give you an analogy of my own about the importance of Christians celebrating the Sacrament of Penance: Suppose that you were going on vacation for three weeks during the summer and you asked your next-door neighbor to cut your grass in your absence. Your neighbor agrees to help you out. Before you leave on vacation you take your neighbor to the shed in your backyard and you show him your lawnmower and give him instructions on how to operate it. After instructing your neighbor, you leave for three weeks. You come back from your vacation and, lo and behold, your neighbor is on his hands and knees in your yard cutting your grass with a pair of scissors. What would your first question to your neighbor be? It would probably be something like, "Why didn't you use the tool that I left behind and instructed you to use?" When Jesus returns to His earthly "home" on Judgement Day after His "vacation" in heaven I think that He might very well ask the same question to Christians who are not actively celebrating the Sacrament of Penance. In going to Jesus directly and by-passing the system that He has already set up and commanded us to utilize would be to, effectively, say to Him, "Thanks, but no thanks, Jesus. I know better than you how my forgiveness is supposed to come about. I'll do it *my* way if you don't mind!"

Have you ever given a gift and find out later that the person put your gift in one of his closets and never used it? How does that make the giver feel? Usually, it offends the giver because his gift was not valued by the recipient. The Scriptures tell us that Jesus Christ has given us the gift of the Sacrament of Penance. Have we been actively utilizing our Lord's gracious gift or have we "packed it away" in one of our "closets" and forgotten about it?

Consider this analogy: Where does water come from? The faucet in our home? No, actually, water falls from the clouds (the heavens) and accumulates in lakes and in underground wells. The faucet in our home is simply the vehicle that we use for the delivery of the heavenly-originating water. One could bypass the faucet in one's home and take an airplane and harvest water from the rain clouds directly but would this be following God's intended design? No. In a similar manner, forgiveness comes from the "heavens" (from God.) At the end of Jesus' mission on earth, He chose the human Apostles to be the vehicles (the "faucets") for the delivery of God's forgiveness in His physical absence (cf. John 20:21-23).[9]

Ask any Christian minister who has healing services in his Church if he has ever healed a person through his ministry. He will probably say, "Yes, but it was God using me and working through me, it wasn't anything that I did myself." In the same way, Jesus uses priests to carry out *His ministry* of reconciliation. It is not the priest himself who forgives sins (the priest is, indeed, a mere human being who is a sinner like anyone else), it is *Jesus* working through the ministry of the priest.

Common Objection #3

"John 20:21-23 says that Jesus gave His *disciples* the authority to forgive sins in His name. A disciple is anyone who is a follower of Christ. Therefore, any two Christians can admit their sinfulness to each other and Jesus will forgive them of their sins."

A Catholic Response

A number of times in the Gospel of Matthew, the 12 *Apostles* are referred to as "the 12 *disciples*." (cf. Matt 10:1; Matt 20:17) In John 20:21-23 Jesus was speaking to the elite group of His disciples called His "Apostles." Refer to the writings of the early Christian community at the end of this chapter to see that not every Christian had the authority to act as an agent of Jesus' forgiveness but only those ordained by the Church to do so: St. Paul writes to Timothy, "Do not neglect the gift you have, which was conferred on you through the prophetic word with the imposition of hands of the presbyterate" (1 Tim 4:14).

Common Objection #4

"In demanding acts of penance in satisfaction to God for sins committed, the Catholic Church is making the statement that the sacrifice of Christ on the cross was insufficient and the sinner is required to add to the already finished work of Christ on Calvary (cf. John 19:30)."

A Catholic Response

In the *Catechism of the Catholic Church* we clearly read what the Catholic Church believes about the effects of Jesus' death and resurrection: "the 'New Adam' [Jesus Christ] who, because he 'became obedient unto death, even death on a cross,' makes amends superabundantly for the disobedience of Adam."[10]

What is the place of "penance" in the life of the Christian? Asking for some external sign of their interior conversion John the Baptist tells his listeners: "Produce good fruits as evidence of your repentance..." (Luke 3:8). In the Letter to the Hebrews we read: "...So strengthen your drooping hands and your weak knees. Make straight paths for your feet, that what is lame may not be dislocated but healed" (cf. Heb 12:5-13). What the Biblical writer is saying here is that, after a person sins, he should fortify himself spiritually so that he can be more resolved in his walk with Christ. The penance that the priest gives the penitent after his confession is simply a prayer or an apostolic deed that is aimed at restoring and strengthening his relationship with God that was strained by his post-Baptismal sinfulness. James writes to the Christian community: "Draw near to God, and he will draw near to you. Cleanse your hands, you sinners, and purify your hearts, you of two minds. Begin to lament, to mourn, and to weep. Let your laughter be turned into mourning and your joy into dejection. Humble yourselves before the Lord and he will exalt you" (James 4:8-10).

St. Paul speaks to the Corinthians about the necessity for discipline in the spiritual life: "...I drive my body and train it, for fear that, after having preached to others, I myself should be disqualified" (1 Cor 9:27).[11] A penance given by the priest to the penitent after confession is simply asking the penitent to pray some specified scripturally-based prayer or to perform some act of Christian charity that is aimed at "driving the penitent's body and soul and training it" so that the person would be more spiritually fit in his faith journey toward heaven.[12]

A priest is concerned with the spiritual well being of a person just as a doctor is concerned with the physical well being of a patient. After a heavy smoker has suffered a heart attack he goes to his doctor and is usually told something like, "O.K. your physical condition is stabilized now but I want you to stop smoking, eat a healthy diet, and walk for 15 minutes a day." In giving this "penance" to his patient, the doctor is simply prescribing a corrective measure that will help the patient to re-gain and strengthen his physical health. In giving a penance, the priest is doing the same thing in the spiritual realm. To give a penitent a penance is certainly making no statement that Christ's sacrifice on the cross was insufficient in forgiving sins. A penance is a corrective spiritual measure aimed at enabling the Christian to be more steadfast in his faith journey. It is also an external visible sign to Jesus of the sinner's invisible interior resolve to lead a more Christ-like life. After the guilt of a sinner's sins has been wiped away, penance is aimed at addressing and offsetting the consequences that the sinner's sins have created. (Cf. Chapter 24 of this book for a further discussion of the consequences of a sin that linger on after the guilt and eternal punishment has been removed by God.)

Seven Good Reasons to Receive God's Forgiveness Through the Ministry of a Priest in the Sacrament of Reconciliation

1) We are seeking forgiveness the way Jesus Christ designed it to be sought (cf. John 20:21-23; Matt 16:18-19; Matt 18:18; James 5:14-15; Matt 9:1-8; 2 Cor 5:17-21.)[13]

2) Not only are our sins forgiven, but Sacramental graces are obtained that strengthen us spiritually.[14]

3) We are *assured* that our sins are forgiven by getting to audibly hear it. Through the personal, concrete encounter of the Sacrament, we are not dependent upon the sometimes-elusive *feeling* that we are forgiven by God.[15]

4) We can obtain sound advice on avoiding sin in the future by someone who is trained in the spiritual life.[16]

5) We are reconciled with the larger faith community whom our sin has adversely affected.[17]

6) We are accountable to someone else for our actions (which often makes a person act more responsibly.) Have you ever observed some employees when the boss is out of town and they are not accountable to anyone for their actions?

7) Mental health professionals tell us that it is psychologically healthy to occasionally "unload" our spiritual and emotional "baggage" in the presence of another human being who can listen in a non-judgmental manner and relate to us with a compassionate heart.[18]

I hope that I have shown in this chapter that, rather than Catholics having to justify why we go to "Confession," our question to Protestant Christians should, instead, be, "Why *don't* you?"

What Did the Early Christians Believe About the Importance of Receiving God's Forgiveness Through the Ministry of a Priest?

- "For it is good for a man to confess his failings rather than to harden his heart." St. Clement of Rome in his *Letter to the Corinthians* (circa 80 A.D.)[19]

- "Confess your offenses in Church, and do not go up to your prayer with an evil conscience." *Didache* (circa 70 A.D.)[20]

- "On the Lord's Day of the Lord gather together, break bread and give thanks after confessing your transgressions so that your sacrifice may be pure." *Didache* (circa 70 A.D.)[21]

- "In regard to this second and single repentance, then: — since it is such a serious affair, so much the more laborious is its examination. It is not conducted before the conscience alone, but it is to be carried out by some external act... Satisfaction is arranged by confession, of confession is repentance born, and by repentance is God appeased." Tertullian in his *Repentance* (circa 203 A.D.)[22]

- "...[A]nd by the Spirit of the high-priesthood to have the authority to forgive sins." St. Hippolytus of Rome in his *The Apostolic Tradition* (circa 215 A.D.)[23]

- "We have often spoken a denunciation of our wickedness: this is, we have often made a confession of sin... Be careful and circumspect in regard to whom you would confess your sins. Test first the physician to whom you would expose the cause of your illness." Origen in his *Homilies on the Psalms* (circa 240 A.D.)[24]

- Circa 244 A.D., Origen praises the Christian "...who does not shrink from confessing his sin to a priest of the Lord." Origen in his *Homilies on Leviticus* (circa 244 A.D.)[25]

- "Although for lesser sins it is required that sinners do penance for a just time, after which, according to the rule of discipline, they may come to confession and, through the imposition of hands by the bishop and clergy, may receive the right of communication..." St. Cyprian of Carthage in his *Letter to His Clergy* (circa 250 A.D.)[26]

- "And if, inasmuch, as the Lord is merciful and kind, we find that none of those imploring and entreating His mercy should be prohibited from doing penance, then peace is able to be extended through His priests." St. Cyprian of Carthage in his *Letter to Antonianus, A Bishop in Numidia* (circa 251 A.D.)[27]

- "And if anyone uncovers his wound before you, give him the remedy of repentance. And he that is ashamed to make known his weakness, encourage him so that he will not hide it from you. And when he has revealed it to you, do not make it public." Aphraates the Persian Sage in his *Treatises* (circa 336 A.D.)[28]

- "Let no one say to himself, I do penance to God in private, I do it before God. Is it then that Christ hath said, 'Whatsoever thou shalt loose on earth shall be loosed in heaven?' Is it in vain that the keys have been given to the Church? Do we make void the Gospel, void the words of Christ?" St. Augustine in his *Sermons* (circa 400 A.D.)[29]

Endnotes

[1] Jesus' words to St. Peter recounted in Matt 16:19.

[2] Note that the twelve Apostles are often referred to in the New Testament as "the 12 Disciples" (cf. Matt 10:1; Matt 20:17; John 20:19-23).

[3] In Matt 10:8 we read about Jesus authorizing and empowering His Apostles to "cure the sick, raise the dead, cleanse lepers, and drive out demons" in His Name.

[4] Cf. Chapters 3 and 13 of this book.

[5] The English word "priest" comes from the Latin word *presby-*

ter — which comes from the Greek word *presbyterous* — which appears numerous times in the New Testament (e.g., James 5:14; Titus 1:5; 1 Tim 5:17, etc...). Cf. *Merriam-Webster's Collegiate Dictionary, Tenth Edition* Copyright 1994 by Merriam-Webster, Inc., p. 921.

6 Note that "human beings" are *plural*. The Divine God/man Jesus was capable of healing physical infirmities and forgiving sins and also He had give to *other human beings* the power to do the same in His Name (cf. John 20:21-23; Matt 16:18-19; Matt 18:18).

7 God the Father sent His Son Jesus into the world to forgive people's sins (cf. Matt 1:21) and, since Jesus was interested in reconciling *all sinners* and not just those who happened to live during His time He, in turn, when His earthly mission was completed, delegated the ministry of reconciliation to His Apostles and disciples so that, in *His* name, the forgiveness of sins could be available to *all people in all ages* after His death.

8 I. e., verbally "confessed" their former sinful deeds.

9 Rev. John A. O'Brien writes about the common objection of not confessing to a priest because he is simply another man: "'Can you pardon a criminal from the state penitentiary...just the same as the governor of Illinois?' I asked. 'No,' replied my friend, 'I'll admit I can't do that.' 'But aren't you a man,' I persisted, 'and isn't the governor a man, the same as you? And didn't you say that you had as much power to forgive a misdeed as any other man?' 'Yes,' replied my friend, 'but I make a distinction. The governor simply as a *man* does not have the power to pardon. It is only because he occupies the *office* of the governor of Illinois that he has such authority.' 'Then you admit,' I pointed out, 'the same basic distinction which the Church makes between a priest simply as a human being and as one who exercises power solely by virtue of the office which he holds. I, in my private personal capacity as Mr. Smith or Mr. Jones, have no more power than you or any other man. But I, in my *official* capacity as an ambassador of almighty God, acting in His name and by His authority, exercise a power which far transcends that of a human being and is in truth, the very power of God Himself." Cf. Rev. John A. O'Brien, *The Faith of Mil-*

lions, (Huntington, IN: Our Sunday Visitor, Inc., 1963, 1974), pp. 170-171.

10   *Catechism of the Catholic Church*, #411.

11   "By kindness and piety guilt is expiated, and by the fear of the Lord man avoids evil" (Proverbs 16:6).

12   The prophet Joel speaks about the process of spiritual conversion: "Yet even now, says the Lord, return to me with your whole heart, with fasting, and weeping, and mourning..." (Joel 2:12).

13   Author's note: In my experience as a Roman Catholic, the major problem that I myself struggle with and a number of Catholics have with "going to confession" is rooted in our own *pride*. Most human beings just don't like to admit that we make mistakes and are sometimes not the people we are called by God to be. Remember the words of Jesus: "...the one who humbles himself will be exalted" (Luke 14:11).

14   St. Paul writes: "...where sin increased, grace overflowed all the more..." (Rom 5:20).

15   The woman caught in adultery had the privilege of getting to hear that her forgiveness had, indeed, come about when Jesus audibly said to her: "Neither do I condemn you. Go, [and] from now on do not sin any more" (John 8:11).

16   "Seek counsel from every wise man, and do not think lightly of any advice that can be useful" (Tobit 4:18).

17   St. Paul writes: "If anyone has caused pain, he has caused it not to me, but in some measure (not to exaggerate) to all of you" (2 Cor 2:5); "If [one] part suffers, all the parts suffer with it; if one part is honored, all the parts share its joy" (1 Cor 12:26).

18   In the very successful non-denominational "12 Step Program" of Alcoholics Anonymous, "step 5" involves the addict having to verbally admit to *another human being* the exact nature of his past sinfulness. Through this in-depth "confession" to another person, addicts of all faiths (and those who have no particular "religious" faith) claim personal responsibility for their past wrongdoing, "get it off of their chest," and then experience the freedom of turning these past wrongdoings over to God in a tangible, personal encounter.

19   William A. Jurgens (editor and translator), *The Faith of the Early Fathers (Volume 1)*, (Collegeville, MN: The Liturgical Press, 1970), p. 12.

[20] *Ibid.*, p. 2.

[21] *Ibid.*, p. 4.

[22] *Ibid.*, p. 130-131,

[23] *Ibid.*, p. 167.

[24] *Ibid.*, p. 204.

[25] Albert Nevins, M.M., *Answering A Fundamentalist*, (Huntington, IN: Our Sunday Visitor, Inc., 1990), p. 76.

[26] *The Faith of the Early Fathers (Volume 1)*, p. 227.

[27] *Ibid.*, p. 231.

[28] *Ibid.*, p. 303.

[29] James Cardinal Gibbons, *The Faith of Our Fathers*, (Rockford, IL: TAN Books and Publishers, Inc., 1980), p. 284.

Chapter 19

"Whoever Can Accept This Ought to Accept It"[1]: Priestly Celibacy

What Does the Catholic Church Teach?

"All the ordained ministers of the Latin Church, with the exception of permanent deacons, are normally chosen from among men of faith who live a celibate life and who intend to remain *celibate* 'for the sake of the kingdom of heaven.'[70] Called to consecrate themselves with undivided heart to the Lord and to 'the affairs of the Lord,'[71] they give themselves entirely to God and to men. Celibacy is a sign of this new life to the service of which the Church's minister is consecrated; accepted with a joyous heart celibacy radiantly proclaims the Reign of God."[72] (*Catechism of the Catholic Church*, #1579.)

Common Objection #1

"St. Paul says that bishops must be 'married only once...' (1 Tim 3:2). In Luke 4:38-39 we read about Jesus healing Simon Peter's mother-in-law. If Simon Peter had a mother-in-law he, obviously, had a wife. In 1 Cor 9:5 we read that Kephas (Peter) "took along a Christian wife." This shows clearly that the first Pope of the Catholic Church was married. Why does the Roman Catholic Church now teach that priests and religious must remain single?"

A Catholic Response

Clerical celibacy is a current *discipline* in the Roman Catholic Church and not a *dogma of faith*. Let's look at Scripture to see if this discipline has any Biblical foundation:

- Jesus carried out His public ministry as an unmarried celibate and, thus, His own lifestyle has become the pattern for the lifestyle for modern-day Roman Catholic clergy and religious.[2] Jesus chose not to marry one particular woman so that He could be free to "espouse" Himself to the whole Church (cf. Rev 21:9). In imitation of the life of our Lord, the celibate Roman Catholic priest does the same.[3]

- The Scriptures see celibacy for the sake of freeing oneself to spread God's Kingdom as a tremendous value. Jesus says to His followers in the Gospel of Matthew: "Then Peter said to him in reply, 'We have given up *everything* and followed you. What will there be for us?' Jesus said to them, 'Amen, I say to you who have followed me, in the new age, when the Son of Man is seated on his throne of glory, will yourselves sit on twelve thrones, judging the twelve tribes of Israel. And everyone who has given up houses or brothers or sisters or father or mother or *children* or lands for the sake of my name will receive a hundred times more, and will inherit eternal life" (Matt 19:27-29). Note that a celibate priest has given up the responsibilities of caring for a wife and children for the sake of freeing himself to spread the kingdom of God with an undivided heart.

- In the Gospel of Matthew, Jesus speaks to His followers about the ideal of renouncing marriage for the sake of freeing oneself to spread the kingdom of God and then He says, "Whoever can accept this ought to accept it" (Matt 19:10-12).[4]

- In 1ˢᵗ Corinthians, St. Paul says: "Now to the unmarried and to widows I say: it is a good thing for them to remain as they are, as

I do, but if they cannot exercise self-control they should marry, for it is better to marry than to be on fire" (1 Cor 7:8-9).

- In 1 Cor 7:32-35, St. Paul speaks about how a celibate man or woman is free to dedicate him/her self to "the things of the Lord." By not being married to *one* person in an *exclusive* love relationship, the celibate minister is freed to love *all* people and to be available to them whenever called upon.

- In the Book of Revelation a certain group of saints in heaven are singled out for special recognition: "These are they who were not defiled with women; they are virgins and these are the ones who follow the Lamb wherever he goes" (Rev 14:4). We can see here how Rev 14:4 is beautifully fulfilled by the lifestyle of the clergy of the Roman Catholic Church as they embrace a consecrated celibate lifestyle in order to free themselves to do the work of the Lord with an undivided heart.

- St. Paul says in 1ˢᵗ Corinthians: "I tell you, brothers, the time is running out. From now on, let those having wives act as not having them" (1 Cor 7:29). Obviously anticipating Jesus' Second Coming to occur at any moment, St. Paul recommends sexual abstinence for those Christian married couples who could accept the challenge so that they could be free to focus wholeheartedly in prayer on their relationship with the Lord.

- St. Paul goes on to say about celibacy: "...It is a good thing for a man not to touch a woman ... the one who marries his virgin does well; the one who does not marry her will do better" (1 Cor 7:1, 38).

- St. Paul says to the married Christian couples in Corinth: "Do not deprive each other [from the conjugal act], except perhaps by mutual consent for a time, to be free for prayer, but then return to one another..." (1 Cor 7:5). We can see here how celibacy would be especially fitting for priests and religious because their whole life is supposed to be "free for prayer."

- In 1 Samuel we read about the regulation that stated that married Jewish priests must completely abstain from sexual relations for three days before partaking of the Holy Bread (cf. 1 Sam 21:5-7; Lev 15:18). Since a Catholic priest partakes of the Holy Bread (the Holy Eucharist) just about every day of his life, it would make sense that he perpetually abstained from sexual relations.[5]

- In 1 Tim 3:2, St. Paul says that a bishop "must be irreproachable, married only once..." St. Paul himself was a bishop and the fact is that he did not marry (cf. 1 Cor 7:8). In 1 Tim 3:2 St. Paul is not *requiring* bishops to marry but saying that, if a man were already married more than once, he could not assume the office of bishop. [6] In 1 Tim 3:2 the Bible also says that a bishop must "keep his children under control with perfect dignity." If a bishop's adolescent children go "out of control" and run away from home and get in trouble, would that disqualify him from being a bishop and cause his ordination to be revoked? Of course not!

- In the Book of the Prophet Isaiah, God says: "...To the eunuchs who observe my sabbaths and choose what pleases me and hold fast to my covenant, I will give, in my house and within my walls, a monument and a name better than sons and daughters; an eternal, imperishable name will I give them..." (Isaiah 56:4-8).[7]

- Just as Jesus took on Flesh through His mother Mary (a virgin — cf. Luke 1:34), Jesus' Flesh also becomes present at each Mass through a person who has vowed to live a celibate life — the Roman Catholic priest.

- In Matthew 13:45-46, Jesus teaches a parable about the importance of the tenacious pursuit of God's Kingdom: "...the kingdom of heaven is like a merchant searching for fine pearls. When he finds a pearl of great price, he goes and sells *all that he has* and buys it." The candidate for the Roman Catholic priesthood has discovered the "treasure" that faith in Jesus Christ can bring and he, thus, freely chooses to divest himself of *all that he has* (including even a future spouse and children) in order to follow Jesus without distraction.

St. Augustine called celibacy "a vacancy for God." Catholic clergy are not *forced* to be celibate, they freely choose it on their own and petition the Church to ordain them as such in order that they may serve the Lord as an ordained minister.

Scripture scholar Raymond Brown, S.S., in his book *Priest and Bishop: Biblical Reflections*, says the following about the scripturally-based discipline of celibacy in the Roman Catholic Church:

> "The fact that the Western Catholic Church has demanded celibacy of its priests may also be seen as an application of the principle of discipleship. Of course, the Church knows that in the NT celibacy was not demanded of all who followed Jesus or even of the Twelve, but it was held up as an ideal to those who were able to bear it (Matt 19:12, 1 Cor 7:7-9). Since this ideal was held up precisely for the sake of the kingdom of heaven, from a very early period the Church has not deemed it illogical to seek candidates willing to live by the ideal of celibacy among those who want to devote themselves in a special way to promoting the kingdom of heaven."[8]

Any reputable psychologist will tell you that freely chosen celibacy is *not* the cause of pedophilia or sexual infidelity (look at the number of married professionals in all lines of work who have, unfortunately, been caught doing such things.) Pedophilia is a mental illness that, sad to say, touches *all* occupations. Statistics tell us that the overwhelming majority of acts of pedophilia are committed by married parents on their own children (i.e., incest.)

In regard to the case of St. Peter being married, James Cardinal Gibbons writes:

> "...[That] St. Peter, after his vocation, did not continue with his wife ... may be inferred from his own words: 'Behold, we have left *all things*, and followed Thee (Matt 19:27).' Among 'all things' must be reckoned the fellowship of his wife, for he could hardly say with truth that he had left all things if he had not left his wife. Our Savior immediately after enumerates the wife among

those cherished objects, the renunciation of which, for His sake, will have its reward (Matt 19:29)."[9]

Alfons Maria Cardinal Stickler writes about clerical celibacy:

"...[Priestly celibacy] configures the priest to Jesus Christ, the head and spouse of the Church...The priest is therefore not without spousal love, he has as his Bride the Church...The essential content of [priestly celibacy] 'is *the gift of self,* the total gift of *self to the Church,* following the example of Christ...*"[10]

It is interesting to observe how a number of evangelical Christian ministers seem to have *much more difficulty* with Roman Catholic priestly celibacy than the vast majority of Roman Catholic priests do. It is a mystery to me why some of them feel a need to attack the considerable sacrifice that we freely make to attempt to follow our Lord in a more whole-hearted manner.

Common Objection #2

"St. Paul talks about the error of someone forbidding Christians to marry: '...[I]n the last times some will turn away from the faith by paying attention to deceitful spirits and demonic instructions through the hypocrisy of liars branded consciences. They forbid marriage and require abstinence from foods that God created...'" (1 Tim 4:1-3).

A Catholic Response

St. Paul is warning his readers in 1 Tim 4 against *false* asceticism, in which certain things were wrongly seen by some as intrinsically dirty or evil and, therefore, to be avoided.

The fact is that the Church (following Jesus' lead) elevates Christian marriage to the level of a Sacrament. When a man petitions his bishop to ordain him as a Roman Catholic priest, he is certainly *not* making the statement that marriage is unholy or undesirable. What his sacrificial decision is saying is that, as valuable and as holy as marriage is, I believe that the *greater good,* for me with my particular set of God-given gifts, would be to spread God's Kingdom unencumbered by the numerous responsibilities associated with family life. Celibacy doesn't put down Holy Matrimony any more than fasting (cf. Acts 13:2-3) puts down good food.

As far as for abstaining from certain foods (i.e., meat during Fridays of Lent), Catholics do this, not because meat is bad or evil but, since Jesus gave up His Flesh on the cross on a Friday for the salvation of the world (cf. Mark 15:33-42), Catholics make the small sacrifice to give up fleshy meat on Fridays during Lent to commemorate this ultimate expression of God's love.

What Did the Early Christians Believe About the Value of Forgoing Marriage For the Sake of Freeing Oneself to Spread the Kingdom of God?[11]

- "It is determined that bishops, presbyters, and deacons, or all clerics stationed in the ministry, are to restrain themselves completely and are to keep themselves away from their wives and are not to beget children. Anyone who does beget children is to be expelled from the honor of the clerical state." *The Council of Elvira* (300 A.D.)[12]

- "If a presbyter has married a wife, let him be removed from the ranks. But if he has fornicated or has committed adultery, let him be thrust out completely and let him subject himself to penance." *The Council of Neocaesarea* (314 A.D.)[13]

- "It is proper that the sacred bishops, priests of God as well as deacons, or those who are at the service of the divine sacraments, should be absolutely continent in order to obtain in all simplicity what they ask for from God: so that what the apostles taught and antiquity itself has observed we might also observe..." *The Council of Carthage* (390 A.D.)[14]

- "That the chastity of the Levites and priests must be preserved...The rule of continence and chastity had been discussed in a previous council. Let it [now] be taught with more emphasis what are the three ranks that, by virtue of their consecration, are under the same obligation of chastity, i.e., the bishop, the priest and the deacon, and let them be instructed to keep their purity...As was previously said, it is fitting that the holy bishops and priests of God as well as the Levites, i.e., those who are in the service of the divine sacraments, observe perfect continence..." *The Council of Africa* (390 A.D.)[15]

- "[H]e who leads a married life is not admitted by the Church to the order of Deacon, Priest, Bishop or sub-Deacon." St. Epiphanius (d. 403 A.D.)[16]

Endnotes

[1] Jesus Himself is the one who first gives the call to celibacy as He teaches His followers about the great value of remaining unmarried for the sake of freeing oneself to spread God's Kingdom: "[Jesus'] disciples said to him, 'If that is the case of a man with his wife, it is better not to marry.' He answered, 'Not all can accept [this] word, but only those to whom that is granted. Some are incapable of marriage because they were born so; some, because they were made so by others; some, because they have renounced marriage for the sake of the kingdom of heaven. *Whoever can accept this ought to accept it*'" (Matt 19:10-12).

[70] *Mt* 19:12.

[71] *1 Cor* 7:32.

[72] Cf. *PO* 16.

[2] Celibate St. Paul (cf. 1 Cor 7:8) writes to the Christians in Corinth: "Be imitators of me, as I am of Christ" (1 Cor 11:1).

[3] One of the reasons why I have undertaken the writing of this book is because some well-meaning people, who do not truly know my "wife" (the Roman Catholic Church), are making erroneous statements about her. Hopefully, I can begin to show the readers of this book how beautiful my "wife" is and clear up some of the misconceptions being spread about her.

4   Albert Nevins writes about celibacy: "Jesus was not placing a mandate on His followers but a counsel. Celibacy was for those able to keep it for the perfection of the kingdom of heaven, where the saved 'neither marry nor are given in marriage, but are like angels in heaven' (Mt 22:30). St. Paul took this counsel as a model for his own life. In his discussion of marriage (1 Cor 7) he observes, 'It is well for a man not to touch a woman.' Being a realist, however, Paul recognized that celibacy was not for all. He concludes (7-9): 'I wish all were as I myself am. But each has his own special gift from God, one of one kind and one of another... To the unmarried and the widows I say that it is well for them to remain single as I do. But if they cannot exercise self-control they should marry. For it is better to marry than be aflame with passion.' Thus the Western Church in mandating the discipline of celibacy for its priests (a deacon is permitted to be married when ordained, but if his wife dies, the deacon cannot remarry) is carrying out the counsel of Jesus and the wish of St. Paul... Celibacy is not only biblical in origin but also a gift of the Spirit, just as faithful married love is a gift of the Spirit." Cf. Albert Nevins, M.M., *Answering A Fundamentalist*, (Huntington, IN: Our Sunday Visitor Inc., 1990), pp. 114-115.

5   In the Book of Exodus we read about the people of Sinai before they received the Commandments from God: "Then Moses came down from the mountain to the people and had them sanctify themselves and wash their garments. He warned them, 'Be ready for the third day. *Have no intercourse with any woman'*" (Exod 19:14-15). Should not the priest, whose vocation it is to preach about the Commandments of God *daily*, abstain altogether from the sexual act? Cf. James Cardinal Gibbons, *The Faith of Our Fathers*, (Rockford, IL: TAN Books and Publishers, Inc., 1980), p. 330.

6   Scripture scholar Raymond Brown, S.S. writes: "The regulation in 1 Tim 3:2 that a widower who has remarried cannot be a presbyter-bishop is not really different *in kind* from the later church law that a married man cannot serve as a priest." Cf. Raymond E. Brown, S.S., *Priest and Bishop: Biblical Reflections*, (New York, NY: Paulist Press, 1970), p. 37.

7   Cf. Jesus' words concerning those Christians who have chosen to be "eunuchs for the sake of spreading God's kingdom" in Matt 19:10-12.

8   Raymond E. Brown, S.S., *Priest and Bishop: Biblical Reflections*, (Paramus, NJ: Paulist Press, 1970), p. 25.

9   James Cardinal Gibbons, *The Faith of Our Fathers*, (Rockford, IL: TAN Books and Publishers, Inc., 1980), p. 328.

10   Alfons Maria Cardinal Stickler, *The Case For Clerical Celibacy*, (San Francisco, CA: Ignatius Press, 1995), pp. 101-102.

11   Alfons Maria Cardinal Stickler writes: "...[W]e can make the following assertion [about clerical celibacy]: that the three higher grades of the clerical ministry were clearly obliged to clerical continence, that such an obligation can be traced to the very beginnings of the Church and that it had been handed down as part of the oral tradition. After the period of the persecution of the Church and especially due to the increasing numbers converting, which also meant an increase in the number of ordinations, we find infractions against this difficult obligation. Against such infractions, both councils and Popes insisted with ever-increasing determination on the obligation to continence by means of written laws or regulations. These particular regulations and provisions appear to be, not innovations, but rather part of an unbroken normative tradition. Even before it had become fixed in written laws, a genuinely binding obligation had been handed on by the oral tradition of the Church." Cf. *The Case For Clerical Celibacy*, p. 40.

12   William A. Jurgens (editor and translator), *The Faith of the Early Fathers (Volume 1)*, (Collegeville, MN: The Liturgical Press, 1970), p. 256.

13   *Ibid.*, p. 274.

14   Aidan Nichols, O.P., *Holy Order*, (Dublin, Ireland: Veritas Publications, 1990), p. 156.

15   *The Case For Clerical Celibacy*, pp. 23-24.

16   *The Faith of Our Fathers*, p. 329.

Chapter 20

Do Catholics Worship Statues?

What Does the Catholic Church Teach?

"...[A]lready in the Old Testament, God ordained or permitted the making of images that pointed symbolically toward salvation by the incarnate Word: so it was with the bronze serpent, the ark of the covenant, and the cherubim.[69] ...Basing itself on the mystery of the incarnate Word, the seventh ecumenical council at Nicaea (787) justified against the iconoclasts the veneration of icons — of Christ, but also of the Mother of God, the angels, and all the saints. By becoming incarnate, the Son of God introduced a new 'economy' of images... The Christian veneration of images is not contrary to the first commandment which proscribes idols. Indeed, 'the honor rendered to an image passes to its prototype,' and 'whoever venerates an image venerates the person portrayed in it.'[70] The honor paid to sacred images is a 'respectful veneration,' not the adoration due to God alone:

> Religious worship is not directed to images in themselves, considered as mere things, but under their distinctive aspect as images leading us on to God incarnate. The movement toward the image does not terminate in it as image, but tends toward that whose image it is."[71]

(*Catechism of the Catholic Church*, #2130–2132.)

Common Objection #1

"God plainly says in the Bible: 'You shall not carve idols for yourselves in the shape of anything in the sky above or on the earth below or in the waters beneath the earth; you shall not bow down before them or worship them' (Exodus 20:4-5). When Catholics put statues of Jesus or the saints in their homes and Churches, they are clearly going against this commandment of the Lord."

A Catholic Response

Let us look through the Bible to see if statues and images were ever commissioned by God for religious usage:

- In the Book of Exodus, God instructs His people to build two *gold statues* of cherubim and place them on top of the Ark of the Covenant (cf. Exod 25:10-22).

- In the First Book of Kings we read that in the sanctuary of the Temple there were two *olive wood statues* of cherubim and numerous carvings and statues of oxen, lions, palm trees, etc... (cf. 1 Kings 6:23; 7:13-51).[1]

- In the Book of Numbers, God ordered Moses to make a *bronze statue* of a serpent and to mount it on top of a pole as an instrument of healing for God's people (cf. Num 21:6-9).

- In the Book of Judges we read that Micah's mother had a "carved image" constructed of silver and consecrated it as a gift to the Lord (cf. Judges 17:1-6).

Did God intend for His people to *worship* these various statues and images that He ordered them to construct? Of course not! God's purpose in using these images was merely to enable the faithful to recall that these were holy places and to turn their hearts and minds toward Him.

An important distinction must be made between an *image* and an *idol*. An image is simply a spiritual "visual aid" that is used by the faithful to increase their spirit of prayerfulness and devotion to God. An idol, on the other hand, is an image that is worshipped by the unfaithful *in place of* the one true God (i. e., the "golden calf" described in Exod 32:7-8).

In the Old Testament, images of God were forbidden because God had not yet taken on a human form. Since no one in the Old Testament had ever seen God face-to-face, artists would, obviously, have had no idea of what He looked like. In the New Testament, however, we read that God *has* taken on a human form (image): "He [Jesus] is the image of the invisible God..." (Col 1:15). "For in [Jesus] dwells the whole fullness of the deity bodily..." (Col 2:9). "What was from the beginning, what we have heard, what we have seen with our eyes, what we looked upon and touched with our hands concerns the Word of life — for the life was made visible..." (1 John 1:1-2).

In the Letter to the Hebrews, the Biblical writer speaks about the faithful saints who lived and died long ago (e. g., Abel, Abraham, Isaac, Jacob, Moses, Samson, David, etc...) and then he says, "Therefore, since *we are surrounded by so great a cloud of witnesses*, let us rid ourselves of every burden and sin that clings to us and persevere in running the race that lies before us" (cf. Heb 11:1 — 12:1). In a number of Catholic Churches, statues of many of the faithful Old and New Testament saints who have lived before us line the walls of the Church, giving worshippers a visual image of the spiritual reality that all of these saints, along with Christ, are witnessing of our faith journey and are prayerfully "cheering us on" in heaven.

Catholic convert David Currie writes: "In an Evangelical church, it is usually the pulpit, the preacher, or the choir that is the predominant feature in the front of the church. That arrangement makes it much harder to direct worship to God alone. All those people can get in the way."[2]

Statues are nothing more than plaster, paint and wood that serve as visual aids for prayer and meditation. Because we humans rely heavily upon our senses to perceive things, paintings of saints and statues appeal to our sense of sight and help us to focus on the good and holy life of the saint that we are thinking about.[3] Statues, paintings and stained glass windows can serve as wonderful educational tools. This was all the more important during those times in history when many of the Christian faithful could not read. But, even today, it is common in a Catholic Church to see mothers walking their children around the Church and teaching them, by means of "show and tell," about the various mysteries of the Christian faith and the stories of the great "cloud of witnesses" (the lives of the saints.)

We put statues in our Churches for the same reason that a person puts pictures of his family on the walls in his house. This is the same reason why a television weatherman shows us a picture of the United States when he speaks to us about the weather. He could just tell us the facts, but the visual picture allows us human beings to more fully grasp the intangible reality that he is speaking about.

We read in the Book of Revelation that the saints in heaven plead with God and ask Him to act on their behalf (cf. Rev 6:9-10). The saints in heaven are, thus, still a vital part of the spiritual family of Catholics.

Catholics *do not* worship statues! Most Christian denominations have crosses in their sanctuaries or images of crosses in the stained glass windows of their churches. Is there anything wrong with that? Certainly not! In order to teach their children, many Christian denominations use religious instructional books and children's Bibles that have pictures of Jesus in them. Aren't pictures of Jesus two-dimensional *images*? Is this breaking God's commandment? Not at all!

Protestant Christians may sometimes hold up their Bibles during worship. Are these Christians worshipping an inanimate book made up of paper, glue, leather and ink or are they worshipping the God in heaven who wrote that book? The latter holds true, of course. In a similar manner, Catholics don't worship or honor the plaster and the paint but the spiritual realities represented by the plaster and the paint.

A Catholic may pray to God *in front* of the visual aid of a statue of a saint but a Catholic would never pray *to* a statue itself because that would clearly constitute idolatry. (Cf. Exodus 32:7-8 where the people prayed *to* the statue of the golden calf which *was* their god.)

What Did the Early Christians Believe About the Use of Images as Visual Aids for Prayer and Worship of the One True God?

- Albert J. Nevins, M.M. writes:

    "The early Church used statues and images as aids to devotion and as expressions of faith. One need only to visit the catacombs in Rome to see statues and frescoes representing not only Christ but also scenes from Scripture. When the Church emerged from the catacombs, it continued to decorate its houses of worship with statues, mosaics, frescoes, and oil paintings, all designed to increase a spirit of prayerfulness."[4]

- "Previously God, who has neither a body nor a face, absolutely could not be represented by an image. But now that he has made himself visible in the flesh and has lived with men, I can make an image of what I have seen of God...and contemplate the glory of the Lord, his face unveiled." St. John Damascene (d. circa 749 A. D.)[5]

Endnotes

[69] Cf. Num 21:4-9; Wis 16:5-14; Jn 3:14-15; Ex 25:10-22; 1 Kings 6:23-28; 7:23-26.

[70] St. Basil, *De Spiritu Sancto* 18, 45: PG 32, 149C; Council of Nicaea II: DS 601; cf. Council of Trent: DS 1821-1825; Vatican Council II: *SC* 126; *LG* 67.

[71] St. Thomas Aquinas, *STh* II-II, 81, 3 *ad* 3.

[1] In the light of God instructing His people to adorn the Temple and other holy places with various images, it appears, from looking at the Ten Commandments (cf. Deut 5:8-10), that God prohibited the use of *pagan* images that were not associated with the worship of the one true God.

[2] David B. Currie, *Born Fundamentalist Born Again Catholic*, (San Francisco, CA: Ignatius Press, 1996), p. 148.

3   A number of Protestant Christian churches sponsor Easter plays in which various members of their congregation dress up in costume as Jesus and the saints (give living images) to the audience in an attempt to get the audience to focus on the lives of these spiritual giants. Is there anything wrong with that? Of course not!

4   Albert J. Nevins, M.M., *Answering A Fundamentalist*, (Huntington, IN: Our Sunday Visitor, Inc., 1990), p. 106.

5   *Catechism of the Catholic Church*, #1159.

Chapter 21

The Seven Biblical Sacraments

What Does the Catholic Church Teach?

"'Adhering to the teaching of the Holy Scriptures, to the apostolic traditions, and to the consensus ... of the Fathers,' we profess that 'the sacraments of the new law were ... all instituted by Jesus Christ our Lord.'[31] '...The purpose of the sacraments is to sanctify men, to build up the Body of Christ and, finally, to give worship to God. Because they are signs they also instruct. They not only presuppose faith, but by words and objects they also nourish, strengthen, and express it. That is why they are called 'sacraments *of faith*.'"[44] (*Catechism of the Catholic Church*, #1114, 1123.)

Common Objection #1

"The word 'sacrament' isn't even in the Bible. How could Christ possibly have instituted them?"

A Catholic Response

St. Paul writes to the Christians in Corinth: "Thus should one regard us: as servants of Christ and stewards of the *mysteries* [Greek: *mysterion*] of God" (1 Cor 4:1). St. John Chrysostom (d. 407) and St. Gregory of Nyssa (d. 394) often used the words *Mysterion*

("Mystery") and *Sacramentum* ("Sacrament") interchangeably. We can see here in Scripture that the Church is, indeed, called to serve as the "steward" of Jesus' Sacraments.

The word "Sacrament" comes from the Latin word *sacramentum* (which means "holy thing"). By His words and actions, Jesus made certain things "Holy Things" or "Sacraments." Although the word "Sacrament" does not appear, as such, in Scripture, the reality of Jesus instituting certain "Holy Things" is solidly rooted in Scripture. The Church simply gave a name to the Biblical reality.

Scripture reveals to us that the merits of Jesus' death and resurrection are applied to us over time and not in one big lump (cf. Phil 2:12; 1 Pet 1:9). The seven Sacraments of the Catholic Church are the "applicators" of the merits of our Lord's Saving Act accomplished on Calvary.

St. Paul writes to the Christians in Colossae: "...I rejoice in my sufferings for your sake, and in my flesh I am filling up what is lacking in the afflictions of Christ on behalf of his body, which is the church" (Col 1:24). St. Paul is certainly not saying here that Jesus' death and resurrection are somehow deficient. What he is saying is that, by uniting his own sufferings to the sufferings of Christ, he is able to draw from the "reservoir" of merits that are a result of Jesus' death and resurrection. Along the same lines, the seven Sacraments are the means of applying the healing and saving merits of Jesus' death and resurrection to the souls of individual believers throughout the course of history.[1]

James Akin writes:

> "In both the Old and the New Testament there are incidents where God uses physical means to convey grace. One striking example is the case of the woman with a hemorrhage: 'When she heard about Jesus, she came up behind him in the crowd and touched his cloak, because she thought, 'If I just touch his clothes I will be healed.' Immediately her bleeding stopped and she felt in her body that she was freed from her suffering. At once Jesus realized that power had gone out from him. He turned around in the crowd and asked, 'Who touched

my clothes?' "You see the people crowding against you,' his disciples answered, 'and yet you can ask, 'Who touched me?' But Jesus kept looking around to see who had done it. Then the woman, knowing what had happened to her, came and fell at his feet and, trembling with fear, told him the whole truth. He said to her, 'Daughter, your faith has healed you. Go in peace to be freed from your suffering' (Mark 5:27-34, NIV).

This passage contains all the elements of the sacramental principle: the woman's faith, the physical means (touching Jesus' clothes), and the supernatural power that went out from Jesus... This is how the sacraments work; God uses physical signs (water, oil, bread, wine, the laying on of hands) as vehicles for his grace, which we receive in faith.

Thomas Aquinas pointed out that, since we are not simply spiritual beings, but physical creatures also, it is fitting for God to give us his spiritual gift of grace through physical means."[2]

Alan Schreck writes about the connection between the ministry of Jesus and the seven Catholic Sacraments:

"Besides using persons to carry on his mission and communicate the grace of God, Jesus also employed specific actions and objects as visible signs of the life and blessings he came to give. Water was one such sign, as when Jesus was baptized by John in the Jordan River and the Holy Spirit descended upon him (Mk 1:9-11). Jesus used ordinary food to show the power of God. His first miracle in John's gospel was to change water into wine (see Jn 2:1-11), and later he multiplied bread and fish to feed the hungry crowds (see Mk 6:35-44, 8:19). Jesus' actions and gestures communicated the grace and power of God. He often touched people when he healed them, even lepers (Mk 1:40-45), and used his own spit to open a blind man's eyes (see Mk 8:22-26). He breathed on the apostles to give them the Holy Spirit

(Jn 20:22), and he gave them his own body and blood on the night before he died in the form of bread and wine (Mk 14:22-25). All of these are instances of Jesus' use of 'sacraments' — specific objects, gestures, and persons that visibly symbolized and conferred God's abundant grace and blessings.

...The sacraments emerged as a distinctive part of the church's life as the apostles followed Jesus' example or carried out his teaching. They anointed the sick for healing (see Mk 6:13). They laid their hands on people and prayed for them to receive the Holy Spirit (see Acts 8:14-17, 19:5-6). They laid their hands on others to be set apart for special ministry or mission in the church (see Acts 6:3-6, 13:1-3). They baptized (see Mt 28:19, Jn 4:2), and forgave sins with authority as Jesus had instructed and empowered them to do (see Mt 18:18, Jn 20:23). They came to understand marriage as a sacrament (which literally means 'mystery'), representing the mystery of Jesus' love for the church (see Eph 5:21-23). And, of course, they offered bread and wine in thanksgiving ('eucharist') for Jesus' death, fulfilling his command to 'do this in remembrance of me' (Lk 22:19).

The apostles knew that they were not Jesus, but they knew that Jesus himself was the one who was present with them and through them when they did those things in his name."[3]

The following are some of the major Biblical foundations for the seven Sacraments of the Roman Catholic Church:

Baptism Matt 3:13-17; John 3:5, 22; Matt 28:19; 1 Peter 3:18-22; Titus 3:5; Luke 3:3; Gal 3:27; Mark 16:16; Acts 22:16; Acts 2:38-39; Rom 6:3-5; Luke 7:30 (*cf. Chapter 22 of this book*)

Penance

John 20:22-23; Matt 16:18-19; Matt 18:18; Matt 9:1-8; 2 Cor 5:17-20; Luke 15:11-32 *(cf. Chapter 18 of this book)*

Holy Eucharist

Mark 14:22-25; Matt 26:26-28; Luke 22:19-20; 1 Cor 11:23-30; John 6:4, 51-68; Heb 10:25-31; 1 Cor 5:7-8; Rev 19:9 *(cf. Chapter 5 of this book)*

Confirmation[4]

Acts 8:14-17; Acts 19:1-6; Acts 2:1-4; Matt 10:32-33; Heb 6:1-2

Marriage[5]

Gen 1:27-28; Gen 2:21-24; Eph 5:25, 31-32; Heb 13:4; John 2:1-12 *(cf. Chapter 25 of this book)*

Holy Orders[6]

Acts 2:1-4; Acts 1:21-26; Luke 24:44-51; Acts 6:2-6; 2 Tim 1:6; 1 Tim 4:14; 1 Tim 5:22; Acts 14:23; Acts 13:3, Rom 15:15-16 *(cf. Chapter 6 of this book)*

Anointing of the Sick

James 5:14-15; Mark 6:13

The 7 Sacraments are the "faucets" that Jesus has instituted to dispense the merits of His death and resurrection to believers throughout the course of history. Consider this visual diagram of the role of Sacraments:[7]

What Did the Early Christians Believe About the Sacraments?

- "Moreover, those things which were created from the waters are blessed by God, so that this might also be a sign that men would at a future time receive repentance and remission of sins through water and the bath of regeneration — all who proceed to the truth and are born again and receive a blessing from God." St. Theophilus of Antioch in his *To Autolycus* (circa 181 A.D.)[8]

- "The Spirit who in the beginning hovered over the waters would continue to linger as an influence upon the waters... All waters, therefore, by reason of the original sign at their beginning, are suitable, after God has been invoked, for the sacrament of sanctification." Tertullian in his *Baptism* (circa 200 A.D.)[9]

- "In the saving sacraments, when necessity compels and when God bestows His pardon, divine benefits are bestowed fully upon believers." St. Cyprian of Carthage in his *Letter to a Certain Magnus* (circa 255 A.D.)[10]

- "...[S]o that whoever has been baptized anywhere in the name of Christ, immediately receives the grace of Christ." *Fragment of a Letter of Stephen of Rome to the Bishops of Asia Minor* (circa 255 A.D.)[11]

Endnotes

[31] Council of Trent (1547): DS 1600-1601.

[44] *SC* 59.

[1] Cf. Rev. John A. O'Brien, *The Faith of Millions*, (Huntington, IN: Our Sunday Visitor, Inc., 1963, 1974), p. 143.

[2] Patrick Madrid (editor), *Surprised by Truth*, (San Diego, CA: Basilica Press, 1994), p. 65.

[3] Alan Schreck, *Catholic and Christian*, (Ann Arbor, Michigan: Servant Books, 1984), pp. 122-123.

[4] Originally, the anointing with oil and laying on of hands was part of the Sacrament of Baptism (cf. Acts 8:14-17). Therefore, Confirmation is linked to Jesus' command to be baptized (cf. John 3:1-5, 22).

[5] It is sinful for married couples to intentionally render the marital act infertile through artificial means (cf. Gen 1:27-28; Psalm 127:3-5; Deut 7:13-14; Gen 38:8-10; Deut 25:11-12; Luke 1:25). Cf. also *Catechism of the Catholic Church,* #2366-2370. For *serious reasons,* the Catholic Church allows "natural family planning" — in which the married couple work with the woman's natural fertility cycles in order to space births. Cf. also (Protestant) Charles D. Provan's excellent book, *The Bible and Birth Control,* (Monongehela, PA: Zimmer Printing, 1989).

[6] Note that, in the Old Testament, all Jews were called "priests" (cf. Exod 19:6), while at the same time God also set aside certain men (Aaron and his sons) to carry out a specialized ordained priestly ministry (cf. Exod 29). Just as in the Old Testament, all Christians are called "priests" (cf. 1 Pet 2:9), while at the same time Jesus set aside certain men (the Apostles and

their successors) to carry out a specialized ordained priestly ministry (cf. Rom 15:15-16; 1 Tim 4:14, Luke 22:7-20, etc.)

Jesus did *many* things throughout His lifetime that went totally against prevailing practice. If He didn't agree with existing structures or practices, He changed them (e.g., John 4:9, 27; Matt 5:38-42; Num 19:11/John 11:38-44; Luke 5:27-30; Mark 3:16-19, etc.) When Jesus hand-picked His twelve Apostles for "ordination", He chose men exclusively (cf. Luke 6:13-16). The Catholic Church assumes that, because Christ could have very well included women among His chosen group of "priests" but deliberately decided *not* to do so, that this is the way that He wished it to be. Jesus certainly had a deep love and concern for women throughout His ministry but, evidently, He felt that these precious and faith-filled disciples should serve the Church in other extremely crucial roles besides ordained ministry.

7   "The *altar* of the New Covenant is the Lord's Cross, from which the sacraments of the Paschal mystery flow..." (*Catechism of the Catholic Church*, #1182).

8   William A. Jurgens (editor and translator), *The Faith of the Early Fathers (Volume 1)*, (Collegeville, MN: The Liturgical Press, 1970), p. 75.

9   *Ibid.*, p. 126.

10   *Ibid.*, p. 235.

11   *Ibid.*, p. 243.

Chapter 22

"Let the Children Come to Me":[1] Infant Baptism

What Does the Catholic Church Teach?

"Born with a fallen human nature and tainted by original sin, children also have need of the new birth in Baptism to be freed from the power of darkness and brought into the realm of the freedom of the children of God, to which all men are called.[50] The sheer gratuitousness of the grace of salvation is particularly manifest in infant Baptism... The practice of infant Baptism is an immemorial tradition of the Church. There is explicit testimony to this practice from the second century on, and it is quite possible that, from the beginning of the apostolic preaching, when whole 'households' received baptism, infants may also have been baptized."[53] (*Catechism of the Catholic Church*, #1250, 1252.)

Common Objection #1

"Baptism is only for individuals who are old enough to profess faith in Jesus Christ as their personal Lord and Savior: "...if you confess with your mouth that Jesus is Lord and believe in your heart that God raised him from the dead, you will be saved" (Rom 10:9). Infants are not yet capable of doing this and, therefore, should not be baptized."

A Catholic Response

In the Book of Genesis, God instructs Jewish parents to bring their eight-day-old baby boys to the Temple to have them circumcised (cf. Gen 17:9-14). Because of the parents' faithful response to God's command, the Jewish baby boy, at the very beginning of his young life (and way before "the age of accountability"), became a full-fledged member of God's Chosen People. Being faithful Jews, Mary and Joseph did as God had requested and brought the baby Jesus to be circumcised when He was a mere eight days old (cf. Luke 2:22-32). One can clearly see in Sacred Scripture that God has called *(and continues to call)* every human being, no matter how young or old, into a covenant relationship with Him.[2]

Just as circumcision was the covenant sign for God's Chosen People in the Old Testament (cf. Gen 17:9-14), Baptism became the covenant sign for God's New Chosen People in the New Testament: *"In [Jesus] you were also circumcised* with a circumcision not administered by hand, by stripping off the carnal body, with the circumcision of Christ. You were buried with him in *baptism,* in which you were raised with him through faith in the power of God, who raised him from the dead" (Col 2:11-12).

Nowhere in the New Testament or the Old Testament do we have any indication that God wishes to exclude children from entering into covenant with Him and nowhere in the Bible is the ancient practice of infant Baptism prohibited. In fact, in the Gospel of Matthew, Jesus clearly tells His disciples: *"Let the children come to me,* and do not prevent them; for the kingdom of heaven belongs to such as these" (Matt 19:14). This particular passage does not explicitly mention Baptism but it clearly shows that Jesus' intent for all people, regardless of their age or ability to reason, is to enter into relationship with Him.[3]

Baptizing infants makes the clear statement that there is nothing that we can do to "earn" salvation *(certainly, the infant is not capable of doing anything on his own.)* God's love reaches out to us before we are even capable of any kind of formal response. On the child's behalf, the faithful parents and godparents promise to support and nurture the child in his faith.[4] At Confirmation, the Catholic reaffirms for himself belief in Jesus Christ as Lord and Savior.

Jesus' public ministry was geared toward adults so it would make sense that the first converts to Christianity were adults. It was only natural that, after their Baptism, these newly-converted adult Christians wanted to share the promise of everlasting life with each member of their own families. Christian parents wanted to form their children in the ways of the Christian faith while they were most impressionable.

In the Acts of the Apostles, Peter says: "Repent and be baptized, every one of you, in the name of Jesus Christ for the forgiveness of your sins...for the promise is made to you and *to your children* and to all those far off, whomever the Lord our God will call" (Acts 2:38-39).

A number of times in the New Testament, one reads about whole households of people being baptized: "After she and her *household* had been baptized..." (Acts 16:15); "...then he and *all his family* were baptized at once" (Acts 16:33); "I baptized the *household* of Stephanas also..." (1 Cor 1:16). Early historical writings testify to the fact that children were, indeed, part of these households mentioned in Scripture *(cf. the writings of the early Church Fathers at the end of this chapter).*

Some evangelical Christians will claim that a person must receive the Holy Spirit first and *then* request Baptism *(thus, infant Baptism is ruled out because a child can't yet do this.)* The fact is that, a number of times in the New Testament, the Holy Spirit was received *after* the Baptism with water had already taken place *(cf. Luke 3:21-22; Acts 8:14-17; Acts 19:1-7).*[5]

What Was the Belief and Practice of the Early Christians Concerning Baptism?

Infant Baptism

- St. Irenaeus — who was a disciple of St. Polycarp — who was a disciple of St. John the Evangelist — writes about Baptism: "Christ came to save all who through Him are born again unto God; infants and children, boys and youths, and aged persons." St. Irenaeus in his *Against Heresies* (circa 190 A.D.)[6]

- "Baptize first the children; and if they can speak for themselves, let them do so. Otherwise, let their parents or other relatives speak for them." St. Hippolytus of Rome in his *The Apostolic Tradition* (circa 215 A.D.) [7]

- "Baptism is given for the remission of sins; and according to the usage of the Church, Baptism is given even to infants." Origen in his *Homilies on Leviticus* (circa 244 A.D.)[8]

- "The Church received from the Apostles the tradition of giving Baptism even to infants. For the Apostles, to whom were committed the secrets of divine mysteries, knew that there is in everyone the innate stains of sin, which must be washed away through water and the Spirit." Origen in his *Commentaries on Romans* (circa 244 A.D.)[9]

- "As to what pertains to the case of infants: you said that they ought not to be baptized within the second or third day after their birth, and that the old law of circumcision must be taken into consideration, and that you did not think that one should be baptized and sanctified within the eighth day after his birth. In our council it seemed to us far otherwise. No one agreed to the course which you thought should be taken. Rather, we all judged that the mercy and grace of God ought to be denied to no man born." St. Cyprian of Carthage in his *Letter to Cyprian and of His Colleagues in Council to the Number of Sixty-Six: To Fidus* (circa 251 A.D.)[10]

Baptism in the Name of the Trinity:[11]

- "In regard to Baptism — baptize thus: After the foregoing instructions, baptize in the name of the Father, and of the Son, and of the Holy Spirit." *Didache* (circa 70 A.D.)[12]

- "The law of washing has been imposed, and the form has been prescribed: "Go," He says, "teach the nations, washing them in the name of the Father and of the Son and of the Holy Spirit." Tertullian in his *Baptism* (circa 200 A.D.)[13]

- "...[L]egitimate Baptism is had only in the name of the Trinity." Origen in his *Commentaries on Romans* (circa 244 A.D.)[14]

Baptism By Pouring:[15]

- "...If you have no living water, then baptize in other water; and if you are not able in cold, then in warm. If you have neither, pour water three times on the head, in the name of the Father, and of the Son, and of the Holy Spirit." *Didache* (circa 70 A.D.)[16]

- "...[I]f water is scarce, whether as a constant condition or on occasion, then use whatever water is available." St. Hippolytus of Rome in his *The Apostolic Tradition* (215 A.D.)[17]

- "As [Novatian] seemed about to die, he received Baptism in the bed where he lay, by pouring..." St. Cornelius 1, Pope, in his *Letter to Fabius of Antioch* (circa 251 A.D.)[18]

- "You have asked also, dearest son, what I thought about those who obtain the grace of God while they are weakened by illness — whether or not they are to be reckoned as legitimate Christians who have not been bathed with the saving water, but have had it poured over them. On this point, my modesty and reservation prejudges no one. Let each one consider what he thinks best; and what he thinks best, let him do." St. Cyprian of Carthage in his *Letter to a Certain Magnus* (circa 255 A.D.)[19]

A Christian is "Born Again" Through the Waters of Baptism:[20]

- "As many as are persuaded and believe that what we [Christians] teach and say is true, and undertake to be able to live accordingly, and instructed to pray and to entreat God with fasting, for the remission of their sins that are past, we pray and fast with them. Then they are brought by us where there is water and are regenerated in the same manner in which we were ourselves regenerated. For, in the name of God, the Father...and of our Savior Jesus Christ, and of the Holy Spirit [Matt. 28:19], they then receive the washing with water. For Christ also said, 'Unless you are born again, you shall not enter into the kingdom of heaven'" (Justin Martyr in his *First Apology* 61 [151 A.D.]).

- "'And [Naaman] dipped himself ... seven times in the Jordan' [2 Kgs. 5:14]. It was not for nothing that Naaman of old, when suffering from leprosy, was purified upon his being baptized, but [this served] as an indication to us. For as we are lepers in sin, we are made clean, by means of the sacred water and the invocation of the Lord, from our old transgressions, being spiritually regenerated as new-born babes, even as the Lord has declared: 'Except a man be born again through water and the Spirit, he shall not enter into the kingdom of heaven'" (St. Irenaeus in his *Fragment* 34 [190 A.D.]).

- "[N]o one can attain salvation without baptism, especially in view of the declaration of the Lord, who says, 'Unless a man shall be born of water, he shall not have life'" (Tertullian in his *Baptism* 12:1 [203 A.D.]).

- "The Father of immortality sent the immortal Son and Word into the world, who came to man in order to wash him with water and the Spirit; and He, begetting us again to incorruption of soul and body, breathed into us the Spirit of life, and endued us with an incorruptible panoply. If, therefore, man has become immortal, he will also be God. And if he is made God by water and the Holy Spirit after the regeneration of the laver he is found to be also joint-heir with Christ after the resurrection from the dead. Wherefore I preach to this effect: Come, all ye kindreds of the nations, to the immortality of the baptism" (Hippolytus in his *Discourse on the Holy Theophany* 8 [217 A.D.]).

- "But you will perhaps say, 'What does the baptism of water contribute toward the worship of God?' In the first place, because that which has pleased God is fulfilled. In the second place, because when you are regenerated and born again of water and of God, the frailty of your former birth, which you have through men, is cut off, and so ... you shall be able to attain salvation; but otherwise it is impossible. For thus has the true prophet [Jesus] testified to us with an oath: 'Verily, I say to you, that unless a man is born again of water...he shall not enter into the kingdom of heaven'" (*Recognitions of Clement* 6:9 [221 A.D.]).

- "[When] they receive also the baptism of the Church...then finally can they be fully sanctified and be the sons of God...since it is written, 'Except a man be born again of water and of the Spirit, he cannot enter into the kingdom of God'" (St. Cyprian in his *Letters* 71[72]:1 [A.D. 253]).

Endnotes

1   Jesus' stern words to His disciples when they tried to prevent children from approaching Him (cf. Matt 19:13-15).

50 Cf. Council of Trent (1546): DS 1514; cf. *Col* 1:12-14.

53 Cf. *Acts* 16:15, 33; 18:8; *1 Cor* 1:16; CDF, instruction, *Pastoralis actio*: AAS 72 (1980) 1137-1156.

2   Many severely retarded people (who are seriously impaired in their ability to understand) are not mentally capable of even knowing who Jesus is much less making a personal commitment to Him as their "personal Lord and Savior." Should handicapped people who don't possess the ability to comprehend intellectually be excluded from the ranks of God's Chosen People? Of course not! Babies don't yet have the ability to reason and understand but that doesn't stop them from being called into covenant with God (cf. Gen 17:9-14). When Catholic Christian children grow older and their ability to understand and reason has developed they are invited to formally make their adult commitment to Christ in the Sacrament of Confirmation. (In much the same way, the Jewish child, who entered into covenant with God at eight days old through his circumcision, is invited to formally make an adult commitment to his faith at age thirteen at his Bar Mitzvah).

3   We read in the Scriptures that *God* is the one who takes the initiative in calling us (many times even before we even are capable of an adult response): "*...before you were born I dedi-*

cated you, a prophet to the nations *I appointed you*" (Jer 1:5); "...The Lord called me *from birth...*" (Isaiah 49:1); "It was not *you* who chose *me*, but *I* who chose *you...*" (John 15:16).

4 A number of times in the New Testament, Jesus responds to the faith of various *parents* who come to Him and ask Him to bestow some spiritual benefit on their child (e.g., the healing of Jairus' daughter [cf. Mark 5:22-23, 35-43]; the healing of the boy with a demon [cf. Mark 9:14-27]). Note that, even though these young children took no initiative and did not yet display any personal faith in Jesus, He responded to the deep faith of the parents (undoubtedly because He sensed that they would be committed to fulfilling their role of spiritually forming their children in the faith as they grew.) Note also how, in Mark 2:1-12, a paralytic is brought to Jesus by his faith-filled friends and, because of the friend's deep faith, Jesus bestows a cure upon the paralytic man — who, by the way, never speaks a word to Jesus.

5 Note that John the Baptist received the Holy Spirit while he was still in his mother's womb (cf. Luke 1:15).

6 Rev. John A. O'Brien, *The Faith of Millions*, (Huntington, IN: Our Sunday Visitor, Inc., 1963, 1974), p. 155.

7 William A. Jurgens (editor and translator), *The Faith of the Early Fathers (Volume 1)*, (Collegeville, MN: The Liturgical Press, 1970), p. 169.

8 *Ibid.*, p. 208.

9 *Ibid.*, p. 209.

10 *Ibid.*, p. 233.

11 In places such as Acts 2:38, we read about Baptism "in the name of Jesus Christ." Many Scripture scholars interpret passages such as this to refer to *Christian* Baptism (as opposed to Jewish) in the manner in which Jesus Christ instructed it to be performed (i.e., "in the name of the Father, and of the Son and of the holy Spirit" — cf. Matt 28:19). For a more extensive selection of writings of the early Church Fathers speaking about Trinitarian Baptism visit the *Catholic Answers* web site at www.catholic.com.

12 *The Faith of the Early Fathers (Volume 1)*, p. 2.

13 *Ibid.*, p. 127.

14 *Ibid.*, p. 209.

15 Note that nowhere in the New Testament does Jesus give His followers instructions as to the precise manner in which Baptismal water was required to be applied. It appears that Baptism by immersion may have been practiced for some Baptisms (cf. Mark 1:10; Acts 8:39) but the New Testament never says that this was the *only* way to validly apply the baptismal water. The Catholic Church does indeed recognize Baptism by immersion. It also recognizes Baptism by pouring — which would have certainly been practiced in the time of Christ in the many desert regions of the Holy Land where water was/is still scarce.

16 *The Faith of the Early Fathers (Volume 1)*, p. 2.

17 *Ibid.*, p. 169.

18 *Ibid.*, p. 216.

19 *Ibid.*, p. 235.

20 For the following quotes and an even more extensive list of the early Church Fathers speaking about being "born again" through the waters of Baptism visit the *Catholic Answers* Internet web site at <http://www.catholic.com>.

Chapter 23

The Catholic Creeds: Biblical Concentrate

What Does the Catholic Church Teach?

"*The Apostle's Creed* is so called because it is rightly considered to be a faithful summary of the apostles' faith. It is the ancient baptismal symbol of the Church of Rome. Its great authority arises from this fact: it is 'the Creed of the Roman Church, the See of Peter, the first of the apostles, to which he brought the common faith.'[13] *The Niceno-Constantinopolitan* or *Nicene Creed* draws its great authority from the fact that it stems from the first two ecumenical Councils (in 325 and 381). It remains common to all the great Churches of both East and West to this day." (*Catechism of the Catholic Church*, #194, 195.)

Common Objection #1

"The Catholic creeds are not found, as such, in the Bible. Therefore, they are human inventions."

A Catholic Response

Let's take both the Apostle's Creed and the Nicene Creed and break them down verse-by-verse to see if they have any basis in Scripture:

The Apostle's Creed:

The Apostle's Creed is an expansion of the profession of faith required of baptismal candidates in the early Church (cf. Acts 8:36-37).[1] Most scholars believe that the Apostle's Creed was not actually written by the Apostles themselves but contains the core beliefs of the faith that were handed down by the Apostles to their communities of disciples. In its twelve articles of faith, the Apostle's Creed presents the Christian believer with "Scriptural concentrate." Catholics pray the Apostle's Creed at the beginning of the rosary.

1) I believe in God *(cf. Deut 6:4)*, the Father almighty *(cf. 2 Cor 6:18)*, Creator of heaven and earth *(cf. Gen 14:19)*

2) And in Jesus Christ, His only Son *(cf. John 1:18)*, our Lord *(cf. Phil 2:11)*

3) Who was conceived by the Holy Spirit, born of the Virgin Mary *(cf. Matt 1:18)*

4) Suffered under Pontius Pilate *(cf. John 19:13, 16)*, was crucified, died, and was buried *(cf. 1 Cor 15:3-4)*. He descended into death *(cf. 1 Cor 15:3)*

5) The third day He rose again from the dead *(cf. 1 Cor 15:4)*

6) He ascended into heaven *(cf. Luke 24:51)* and is seated at the right hand of God, the Father almighty *(cf. Col 3:1)*

7) From thence He shall come to judge the living and the dead *(cf. 2 Tim 4:1)*

8) I believe in the Holy Spirit *(cf. John 4:24)*

9) The holy *(cf. Eph 5:25-27)* Catholic Church *(cf. 1 Cor 12:13; Matt 28:19-20)*, the communion of saints *(cf. Eph 2:19-22)*

10) The forgiveness of sins *(cf. Acts 2:38; John 20:22-23)*

11) The resurrection of the body *(cf. Rom 6:5)*

12) And life everlasting *(cf. John 3:16)*. Amen *(cf. Rom 9:5)*.

The Nicene Creed:

The Nicene Creed is a further elaboration on the earlier Apostle's Creed. Each of the twelve articles of faith of the Apostle's Creed were expanded upon to combat doctrinal errors being spread by heretics at the time.[2] The Nicene Creed was formulated at the Catholic Council of Nicaea in the year 325 A.D. Catholics pray the Nicene Creed at Mass.

1) We believe in one God *(cf. Deut 6:4)*, the Father almighty *(cf. 2 Cor 6:18)*, maker of heaven and earth *(cf. Gen 14:19)*, of all that is seen and unseen *(cf. Col 1:16)*

2) We believe in one Lord, Jesus Christ *(cf. Phil 2:11)*, the only Son of God *(cf. John 1:18)*, eternally begotten of the Father *(cf. John 1:1)*. God from God, Light from Light, true God from true God *(cf. John 10:30)*, begotten, not made *(cf. John 1:1)*, one in Being with the Father *(cf. John 10:30)*. Through Him all things were made *(cf. John 1:3)*. For us men and for our salvation he came down from heaven *(cf. John 3:13)*

3) By the power of the Holy Spirit, He was born of the Virgin Mary and became man *(cf. Matt 1:18)*

4) For our sake, He was crucified under Pontius Pilate *(cf. John 19:13, 16)*, He suffered, died, and was buried *(cf. 1 Cor 15:3-4)*

5) On the third day He rose again in fulfillment of the Scriptures *(cf. 1 Cor 15:4)*

6) He ascended into heaven *(cf. Luke 24:51)* and is seated at the right hand of the Father *(cf. Col 3:1)*

7) He will come again in glory to judge the living and the dead *(cf. 2 Tim 4:1)* and His Kingdom will have no end *(cf. John 3:16)*

8) We believe in the Holy Spirit, the Lord *(cf. John 4:24)*, the giver of life *(cf. John 6:63)*, who proceeds from the Father *(cf. John 15:26)* **and the Son** [3] *(cf. Phil 1:19)*. With the Father and the Son He is worshipped and glorified *(cf. John 4:24)*. He has spoken through the prophets *(cf. Isaiah 61:1)*

9) We believe in one *(cf. John 17:11)*, holy *(cf. Eph 5:25-27)*, Catholic *(cf. 1 Cor 12:13; Matt 28:19-20)*, and apostolic *(cf. Eph 3:4-6)* Church

10) We acknowledge one baptism *(cf. Eph 4:5)* for the forgiveness of sins *(cf. Acts 2:38)*

11) We look for the resurrection of the dead *(cf. 1 Thes 4:14)*

12) And the life of the world to come *(cf. 2 Peter 3:13)*. Amen *(cf. Rom 9:5)*.

The Word "Catholic" Describing the "Universal" Scope and Mission of the One Church Historically Founded by Jesus Christ Himself:[4]

- "Wherever the bishop appears, let the people be there; just as wherever Jesus Christ is, there is the Catholic Church." St. Ignatius of Antioch in his *Letter to the Smyrnaeans* (circa 110 A.D.)[5]

- "When finally Polycarp had finished his prayer, in which he remembered everyone with whom he had ever been acquainted, the small and the great, the renowned and the unknown, and the whole Catholic Church throughout the world." *The Martyrdom of St. Polycarp* (circa 155 A.D.)[6]

- "You wrote also, that I should forward to Cornelius, our colleague, a copy of your letter, so that he might put aside any anxiety and know immediately that you are in communion with him, that is, with the Catholic Church." St. Cyprian of Carthage in his *Letter to Antonianus, A Bishop in Numidia* (circa 251 A.D.)[7]

- "...We are not ignorant of the fact that there is one God, and one Christ the Lord whom we confess, and one Holy Spirit; and that there must be one bishop in the Catholic Church." St. Cornelius I, Pope, in his *Letter to Cyprian of Carthage* (circa 252 A.D.)[8]

- "For the Church, which is One and Catholic, is not split or divided, but is indeed united and joined by the cement of priests who adhere to one another." St. Cyprian of Carthage in his *Letter to Florentius Pupianus* (circa 254 A.D.)[9]

Endnotes

[13] St. Ambrose, *Expl. symb.* 7: PL 17, 1196.

[1] The footnote in the *New American Bible With Revised New Testament* for Acts 8:37 gives us the eunuch's profession of faith before his Baptism: "And Philip said, 'If you believe with all your heart, you may.' And he said in reply, 'I believe that Jesus Christ is the Son of God.'" Cf. *New American Bible With Revised New Testament*, (New York, NY: Catholic Book Publishing Co., 1986), p. 192.

[2] E.g., the early heresy of "Arianism" claimed that Jesus was merely a creature and inferior to the Father; the early heresy of "Nestorianism" stated that Jesus was actually two persons: a human person *and* a divine person. In an attempt to further clarify orthodox teaching, the Church further elaborated upon the twelve articles of faith first put forth in the Apostle's Creed.

[3] Latin: *filioque*. To further articulate the Scriptural truth that the Holy Spirit proceeds also from God the Son: "Indeed I shall continue to rejoice, for I know that this will result in deliverance for me through your prayers and support from the Spirit of Jesus Christ" (Phil 1:18-19), the Latin Church's Creed was

expanded to read: "We believe in the Holy Spirit, the Lord, the Giver of Life, who proceeds from the Father *and the Son...*"

4   Originally, the word "Catholic" (Greek: *kata holos* [meaning "according to the whole"]) was an adjective used to describe the universal scope of the one Church established by Jesus Christ on the "rock" of St. Peter (cf. Matt 16:18-19). Names like "The Church of Christ" (cf. Rom 16:16), "The Church of God...in Christ" (1 Thess 2:14), etc. are all referring to this one Church established by Jesus under the prime ministry of St. Peter. As Jesus' one Church began to combat various heresies in the early centuries, the word "Catholic" was used to differentiate Jesus' Church from the false doctrines being promoted by the theologically misguided.

5   William A. Jurgens (editor and translator), *The Faith of the Early Fathers (Volume 1)*, (Collegeville, MN: The Liturgical Press, 1970), p. 25.

6   *Ibid.*, pp. 30-31.

7   *Ibid.*, p. 230.

8   *Ibid.*, p. 216.

9   *Ibid.*, p. 234.

Chapter 24

Indulgences and the Bible

What Does the Catholic Church Teach?

"'An indulgence is a remission before God of the temporal punishment due to sins whose guilt has already been forgiven, which the faithful Christian who is duly disposed gains under certain prescribed conditions through the action of the Church which, as the minister of redemption, dispenses and applies with authority the treasury of the satisfactions of Christ and the saints.'[81] 'An indulgence is partial or plenary according as it removes either part or all of the temporal punishment due to sin.'[82] Indulgences may be applied to the living or the dead... To understand this doctrine and practice of the Church, it is necessary to understand that sin has *a double consequence*. Grave sin deprives us of communion with God and therefore makes us incapable of eternal life, the privation of which is called the 'eternal punishment' of sin. On the other hand every sin, even venial, entails an unhealthy attachment to creatures, which must be purified either here on earth, or after death in the state called Purgatory. This purification frees one from what is called the 'temporal punishment' of sin. These two punishments must not be conceived of as a kind of vengeance inflicted by God from without, but as following from the very nature of sin. A conversion which proceeds from a fervent charity can attain the complete purification of the sinner in such a way that no punishment would remain...[83] The forgiveness of sin and restoration of communion with God entail the remission of the eternal punishment of sin, but temporal punishment of sin remains. While patiently bearing suffering and trials of all kinds and, when the day comes, serenely facing death, the Christian must strive to accept this temporal punishment of sin as a grace. He should strive by works of mercy and charity, as well as by prayer and the various practices of penance, to put off completely the 'old man' and to put on the 'new man.'"[84] (*Catechism of the Catholic Church*, #1471–1473.)

Common Objection #1

"St. Paul says, "For by grace you have been saved through faith... it is not from works..." (Eph 2:8-9). A Catholic indulgence makes the statement that a person can save himself through his own works."

A Catholic Response

The term "indulgence" originally meant "favor," "remission," or "forgiveness." The current usage of the term by some, however, has distorted its original meaning. Today the term "indulgence" is wrongly understood by some to mean "a stamp of approval for some wrongdoing" or, as one former televangelist once (mistakenly) defined it, an indulgence is "the Catholic Church's permission for a person to indulge in sin." Hence, when some hear that the Catholic Church has granted an indulgence, the wrong image of the Church granting a "license to sin" comes to the mind of some.

Let me present an analogy that may help to illustrate that a sin has both guilt *and* consequences attached to it: Suppose that two young boys are playing in their back yard and one of the boys bets the other that he can't throw a rock through a neighbor's window. Suppose that the boys are successful in breaking the window and, after discovering the broken window, the neighbor contacts his personal lawyer (who has been given the authority to represent him and make decisions in his absence). Suppose the appointed lawyer tells the boys that his client has forgiven them for what they had done but they are still, nonetheless, responsible for replacing the broken glass in his client's window. In this example, the boys are forgiven of the guilt of their sin but still, out of justice, they are required to pay the price to repair the wrong that they had done.

Suppose that the lawyer, representing the client with the broken window, was to tell the mischievous boys that they are excused from paying the full price of replacing the glass in the window ($40.00) and that they only had to pay $5.00 (which he knew that they could earn by mowing their parents' yard one time.) To go one step further, could not the lawyer representing the client with the broken glass totally excuse the boys from any and all liability to repair the window? Yes, he could. That would be his decision and the decision would, in turn, be ratified by the man whom he represents.

We often see an example of the concept of indulgences illustrated in everyday life: Suppose that a certain drug-addicted young man commits a very serious crime and is arrested by the police. Suppose that this criminal is then sentenced by the judge to spend 40 years of his life in jail in order to pay the consequences of his wrongdoing. Suppose that 25 years go by and the criminal in question has really reformed his life and has displayed, by his model behavior, that he, indeed, has turned over a new leaf. Don't we hear all the time about parole boards waving the remainder of the sentences of criminals who have shown, by their actions, that they are serious about reforming their lives? The rehabilitated criminal is set free and is allowed back into the community and his debt to society is considered paid. Notice the presence of all of the elements of the concept of indulgences: (a) a sin is committed, (b) the person is judged guilty of the sin, (c) the sinner now has consequences to suffer because of his sin, (d) the authorities have the power, if they so choose, to diminish (or totally cancel) the sinner's responsibility to pay the consequences of his sin and, (e) reconciliation is achieved.

Consider these passages from Scripture that indicate that a forgiven sinner is still required to face the consequences brought about by his sin:[1]

- In 2 Samuel 12:9, 13-18 we read that the Lord forgave David of the guilt of his sin but he still had to pay the consequences of what he had done — his child still died.

- In Numbers 5:5-8 God tells Moses that, if a person steals something from his neighbor, "he shall confess the wrong he has done [*i. e., have the guilt removed*], restore his ill-gotten goods in full, and in addition give one fifth of their value to the one he has wronged [*i. e., make restitution for the damage that the sin has caused*]."

- In Numbers 12:1-15 we read that Miriam was forgiven by the Lord of the guilt of her sin but she still had to pay the consequences of what she had done — she still was afflicted with leprosy.

- Moses, in spite of the remission of the guilt of his sin of doubting God (cf. Num 20:10-12, Deut 32:48-52), was still required to pay the consequences of his sin and, thus, was not able to enter into the Promised Land (cf. Num 32:10-13).

- In Psalm 99:8 we read: "O Lord, our God, you answered them; you were a forgiving God, though you punished their offenses." We see here that God forgives the guilt of the sinner but still makes him pay the resulting consequences of his wrongdoing.

- In James 5:20 we read: "...whoever brings back a sinner from the error of his way will save his soul from death and will cover a multitude of sins." Can an individual's pious works (e. g., ministering to a sinner and leading him back to God) forgive the guilt of a person's sins? No. That is Jesus' domain (and a ministry that He asked His Apostles to exercise in His Name — cf. John 20:21-23). We read in James 5:20 how an individual's pious works can have an effect in offsetting the consequences of his sins after Jesus has already forgiven the guilt of those sins.

- In Sirach 3:14 we read: "kindness to a father will not be forgotten, it will serve as a sin offering..." Again, a good work offsets the consequences of sin after its guilt has already been forgiven by God.

- In 1 Pet 4:8 we read: "Above all, let your love for one another be intense, because love covers a multitude of sins." Again, we see how a good work (i. e., loving someone) can offset the consequences of sin after God has already taken away its guilt and the resulting eternal punishment.

- In Sirach 3:29 we read: "Water quenches a flaming fire, and alms atone for sins." We see here how a good work (i. e., almsgiving to the poor) can offset the consequences of sin after God has already taken away its guilt and the resulting eternal punishment.

- In 2 Cor 2:6-10, St. Paul tells us that, in his judgement, a certain sinner in the community had suffered long enough and, appealing to his Christ-given authority to "bind" and to "loose" (Matt 16:18-19), he remits the remaining consequences of the person's sin.

- In 2 Cor 5:10, St. Paul (a "saved" Christian) tells us that our sins in this life will have consequences in the next life. In others words, we will *all* be held accountable for the consequences of our sins after the guilt (and, thus, the eternal punishment) has been remitted.

- In Matt 16:18-19, Jesus gives St. Peter *(and his successors)* the authority to make "binding" and "loosing" decisions.

- In James 2:14, 17, 22, 24, we read that "faith without works is dead" and that good works "complete" our faith. After one has received the free gift of faith from God, his thankful response is good works. Nowhere in the Bible does it say that faith *alone* ("*sola fide*" of Martin Luther) is the only thing that is necessary for our salvation. Passages like Eph 2:8-9 that speak about the importance of faith have to be read in conjunction with James Chapter 2.[2] Indulgences certainly *do not* make the statement that we can save ourselves. God is the one who forgives us of the guilt of our sins and saves us through grace. After we have been forgiven of the guilt of our sins by God, we, out of justice, must take the necessary actions to address the consequences that our sins have caused.

- In Rev 14:13, Scripture tells us that a saintly person's good works accompany him as he enters into heaven. This accumulated "pool" of saintly merit, then, is part of the "treasury of merit" that the Church draws from and, in turn, applies to the faithful who request it.[3]

Through the merits of Jesus' death and resurrection, God has made the guilt of our sins forgivable — if we turn to Him with contrite hearts. But, out of Divine justice, we must still make satisfaction to God in order to offset the consequences of our sins. St. Paul tells the "saved" Christians in Corinth: "For we must all appear before the judgment seat of Christ, so that each one may receive recompense, according to what he did in the body, whether good or evil" (2 Cor 5:10). In other words, St. Paul is saying that we Christians must clean up the "mess" that our sins have caused. By appealing to the "power of the keys" (cf. Matt 16:18-19), the Church, in Jesus' Name, has the prerogative of lessening *(partial indulgence)* or totally eliminating *(plenary indulgence)* the satisfaction owed to God because of the remaining consequences of a forgiven sin. Note that, in Matt 16:18-19, Jesus made Peter his representative and gave him the keys to "run His institution" and make necessary decisions in His absence.

Ronald Lawler, O.F.M., Donald Wuerl, and Thomas Lawler (editors) in their book *The Teaching of Christ* write:

> "The principle underlying indulgences is as old as the Church. It is based on the doctrine of the Mystical Body of Christ. All members of this Body, St. Paul wrote (cf. 1 Cor 12:21-26), should contribute to the well-being of an ailing member. Fully aware of the infinite and decisive value of Christ's atoning death, Paul rejoiced that his own sufferings could benefit the Christians of Colossae, and he added: 'In my flesh I complete what is lacking in Christ's afflictions for the sake of His body, that is, the Church' (Col 1:24). The Church teaches that in virtue of the authority given it by Christ, it may grant to sinners who have already received forgiveness of their sins a share in the merits of Christ and the saints, so that the burden of temporal punishment due for sins may be removed or lightened."[4]

The practice of the Church granting indulgences certainly *does not* make the statement that Jesus' death and resurrection was ineffectual in forgiving our sins. The practice of granting indulgences simply recognizes the scriptural truth that sin cannot enter into heaven (cf. Rev 21:27), that we are all sinners (cf. 1 John 1:8-10), that we will *all* be held accountable for the sins that we commit during our lifetime (cf. 2 Cor 5:10) and that St. Peter (the first Pope of the Roman Catholic Church) received the authority from Christ to bind and to loose in Jesus' Name (cf. Matt 16:18-19). *(For a further discussion of what Jesus' death and resurrection has accomplished refer to Chapter 10 of this book.)* [5]

Historical Background

The Church has been exercising the prerogative of granting indulgences from the very beginning of its existence. In numerous historical writings, we find the Bishops of the early Church imposing various canonical penances on serious sinners *(who were subjected to long fasts, severe abstinences for periods of years, exclusion from participation in the Church — even for a lifetime in extreme cases.)* St. Paul writes about the issue of the reconciliation of serious sinners: "For it is impossible in the case of those who have once been enlightened and tasted the heavenly gift and shared in the holy Spirit and tasted the good word of God and the powers of the age to come, and then have fallen away, to bring them to repentance again..." (Heb 6:4-6).

In 1 Cor 5:1-5 we read about an individual receiving the penalty of ex-communication by the leaders of the Church for committing the serious sin of incest. These penalties were, in some instances, lessened or canceled by the Church, according to the Church's discretion (which was granted her by Christ [cf. Matt 16:18-19]). Note that Jesus gave His Church power not only to *bind* but to *loose.*

A partial remittance used to be given in a certain number of "days" to recall the time when, in the early Church, contrite sinners could come back into the Church so many days early if they truly displayed sincere sorrow for the wrong they had done. Can one measure "God time" in years and days? No. It is simply a

345

human way to state that certain acts of charity have a value in off-setting the consequences of sin.

Fr. Chas. M. Carty and Fr. Dr. L. Rumble, M.S.C., in their book *Indulgence Quizzes to a Street Preacher*, make the following point concerning charges of the so-called abuse of indulgences in the 16th century:

> "The Pope granted the favor of certain indulgences to those who would give alms towards the building of St. Peter's in Rome. But there is a difference between giving alms to a good work, and giving money to purchase something of equivalent value. Remember that Christ had a special blessing for the widow who gave her mite as an alms to the temple in Jerusalem. Would you accuse Him of selling that blessing for a mite? Canon 2327 of the Church excommunicates anyone who seeks material profit from indulgences."[6]

The Theology of Indulgences in the Writings of the Early Church Fathers:

- "[S]ome...are accustomed to beg from the martyrs in prison; and therefore you should possess and cherish and preserve it in you so that you perchance may be able to grant it to others." Tertullian (d. circa 245 A. D.)[7]

- "Those who have received a memorial from the martyrs and their help can, before the Lord, get relief in their sins. Let such, if they be ill and in danger, after Confession and the imposition of your hands, depart unto the Lord with the peace promised them by the martyrs." St. Cyprian of Carthage (circa 250 A. D.)[8]

Endnotes

[81] Paul VI, apostolic constitution, *Indulgentiarum doctrina*, Norm 1.
[82] *Indulgentiarum doctrina*, Norm 2; cf. Norm 3.
[83] Cf. Council of Trent (1551): DS 1712-1713; (1563): 1820.

[84] *Eph* 4:22, 24.

[1] "Protestants often deny that temporal penalties remain after forgiveness of sin, but they acknowledge it in practice — for instance, when they insist on people returning things they have stolen. Thieves may obtain forgiveness, but they also must engage in restitution. Protestants realize that, while Jesus paid the price for sins before God, he did not relieve our obligation to repair what we have done. They fully acknowledge that if you steal someone's car, you have to give it back; it isn't enough just to repent... Protestants also admit the principle in practice when discussing death. Scripture says death entered the world through original sin (Gen 3:22-24; Rom 5:12). When we first come to God we are forgiven, and when we sin later we are able to be forgiven, yet that does not free us from the penalty of physical death. Even the forgiven die; a penalty remains after our sins are forgiven." James Akin, *A Primer on Indulgences*, The Catholic Resource Network, http://www.cwtn.com/library/ANSWERS/PRIMINDU.TXT.

[2] Cf. Chapter 4 of this book for a further Biblical discussion of how a Christian is justified before God.

[3] It appears that the often-heard phrase "you can't take it with you when you die" applies only to material things. The New Testament teaches us that we are able to take with us to heaven the merits of our loving works of obedience to God performed while here on earth (which were, of course, accomplished by God's free gift of grace, in faith, with the assistance of the Holy Spirit!) Cf. *Catechism of the Catholic Church*, #1476-1477.

[4] Ronald Lawler, O.F.M., Donald Wuerl, Thomas Lawler (editors), *The Teaching of Christ (Second Edition)*, (Huntington, IN: Our Sunday Visitor, Inc., 1976, 1983), pp. 477-478.

[5] Albert Nevins, M.M. writes: "The notion that a misdeed can be made up by good behavior exists in most families, and even civil law is assigning community service for prison sentences in many cases." Cf. Albert Nevins, M.M., *Answering A Fundamentalist*, (Huntington, IN: Our Sunday Visitor Inc., 1990), p. 95. (Note that when a criminal is assigned to do community service after committing a misdeed, this certainly doesn't imply that the judge doesn't have the power to forgive him.)

6   Fathers Rumble and Carty, *Indulgence Quizzes to a Street Preacher*, (Rockford, IL: TAN Books and Publishers, Inc., 1976), p. 15.

7   *Ibid.*, p. 19.

8   *Ibid.*, p. 19. Cf. also the writings of St. Ignatius of Antioch, St. Polycarp, Origen, and St. Ambrose.

Chapter 25

Annulments and the Bible

What Does the Catholic Church Teach?

"The consent must be an act of the will of each of the contracting parties, free of coercion or grave external fear.[128] No human power can substitute for this consent.[129] If this freedom is lacking the marriage is invalid... For this reason (or for other reasons that render the marriage null and void) the Church, after an examination of the situation by the competent ecclesiastical tribunal, can declare the nullity of a marriage, i.e., that the marriage never existed.[130] In this case the contracting parties are free to marry, provided the natural obligations of a previous union are discharged."[131] (*Catechism of the Catholic Church*, #1628–1629.)

Common Objection #1

"The Bible mentions nothing about annulments. It is simply a Catholic money-making scheme!"

A Catholic Response

One of the toughest teachings proclaimed by Jesus in the New Testament has got to be His teaching on divorce and re-marriage:

- "Everyone who divorces his wife and marries another commits adultery, and the one who marries a woman divorced from her husband commits adultery" (Luke 16:18).

- "Whoever divorces his wife and marries another commits adultery against her; and if she divorces her husband and marries another, she commits adultery" (Mark 10:11-12).

- "Whoever divorces his wife (unless the marriage is unlawful)[1] causes her to commit adultery, and whoever marries a divorced woman commits adultery" (Matt 5:31-32).

- "Whoever divorces his wife (unless the marriage is unlawful)[2] and marries another commits adultery" (Matt 19:9).

- St. Paul echoes Jesus' teaching about the permanence of the covenant of marriage: "To the married, however, I give this instruction (not I, but the Lord): a wife should not separate from her husband — and if she does separate she must either remain single or become reconciled to her husband — and a husband should not divorce his wife... A wife is bound to her husband as long as he lives. But if her husband dies, she is free to be married to whomever she wishes, provided that it be in the Lord" (1 Cor 7:10-11, 39).[3]

Webster's dictionary defines "adultery" as: "voluntary sexual intercourse between a married man and someone other than his wife or between a married woman and someone other than her husband." What Jesus is saying in the four previously-mentioned Gospel passages is that, when a person divorces his first spouse and then re-marries another individual while his original spouse is still living, he is engaging in sexual intercourse with someone other than his spouse because, in God's eyes, his first (presumably) valid marital covenant is still standing and he is sharing the conjugal act with someone other than his Divinely-recognized mate.

Consider the following illustration that graphically depicts the two components of a marriage: (a) **the civil/legal** *(which is cancelable at the discretion of the spouses)*, and (b) **the spiritual/moral** *(which the Scriptures tell us is non-cancelable.)*

| **Civil Union** - a legal contract that binds the spouses to one another in civil matters. This contract is able to be voided, at the discretion of one or the other spouse, through a civil divorce. | **Covenant** - a lifelong covenantal oath that binds the couple spiritually and morally to God and to each other "until death do they part" (cf. Mark 10:1-12; 1 Cor 7:39). |

In light of Jesus' strong New Testament prohibition on divorce and re-marriage while the original spouse is still living, it would seem that *all* Christian ministers would be called to thoroughly investigate the request of a previously-married person who asks to be married, once again, to someone else while his/her original spouse is still living. Many Protestant ministers serve as their own "tribunal" in that they inquire into the previous marriage themselves until they are satisfied that the original couple did not, for one reason or another, have the capacity to enter into a true marital covenant.[4]

Because the Catholic Church (following Jesus' lead) takes the covenant of marriage so seriously, we have an in-depth investigation procedure in place to make certain, as much as humanly possible, that the testimony being given by the former spouses about their previous marriage is accurate and complete. (Author's note: In my experience as a marriage counselor, to listen to only one spouse's side of the story rarely gives a true picture of what is actually happening in his/her marriage. It seems that we human beings often prefer to project our own shortcomings onto others rather than to claim them and deal with them ourselves! The Catholic marriage nullity process gives *both spouses* the opportunity to present their side of the story in its entirety in hopes that the *full truth* about their former marital relationship would be revealed. After this thorough investigation process has been completed the Church, going on the testimony submitted by the petitioning spouse, the former spouse if he/she chooses to respond, and two or more witnesses, exercises the "binding and loosing" authority bestowed upon it by Jesus Christ [cf. Matt 16:18-19]).

"But I asked God for forgiveness for my divorce, therefore, I am no longer living in adultery with my second spouse," one person once said. It is, indeed, commendable that this person has asked for God's forgiveness for canceling the civil/legal component of his marriage with his first spouse through a divorce. The fact remains, however, that he is continuing to share the marital act with another person while his (presumably valid) indissoluble marital covenant/oath with his original spouse still stands in the eyes of God. (Please note that lawyers can fill out the necessary paperwork to sever the *legal ties* between two spouses but lawyers or civil courts have no authority whatsoever to dissolve the couple's [presumably valid] covenant of marriage.)[5]

In Matt 16:18-19 and Matt 18:18 we read about Jesus giving the authority to "bind" and to "loose" to Peter and His Apostles (His Church.) Note that Jesus does not bestow this authority upon every individual Christian, allowing them to make personal "declarations of nullity." (Cf. Matt 18:15-17 where Jesus asks that His Church be brought in to mediate irreconcilable disputes between Christians. Cf. also Deut 17:8-10 and read about God authorizing the Levitical priests to render judgement on various types of cases brought to them by the Israelite people.)

Note how, even in civil law, certain types of people are viewed as not having the competence of entering into valid contracts with other people (e.g., minors — because of their immaturity, mentally or emotionally impaired people, people who have been deceived in some manner by the other contracting party, people who are under some type of force or duress, etc...) Civil courts often rule that these types of people, even though they may have fulfilled all of the normal formalities of entering into a contract, were not capable of doing so. If the evidence supports it, the civil court makes the declaration that the attempted contract never existed in the first place. A similar thing happens in a marriage declaration of nullity proceeding. If the submitted testimony and facts support it, the Church declares that, even though all of the elements of a marriage ceremony were performed by the couple, one or the other or both spouses did not possess the competence/capacity to enter into a true marriage covenant.

The three conditions on which declarations of nullity can be sought are as follows:

1) **Lack of or defect of canonical form:** *(the marriage ceremony in which a Catholic was involved was not performed properly — cf. 1983 Code of Canon Law 1108-1117.)*
2) **Various invalidating impediments:** *(one or the other or both spouses were not eligible, for one reason or another, to enter into the covenant of marriage — cf. 1983 Code of Canon Law 1083-1094.)*
3) **Defect of consent:** *(one or the other or both spouses were unable to enter into a true marital covenant due to the existence of factor[s] that blocked the free and total exchange of consent — cf. 1983 Code of Canon Law 1095–1103.)*

Our lives are often lived in the midst of many limitations, problems, and dysfunctional influences. What the Catholic Church does in a marriage nullity proceeding is to ask the question, "Was this union able to be a true marital covenant?" For their union to be a true covenant, the husband and the wife must have had the capability to give their free and total consent to one another on the day of their wedding. Are there conditions and problems that could prevent the couple from giving their entire selves to one another on the day of their wedding? The following are some of the "grounds" to investigate the possibility of a declaration of nullity under the "defect of consent" category mentioned previously:

• **Emotional problems:** *(serious emotional conditions that could make one or the other or both spouses behave irrationally and unpredictably to the degree that they could not exchange free and total consent)*

353

- **Alcoholism/Drug Abuse:** *(active substance abuse and/or addictive behaviors on the part of one or the other or both spouses could block the couple's free and total consent)*

- **Force and fear:** *(e.g., a pre-marital pregnancy could have forced the couple to enter into marriage under duress before they were truly ready to make a life-long covenantal commitment; one or the other or both spouses got married to escape a bad situation at home and, thus, free and total consent did not come about)*

- **Exclusion of permanence:** *(marriage was not seen as a commitment for life by one or the other or both spouses — e.g., "We'll stay married as long as we are happy...")*

- **Exclusion of fidelity:** *(one or the other or both spouses do not intend to be faithful to the other spouse in an exclusive relationship and have left open the possibility of extra-marital affairs with other people)*

- **Exclusion of children:** *(children are an integral part of marriage and cannot be intentionally ruled out from the beginning by one or the other or both spouses)*

- **Conditional consent:** *("strings" are attached to the marriage commitment concerning the fulfillment of some future promise by one or the other or both spouses — e.g., "I'll marry you if...")*

- **Immaturity:** *(one or the other or both spouses are not able to function as a responsible, mature adult)*

In the marriage nullity process, the Church is not out to blame one or the other spouse for the failure of the marriage. The Church does not take the side of one or the other spouse. All that the Church is doing is asking if the covenant of marriage was able to be instituted by the couple on their wedding day. (Note that the "minister" of marriage is not the Catholic priest, other Christian minister, or civil official who may conduct the ceremony — they are only the official *witnesses* for the Church and/or the State. The "ministers" of marriage are *the bride and the groom themselves*. The marriage nullity process seeks to discover if these "ministers" of marriage had the capability of totally surrendering their lives to one another and to the Lord on the day of their marriage.)[6]

Some parents are concerned that if, by a declaration of nullity, the Church says that a true *covenant* didn't have the chance to exist, that means that their *marriage* didn't exist — and if their marriage didn't exist, then their children would be considered illegitimate (i.e., born out of wedlock). Nothing is further from the truth! The Church is not denying the existence of a valid civil union (the couple was fully legally married and have a copy of the civil marriage license to prove it!) Because the couple was validly civilly married, any children born within that union would be considered fully legitimate in the eyes of the Church and in the eyes of the State. In an declaration of nullity the Church is saying that, for one reason or another, *the covenant was not able to be brought about*. This in no way effects the legitimacy of the children!

As far as for the charge that declarations of nullity were devised by the Catholic Church in order to make money, the fact is that operating the tribunal is a money *losing* proposition for the Church. The costs incurred in the processing of each marriage nullity case *far outweighs* the voluntary contribution that petitioners give to help offset the expenses incurred. The office of the tribunal exists to be a pastoral outreach to individuals whose relationships have painfully terminated and who wish to enter into a true covenantal marriage with another partner.

What the Church is trying to do through the marriage nullity process is to: (1) be faithful to Jesus' clear scriptural teaching that the covenant of marriage is permanent and, (2) to be compassionate to people as Jesus would be compassionate when their own personal woundedness and limitations prevent them from entering into a true marital covenant.

One final thought concerning the reception of Holy Communion: Catholics who find themselves divorced and remarried again outside of the Church are confronted with the Church's moral teaching that they are prohibited from receiving the Holy Eucharist. Please note that civil divorce, by itself, does not prohibit a Catholic from receiving the Holy Eucharist because the Catholic would be (presumably) living as a chaste single person and not sharing the marital act with someone other than his valid spouse. What prohibits a Catholic from receiving the Holy Eucharist is *re-marriage* after a civil divorce before having his/her previous (and presumably valid) marriage declared null. The reason is simple: based on Jesus' Scriptural teachings on divorce and re-marriage, the Church presumes that all marriages legitimately entered into are valid and binding. Until the opposite is proven and declared as such, or through the death of one of the spouses, these spouses are still morally bound to the unity *(fidelity)* and indissolubility *(permanence)* of their previous bond — even if they are no longer living together as husband and wife. To re-marry outside of the Church would constitute a continuing objective state of adultery.[7] It is because of this continuing state of adultery that Catholics are morally prohibited from partaking of the Holy Eucharist (cf. 1 Cor 11:27-30 and *Catechism of the Catholic Church*, #1385). This is why it is so important that Catholics accept the Church's willingness to help them in the aftermath of a civil divorce. The marriage nullity process is one of the principal means at the Church's disposal to render such help and, if possible, to declare the spouses free to re-marry in the Church or have a subsequent civil marriage "blessed" (i.e., recognized by the Church.)

In my ministry as a parish priest I have come to discover that, behind the stories of a number of ex-Catholics are, oftentimes, stories of their divorce and re-marriage again outside of the Church. When their first marriage ended in divorce and they re-married again (before obtaining a declaration of nullity) and their Catholic Church held steadfastly to Jesus' tough teaching on divorce and re-marriage, a number of these people began shopping for other Christian denominations that were not as demanding on this moral issue.

Far from promoting the casual obtaining of a civil divorce and a Church declaration of nullity, this informational chapter on Church declarations of nullity is presented to help divorced Catholics who wish to enter into another Church marriage to understand their rights. Obviously, at the first *hint* of difficulties in the marriage, *both spouses* should seek immediate professional Christian counseling so that they can persevere in their covenant commitment to the Lord and to each other. To quote the slogan from the Catholic Marriage Encounter program: "Love is a *decision* — not just a feeling!" In other words, entering into the covenant of marriage involves *an act of the will*. Sometimes married couples will experience the warm "feelings" of love — and sometimes they will not. When the emotional "dry spells" hit, the covenantal commitment/oath with God and each other (which is an act of the will) still stands. During these times of vocational desolation *all* Christians, regardless of vocation, should call upon the Lord and ask Him for the grace to remain faithful to our commitment.

Hopefully, this chapter will give Catholics a fuller understanding of our Lord's teaching on divorce and re-marriage found in Scripture. Please contact your parish priest if you have been civilly divorced and sincerely feel that you may have possible grounds for a declaration of nullity to be considered. He is ready to welcome you warmly and walk with you through the healing process.

Endnotes

128 Cf. CIC, can. 1103.

129 Cf. CIC, can. 1057 paragraph 1.

130 Cf. CIC, can. 1095-1107.

131 Cf. CIC, can. 1071.

1 The so-called divorce "exception clauses" that appear twice in Matthew's Gospel are interpreted by some Protestant Christians to be a modification of Jesus' absolute prohibition of divorce recounted in Mark 10:11-12, Luke 16:18 and 1 Cor 7:10-11, 39. How should one harmonize Matthew's two exceptions with the other places in Scripture where Jesus does not permit divorce and re-marriage for any reason whatsoever? The footnote in the *New American Bible With Revised New Testament* for "unlawful" (Greek: *porneia*) says that it seems to be a reference to improper marriages that were taking place between close blood relatives — which would have been invalid from the start in both Jewish and Christian communities (cf. Lev 18:6-18; 1 Cor 5:1). The *King James Bible* translates *porneia* in the Matthean exception clauses as "fornication." The *Revised Standard Version Bible* translates *porneia* in the exception clauses as "un-

chastity." The *New American Bible* translates *porneia* in the exception clauses as "lewd conduct." *The New Strong's Exhaustive Concordance of the Bible* (Cf. #4202, pg. 59) notes that the Greek word *porneia* can be used to refer to harlotry (cf. 1 Cor 6:18), to adultery (cf. Gal 5:19) *or* to incest (cf. 1 Cor 5:1). Catholics claim that it is a reference to incestuous relationships — to illicit marriages between close blood relatives (that is how St. Paul uses the word *porneia* in 1 Cor 5:1). The pagans permitted incestuous marriages to take place. If a person living in an incestuous marriage converted to Christianity *(which apparently was happening)* the new Christian would be obliged to terminate the incestuous union in which he was living. Looking at the numerous passages where Jesus and St. Paul absolutely prohibit divorce, the case of incest can be the only proper interpretation of *porneia* when it is used in Matt 5:31-32 and Matt 19:9.

2   Cf. previous footnote on the meaning of the word "unlawful" (Greek: *porneia*).

3   The reason why St. Paul instructs separated husbands and wives to either reconcile with each other or to remain single is because marriage to another person, while the original spouse is still living, would constitute adultery (cf. Jesus' teaching on divorce and re-marriage recounted in Luke 16:18; Mark 10:11-12; Matt 5:31-32; Matt 19:9).

4   In Catholic circles, the "tribunal" is the name of the diocesan office that represents the local Catholic bishop in marriage nullity cases. The priests, religious, and lay people who staff the tribunal do all that they can to minister the compassion and understanding of Christ to individuals who are involved in declaration of nullity proceedings.

5   When two baptized Christians marry their "covenant of marriage" is also a Sacramental union with/in Jesus Christ.

6   In this chapter the reader may have noticed that, instead of the word "annulment," I have used the phrase "declaration of nullity." The reason for this is that the word "annulment" might wrongly be understood by some as meaning that the marital covenant existed up until a certain point in time and then, on a certain date, was voided. The phrase "declaration of nullity" more clearly describes what the Church is actually doing: de-

claring that, because of the existence of invalidating impediment(s), or a lack of or defect of form, or a defect in consent, a true marital covenant never had the chance to come into existence.

7 St. Paul says in his First Letter to the Corinthians that "...adulterers...will [not] inherit the kingdom of God" (1 Cor 6:10). Cf. also Exod 20:14.

Conclusion

This first book of mine has definitely proven to be one of the most challenging undertakings that I have ever attempted in my life.[1] How does one boil down 2,000 years of theological reflection into a single book containing twenty-five chapters? After beginning this project, I quickly realized that it would be impossible for me to give each topic the depth of discussion that it deserved. This book is my attempt to present a minute portion of the intricate tapestry of truth that is the Roman Catholic faith. Hopefully, I have presented the truths of our Catholic faith to the reader in an understandable, respectful, and inviting way.[2]

In the process of putting this book together I have really come to discover that writing about matters of theology is an *extremely* precise art in which the addition or deletion of one single word can drastically change the meaning of a statement. It is my prayer that what I have written is completely accurate and in total harmony with the Magisterium of the Church. I also pray that I have represented the beliefs of my evangelical and fundamentalist Christian brothers and sisters in a fair and accurate manner. Although I am certainly *proud* to be a Roman Catholic, I pray that I did not fall into the sin of *spiritual pride* and come across in an arrogant or uncharitable fashion. I hope that, like St. Peter, I have given an explanation for the reason for my hope and have done so with gentleness and reverence (cf. 1 Pet 3:15-16). The more that I learn about my Catholic faith, the more I realize just how little I do know — and how much more I have yet to learn! I have come to realize that understanding our Christian faith is a *lifelong task* that is guided by the Light of the Holy Spirit.

In this book I have tried to show how Roman Catholicism is, indeed, "unabridged Christianity." To be an articulate Roman Catholic requires a considerable amount of knowledge of both Sacred Scripture and world and Church history — which is why some Catholics have difficulty giving "easy" comprehensive answers to the apparently "simple" questions sometimes posed to them by evangelical Christians.

Catholic convert Dave Armstrong writes:

> "In fact, many Evangelicals (myself included, at that point) take pride in the fact that their gospel is so simple. But the more I studied the theological details of the Christian faith, as expressed, for example, by the early Church Fathers of the first five centuries, the more it became clear that the Gospel is both complex and simple. The principles of the Gospel — such as the Trinity, the divinity of Christ, salvation by grace alone, and baptismal regeneration — can be articulated in very simple terms, but explaining and exploring them is anything but simple."[3]

What I have tried to show in this book is that Catholic beliefs are, indeed, *very* Biblical. When an evangelical Christian makes the claim that Catholic beliefs are "un-Biblical" what he is often saying is: "The Catholic interpretation of the Bible does not square with our pastor's/denomination's interpretation of the Bible." I have shown in this book that the Bible is not self-interpreting (cf. Chapter 12 of this book). How does one determine which interpretation of the Bible is the authentic one that was believed by the first Christians in the early Church? By looking at the writings of the first generations of Christians. In this book, after I have given the scriptural support for some of the more commonly misunderstood Catholic teachings, I have backed it up by showing, historically, that this was, indeed, the belief and practice of the first generations of Christians.

The late Archbishop Fulton Sheen once said something to the effect that "there are only a handful of people who hate the Catholic faith. A number of people, however, hate what they *think* is the Catholic faith." I hope that this book has begun to clear up a few of the common misunderstandings about the Roman Catholic faith and has shown how our faith is, indeed, the *most Biblical* of all Christian denominations.

Since I have been a priest, I have heard a few uninformed Catholics make the comment: "We all pray to the same God. Therefore, it really doesn't matter what particular Christian church a person belongs to..."

Indeed, there is *one* God. That one God sent His *one* Son, Jesus Christ. That one Son, Jesus Christ, founded *one* Church that professed *one* set of beliefs (cf. Matt 16:18-19; Eph 4:5). What I hope that I have shown in this book is that the Roman Catholic Church is the *one Church* historically established by the *one* Son of God, Jesus Christ.

Just as the New Testament is the fulfillment of the Old Testament (cf. Matt 5:17), the Roman Catholic Church is the fulfillment/fullness of the one true Church established by Christ Himself. When a Protestant Christian becomes a Roman Catholic Christian he does not "throw away" his former Christian faith — he has it fulfilled and completed. My intent in writing this book is to invite Protestant Christians (who are right on so many theological issues) to be even *more right* than they already are.

The teachings of the tens of thousands of Christian denominations in existence today are not equally true. I have overheard some Christians make the comment that switching to another Christian denomination is simply choosing to practice Christianity "in a different style." I hope that I have shown in this book that there is no such thing as "generic Christianity." When one leaves one Christian denomination and joins another he is trading in one set of interpretations of Scripture/doctrines/religious practices for another. When a Christian changes denominations he changes much more than the *style* of his worship — he changes the *substance* of his beliefs. The first question that one should ask before switching to any Christian denomination is: "Which denomination will present me with the fullness of the Christian Truth taught by Jesus Christ and historically practiced by the Apostles and their successors?" The sole criteria for joining a Christian denomination should be *truth of doctrine.* Fantastic youth programs, great fellowship, wonderful choirs, a powerful preacher who can stir up your emotions, etc... are *not* reasons for joining a particular Church (although they are certainly nice when you have them!) What matters is *doctrinal truth.* Youth programs, fellowship, choirs, and preaching are all things that can be developed (and we Catholics can take many cues from our Protestant brothers and sisters in these areas!)

If you are already a Roman Catholic, won't you join me in praising God for the tremendous treasure that He has given to us? If you are not presently a Roman Catholic, won't you prayerfully consider enriching our Church with your presence?

After composing some of the most profound theological treatises in the history of Christianity, St. Thomas Aquinas called his writings "straw" because he knew that they didn't even begin to communicate the vastness of Truth that finds its origin in God. If St. Thomas Aquinas' writings were "straw," this book is not even a particle of dust.

**"How can I repay the Lord for all the good done for me?
I will raise the cup of salvation and call on the name of
the Lord... I will offer a sacrifice of thanksgiving
and call on the name of the Lord."**
(Psalm 116:12-13, 17)

Endnotes

¹   As a reader of this book will quickly gather, I am *not* a professional writer! I am only a lover of Jesus and His Church! Please excuse my mistakes in grammar, the structure of some of my sentences, and my punctuation boo-boos!

²   I have attempted to support just about every statement that I have made in this book with applicable passages from Scripture. No doubt there will probably be a few Christians who will read my book and write to me offering an equal number of Bible verses that they believe "disprove" the Bible verses that I have used to support our Roman Catholic beliefs and practices. At that point the discussion would move from a "that's not in the Bible" discussion to a discussion over correct *interpretation* of the Bible. The challenge for the objecting Christian would then be to support his interpretations of various Scripture passages with writings from the first generations of Christians that would give historical *precedence* to his interpretations of the Bible. Supported by the writings of the early Church Fathers quoted in context, I would welcome any kind-spirited dialogues concerning correct interpretation of Biblical texts. If you wish, please correspond with me c/o Queenship Publishing Company.

³   Patrick Madrid (editor), *Surprised by Truth*, (San Diego, CA: Basilica Press, 1994), pp. 246-247.

Greek Capital Letter	Greek Small Letter	English Equivalent	Name of Letter
A	α	a	alpha
B	β	b	beta
Γ	γ	g	gamma
Δ	δ	d	delta
E	ε	e	epsilon
Z	ζ	z	zeta
H	η	ē	eta
Θ	θ	th	theta
I	ι	i	iota
K	κ	k or c	kappa
Λ	λ	l	lambda
M	μ	m	mu
N	ν	n	nu
Ξ	ξ	x	xi
O	o	o	omicron
Π	π	p	pi
P	ρ	r	rho
Σ	σ or ς	s	sigma
T	τ	t	tau
Y	υ	u or y	upsilon
Φ	φ	ph	phi
X	χ	ch	chi
Ψ	ψ	ps	psi
Ω	ω	ō	omega

That's Greek to Me!: An Introduction to Biblical Greek

To form English equivalents (known as "English transliterations") of Greek words, simply use the chart of the Greek alphabet on the facing page and convert each Greek letter into its English equivalent (*e. g., the Greek small letter "λ" = the English letter "l," the Greek capital letter "Ξ" = the English letter "X."*) Let's practice converting a few of the original Greek words of the New Testament into English to see if any of them sound familiar:

- "…then He took a cup, gave thanks [ευχαριστησας],[1] and gave it to them, saying, 'Drink from it, all of you, for this is my blood…'" (Matt 26:27-28).
- "…Behold, I come to do your will, O God [Θεος][2]…" (Heb 10:7).
- "The book [Βιβλος] [3] of the genealogy of Jesus Christ [Ιησου Χριστου][4]…" (Matt 1:1).
- "Then Jesus spoke to the crowds and to his disciples, saying, 'The scribes and the Pharisees have taken their seat on the chair [καθεδρας][5] of Moses. Therefore, do and observe all things whatsoever they tell you, but do not follow their example…'" (Matt 23:1-3).
- "…I would rather speak five words with my mind, so as to instruct [κατηχησω][6] others also, than ten thousand in a tongue" (1 Cor 14.19).

- "…and from Jesus Christ, the faithful witness [μαρτυς],[7] the firstborn of the dead…" (Rev 1:5).
- "The revelation [Αποκαλυψις][8] of Jesus Christ, which God gave to him, to show his servants what must happen soon" (Rev 1:1).

Endnotes

1   *eucharistēsas* (which is where the word "Eucharist" comes from.)
2   *Theos* (which is the root word in "theology"— the study of God.)
3   *Biblos* (which is where the word "Bible" comes from.)
4   *Iēsou Christou* (note that the first two Greek letters in the word "Christ" are "X" and "ρ". The early Christians often drew the Greek letter "X" (chi) and put the Greek letter "ρ" (rho) in the center of it (☧) as an abbreviation for "Christ" — which means "Messiah.")
5   *kathedras* (which is where the word "cathedral" comes from.)
6   *katēchēsō* (which is where the word "catechism" comes from.)
7   *martus* (which is where the word "martyr" comes from.)
8   *Apokalupsis* (which is where the word "apocalypse" comes from.)

Bibliography

Alpha, Veralyn R., *A Heavenly Journey*. Milford, OH: Faith Publishing Co., 1994.

Boadt, Lawrence, *Reading the Old Testament*. New York, NY: Paulist Press, 1984.

Broderick, Robert C. (Editor), *The Catholic Encyclopedia (Revised and Updated Edition.)* Nashville, TN: Thomas Nelson Publishers, 1987.

Brown, Raymond E., S.S, Fitzmyer, Joseph A., S.J., Murphy, Roland E., O. Carm. (Editors), *The New Jerome Biblical Commentary*. Englewood Cliffs, NJ: Prentice Hall, 1990.

Brown, Raymond E., S.S., *Priest and Bishop: Biblical Reflections*. Paramus, NY: Paulist Press, 1970.

Butler, Scott, Dahlgren, Norman, and Hess, David, *Jesus, Peter & the Keys: A Scriptural Handbook on the Papacy*. Santa Barbara, CA: Queenship Publishing Company, 1996.

Catechism of the Catholic Church. Liguori, MO: Liguori Publications, 1994.

Chervin, Ronda De Sola and Pollard, Joseph Msgr., *Tell Me Why: Answering Tough Questions About the Faith*. Huntington, IN: Our Sunday Visitor, Inc., 1994.

Currie, David B., *Born Fundamentalist Born Again Catholic*, San Francisco, CA: Ignatius Press, 1996.

Famighetti, Robert (Editor), *The World Almanac and Book of Facts (1996 Edition.)* Mahwah, NJ: Funk and Wagnalls, 1995.

Fitzmyer, Joseph A., S.J., *A Christological Catechism.* New York, NY: Paulist Press, 1982.

Gibbons, James Cardinal, *The Faith of Our Fathers.* Rockford, IL: TAN Books and Publishers, Inc., 1980.

Glazier, Michael and Hellwig, Monika (Editors), *The Modern Catholic Encyclopedia.* Collegeville, MN: The Liturgical Press, 1994.

Hahn, Scott, *Calling Catholics to be Bible Christians & Vice Versa; Answers For Catholics; A New Look at Our Lady: A Biblical Understanding of Mary; On Your Marks!: Understanding Our One, Holy, Catholic & Apostolic Church; Answering Common Objections; Eucharistic Day at Marytown; The Bible Alone?; The End: A Study of the Book of Revelation* (audio tapes). West Covina, CA: St. Joseph Communications.

Hahn, Scott and Kimberly, *Rome Sweet Home: Our Journey to Catholicism.* San Francisco, CA: Ignatius Press, 1993.

Harrington, Wilfrid J., O.P., *Sacra Pagina Series: Revelation.* Collegeville, MN: The Liturgical Press, 1993.

Ihm, Claudia Carlen, *The Papal Encyclicals 1903-1939.* McGrath Publishing Co., 1981.

John Paul II, Pope, *Redemptoris Mater: The Mother of the Redeemer.* Washington, DC: United States Catholic Conference, 1987.

Jurgens, William A., *The Faith of the Early Fathers (Volumes 1, 2, 3).* Collegeville, MN: The Liturgical Press, 1970, 1979, 1979.

Kaler, Patrick, C.SS.R., *You and the Bible: Tough Questions and Straight Answers*. Liguori, MO: Liguori Publications, 1985.

Keating, Karl, *Catholicism and Fundamentalism*. San Francisco, CA: Ignatius Press, 1988.

Keating, Karl (editor), *This Rock* Magazine. San Diego, CA: Catholic Answers, Inc.

Keating, Karl, *What Catholics Really Believe*. Ann Arbor, Michigan: Servant Publications, 1992.

Kodell, Jerome, O.S.B., *The Catholic Bible Study Handbook*. Ann Arbor, Michigan: Servant Books, 1985.

Lawler, Ronald, O.F.M., Wuerl, Donald W., Lawler, Thomas Comerford (Editors), *The Teaching of Christ (Second Edition)*. Huntington, IN: Our Sunday Visitor, Inc., 1983.

Madrid, Patrick, *Any Friend of God Is A Friend Of Mine*. San Diego, CA: *This Rock* Magazine, September 1992.

Madrid, Patrick, *Any Friend of God Is A Friend of Mine*. San Diego, CA: Basilica Press, 1996.

Madrid, Patrick (Editor), *Surprised By Truth*. San Diego, CA: Basilica Press, 1994.

Manelli, Stefano Fr., O.F.M., *Jesus Our Eucharistic Love*. Brookings, SD: Our Blessed Lady of Victory Mission, 1973.

Mbukanma, Jude Rev., *Is It In The Bible?* Clifton, VA: M. E. T. Ltd., 1987.

McKenzie, John L., S.J., *Dictionary of the Bible*. New York, NY: Macmillian Publishing Co., 1965.

Mead, Frank S., *Handbook of Denominations in the United States (Eighth Edition)*. Nashville, TN: Abingdon Press, 1985.

Metzger, Bruce M., Coogan, Michael D. (editors) *The Oxford Companion to the Bible.* New York, NY: Oxford University Press, 1993.

Miller, J. Michael, C.S.B., *What We Believe About The Saints.* Huntington, IN: Our Sunday Visitor, Inc., 1992.

Miravalle, Mark, *Introduction to Mary: The Heart of Marian Doctrine and Devotion.* Santa Barbara, CA: Queenship Publishing Co., 1993.

Montague, George T., S.M., *The Apocalypse: Understanding the Book of Revelation and the End of the World.* Ann Arbor, Michigan: Servant Publications, 1992.

Nevins, Albert J., M.M., *Answering A Fundamentalist.* Huntington, IN: Our Sunday Visitor, Inc., 1990.

New American Bible With Revised New Testament. New York, NY: Catholic Book Publishing Co., 1986.

Nichols, Aidan, O.P., *Holy Order.* Dublin, Ireland: Veritas Publications, 1990.

O'Brien, John A. Rev., *The Faith of Millions.* Huntington, IN: Our Sunday Visitor, Inc., 1974.

O'Connor, James T. Rev., *The Hidden Manna: A Theology of the Eucharist.* San Francisco, CA: Ignatius Press, 1988.

Ott, Ludwig, Dr., *Fundamentals of Catholic Dogma.* Rockford, IL: TAN Books and Publishers, Inc., 1960.

Provan, Charles D., *The Bible and Birth Control.* Monongahela, PA: Zimmer Printing, 1989.

Rumble, Leslie Dr. Rev., M.S.C. and Carty, Charles Rev., *Indulgence Quizzes to a Street Preacher.* Rockford, IL: TAN Books and Publishers, Inc., 1976.

Rumble, Leslie Dr. Rev., M.S.C. and Carty, Charles Rev., *Radio Replies (Volumes 1, 2, 3.)* Rockford, IL: TAN Books and Publishers, Inc., 1979.

Schreck, Alan, *Catholic and Christian.* Ann Arbor, Michigan: Servant Books, 1984.

Shea, Mark P., *By What Authority?: An Evangelical Discovers Catholic Tradition.* Huntington, IN: Our Sunday Visitor Publishing Co., 1996.

Shea, Mark P., *This IS My Body: An Evangelical Discovers the Real Presence.* Front Royal, VA: Christendom Press, 1993.

Sheedy, Father, *Father Sheedy's Ask Me A Question.* Huntington, IN: Our Sunday Visitor, Inc., 1989.

Stravinskas, Peter Rev., *The Catholic Answer Book (Volumes 1, 2).* Huntington, IN: Our Sunday Visitor, Inc., 1990, 1994.

Stravinskas, Peter Rev. (Editor), *Our Sunday Visitor's Catholic Encyclopedia.* Huntington, IN: Our Sunday Visitor Publishing, Inc., 1991.

Stravinskas, Peter Rev., *The Bible and the Mass.* Ann Arbor, Michigan: Servant Publications, 1989.

Stravinskas, Peter Rev., *The Catholic Church and the Bible.* San Francisco, CA: Ignatius Press, 1987.

Stravinskas, Peter Rev., *The Mass: A Biblical Prayer*, Huntington, IN: Our Sunday Visitor, Inc., 1989.

Stickler, Alfons Maria Cardinal, *The Case For Clerical Celibacy.* San Francisco, CA: Ignatius Press, 1993.

Stoddard, John L., *Rebuilding A Lost Faith.* Rockford, IL: TAN Books and Publishers, Inc., 1990.

Strong, James, *The New Strong's Exhaustive Concordance of the Bible*. Nashville, TN: Thomas Nelson Publishers, 1990.

Swete, Henry Barclay, *An Introduction to the Old Testament in Greek*. Peabody, Mass.: Hendrickson Publishers, 1989.

Whitaker, Richard E. (Compiler), *The Eerdmans Analytical Concordance to the Revised Standard Version of the Bible*. Grand Rapids, Michigan: William B. Eerdmans Publishing Company, 1988.

Willis, John R., S.J., *The Teachings of the Church Fathers*. New York, NY: Herder and Herder, 1966.